Guerilla Guide to Teaching

2nd Edition
The Definitive Resource for Trainee Teachers

Sue Cowley

continuum

To Álvie and Edite,
with all my love.

Continuum International Publishing Group

The Tower Building
11 York Road
London SE1 7NX

80 Maiden Lane, Suite 704
New York,
NY 10038

www.continuumbooks.com

British Library Cataloguing-in-Publication Data
A catalogue record for this book is available from the British Library.

ISBN: 0-8264-9292-4 (paperback)

Library of Congress Cataloging-in-Publication Data
A catalog record for this book is available from the Library of Congress.

Typeset by Ben Cracknell Studios | www.benstudios.co.uk
Printed and bound in Great Britain by Ashford Colour Press, Gosport, Hampshire

Contents

Acknowledgements

It never ceases to amaze me how generous those in the teaching profession are with their time and expertise, especially considering the huge workload that comes with the job. This book would not have been possible without the help of a large number of teachers, trainee teachers, and other people working in the world of education. A huge 'thank you' goes to everyone who contributed their thoughts and experiences to make this book possible.

Special thanks must go to Karen Garner and Carl Smith, teachers who went out of their way to help me, and who were happy to answer a seemingly endless stream of questions without a murmur of complaint. A heartfelt 'thank you' goes to Tabby Rayment, whose research skills have been invaluable to me in putting this new edition of the book together. Thanks must also go to Alexandra Webster and all the team at Continuum, and of course to Tilak, for his continued support and expertise.

Introduction

Teaching really is one of the most wonderful jobs in the world. Of course, it has its difficulties, and if you're going to do your job properly you've got to be really dedicated and hard working. But for every downside, and for every difficult day, there are a million reasons for teachers to love their work. What other job gives you so many rewards: the chance to build bonds with young people, to work with the subject you love, to see a student learn something new, to be your own boss in your own classroom? And what other job gives you the opportunity to inspire future generations, to hear those priceless words: *'you made a difference to my life'*?

This book will help you negotiate the minefield that is the teaching profession. It's realistic, practical, and stuffed with valuable information. My hope is that it will prove a useful reference source for a wide range of people: for student trainees, for teachers in their first couple of years in the job, for overseas trained teachers coming to work in the UK, for more experienced staff, and also for those interested in taking up support roles within a school.

One of the key elements of this book is a series of interviews with people working in education, in all sorts of different areas. As you read, you'll hear from student teachers and teachers who've spent their lives in the profession. You'll find out the truth about the first year from newly qualified teachers. You'll hear what life is like at the top of the management and advisory structure. If you have a question or concern about teaching, you'll find the answer here.

As a profession, teaching gets a lot of press attention, sadly quite a lot of it negative. All parents have to educate their children, and consequently it's a subject close to many people's hearts. We can all remember the good and bad bits of our own time in education. For some of us, though, our school days were a long time ago, and there have been huge changes in the years since we last walked out of the school gates. This book will help you understand the world of education as it is today. It gives you an insight into what working as a teacher is really like. Above all, if your quest is to become a good teacher, this book will help you fulfil your goal.

Teaching is a profession in a constant state of change. Every five minutes, it seems, a fresh initiative is launched, an extra set of tests is brought in or a new curriculum idea is tried out. For many of my interviewees, this constant flux, and all the administration and paperwork that go with it, was one of the biggest causes of stress in their working lives. There is no doubt that handling the behaviour of some young people can be tough and really hard work. I don't try to hide the less wholesome facts about teaching here. However, the overall message of this book is that it really is worthwhile entering the profession if you've got the requisite dedication and energy.

I'd like to wish you luck in your quest to work as a teacher, or in the field of education. As I said at the start of this introduction, it really is one of the best jobs in the world. If you're willing to give it your best, and to dedicate your life to helping children succeed, you really couldn't make a better choice of career.

Sue Cowley
www.suecowley.co.uk
Additional research by Tabatha Rayment.

Please note:
Acronyms are rife in teaching, but confusing for the newcomer and, indeed, for some of us 'old hands' as well. For explanations of all abbreviated terms used in this book, see the 'Guide to edu-speak' on pages xii–xv.

Both government policies and website addresses are subject to seemingly constant change. Although every effort has been made to include up-to-date information, please be aware that some of the details in this book may have changed since the time of writing.

As a result of devolution, educational policies vary across the UK. Where there is space, I explain the situation as it applies to the different regions. However, in some sections of this book I refer to the system as it is in England (the National Curriculum, etc.) because this is where the majority of teachers will work.

Before you begin … a guide to edu-speak

Education has a language all of its own: a language with loads of acronyms, abbreviations and impenetrable bits of jargon. Sometimes these terms make a lot of sense – it would make for a exhausting conversation if you had to talk about a child with 'special educational needs' for an hour, rather than simply one who has 'SEN'. There are, however, various problems with these terms. For a start, they seem alienating to new entrants to the profession and to parents and others who don't work in schools. They also change so regularly that keeping up to date is a thankless task.

Anyway, unless you are already fluent in edu-speak, you'll need the dictionary given below to understand this book and to navigate your way through the teaching profession. You might want to turn over the corner of this page now, so that you can refer back to it as you read.

A

ADD	Attention Deficit Disorder
ADHD	Attention Deficit Hyperactivity Disorder
AFL	Assessment for Learning
ASN	Additional Support Needs (term used in Scottish schools)
AST	Advanced Skills Teacher

B

BA	Bachelor of Arts
BECTA	British Educational Communication and Technology Agency
BEd	Bachelor of Education
BIP	Behaviour Improvement Plan
BSc	Bachelor of Science
BT	Beginning Teacher

C
CACHE   Council for Awards in Children's Care and Education
CAL   Computer-Aided Learning
CEDP   Career Entry and Development Profile
CPD   Continuing Professional Development
CRB   Criminal Records Bureau

D
DENI   Department of Education in Northern Ireland
DfES   Department for Education and Skills
DRB   Designated Recommending Body

E
EAL   English as an Additional Language
EBD   Emotional and Behavioural Difficulties
ECM   Every Child Matters
EOTAS   Education Other Than At School
ERIC   Everybody Reads in Class
ESBD   Emotional, Social and Behavioural Difficulties
ESOL   English for Speakers of Other Languages
EWO   Education Welfare Officer

G
G&T   Gifted and Talented (although to my mind, this will always
        translate as 'Gin and Tonic')
GCSE   General Certificate of Secondary Education
GNVQ   General National Vocational Qualification
GRTP   Graduate and Registered Teacher Programmes
GTC   General Teaching Council
GTCE   General Teaching Council for England
GTCS   General Teaching Council for Scotland
GTP   Graduate Teacher Programme
GTTR   Graduate Teacher Training Registry

H
H&S   Health and Safety
HoD   Head of Department
HoY   Head of Year
HMCI   Her Majesty's Chief Inspector of Schools
HMI   Her Majesty's Inspector of Schools

I
ICT   Information and Communications Technology
IEP   Individual Education Plan
ILO   Intended Learner Outcomes
INSET   In-Service Training/In-Service Education of Teachers
ITT   Initial Teacher Training
IWB   Interactive White Board

K
KS   Key Stage

L
LEA   Local Education Authority
LSA   Learning Support Assistant
LSDA   Learning Skills and Development Agency

M
MFL   Modern Foreign Languages
MLD   Moderate Learning Difficulties

N
NC   National Curriculum
NGfL   National Grid for Learning
NLS   National Literacy Strategy
NNS   National Numeracy Strategy
NPQH   National Professional Qualification for Headship
NQT   Newly Qualified Teacher
NT   National Tests (formerly SAT – Standard Assessment Tasks)
NVQ   National Vocational Qualification

O
Ofsted   Office for Standards in Education

P
PANDA   Performance and Assessment Report
PGCE   Post Graduate Certificate in Education
PPA   Planning, Preparation and Assessment time
PRU   Pupil Referral Unit
PSHCE   Personal, Social, Health and Citizenship Education
PSHE   Personal, Social and Health Education

Q
QCA   Qualifications and Curriculum Authority
QTS   Qualified Teacher Status

R
RSM   Recruitment Strategy Manager
RTP   Registered Teacher Programme

S
SATs   Standard Assessment Tasks
SCITT   School Centred Initial Teacher Training
SEAL   Social Emotional Aspects of Learning
SEF   Self-Evaluation Form
SEN   Special Educational Needs
SENCo   Special Educational Needs Coordinator
SLD   Severe Learning Difficulties
SLT   Senior Leadership Team
SMART   Specific, Measurable, Achievable, Realistic, Time-related
SMT   Senior Management Team
SNS   Standard National Scale
SoW   Scheme of Work
STRB   School Teachers' Review Body

T
TA   Teaching Assistant
TDA   Training and Development Agency for Schools (formerly the TTA)
TEFL   Teaching English as a Foreign Language
TESOL   Teaching English to Speakers of Other Languages
TES   *The Times Educational Supplement*
TLR   Teaching and Learning Responsibilities
TPS   Teachers' Pension Scheme
TTA   Teacher Training Agency

U
UCAS   Universities and Colleges Admissions Service

V
VAC   Very Able Children
VAK   Visual, Auditory, Kinaesthetic

W
WALT   We Are Learning To
WILF   What I am Looking For

Part One
BECOMING A TEACHER

A career in teaching

So, you're looking at a career in teaching. You might be just turning the idea over in your mind, unsure about whether it's the right choice for you. If you've mentioned your prospective career to others, you've probably had reactions ranging from 'are you sure that's a good idea?' to 'you're completely insane'. Maybe you're at the stage of applying for a PGCE, or have already embarked on your training. Perhaps you are in the first few years of your teaching career, and you're questioning whether you've made the right decision. This chapter gives you information and advice about teaching as a career choice. It explores the upsides and the downsides of a teaching job, and looks at the facts about teacher recruitment and retention. It also gives you the chance to hear from some 'voices of experience' – those teachers who have stuck it out in the job for a substantial part of their working lives.

The upsides

Why go into teaching, then, or why stay in teaching for the long term? Here's a list of just some of the upsides of the job:

- Above all else, a job in teaching is rewarding and worthwhile. If you like children, and are willing to work hard to help them succeed, then there is nothing quite like teaching for a sense of personal satisfaction.
- Teaching is both a profession and a vocation. Although it's perhaps not respected as much as it once was, it is still a good career choice for graduates.
- Teaching will stretch you in a number of ways – intellectually, physically, emotionally, psychologically. If you want to challenge yourself on a daily basis, teaching is a great option.
- Teaching gives you a good range of transferable skills. Times are changing, and the tendency is increasingly towards moving between different jobs during your working life. As a teacher, you develop skills that other employers are keen to utilize.

- The job offers good long-term security. There will always be a need for teachers; once you are qualified it is unlikely that you will ever be out of work for too long.
- Teaching is a 'mobile' profession – you can work pretty much anywhere in the country, or even in the world. Teachers who speak English are in great demand in international and language schools as well as in the UK.
- The job is reasonably well paid, and there is a defined and rising salary scale as you gain more experience or take promotion.
- The teachers' pension offers an excellent deal, especially if you stay within the profession for many years.
- You will be working alongside other, like-minded people, who are educated to the same level as you, and who share your sense of vocation.
- You will be working, and forming bonds, with young people. This is not only enjoyable, but it can provide you with a youthful buzz, energy and zest for life.
- On the whole, teaching does get easier the longer you do it and the more experienced you are, a point that is well worth remembering if you're finding life hard as an NQT.
- In a secondary school, or in higher education, you get the chance to work with the subject you love, day in and day out.
- In your own classroom, despite all the dictates from above, to a large extent you are still your own boss.
- Although it might be tiring and stressful, the job is never boring. You might be learning about a new topic, or going out on a trip with your students – every single day offers a different challenge.
- Potentially, the job combines well with raising a family.
- You have the opportunity to make a difference to the lives of others.
- Some teachers have a genuine, long-term impact on the young people with whom they work.
- The holidays are great!

The downsides

Of course there are also some negative aspects to working in education. The decision you have to make, when considering a career in teaching, is whether the upsides outweigh the downsides for you. As far as I'm concerned, with teaching, there is no middle ground. The job is far too important to do half-heartedly, or to spend your time moaning about what's wrong. Here are some of the downsides for you to consider:

- Although it's not true in every school, there is some seriously bad behaviour out there. There are some students (and even parents) who will abuse you verbally and possibly even physically.
- There is a lot of stuff in teaching that has nothing to do with the actual teaching. Paperwork and meetings often get in the way of the important bits of the job, such as teaching good lessons and building positive relationships with a class.
- The job can be very stressful, whether this is to do with excessive workload or poor behaviour. It can also 'take over' your life if you let it.
- The job is very tiring. Some teachers suffer from work-related illnesses such as stress and nervous breakdowns.
- If you want promotion, you must be willing to take all the additional paperwork, pressure and politics that come with a management post.
- To earn a really high salary, you will need to leave the classroom (perhaps the reason you entered the job in the first place) and move into a senior management role.
- The pay will never be all that great. Even right at the 'top of the tree', there is still a gap between a headteacher's pay and that of a company director in the business world.
- You'll never be given a company car, health insurance scheme, gym membership, bonus, or any of the other potential perks of a job in the commercial sector.
- Many teachers work very long hours in order to do the job as well as they can, or even simply to get the job done at all.
- Teaching is often used as a 'political football', and there is a lot of interference from governments of whatever persuasion. You are likely to find yourself battling to keep up with new initiatives and seemingly endless changes to the curriculum.
- There is less and less freedom for teachers to move outside the statutory curriculum areas, and to be creative in their approaches to the job.
- The nature of the job has the potential to lead to cynicism and a negative attitude. Some teachers do have a tendency to moan.
- There are a few teachers in the job who are not up to it, or who have been worn out by it. You will find yourself covering for these people, both in dealing with the issues that arise in their classrooms, and literally covering for them, when you have to take their classes because they're not in school.
- You may find yourself spending much of those lovely long holidays dealing with all the work you couldn't fit in during term time.
- There is no flexibility in when you take your holidays, and you will be taking them at the time when they are most expensive.

The facts

Although plenty of surveys and reports have been done, it's surprisingly difficult to find any official figures about the number of people entering and leaving the teaching profession. Statistics for September 2005 from the Graduate Teacher Training Registry (GTTR) show a total of 29,662 applicants accepted onto UK training courses. However, these numbers only cover those applying through the GTTR. The Training and Development Agency for Schools (TDA – formerly the TTA) has published figures showing that the actual number of trainee teachers is around 41,900. A research report written for the DfES in 2005 found that 1 in 4 qualified teachers left the profession within five years.

You can find some of the reported figures and other details below, although the numbers given do vary considerably. Be warned: these figures make worrying reading. The information given below is taken from the *Guardian* education website (www.education.guardian.co.uk), and from a report by Alan Smithers and Pamela Robinson of Liverpool University for the National Union of Teachers (www.teachers.org.uk).

- 2 out of 5 teachers leave the profession within 5 years.
- Up to 40 per cent of teachers leave within the first 3 years.
- 58 per cent leave teaching within the first 3 years (this figures includes those leaving during and after teacher training).
- Out of 100 final year student teachers, 40 don't go into the classroom, and another 18 leave within the first 3 years.

Primary school teachers who do not expect to be teaching:

- 31 per cent in 5 years
- 56 per cent in 10 years
- 77 per cent in 15 years

Secondary school teachers who do not expect to be teaching:

- 26 per cent in 5 years
- 51 per cent in 10 years
- 71 per cent in 15 years

Reasons given for leaving the profession included workload, long working hours, pupil behaviour, government initiatives, salary levels and stress.

Voices of experience

The interviews that follow give you a good idea about what it's like to spend a large part of your working life as a teacher. My interviewees don't pull their punches, but from each of them comes a sense of the joy of teaching, as well as an honest appraisal of some of the more difficult aspects of the job.

Primary school teacher (retired, 33 years' experience)

Now a freelance journalist

Anne Cowan

Q. What made you go into teaching in the first place?

Anne – On the rebound from a Bob Cratchit-like year as an insurance clerkess, I decided to be a teacher because I had loved my own primary school days.

Q. And what teaching qualification did you take?

Anne – I took the 3-year course for primary teachers at Moray House College of Education, Edinburgh, qualifying in 1962.

Q. What about your 33 years as a teacher? Where did you work and in what type of schools?

Anne – After two difficult years in a Glasgow housing scheme, I gave up and worked my way to San Francisco. On my return to Scotland there followed three years in the inner city, 16 in a former mining community and 12 years in the small-town school I went to myself. Each time I changed job, teaching got easier and more enjoyable.

Q. Why do you think some people stay in the profession long-term, while others leave after a few years?

Anne – If there's one thing which keeps the unpromoted teacher's nose to the chalkface it's pay, followed a close second by pension prospects. Many of us who qualified in the 1960s are from the first generation of our families to have stayed on at school beyond the age of 14. We've seen what long hours in menial jobs for low pay are like and do not want to be old and cold. Lots of teachers who have children expensively educated at university spring from a respectable working class which abhorred debt. If that's where you're coming from, you stick in at school. I didn't give up teaching for writing, but by a stroke of luck got early retirement at 55. Much as I had enjoyed my job I had been at it too long and was exhausted.

Q. What advice would you give young teachers who hope to stay in the profession long term? How did you stick it for so long?

Anne – How did I survive at the chalkface for 33 years? The ability to switch off, to forget all about work once you're off the premises, is crucial. There is life beyond the school gates, so don't be scared to get out there, relax and enjoy it. Anybody needs to get out and meet people, to do something different after work, all the more so teachers, whose work involves controlling and educating conscripts.

Q. And on a day to day basis in the classroom? How did you survive in the tougher schools?

Anne – Surviving teaching reminds me of aircraft safety demonstrations. Adults, fix your own oxygen mask first or you won't be able to help the children. Teacher, save yourself. At tougher schools we showed more TV programmes than was strictly necessary. It settled difficult classes and gave the teacher a breather to catch up with correction. If uproar is about to break out, play a quiet game for five minutes. I must confess to being a closet whole-class teacher when juggling groups was driving me to despair. The old-fashioned arrangement, rows of seats facing the front, concentrates juvenile minds wonderfully, if you can get away with it. One thing I would have appreciated is the book *Getting the Buggers to Behave*.

Q. Have you got any advice for new teachers?

Anne – Unfortunately many young teachers feel pressurized and fall victim to the creeping cult of presenteeism. Where competitive parking is the norm, they put themselves into self-imposed detention under the illusion that a car on show is an indicator of commitment to the job. Also when new schemes are introduced, there's the temptation to think that this is the right way to go about things. Teaching is not an exact science. There is not one right way. Do it your way. One golden rule is to be in class before the pupils and start the lesson immediately they settle down.

Q. What do you feel makes primary school teaching such a great job?

Anne – One of the best things about primary teaching comes when the class feels like a family. Everyone gets to know each other, they gel and when something absurd happens, you roll your eyes and they all laugh with you, not at you. There's something very nice about gathering them all round to tell a story, go off at a tangent and have a blether. The sad thing is that so much of the spontaneity has been knocked out of the primary school. With strict guidelines and having to keep written pupil assessments of everything except how they blow their noses, teachers are stressed out. Another innovation I would have found disconcerting and inhibiting is having other adults in the class most of the time.

Q. And what sort of teacher would you say you were?

Anne – You'd have to ask my former pupils what kind of teacher I was! I'd say that I was never a perfectionist, that I liked a firm but informal approach, and that I loved teaching creative writing and art and doing projects which involved both of them with getting out of school.

Q. Could you describe some of the best memories of your teaching career?

Anne – One of my favourite things was sussing out the Edinburgh Festival Fringe and taking a new class of a couple of days up to town 23 miles away. We'd go with parent helpers to one of the children's events at Edinburgh International Book Festival in Charlotte Square in the morning, eat lunch sitting watching the jugglers and fire eaters at the foot of the Mound, then walk up to the Old Town to see free exhibitions, street theatre and performances up closes and in back yards. Then back at school next day we'd plunge into the creative explosion of words and colour and enthusiasm. I always thought that the epitaph to my teaching would read 'she muddled through' and was genuinely astonished at the nice things people kindly said when at the age of 55 I finally tottered out the school.

Another surprise was the joy of continuity. I ended up teaching with people who had taught me and who had been at school with me. There were pupils from families of which I knew/had known four generations. That was really interesting and they do say that a sense of belonging is one of the most important things in life. It came as an unexpected bonus and I'm glad I was part of East Lothian small-town life again. I loved teaching at my old school.

I used to joke that the two great educational advances were women teachers being allowed to wear trousers and the October break. Seriously though, parents' nights make the world of difference. So much good can result and misery be avoided now that teachers get the chance to speak to the people who know the child best. Parents' nights help everybody.

Q. You stayed in the classroom. Was that a deliberate decision? What do you think about going for promotion?

Anne – What do I think of promotion? I hardly give it a thought. As one of nature's employees and not officer material, I've never been interested in it. One thing is certain, the headteacher sets the tone and a good head is vital to the morale of other staff. Having smashing colleagues who become friends makes all the difference in the world.

Q. You moved into another career after you left the classroom. Why did you start writing, and how did you go about it?

Anne – There was a time when each morning as I wrote the date on the board, it seemed as if this heralded another long day of my life to be spent between four classroom walls. It was freelance journalism that saved my sanity and opened many doors. For a while, after school on a Thursday, I'd go up to *The Scotsman* office in Edinburgh, go through the press releases, find a fashion theme and write it up. Work for *The Herald* and *Times Educational Supplement Scotland* and various London papers followed. But my escape might just as well have been into hillwalking, salsa dancing or advanced patchwork quilting, though journalism paid better.

Q. And how do you think things have changed since you left teaching? Are the changes for the better or not?

Anne – In the ten years I've been a freelance journalist I've been hearing of the ever-changing new regimes and pressures being inflicted on primary schools. Preplanning every dot and comma and assessing to the nth degree is a time-consuming nightmare. Teachers are floundering in an ocean of unnecessary paperwork. Who is it supposed to benefit? Nobody's going to read the half of it. At times it seems as if the relaxed atmosphere and much of the fun are but fond and distant memories.

Q. Finally, what could be done to make teaching a more attractive profession?

Anne – Teachers' pensions, like those of forces and police, should not be based on 40 years' service. It keeps too many tired, burnt-out people at the chalkface. It is doing pupils no favours and more early retirement or the adoption of a 30 year career structure would breathe fresh life into the schools. On the other hand, the plain speaking of the old staffroom cynic is the perfect antidote to all the jargonese and daft innovations to which teachers are subjected.

'Surviving teaching reminds me of aircraft safety demonstrations. Adults, fix your own oxygen mask first or you won't be able to help the children. Teacher, save yourself.'

Secondary school teacher – 25 years' experience

Head of Faculty – Design & Technology

Name withheld

Q. Why did you decide to go into teaching?

A. I came into teaching when I was 25 after working in industry, mostly in chemical and aerospace companies. Reasons? Well I felt I'd enjoy it having had spells as an instructor to engineering apprentices; it would be a challenge and seemed at that time to provide a good career structure. Money was not an issue. To be honest I also liked the holidays as it fitted in with my climbing passion and allowed me to go abroad on expeditions.

Q. What route did you take into teaching?

A. I left school at 16 with six O levels. Then I did five years in further education to HNC standard in Product Design. My PGCE course was at Manchester University. After that I did some teaching in further education then moved into secondary teaching.

Q. Do you think it's better for teachers to gain work experience like you did, before going back to work in education?

A. Certainly it was (for me) better to enter teaching with experience at 26 than it would have been to have followed a more conventional sixth-form route and entered earlier.

Q. How long have you been teaching, and what's your current job?

A. Twenty five years this September. I work at an 11 to 16 comprehensive. I'm the Head of Faculty for Design and Technology. I teach all years, with a high percentage of GCSE in Electronics.

Q. What has been your best moment in teaching?

A. There are too many to recall. The best times seem to revolve around personalities, relationships and situations. I've enjoyed foreign visits with students, outdoor challenges, absorbing project work and the satisfaction of getting results. It's also nice to have ex-students come back years later and say you made a difference; something that is not always evident at the time.

Q. And what about the worst moments?

A. Again, many. Aside from personal tragedies that have affected colleagues and students it has to be the depressing grind of trying to be an effective teacher when paperwork, lack of funds, lack of time, poor facilities get in the way. It was good until the mid-1980s but has got worse year on year since then. It is depressing to see once-good teachers crack under the strain.

Q. What are the best and worst things about teaching your subject and age group?

A. I enjoy my subject because it allows me to be creative and still challenges me. The worst thing is the lack of resources. Never enough time to prepare lessons as I'd wish. Masses of admin and chasing faculty problems. Behaviour has declined markedly over the past five years. It's hard to get any time for decent INSET.

Q. Tell me about being promoted. What's it really like? Is it worth the hassle?

A. I've been promoted several times to my current position. I turned it down initially … not worth the money, I'd rather have a life. Only my own self-esteem keeps me going. I thought I would have a chance to really develop a faculty and weld a team, instead you are given no management time (time to have a vision, think, plan, etc.) I have moved a faculty on and am proud that it's one of the best in the area and has excellent results, but it has been at a cost.

Q. Has being promoted taken you away from the classroom?

A. I wish it had! One of the great myths. Just about all middle managers retain their full teaching load and run a faculty … an impossible task. I teach 34 lessons out of 40; 50 per cent is GCSE work and I lose more doing cover each week. Only at SMT level does the teaching load drop away.

Q. And what about the future? Would you like to be promoted further?

A. I'd like to move out of teaching. Certainly no higher in a school.

Q. What support have you experienced during your teaching career?

A. I've had support from many sources. My wife (excellent), my colleagues (very good), the unions (OK), senior staff (varied … some good, some not so good escapees from the classroom), the LEA (has fallen away over the years).

Q. Would you recommend a teaching career to others?

A. Absolutely not! This is not the profession it was. The workload is horrendous, the support is often poor, politicians will lay every ill of society at your door; you will work in poor conditions with limited resources. Morale is very low and

I can't see where the next generation of teachers will come from. It is rare indeed to find a student who says they wish to become a teacher ... and many will try to dissuade them. Only if you are teaching full time in the current climate and have been for a while will you understand.

Q. What could be done to make teaching a 'better' career, then?

A. Time, resources and some appreciation. Time to prepare/plan. A year out every seven years. A better career structure.

Q. What was it like when you first started teaching? Has education changed? Are the changes for the better or not?

A. I enjoyed teaching when I started. It seemed more relaxed. People had time for you and vice versa. You got to know students better. Class sizes were smaller (considerably). I had a good induction year. NQTs now seem to be thrown in the deep end so it's little wonder many quit within a year or two. I have seen change upon change for over ten years with much of that soon ditched and no one held accountable for the lost energy, time and money thrown at it. We were recently (as a staff) forced to watch a DfEE video as an INSET activity that told us that the new thinking was that lessons should have a beginning, middle and end (which would be called a plenary) and should be structured to be effective ... to think we'd missed that over the years.

Q. What about the future? What are your plans?

A. Not too sure. Maybe to change schools and have a fresh challenge with a new set of faces; that could be revitalizing. Failing that to expand a business venture I've been involved in for several years and see how far that goes. I have two children to put through university and the expense of that is now starting to weigh so a decent income remains a priority.

Teacher training **2**

This chapter covers the 'nuts and bolts' of becoming a teacher. It gives you information about the different routes that you can take into the profession, and looks at the decisions you need to make before entering teacher training. It will also give you an idea of what these different routes involve, and how to go about applying for them. In addition, you'll hear from two trainees taking different routes into the profession, and from a lecturer on a PGCE course.

Routes into teaching (England and Wales)

There are a variety of different routes into teaching. To be a fully qualified teacher in a state-maintained school in England or Wales, you need to gain your Qualified Teacher Status (QTS). This usually means you need to complete a programme of Initial Teacher Training (ITT) as well as passing the QTS Skills Tests.

The two most common routes into teaching are via an undergraduate or postgraduate university course. There are 83 ITT providers in England and Wales. There are also employment-based and QTS assessment-only options available, where you can learn 'on the job'. While this might seem an attractive and financially beneficial option, it can be difficult to secure a placement. You'll find details about this and the 'traditional' routes below.

Routes into Teaching

STEP ONE		STEP TWO		STEP THREE
You must have: GCSE in English and Maths – Grade 'C' or higher (or equivalent) (Applicants born on or after 1 September 1979, who want to teach primary or Key Stage 2/3 (ages 7–14), must also have achieved a grade C or equivalent in a GCSE science subject.)		A minimum of two A levels or Access Course (depending on the course)		Degree/Postgraduate Certificate

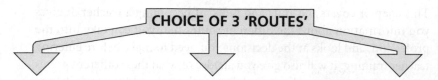

CHOICE OF 3 'ROUTES'

ROUTE ONE
Undergraduate route

'Teaching degree', with subject specialism

- BEd/BA/BSc with QTS
- Usually primary level
- Full or part-time
- 3 or 4 years (5-year part-time courses available)

If you are one year into a non-teaching degree, you can apply for a 2-year course. This is especially suitable for mature entrants.

ROUTE TWO
Postgraduate route

'Subject-specific degree', then teaching qualification

First degree:

- For primary preferably related to the National Curriculum.
- For secondary the subject or subjects you want to teach.

Postgraduate qualification – PGCE:

- 1 year (some 2 years)
- Full, part-time, flexible learning
- Flexible learning = distance learning, evenings, weekends

School Centred Initial Teacher Training (SCITT)

- 1 year full time
- Based in one school within the consortium (lead school) while completing teaching practices at others from the group.

ROUTE THREE
Employment based and assessment-only based route

Training for QTS while employed by a school

- Work as an unqualified teacher while gaining QTS.
- Follow an individual programme of training while you work.
- School pays you an unqualified teacher's salary while you train – from £14,000 per annum.
- Can take 3 months to 1 year, depending on previous teaching experience.
- You must find a school willing to train you on GTP/RTP.
- Highly competitive – can be difficult to secure a placement and funding is not always available.
- Places tend to go to those offering a secondary shortage subject.

Note: The different routes into teaching are subject to frequent changes. You can find out a great deal more information about getting into the profession from the Training and Development Agency for Schools (TDA), formerly the Teacher Training Agency (TTA). Visit their website at www.tda.gov.uk.

Routes into teaching (Scotland and Northern Ireland)

There are seven universities in Scotland that offer teacher training at various levels: Aberdeen, Dundee, Edinburgh, Glasgow, Paisley, Stirling and Strathclyde. You can find details of these on the Teaching In Scotland website, www.teachinginscotland.com.

As in England and Wales, you can choose between a postgraduate course for primary or secondary, or an undergraduate course (in a limited range of subjects). Postgraduate trainee teachers studying in Scotland follow a PGDE – a Professional Graduate Diploma in Education, the Scottish equivalent of a PGCE. Distance and part-time options are only available at the University of Aberdeen and the University of Strathclyde.

There are six ITT providers in Northern Ireland that offer both primary and secondary PGCE courses. These universities do not take part in the GTTR scheme and applicants should apply directly to the registrar/admissions officer at the college or university at which they are interested in studying. There are no financial incentives available, and there are high levels of competition for teaching posts in Northern Ireland. You can find out more information from the teaching section of the Department of Education website for Northern Ireland, www.deni.gov.uk/index/teachers_pg/teachers-teachinginnorthernireland_pg.htm

Decisions, decisions

Before deciding which route to take into teaching, there are various things that you'll need to consider.

- *Which 'route' is best for me?* For instance, if you are completely certain that you wish to teach at secondary school level, the normal approach would be to take a subject-specific degree and then follow this with a PGCE. When making the choice between a 'straight' teaching degree, or a first degree/PGCE, think carefully about the benefits and drawbacks of each route:
  - *The teaching degree (BEd; BA/BSc with QTS)* – gives you more time to practise and develop your teaching skills, but has less flexibility should you decide to leave (or not enter) the profession.
  - *A first degree + PGCE* – gives you a much more condensed opportunity to learn while on teaching practice, but is a more flexible route for those unsure about teaching, and (in England) attracts a financial incentive (see below).
- *Which degree subject is best for me?* If you wish to teach at primary level, and decide to take the degree/PGCE route, you should ensure that

your subject choice is related to the National Curriculum. If you're planning to teach at secondary level, be aware that some subjects are far more popular than others. As a consequence there is more competition when trying to secure a teaching post within that subject area. If you train to teach a 'secondary shortage subject', you are likely to find it far easier to get a job, and to gain promotion quickly.

- *What age group do I want to teach?* You can train to teach in the whole of the primary or secondary sector, or a specific age group, such as 3–8, 14–19 or Post Compulsory (16+).
- *How am I going to finance my training?* At present, some teacher training courses attract additional funding from the government. See 'Financial incentives', below, for more information.

What's in the degree?

Primary school teachers are trained to teach English, maths and science, plus one or more specialist subjects. The undergraduate route involves a substantial amount of time spent in school, currently a minimum of 24 weeks for a 3-year course and at least 32 weeks for a 4-year course. These teaching practices (TPs) are 'staggered' over the years of the course, so that they build up gradually in length and intensity.

For the PGCE course, you can expect to spend between 18 to 26 weeks teaching in a school, depending on your ITT provider and whether you are studying for a Primary or Secondary PGCE. You can find lots more information about teaching practice in the next chapter.

Applying for teacher training

There are various ways to apply for training, depending on the particular route you wish to take:

- *Undergraduate route:* Applications in England, Wales and Scotland must be made online through the University and Colleges Admissions Service (UCAS) at www.ucas.com. The application fee is £15.
- *Postgraduate route*: Apply online via the Graduate Teacher Training Registry (GTTR) at www.gttr.ac.uk. The application fee for 2006 is £12.
- Northern Ireland: Postgraduate students should apply directly to the training institution.
- *Employment-based ITT routes:* Contact your local designated recommending body (DRB). You can find your local DRB through the TDA website at www.tda.gov.uk/Home/partners/recruiting/ebr/drbs/drbregions.aspx.

The earlier you make your application, the more likely it is to be considered by the training provider. The application cycle usually begins in September and concludes in December, with the clearing process in July. You can find full contact details for the GTTR and UCAS in the Directory at the back of this book.

Fees and grants

Of course, the 'good old days' of free university education are now long gone. The situation is very complicated, but the following information should help you negotiate the ins and outs of how much you will have to pay to train to be a teacher. (Some trainees will be eligible for financial incentives – see below, pp. 18–19.)

England/Northern Ireland

- All undergraduates now have to pay tuition fees towards their teaching degrees.
- From September 2006, ITT providers in England and Northern Ireland will be able to charge undergraduate and postgraduate students variable tuition fees of up to £3,000 per year.
- The Student Loans Company will allow students to take out larger loans to cover these fees.
- You will not have to repay anything until you have completed your ITT course and are earning a salary of over £15,000 per year.
- Some training providers who are charging the full amount of £3,000 will give you a grant of £300 towards this fee.
- Some students may be eligible to receive a non-repayable maintenance grant of up to £2,700 from their LEA. Of this, £1,200 is not means-tested for PGCE students.
- If your family income is less than £17,500 you can get the full amount.
- Students with higher family incomes may receive a means-tested portion of the full amount.
- You may also get further financial support from your training provider.

Wales

- ITT providers in Wales charge fixed tuition fees for all PGCE students, currently £1,200.
- This will rise in the academic year 2007/2008 to £3,000.
- A non-means-tested, and non-repayable fees grant of up to £1,800 will be available to some students.
- Maintenance grants and student loans will also be available to Welsh trainee teachers.
- They can use either of these financial options to pay their course fees.

Scotland

- Financial support and fees for all ITT courses in Scotland are the same as for any undergraduate course.
- Students may apply for a loan through the Student Awards Agency for Scotland (SAAS).
- They may also be eligible for a bursary or any applicable supplementary grant.
- The SAAS will pay the living costs and course fees for students studying PGDE/PGCE courses in priority subjects. The priority subjects for 2006/2007 are: maths, English, Gaelic, home economics, modern languages, physics, technological education, art, chemistry, drama, geography, music, physical education, religious education and primary.

Financial incentives

In Northern Ireland and Scotland, competition for teaching posts means that there is no need to offer financial incentives to attract additional graduates into teaching. Teaching salaries in Scotland are also slightly higher than elsewhere in the UK.

Financial incentives are currently available for students doing a PGCE in England or Wales. Some undergraduate students may also be eligible for special funding. Details of financial incentives from September 2006 are as follows:

England

- Undergraduates can apply for a means-tested grant from the DfES of up to £2,700 per year (although there is no guarantee that you will receive anything).
- All PGCE students receive a £6,000 'training bursary'. Trainees in the 'priority subjects' receive a bursary of £9,000 (these subjects are secondary maths, science, English (including drama), ICT, design and technology, modern languages, RE and music.)
- Those who teach a priority subject may be eligible for a one-off, taxable 'Golden Hello' payment of between £2,500 and £5,000 (for secondary maths and science) after they have passed their induction.

Further information explaining financial incentives for trainee teachers can be found on the Directgov website (www.direct.gov.uk), the 'want to teach?' section of the GTTR website (www.gttr.ac.uk/teach/index.html) and via the TDA (www.tda.gov.uk).

Wales

- Eligible secondary maths and science PGCE trainees get a £7,200 training grant and a £5,000 teaching grant.
- Eligible trainees on PGCE courses for other priority secondary subjects receive a £7,200 training grant and a £2,500 teaching grant. The other priority subjects are now modern languages, design and technology, ICT, English (including drama), Welsh as a second language, music and RE.
- Eligible trainees on all other secondary PGCE courses (including art, geography, history, PE) and all primary PGCE courses will receive a £4,200 training grant.
- Undergraduates in Wales training to be secondary teachers may be eligible for a Secondary Undergraduate Placement Grant from £600–£1000, depending on the subject.

For more information see www.wales.gov.uk.

QTS

In order to teach in a state-maintained school you need to achieve QTS, or 'qualified teacher status'. You do this by completing your teacher training and showing that you have met the relevant standards (see below).

The QTS standards

You can find a downloadable document that explains the QTS standards in full from the 'Partners' section of the Training Development Agency for Schools website (www.tda.gov.uk) and via the DfES website (www.dfes.gov.uk). You can get copies of the booklet 'Qualifying to Teach' free of charge by phoning 0845 6060 323.

Briefly, the QTS standards deal with the areas of your work explained below:

- *Professional values and practice*: This covers areas such as having high expectations of your students, treating the children with respect and consistency, and improving your own teaching.
- *Knowledge and understanding*: In this section are attributes such as good subject knowledge, understanding the National Curriculum, using ICT effectively, and knowing a range of strategies to promote effective learning and good behaviour.
- *Teaching*: This section looks at three different areas. The first is planning, expectation and targets, for example setting challenging objectives and selecting and using resources. The second is monitoring and assessment,

for example assessing and recording student progress, and reporting on it to parents and others. The third is teaching and class management, which covers areas such as having high expectations and organizing and managing the learning environment.

The QTS skills tests

Students training in England also have to pass the QTS 'skills tests'. These are in literacy, numeracy and information and communications technology (ICT). At present, skills tests are not required for teachers training in Wales. You can find lots of information about these tests, including some practice materials, on the TDA website (www.tda.gov.uk/skillstests.aspx). You'll also find some comments about the skills tests in the student interviews below.

First steps

The interviews that follow give you an insight into what it's like to be a trainee teacher. You'll hear about a couple of different ways of becoming a teacher – the traditional PGCE course, and the relatively new GTP route into teaching. You'll also hear from a tutor working with trainees, who will give you an insight into how to be successful on a PGCE course.

PGCE student

Laura Jenkinson

Q. Hi Laura! You went to a school where I used to teach, and we worked together on a school play, although I never actually taught you. How would you describe your own experiences of education?

Laura – I really enjoyed my education. I never had a problem with school, was quite accepting of it, and wanted to do my best. There were certainly some subjects I was rubbish at, like maths and electronics, but my teachers were all so interesting – even if just because they were weird – that I didn't really think of it as work. I had a pretty fun time. It's interesting looking back with what I know now, I can recognize lots of the techniques that were used by my teachers.

English is definitely the subject I remember most clearly, aside from my A-level subjects (classical civilization and Latin). The fact that I remember them I think shows that I really enjoyed them. And I remember every minute of the play! I was just in awe of the whole production; it took me ages to stop giggling with excitement at rehearsals. It gave me a taste for more and it was such a positive experience for me that I look forward to working on one with my future students.

Q. What was your background before you became a trainee teacher?

Laura – I was working as a bookseller at Blackwell in Oxford. I'd graduated from Durham Uni two years before with a 2.1 in English Studies. I worked with a few student theatre companies, first acting and then doing publicity and production for shows – I love having projects! When I graduated I moved back to London to live with my parents, and got a temporary job at Waterstones in Gower Street for a bit – bliss to be surrounded by books. When the contract was up, I moved to Oxford to be with my (now) fiancé, and started to work at another academic bookshop.

I thought about moving into something in publishing with the production and publicity design experience I got from working in student theatre at Durham, but despite having lots of interviews I wasn't successful. I'd realized by then I didn't particularly want to work in an office. I was a bit bored at work, despite the lovely people and running my own section, and my fiancé suggested teaching. I got a deferred place at one of the local universities, and spent the year in-between working at lots of literary festivals and spending my bookshop staff discount.

Q. What made you decide that you really wanted to go into teaching?

Laura – It was always being suggested to me by teachers and my friends at school – I seemed to have a way of getting things across to people – but I didn't like the idea because you just don't when you're 15 and at school already. When my parents and partner suggested it later I'd had time to think about it and it seemed a much more interesting idea. I'd always chosen to work in the more academic bookshops, and loved helping the kids who brought their school prize book tokens to the shop to make their choices. I'd even arranged a children's storyteller for Saturday mornings (my fiancé!). I thought a career in education could be satisfying and include all of my interests.

Q. Tell me about the route that you're taking to become a teacher. Why did you choose this particular course?

Laura – I'm doing a PGCE Secondary in English, partly because it seemed the most sensible route for me – a mix of college and in-school training – but mostly because I wasn't aware of the other options. I'd also heard that my local university had a great course, so I decided to stick with that.

Q. What's the best thing so far about the PGCE?

Laura – Knowing that it's the best decision I ever made! I'm in my last placement now and I still love it. Quite a few people did drop out in the first term (not from English), but it didn't even cross my mind. I've realized how much I love working with children, which is something I, oddly, didn't consider before. I have to say also that I've made some brilliant friends doing the course that I know I'll keep in touch with.

Q. And the worst?

Laura – The worst (and I hear this is normal for these courses) is the travelling and course organization. I'm sure they do their best and it can't be easy to arrange placements for 100-or-so people, but it's so disappointing to live near several schools in Oxford and then get posted to Buckinghamshire or Milton Keynes, especially when you don't drive. You're only meant to have one marathon journey out of the three placements, but it's not worked out like that for some, but then everybody copes and most love the schools they're at.

Some of the lectures have been rather weighty – we're taught that people can't concentrate for more than an hour, but some of them are longer. And some issues have been over emphasized at the expense of under-representation of other real issues. But they do take our suggestions quite seriously and, as a result of one very interesting 1½ hour lecture, I'm participating in a brain-scanning experiment next month.

Q. Tell me about the placements you've had this year: how long were they, and how have they gone?

Laura – I've had two placements during the course, at very different schools, one very large newish one and a smaller, older one (with a very exciting cross-country bus ride to get there). The first lasted around seven weeks, at least two weeks of which were observation. I had to teach a class from nearly every year group, and team-taught a Year 10 and a form group with another student on the course, which was interesting because we had such different ideas. The second and third placements, both at the second school, have been around six or seven weeks long, and with 60 per cent and 40 per cent timetables respectively.

Both placements have gone well overall, and it's been useful to see the very different ways the schools approach things like lesson structure and behaviour management. I've been lucky as my mentors have all been supportive and professional – there have been a few horror stories from the rest of the group. It's also nice to be at the same school for two terms. The kids react differently to you when they know you're around for the long haul.

Q. What about the QTS skills tests, any thoughts about those?

Laura – I did all my QTS tests last week (before starting my last placement) – and passed! It was difficult to schedule them as they get booked up in advance and they're only really do-able in college time. I was really worried about the possibility of having to reschedule them when I took the two numeracy practice tests home and failed incredibly poorly twice – what on *earth* is a Box-and-Whisker diagram and why have I never seen one before?! Once in the proper test, with headphones and scrap paper, it's an awful lot easier.

I managed to finish the ICT and literacy tests in under an hour the next morning, without practice, so they can't be that hard. I think it's just important to prepare yourself for whichever one you fear the most. There's so much importance attached to the tests but they're really just to check basic skills. It was almost fun in the end!

Q. Could you tell me about the support that you've received from your university?

Laura – Uni support has been great. My uni group had such a wide range of background and experiences, and we all try and meet up for a drink every couple of weeks and have a supportive moan. My uni mentor is a legend and he is a tower of strength. He's always on the end of the phone, helping us with resources, keeping us in touch with each other when we're on placement, and helping us remember how to think. I was at my second placement, upset after my fifth unsuccessful interview that had had all the appearances of going well, and he came to see me the very next day to talk it through.

Q. What kind of planning are you having to do, and in how much detail?

Laura – I'm planning for all of my classes now. Last term, I managed to get all my planning done in free periods and on the bus home (useful as I get home quite late and still have a Saturday job at the bookshop, so I don't have much free time). The uni gave us a planning guide for our lesson plans that I generally use for all my lessons. It requires us to fill in columns for content, time needed, teaching strategies, resources needed, differentiation, and possibilities for cross-curricular learning, all of which I think are really important to think about at this point. Using the same guide for each lesson helps you compare your progress in these areas.

We're encouraged to use the three-part lesson, although my second placement school has given me space to experiment with what works best for each class, for example simply using quiet reading as a starter, literacy aid and calming tool for a boisterous group.

I try and write my plans in a lot of detail as it helps me remember what I want to do in class and stops me getting flustered. I'm a lot more confident in my planning and delivery now, so I refer to those details less and less. I always write an evaluation after I've taught a lesson, which helps me when I need to look back and see what's worked with a group and what hasn't.

Q. Has there been a lot of written work on the course?

Laura – We've only had three written assignments: a scheme of work project on a children's book, an essay assessing the progress of KS3 pupils as you taught them, another essay on an aspect of school practice. These were only about 2,000 words long (although most of us found this limiting and wrote 3,000 plus an appendix). There have also been cumulative projects, mining information about your placement school or its equal opportunities or transition policies.

Everyone moans that they're boring but in the end they're practically useful in that they make you do a bit of work now in an area that'll help you in the long term. We also keep an audit of our subject knowledge – there's got to be a lot more in it at the end of the course than it had at the start.

Q. What's the best thing about doing TP?

Laura – The fact that you get a chance to discuss and practise teaching skills and techniques on fellow students before getting to school is great – those GTP folk are very, very brave. And then the placements themselves are so intense, six or seven full weeks in school, which allows you to have a more realistic experience and build proper relationships with the pupils, uninterrupted by college.

Q. Any advice for other student trainees about making a success of TP?

Laura – Keep an open mind. It may all look like chaos, but it's only for a year and you'll get through it. But then, if you can't find a reason to get up in the morning by placement 2, it's probably not for you.

Milk your placement school departments for any resources you can while you're there – you should find that your course pays for the photocopy costs. Try and do as much as possible in school, but do be sensible about your workload. Sounding a bit cynical, only commit if you can reasonably fit it in and it will help you reach your standards.

Very important – try not to live in a tiny studio flat with another person who works full time while you do this course. You will see your furniture slowly disappear under mounds of paper which, I promise, you will never get round to filing.

Q. Why did you choose to work with this particular age group? How are you finding the students?

Laura – I was tempted by primary, which I think a lot of people are because it seems so creative. But I like the intricacies of my subject too much to miss out on teaching them, and the range of ages in secondary is so wide that there's an absolute wealth of opportunities to try different things for each.

Although the students in my first school weren't particularly friendly, those at the second school are. It's nice to find children who act the age they are, and most do under the surface. I've started smiling at random kids in the street these days. And they smile back! It's very weird.

Q. And what are your plans for the future? Do you have a job lined up yet?

Laura – I've actually managed to find a job where I can teach English, classics and Latin – all my A-level subjects – and it was the fifth interview I had. Lots of others on my course have had a similar experience, in that they're actually more likely to get the job they're more suited for, rather than the first one they apply for. It's not the end of the world when interviews go pear-shaped, and there's probably something for you just waiting to be advertised.

I'm looking forward to teaching my three subjects, although I hope I'll be able to do a lot of extracurricular things. I'm trying to think of interesting places to visit, I want to get my pupils out into the environments where the texts they're studying were written. I want to get involved with drama too, and put on a play or two. I really want to get my kids writing all the time –

I've seen a lot of pupils who don't know how to write an essay by the end of Year 9 – and reading as much various material as possible, and loving it. Frankly I just can't wait to get into a classroom I can call my own and to classes who can view me as their 'proper' teacher.

For the future, I'm toying with the idea of maybe going into educational psychology, but for now I'm more than happy in the classroom.

GTP trainee

Claire Gill

Q. Could you tell me a bit about what you did before you decided to train as a teacher?

Claire – Having always being a nosey parker, I chose the journalistic career route and went on to complete a 3-year degree in Multi-Media Journalism at Bournemouth University. This provided me with excellent experiences in the industry from working at *New Woman* online and reviewing bust creams to working on national TV programmes. After graduation I went on to work for a Lycos entertainment website which led to my dream job of working on the infamous BBC TV programme and website, *Newsround*.

Q. And what made you decide to go into teaching?

Claire – With three teachers in the family I guess it was inevitable, I just chose to ignore it for a while and gain experiences outside the classroom. I was well aware of the hard work, long hours and bureaucracy involved. However, after enjoying working with children on shoots for *Newsround*, I started to warm to the idea. A big bonus was that I could make my own decisions in my own work space, be creative and not get bombarded by wannabee boy bands' CDs. I went in and spent some time with my Mum's class and enjoyed being in the classroom environment. The last straw was the impossibility of buying a house in London. I went into teaching with an open mind and the idea that I could always return to journalism if it didn't work out.

Q. Why did you choose the GTP route rather than the more traditional PGCE?

Claire – I had worked for three years and couldn't afford to be a student again. But above and beyond this, was the need for getting real experience as a teacher day by day so that I could really make my mind up whether it was for me.

Q. How did you find it doing the GTP? What was it like being thrown 'in at the deep end'?

Claire – Where do I start?! Within a month of starting my GTP I was doing four days of supply in a Reception class, pretty scary since my only teaching experience prior to this had been in Year 6. I taught in every year group and got to see many different ways of teaching and planning.

On the downside, the paperwork was horrendous – you had to gather evidence on everything and anything. I loved the teaching aspect of my training: being able to get stuck in, but a lot of time was wasted 'ticking boxes'. Oh – and my social life suffered. Furthermore, you were an employee and felt under a certain pressure to perform, unlike placements where you could go and make mistakes – you had to live with them for a year.

Q. What kind of support were you given while doing the GTP?

Claire – I had an understanding headteacher who allocated me time every week to complete my paperwork and to do planning. My mentor was also helpful. The main problem was that my GTP year was done through the LEA, rather than a university, so I didn't get the chance to touch base as often as I would have liked with the other GTP trainees and there were times when I felt isolated.

Sometimes I would be asked to cover lessons on my own when I didn't feel ready for it and the external mentor was more of an assessor than a figure looking after my welfare. The main problem with GTP is that your school employs you and therefore you don't want to put a foot wrong. If they do things incorrectly, such as asking you to cover lessons on your own, you go along with it because you want to pass.

Furthermore, the DRB didn't really provide us with enough opportunities to boost our subject knowledge. Many of us hadn't done science since we were 16 so we could have done with some refresher lectures.

GTP is a fantastic way of preparing for being a classroom teacher, it provides you with all the experience you need, but there are times when you are really on your own, and other teachers/staff are often too busy to notice or understand. You really need to be determined and grit your teeth.

Q. What difference do you think this route has made to you and your teaching now?

Claire – I feel confident teaching in any year group which is something a lot of teachers have not had experience of. I was also used to the exhaustion of the teaching year and how to cope with the times when you are flagging. Furthermore, teachers were generally more honest with me and shared honest, practical advice on how they survive the demands of the profession. One teacher nearing retirement opened my eyes to the art of 'basketwork' when it all gets too much.

Doing the GTP taught me that you need to be healthy and energized to be a good teacher and that getting bogged down in planning and marking does not always make for the best learning opportunities in the classroom. Something most training shies away from.

Q. Tell me about your current post and the kind of things you're doing. What are you enjoying most about teaching, and what are you finding hardest?

Claire – I'm nearing the end of my NQT year at the same school where I completed my GTP training, teaching a lovely Year 4 class. I am looking for a new post for September, as I want to gain experience in another school, having trained and completed by GTP at my present school. I feel it's time to move and get my foot in the door for managing a curriculum area.

I love having my own class, hearing them telling me about their lives, seeing them enjoy their lessons and believing in themselves. It's been great having my classroom how I want, being creative with displays and doing the second round of parents' evenings in a more confident manner. On the downside, school politics, changing policies, illogical initiatives from the government and the endless pressures of paperwork, feeling like you are never quite doing enough have got me down.

Having helped out with after-school clubs and extra activities in school I have also learnt the art of saying no, occasionally. With a wedding to plan, and a house to find, I have learnt that you have to get some kind of work–life balance – otherwise your teaching suffers. Teaching is a great job and while the last two years have been very hard work, I feel more confident and happier to go into my second year of teaching – there is a light at the end ... somewhere!

Lecturer on PGCE course

Name withheld

Q. What kind of attributes do you look for in a prospective trainee teacher?

A. A degree of 2.2 and above or, if not, ample work experience as an LSA in the year before is VERY valuable. They need to have been into school, and to be able to say something about their time there – what was a good lesson and why? They need to be able to reflect on their own experience as a pupil – who was their favourite teacher and why? Also, long-standing evidence of an interest in children and the ability to 'get on with them' is helpful.

Q. Why do you think some students make successful trainees, while others really struggle?

A. It depends on how quickly and easily they can take criticism: some find it difficult adapting to the school culture. Some trainees can't break out of the model of their own schooling, which may not be appropriate for their placement school.

Q. What makes a 'good' teacher?

A. That's too vast a subject to say. However, it would include a willingness to continue to learn, and continue to reflect on their practice in light of their professional experience, colleagues' advice and research evidence.

Q. What advice could you give trainees about successful teaching placements?

A. Know your place! Be considerate of busy teachers. Try to run as much as you can yourself. Give teachers feedback forms. Think about targets you want to work on. Work on your targets each week.

Q. What advice could you give trainees about being successful on the course as a whole?

A. Be prepared for it to be hard, for you to feel very small sometimes, and completely exasperated, but enjoy the good bits! It gets better in your second year of teaching!!

Useful books for trainee teachers

How to Survive your First Year in Teaching
Author: Sue Cowley
Publisher: Continuum
Price: £12.99
ISBN: 0-8264-6465-3

I wrote this book after surviving my own first year in teaching. I realized that there weren't any books available that told you about that first year *as it really is*, so I decided to write one. The book covers the whole range of important things that you need to know about – classroom and behaviour management, dealing with paperwork, induction, professional development, and so on.

Essential Teaching Skills
Author: Chris Kyriacou
Publisher: Nelson Thornes
Price: £15
ISBN: 0-7487-3514-3

An overview of the key skills needed to become a successful teacher. This book has quite a 'dry' tone which I didn't find particularly engaging. However, it could prove useful for university essays because it gives references to other writers/researchers and suggestions for further reading.

The Craft of the Classroom
Author: Michael Marland
Publisher: Heinemann Educational
Price: £14.25
ISBN: 0-435-80579-7
This book is a true 'classic' – over 30 years old and still in print. Its age means that it sometimes reads in an old-fashioned way, but the ideas that it contains are still useful in the modern classroom. It provides more of a philosophy for teachers than a set of strategies or tips, but will be helpful for the new teacher nonetheless.

3 Teaching practice

For many trainee teachers, teaching practice (TP) is the most exciting (and scariest!) part of the teacher training course. It is during your TPs that you get the chance to put all that theory and reading into practice, and that you discover how challenging and rewarding the job can really be. In this chapter you'll find lots of information, tips and ideas about surviving and succeeding on TP. The advice that I give will help you cope with the practical issues you might face on TP, and also to feel better prepared for any problems that could crop up.

Preparing for teaching practice

Getting ready to go on your first teaching practice (TP) can feel like a daunting prospect. It may be a number of years since you last set foot in a classroom and, in any case, working in a school as a teacher is very different to attending a school as a student. You may have heard worrying stories about the type of bad behaviour you're likely to come across. You will certainly be feeling at least a little unsure and anxious about what lies ahead. If you're anything like me, you probably have a bit of a sick feeling in your stomach about facing your first class of children.

There are lots of things that you can do to prepare yourself for, survive, and succeed on TP. And with at least some advance knowledge and tips about the process, you can lessen the stress of your first TP.

Common concerns and how to address them

Here are some of the more common concerns and questions about TP, both ones to do with being in the classroom, and also the more practical aspects of the whole experience. Hopefully my answers will help you feel more confident in the days and weeks leading up to your own first school experience.

Should I plan some work for the children?

Will I be thrown in 'at the deep end'?

Should I prepare anything at all?

How can I find out more about my TP school?

Do I need to bring my own drinks with me?

What about lunch?

How early should I arrive?

What should I do when I arrive at the school?

I start my first TP tomorrow, and I'm feeling completely terrified – is this normal?

- *Should I plan some work for the children?* In short, no. Although it is very tempting when you're a keen student teacher, it is not really worth your while to do too much lesson preparation in advance. One of the most crucial things about planning is that it suits the children you are teaching – at this point children you haven't yet met.
- *Will I be thrown in 'at the deep end'?* Again, probably not. On your first teaching practice it is highly unlikely you will be given completely free rein with a class. At this point you will not have sufficient experience, and the class teacher is unlikely to want to hand over his or her students immediately. Rather, you might simply be observing what goes on, or the class teacher could ask you to work with some small groups at first. Don't worry, eventually you will be given the freedom to prepare and teach some lessons of your own.
- *Should I prepare anything at all?* It may help you feel better prepared if you have some ideas ready. These could be for quick games, fun activities or interesting exercises that you could use if you are asked to look after the class. In any case, this type of 'mini' planning will come in handy later on.
- *How can I find out more about my TP school?* With the advent of the internet, this is now fairly straightforward. Look up the school's latest Ofsted report at www.ofsted.gov.uk. Find out its 'vital statistics' on the performance tables webpage (www.dfes.gov.uk/performancetables). Remember, though, that reports and statistics can only ever give you a 'snapshot' view of a school – you may find that the reality of the place is actually very different.

- *Do I need to bring my own drinks with me?* The 'tea and coffee' situation varies from school to school. Some schools provide their staff with mugs, tea bags, coffee, milk and hot water, but in my experience this is actually quite rare. In many schools, teachers are expected to bring in their own refreshments. You may experience some resentment if you turn up in the staffroom expecting to 'borrow'. To avoid any possibility of treading on toes, take in your own mug and whatever drink-making equipment you might require on the first day at school.
- *What about lunch?* Remember that the school could be a fair distance from the nearest shops, and that the catering at lunchtime might not be to your taste. Better to take your own packed lunch with you, at least on the first day, until you have sussed out the situation.
- *How early should I arrive?* Aim to arrive extra early on your first day of TP. At this point, you won't be sure about how long travelling to the school will take, and it's better to be safe than sorry. Nothing makes a worse impression than a teacher who arrives late. In the teaching profession it is absolutely vital that you are in school and ready to start work when your children arrive. Remember that schools are very busy places first thing in the morning. It could be that you are left hanging around for a while before somebody is available to deal with you.
- *What should I do when I get to the school?* When you arrive, make sure that you report to the main school reception. You will probably be asked to 'sign in' and perhaps be given a badge to wear, identifying you as a visitor to the school. You might then be taken up to the staffroom to wait until someone can see you.
- *I start my first TP tomorrow, and I'm feeling completely terrified – is this normal?* In short, yes! You may well find that you have trouble sleeping the night before your first day at school, or that you have a nervous, sick feeling in your stomach. Don't worry about this – it is perfectly normal, and indeed even experienced teachers often feel this way at the start of a new school year or term (I know I do).

The first day

It is extremely unlikely that you'll be thrown in at the deep end on your first day at school, and expected to actually look after a class on your own. What is more likely is that you will be asked to observe the class or the teacher, perhaps helping out with a small group of students once they have been set a task on which to work. Here's a checklist of tips for what to do (and what not to do) on that crucial first day, followed by a more detailed explanation of each piece of advice:

> ## Surviving the first day
>
> Get your bearings
>
> Locate the facilities
>
> Find out about timings
>
> Get some information
>
> Make useful contacts
>
> Approach the staffroom with care

- *Get your bearings*: Begin to learn the layout of the school. If you're not automatically given a map, ask for one at school reception and spend time studying it. If you get time during the day, do a walkabout around the school buildings to familiarize yourself with them.
- *Locate the facilities*: Find out where the vital amenities are: especially important are the toilets, the staffroom, the assembly hall, the canteen, the school office and the photocopying machine.
- *Find out about timings*: You will need to become completely au fait with the timing of the school day. Timetables vary considerably from school to school, so make sure you learn:
  - What time the school day starts and finishes
  - How long the lessons are
  - Whether time is given (in a secondary school) for students to move between lessons
  - How long the breaks are, and whether these are the same for all students (some schools run different lunch timings for different age groups or Key Stages)
  - Whether there is a daily or weekly assembly, and when this takes place
  - In a secondary school, whether the timetable runs over one or two weeks
- *Get some information*: If you can, get hold of a copy of some of the more important school policies. It will prove especially useful to read about the school rules and the whole-school behaviour policy, especially if you are working in a 'challenging' school. That way you have some advance knowledge about what to do if a child does misbehave.
- *Make useful contacts*: Find out, and memorize, the names of key members of staff. As well as the class teacher, identify a couple of senior managers in case you need to refer a student. Make a real effort to get

to know the school secretary and the office staff. These people know a lot about the way that the school runs, and they can make your life much easier by answering many of the questions that you have.

- *Approach the staffroom with care*: A word of warning: do watch where you sit in the staff room. It may seem petty, but teachers can be extremely territorial about their favourite chairs. Before you park yourself in a seat, ask 'is it OK if I sit here?' This might seem silly to you right now, but just wait until you've got a full-time teaching job and you find a trainee in your own favourite seat in the staffroom.

Observations

One of the most valuable parts of any teaching practice is the chance to watch others in action. In fact, even very experienced teachers can still find observations a very worthwhile and helpful activity. Do bear in mind that being observed can be a little intimidating, and be sensitive to your teacher's feelings. Remember, too, that it is not just the teacher you are observing, but also the students. You can find lots of specific advice and practical ideas below for making the most of time spent doing observations.

Observing the class

At the start of a teaching practice, you'll be given a chance to observe the class or classes of the teacher with whom you're going to be working. Your college might ask you to fill out an observation sheet as you do this. Having the time to do these observations is a wonderful opportunity – in fact one that would benefit many working teachers, who rarely get the chance to watch their colleagues at work. What, then, should you be watching out for and learning about as you observe your TP class or classes?

Observation checklist

- ☐ The whole class
- ☐ Individual children
- ☐ Patterns
- ☐ Rules and control mechanisms
- ☐ Expectations
- ☐ Behaviour
- ☐ Rewards and sanctions
- ☐ Resources and equipment
- ☐ Classroom environment
- ☐ The teacher

- *The children as a whole class*: On a general level, how do the children work and behave? Are they keen to learn, concentrating well on what the teacher says and the tasks at hand? Alternatively, are they what is euphemistically known as 'challenging' children, whose behaviour must be closely regulated? Remember that you are probably watching a fairly experienced teacher, and one whom the children already know well. This will have an impact on overall levels of behaviour and work, so please do not expect exactly the same responses from them when you do get the chance to teach.
- *Individual children*: Are there any 'personalities' in the class, or any children who have special learning needs? You might like to talk to the teacher further about these children after the lesson, to get more information about their particular difficulties. Try to avoid making judgements about your students before you get to experience them for yourself: children respond very differently to different teachers.
- *Patterns*: Does the class or day follow a specific pattern? For instance, at what point is the register taken? Do the children sit and listen to a story at the end of the day? What is the 'routine' for going to and coming in from break and lunch? Do the children stand behind their chairs at the end of the lesson? Consider using these patterns yourself when you do get to teach the class – it will give the students a sense of consistency and help you control them.
- *Rules and control mechanisms*: What classroom rules are already in place that you can use to your benefit? Are there school rules that the children must follow? Does the teacher use any control mechanisms that you can take advantage of, for instance 'hands up' for silence, or a 'silent seat' for when he or she wishes to address the class?
- *Expectations*: What kind of expectations does the teacher have of the class? Does he or she expect perfect work and behaviour, or is a little more leniency applied? Remember, teachers are individuals; your own expectations may vary from those of the teacher you observe.
- *Behaviour*: If there is poor behaviour in the class, when and why does it happen? Are there 'triggers' that set off this bad behaviour, such as a lack of space or issues over the pacing of the lesson? Do the students sit and listen in complete silence to the teacher, or does he or she have to struggle for their attention?
- *Rewards and sanctions*: To what extent does the teacher use (or need to use) rewards and sanctions? What rewards are available for you to use? (Remember, these include verbal and written praise, as well as more tangible rewards such as merits and stickers.) When sanctions are used, when and how are they applied? Is there an 'ultimate'

sanction for extreme behaviour? If detentions are set, how and when are these served?

- *Resources and equipment*: Are the children responsible for bringing in their own resources and equipment? When do they get their pencil cases and books out, and what happens if they have forgotten them? If the school provides equipment, where is this kept and how do the children access it?
- *Classroom environment*: What type of environment is provided for the students, and does this contribute to the way that they work and behave? What are the displays like, and how do the children respond to and interact with these? Are there issues with excessive heat or cold, or a lack of space?

Remember that an observation does not have to be a static event (unless your college has specifically asked you not to get involved just yet). The teacher might set an activity then start to move around the classroom helping individuals. This would be the perfect opportunity for you to join in – you might go to the assistance of a child with his or her hand up, or you might simply sit with one group to talk about the work. Show a bit of willing and initiative – every teacher is grateful for help.

Often, the children will question you about your presence in the classroom, perhaps saying 'are you going to be our new teacher?' Consider how you're going to respond if they do ask. You might be direct, saying 'in a little while'; you could give a more tongue-in-cheek answer such as 'only if you're really, really lucky'.

Observing the teacher

In addition to general observations of the class, watching an experienced teacher at work also gives you a great chance to see which teaching techniques work (and which ones don't). There is no guarantee that you will be watching or working with an exceptionally good teacher, but you can also learn a great deal from observing an ineffective teacher. The truth is that most of us teachers fall somewhere in between the two extremes of brilliant/rubbish, especially on days when we are tired, stressed, or simply in a bad mood.

Avoid making snap judgements until you've actually had a chance to teach these children yourself. You may find out that it is not as straightforward as it at first appears. As you observe the teacher, think about some of the following aspects of the way that the classroom is run:

Classroom control

The way that a teacher controls his or her class can have a huge impact on learning and behaviour. Think about the following:

- How does the lesson start and finish? Is there a pattern to the opening and ending of class time?
- What does the teacher do if it looks like a student is going to misbehave?
- How does the teacher deal with poor behaviour when it does occur?
- How does the teacher move the children from one activity to the next?
- Are there specific ways that the teacher organizes any group work?
- What techniques does the teacher use to put the curriculum across?

Verbal and non-verbal signals

The teacher is constantly giving out signals to a class, subconsciously or otherwise. The more aware you can be of these signals, the more effective you will be as a teacher. Consider the following:

- When the teacher wants the class to pay attention, what verbal and non-verbal signals does s/he use?
- How does the teacher use her/his voice?
- Does s/he ever seem tense or out of control vocally?
- Does s/he feel the need to shout? When does this happen?
- How does s/he use her/his face and body?
- How often does the teacher smile or frown at the class?
- What other facial expressions does s/he use?
- How static or active is s/he within the room?
- How does the teacher use different height levels?
- Does the teacher go to the children when they need help, or do they come to her/him?

Behaviour management

Effective behaviour management is vital for ensuring that learning can take place. Here are some points for you to consider:

- Does the teacher's 'mood' have an influence on behaviour?
- Does he or she approach and talk to the class in a negative or a positive way?
- What part do rewards and sanctions play in behaviour management?
- How are small incidents of misbehaviour dealt with?
- How does the teacher handle any more serious incidents?
- At what stage in an incident does the teacher intervene?
- Does the teacher ignore low-level or 'attention-seeking' misbehaviour?
- Which of the teacher's strategies could you use yourself?
- What is the connection between the teacher's expectations and the way that the students behave?

TOP TIP

At some point during your observation, aim to see the teacher from the children's perspective. How would you feel about this teacher if you were a young person in his or her class? How engaged with and focused on the work would you be? Would you be inclined to behave yourself or not? Use these perceptions to inform your own teaching style.

Getting on with the class teacher

Developing a good relationship with the class teacher is essential for a successful teaching practice. Do remember that the teacher will also have been on TP in the past, and will be aware of your worries and concerns. In the vast majority of cases, he or she will be keen to help and support you. Here are some tips for building a positive relationship.

- *Be sensitive about the space*: Teachers can be surprisingly territorial about their rooms. This is especially so in the primary school where all the teachers will have their own classrooms. (Some secondary school teachers also have their 'own' rooms; others are not so lucky and have to travel around the school to different spaces.) Be sensitive – don't just dump down your stuff wherever you like without asking first. Be careful not to give the feeling that you are 'taking over'. (After all, you'll have a classroom of your own shortly, and you'll want it to be treated with respect.)

- *Be sensitive about the children*: Some teachers are also possessive about their classes, perhaps a secondary school teacher with a top-set GCSE group, where there is a lot of pressure to achieve good results. Remember that the teacher might have some insecurities about handing over the children to you (although most teachers will just be grateful to have your help).

- *See the teacher as an 'expert'*: You can learn a huge amount from the experienced teacher – ask the teacher questions and learn as much as you can. Treat your classroom teacher as an 'expert' on the subject of teaching and pick his or her brains whenever you get the chance.

- *Don't be judgemental*: Don't be too quick to judge the teacher with whom you find yourself working. We all have different teaching styles, and you may have a very different opinion of what constitutes good teaching. If it appears that the teacher cannot control the children, bear in mind that this could indicate a group of very difficult students rather than an ineffective teacher.

- *Be subtle and polite*: It's wise and of course respectful to keep your opinions to yourself. Do not, on any account, gossip about 'your' teacher in the staffroom.

- *Let your teacher have a rest*: Remember that your teacher needs to take breaks – don't spend the whole of lunchbreak grilling him or her on the minutiae of the lesson you just saw.

- *Make yourself useful*: If you are not kept busy with teaching at first, do offer to help put up displays, sort resources, anything that will alleviate some of the load on the teacher.

- *Find a chance to chat*: If your other commitments allow, don't rush off the minute the bell goes at the end of the day. Take time to help clear up any work and tidy the classroom. Perhaps sit down with your teacher and chat about the day over a cup of tea or coffee. This may be the only time that you get a chance to relax together, so make the most of the opportunity.

Problems on teaching practice

Of course, you might encounter some problems while on TP, and it's important to solve any issues as quickly as possible. Here are some of the more common concerns of trainee teachers, along with a suggested course of action to take:

- *'The school treats me as an unpaid supply teacher'*: Occasionally, and it is rare (although certainly not unheard of), some schools do view trainee teachers as useful, free of charge, supply staff. If you find yourself pretty much abandoned to take care of a class or classes, without any decent support, your first response should be to talk to your university tutor about the situation. The school has a responsibility to take your training (and your non-contact time) seriously. Until the situation is remedied, view this kind of 'in at the deep end' situation as a learning experience.

- *'I don't get on with my supervisory teacher'*: It's inevitable that there will be occasions when a student teacher does not get on with his or her supervisory teacher. This can be an awkward situation: it is unlikely that your complaints are going to lead to any changes being made, unless there is something seriously wrong with the teacher's supervision of your practice. Have a word with your college tutor, and ask for some advice. Alternatively, just grin and bear it: keep quiet, do your best, focus on the kids, and wait for the end of TP to come.

- *'I can't control the kids!'*: Behaviour management can seem incredibly difficult when you are a student teacher (indeed it's often tricky for experienced teachers as well). Although you should not be given a class that is completely out of control, you are likely to encounter at least some children who refuse to do as you ask. Developing your behaviour management skills is a crucial part of learning to be an effective teacher, and you are still at the 'learning' part of the process. Look closely at the section in this chapter entitled 'Getting your class to behave', preferably before you start your TP. Look at Chapter 8 ('Classroom and behaviour management') as well; it gives lots of information on behaviour management. Buy yourself a general and practical book on dealing with difficult behaviour (you'll find some suggestions at the end of this chapter). If you are having really horrendous problems, talk to your university tutor, or ask your classroom teacher to come in and assist you for a while. Make your children's safety, and your own safety, the top priority, and don't feel guilty about asking for help.

Planning

Your university may specify the format that you must use when planning lessons during TPs. Alternatively, they may give you a list of areas that must be included (see below for some likely points) then leave the actual layout to your discretion. You will probably be asked to prepare 'Schemes of work' which detail how a whole series of lessons fit together over a longer period, to cover a topic or a particular National Curriculum area. You can find some more information about planning as a working teacher in Chapter 6 ('Preparing to teach'). Once you become a full-time teacher it is very unlikely that you will have the time or the inclination to plan in this much detail ever again.

There are a huge number of ways that you might plan a lesson, but there really is no one 'correct' or definitive way. When you first start out as a trainee teacher, you will probably want to include plenty of detail in your plans. Once you become a working teacher, you'll probably look back at the planning you did as a student in amazement, wondering how on earth you had time to fit it all in! However, there are a number of reasons why detailed planning is actually a good idea at this stage in your teaching career:

- To please your university tutors and pass the course!
- To demonstrate that you are fulfilling the standards for becoming a qualified teacher.
- As part of your initial experimentation in what works for you and what doesn't, when it comes to lesson planning and delivery.
- To help you think through your lessons before you actually teach them.
- To assist you in getting the timing of the lesson right (one of the trickier aspects of lesson delivery when you first begin teaching).
- To give you a sense of security, so that you know exactly what will happen (or should happen) at every point in the lesson.
- To enable you to remember what happened during each lesson, and to reflect on your success (or otherwise) after the event.
- To develop some top-quality lessons, resources and materials that can be re-used at a later stage in your teaching career.

What will be in the lesson plans?

You may be asked to include some or all of the following areas in your lesson plans. As you will see from the length of the list below, planning in this much detail will take a considerable amount of time. It is very helpful to create your own format for planning on a computer, so that you can use this as a basis for each individual lesson. You can find a sample 'student lesson plan' in the section below.

- *Aims*: These describe the overall purpose of the lesson, giving a 'map' to show where you are going with the learning. They say what the teacher is aiming to achieve during the session.
- *Objectives*: Objectives are more specific than aims, and explain exactly what the children will learn during the lesson.
- *Learning outcomes*: This term describes what the children will be able to do as a result of being in your lesson.

- *National Curriculum and QCA references*: You should be able to demonstrate which of the statutory criteria your lesson is going to fulfil.
- *Literacy and Numeracy Strategy references*: If you are teaching within the National Literacy Strategy (NLS) or National Numeracy Strategy (NNS), you will need to show how the activities you use correspond to the learning objectives of these strategies.
- *Activities*: A list of the different activities that will take place during the lesson – this might be simply brief bullet points or a more detailed explanation.
- *Organization*: The 'nuts and bolts' of delivering the lesson. For instance, details of whether work will be done individually, in pairs or in groups, and how these groupings will be organized.
- *Timing*: Sometimes trainees are encouraged to give quite a detailed account of the amounts of time allocated to each activity. In reality, you are unlikely to be able to (or want to) stick too closely to exact timings.
- *Resources and equipment*: Details of any resources or equipment that you will be using during the lesson – what they are, when they will be used, and so on.
- *SEN*: Information about any children in the class with special needs, and how your lesson and activities will cater for these students.
- *Differentiation*: Information about those tasks which will be differentiated for students of varying abilities, and how this will be organized.
- *Evaluation*: Information about how the children or the teacher will evaluate the work that has taken place during the lesson.

You can see an example of a numeracy lesson plan below. This plan was written by teacher Steph Leach when she was a PGCE student (you can see an interview with Steph on pp. 190–2).

Teaching

As you progress through your teaching practices, you will gradually be asked to teach more lessons, and to do so with greater independence from the class teacher. However, you will be given a reduced timetable which should help you manage your time. There will also be no statutory requirement for you to attend meetings, parents' evenings and so on. However, if you are offered the chance to experience these aspects of the job, I'd recommend that you do so.

Lesson: Numeracy – addition and subtraction

Date: Tue 12 March 2002   Working with: Whole Class

Learning Objectives:

We are learning…

To recognize the relationship between addition and subtraction

Links to NC, NNS, NLS, QCA:

Calculations

Mental calculations strategies (+ and –)

- Add or subtract the nearest multiple of 10 or 100, then adjust
- Develop further the relationship between addition and subtraction

Resources:

'Round the Class Maths' Cards (25)

Pre-prepared +, –, =, 20, 30, 50, 500, 250, 750, 1000, 150, 850, 899, 440, 459

Textbooks

Computer example sheets x 2

Whiteboard and pens

Key questions/vocabulary:

Is this statement true?

Is there any other way that this statement could be written and still be true?

How many are there altogether?

Is there always this number? Why?

Is there anyone who is still unsure of what we have been doing?

Extension activities:

Write a sum for your partner to solve adding 3 numbers. How many other ways can they write these numbers to make statements that are true using only + and –?

Use of ICT:

Top group do work on 3 PCs.

Mental/Oral Starter:

'Round the Class Maths'

Each child gets one card which reads 'I have (no.)' and 'I need (sum)'

One child starts by saying I need (sum) and whichever child has the answer to this sum on their card says 'I have …, I need …' and so on until the game gets back around to the first child that started.

If no child volunteers an answer, ask class if they know the answer to the sum and then ask if anyone has this number.

Main Activity:

Using pre-prepared number and function cards put up sum

20 + 30 = 50

Is this statement true?

Is there any other way that this statement could be written and still be true?

Get child to come and move numbers around.

Add the   card.

Could this sum be written another way and still be true?

How many ways can this sum be written in total?

Let's do another one.

500 + 250 = 750

Put up the cards **+, –, =, 1000, 150, 850**

Ask a child to use these numbers to make a statement that is true.

Ask another child to do a different statement.

How many are there altogether?

Is there always this number? Why?

Again with **+, –, =, 899, 440, 459**

Is there anyone who is still unsure of what we have been doing? (If so, they could stay on the carpet and work through exercises together with support).

Introduce independent work and explain how it is to be written in their books/on PC (do example).

Plenary:

Did anyone get onto the extension task on the chalkboard?

Can someone give me an example of the sum they gave their partner? (If not, make one up.)

What other ways could this be written?

Do another one.

Progression:

The relationship between multiplication and division.

How and what should I teach in my TP lessons?

Your teaching practices are a time when you should be able to enjoy and experiment with your teaching, so try to take full advantage. Put as much time as you can into planning and delivering exciting and interesting lessons, and think carefully about how well the children respond to this high quality learning experience. Here are some ideas about the type of approaches and activities you could use in your TP lessons, to really motivate and excite your students.

- *Use unusual teaching strategies*: Take a few risks – try out some original or unusual ideas with your classes. There is always the chance that these activities will fall flat, but it is more likely that they will really inspire and motivate your children. It's a great idea to experiment now, while you have the chance and nobody really minds you 'getting it wrong'. However, it is probably best to save your wildest experiments for those times when you are not being observed.
- *Keep it active and practical*: Incorporate active, practical exercises into your teaching whenever you can, whatever the subject you are teaching. Getting the children actively involved with their learning is an excellent way to ensure that the work sticks with them. It will also help you avoid the minor misbehaviour that happens when the children get bored. At first, it can feel quite scary to take this approach, but you'll soon get the hang of it. For instance, in a primary maths lesson, you might teach addition by asking the children to come to the front of the room as you 'add' more to your total. As well as being a good motivator and learning tool, practical exercises teach you lots about the logistics of managing large numbers of people in a confined space.
- *Think laterally*: Take the chance offered by TPs to think 'outside the box', approaching familiar topics in a lateral way. For instance, if you are doing a piece of writing about the local area, you might do so from the perspective of a visiting alien. Think also about how you can incorporate cross-curricular activities or ideas into your teaching. You might be writing, playing and recording 'raps' in a foreign-language lesson, or designing and building monsters in an English lesson on *Frankenstein*.
- *Keep it topical and relevant*: Young people are always better motivated by work that they see as topical and relevant to their own lives. You might find some way to incorporate the latest toy craze into your teaching, or use the format of a familiar television show (such as *Jerry Springer*) to create a forum for discussion.
- *Plan for the future*: See your TPs as the 'information-gathering' stage in your teaching career. As well as gathering information about how to become an effective teacher, you can also start to gather useful ideas

and resources. Start to build a 'bank' of useful games and short starter or filler activities for your subject. Spend time making really top-quality resources (such as board games) that you will be able to re-use later on.

Getting your class to behave

Behaviour management is a hugely complex aspect of teaching, and one that concerns many trainee teachers, and indeed many experienced teachers as well. You may be lucky enough to find yourself in a relatively 'easy' school, where the children are naturally inclined to behave well (although not necessarily all that well for a trainee teacher). Alternatively, you may be given the greater challenge of working in a 'difficult' school, where behaviour management concerns take up a great deal of your time and energy. Many of the issues faced by trainee teachers are also of concern to supply teachers; look at the ideas in Chapter 14, 'Tips for supply teachers' (pp. 237–9) for some additional strategies.

See your TPs as a chance to develop your behaviour management skills: an opportunity to make mistakes and learn from them, as you begin the process of becoming a teacher. You won't get it right straight away, but persist and it will gradually get much easier. Here are some top tips that you may find useful:

- *Be confident*: Yes, I do know how hard it is, especially when you feel terrified inside. But if you look like you know what you're doing (even when you don't) this will communicate itself to the children and make them feel more secure about working with you. If you look scared and uncertain, the children will quickly notice this and try to take advantage. A lot of behaviour management is 'bluff': it's more about the strength and clarity of the verbal and non-verbal signals that you send, than the reality of your skills as a teacher.
- *Be well informed*: Your school should have a 'whole-school behaviour policy', hopefully an effective one. Before you start working with the children, take time to study this policy and to understand it as fully as you can. The key is to know what is and what isn't allowed in the classroom, and what you should do when children misbehave. If you're not entirely sure, the students will pick up on this and very quickly start to try it on. Make sure you are totally up to speed on the kind of rewards and sanctions that are available for you to use.
- *Make your expectations clear*: Children need to know what is expected of them, to be told where they stand, and what they can and can't get away with. The first time that they meet you, they will know as little about you as you do about them. The key to keeping control is to show

them that you have clear and consistent expectations of their behaviour. Children seem to have an innate sense of when their teacher is unsure about his or her expectations. They are usually aware of the (exciting) possibilities of 'getting one over on' the supply or student teacher. So, talk to your class about what you expect, giving them as much clarity as you can. It's hard at first, because you probably are not totally sure about what you actually do want. It does, however, get much easier with time and experience.

- *Use 'I expect' statements*: These offer a very useful way of establishing your expectations. Aim to give at least three 'I expect you to' statements the first time you teach the class. Here are three suggestions that you might like to use:
  - 'I expect you to look at me and listen in complete silence when I'm talking.'
  - 'I expect you to work to the best of your ability.'
  - 'I expect you to stay in your chair and put your hand up if you need help.'
- *Don't get defensive*: It's the most natural thing in the world to become defensive if a student 'takes you on', or if a class is messing around and won't do what you say. The problem is, if the children manage to make the teacher defensive, they know that they are winning. If you start shouting and getting wound up, this will only give the students more reason to misbehave.
- *Keep it calm*: In teaching, a calm approach really does pay dividends. For instance, it's very tempting at first to give the children work that gets them overexcited, because you believe that this will make them like you. But until you are more experienced in classroom management it will often simply lead to chaos. Similarly, aim to stay calm when you are managing children's behaviour, as well as their learning. A teacher who refuses to get wound up or angry will deal with behaviour issues much more effectively; it will also encourage the children to stay calm as well.
- *Be positive*: An assertive (not aggressive) and positive manner demonstrates that you are a confident and decent person. When you are in a bad mood, for whatever reason, or not feeling particularly well, try not to let this filter through into the way that you treat your children. Consider how they will perceive your behaviour and attitude from their side of the desks.
- *Use your voice carefully*: Think carefully about how you use your voice when you first start teaching. Good modulation is very important, especially with young children: for instance being able to move between a happy and a disappointed tone. Avoid shouting at all costs: it can damage your voice and it is very rarely an effective means of discipline.

- *Try to focus on rewards*: When you're finding behaviour hard to manage, it's tempting to dish out sanctions right, left and centre in an attempt to regain the upper hand. Unfortunately, this can actually make the situation worse, because it will create a very negative atmosphere in your classroom. Instead of focusing on punishment, try giving rewards to those children who are doing what you want. Ignore low-level misbehaviour as appropriate, especially any attention-seeking behaviour. A quick word of praise to a well-behaved child can refocus the rest of the class very easily.
- *A learning process*: Remember that learning to teach is difficult, a process that takes many years (and one, of course, which is never truly 'completed'). One of the best ways for us to learn is to make mistakes, to reflect on what went wrong, and to understand how to improve things for the next time. In fact, all the best teachers are still learning from day to day, even right at the end of their careers. As a student teacher you are just at the very start of that process: don't expect too much too soon.
- *Keep a perspective*: It's very easy to lose sight of what really does and doesn't matter. At the end of the day, a few children messing around in your lesson is not a total disaster. The world really won't end if you don't get it right the very first time.
- *Get help, support and advice wherever you can*: Teachers are brilliant at supporting each other, and they will understand what you're going through because they have been there themselves. Turn to the staff at your school for tips and suggestions if you are struggling to manage behaviour. Other sources of support will include your tutors at college, message boards on the internet, such as the *TES* staffroom, and your family and friends. Don't struggle on alone, it really isn't necessary.
- *Read a good book*: There are lots of excellent books which deal with behaviour management, so take the time to read them, preferably before you go on TP. Instead of the theoretical stuff that you might have been encouraged to read at university, look through a practical book on the subject. The section below gives some ideas.

Useful books on behaviour management

Getting the Buggers to Behave (Third Edition)
Author: Sue Cowley
Publisher: Continuum
Price: £14.99
ISBN: 0-8264-8912-5

I wrote this book after (just about) surviving in a pretty challenging school, and it's gone on to be a bestseller. It contains loads of practical tips, suggestions and strategies for dealing with misbehaviour and encouraging better behaviour.

Cracking the Hard Class: Strategies for Managing the Harder than Average Class
Author: Bill Rogers
Publisher: Paul Chapman Publishing
Price: £18.99
ISBN: 0-7619-6928-4
A useful guide for when you have one (or more) classes with particularly difficult behaviour. Plenty of anecdotes from Bill Rogers' own teaching experiences and some interesting case studies. Some useful suggestions for supply teachers (he calls them 'relief' teachers).

Surviving and Succeeding in Difficult Classrooms
Author: Paul Blum
Publisher: Routledge
Price: £17.99
ISBN: 0-415-39720-0
A book that 'tells it as it is' about working in a challenging school. It gives some useful, practical and realistic tips for surviving the toughest teaching jobs. This book would mainly be of interest to secondary school teachers, particularly those working in an inner-city environment.

Managing Boys' Behaviour
Author: Tabatha Rayment
Publisher: Continuum
Price: £9.99
ISBN: 0-8264-8501-4
This book gives an interesting overview into why boys misbehave. It offers useful strategies and techniques for teachers to use with their difficult students.

Managing Very Challenging Behaviour
Author: Louisa Leaman
Publisher: Continuum
Price: £9.99
ISBN: 0-8264-8539-1
This is a useful guide to dealing with different kinds of 'very challenging' behaviour. Chapter headings deal with a variety of tricky student attitudes, ranging from 'Yeah, Whatever!' to 'Go On Then ... Make Me'.

4

Job hunting

This chapter will help you find a job in teaching. It may be that you are a trainee teacher, just starting the hunt for your first post; it could be that you've got a year or more of experience and now want to move on to another school, perhaps into a promoted post. Alternatively, you might be a mature entrant to the profession, moving into teaching from the commercial world, and wondering exactly what the job-hunting process involves. You will find all the information, advice and tips that you need here.

Finding a job

The nature of schools means that teachers are required to give a relatively long period of notice (roughly a full half term before you wish to leave a school). Teachers are only allowed to leave at the end of a school term. This gives the school plenty of time to find and employ a new teacher. In addition, working to the end of a school term means that students are given reasonable continuity in their education.

The dates of the three school terms are deemed to be:

Autumn term – 1 September to 31 December inclusive
Spring term – 1 January to 30 April inclusive
Summer term – 1 May to 31 August inclusive

(Although don't panic, these term dates *include* the holidays!)
The actual deadlines for handing in your notice are:

- Autumn term: 31 October
- Spring term: 28 February
- Summer term: 31 May

This of course means that there are peaks in the number of job adverts around these times of the year. In fact, you'll notice this reflected in the size of the jobs section of the *Times Educational Supplement* (*TES*), which swells to the thickness of a small tree.

Publications

When you're hunting for a job, you'll find that the *TES* becomes your bible. It is published every Friday and most schools (and universities) will provide at least one copy for their staff or students to browse. However, this single copy of the *TES* can prove like gold dust (especially in a school where the teachers are keen to escape) and the jobs section has usually done a disappearing act by the end of morning break. So, when you are job hunting it is well worth buying your own copy. Alternatively, use one of the internet sites listed below.

Jobs in education can also be found in the broadsheet newspapers, such as the *Guardian* and the *Independent* (see the Directory, pages 353–4 for details). If you're interested in a post in a single-faith school, you could also look at the religious press.

The internet

The internet has made it very easy for teachers to access and search for jobs. The *TES* jobs website (www.jobs.tes.co.uk) is updated each Friday morning, and contains the same jobs as you will find in the printed publication. You can search for jobs in various different subject areas, age ranges, locations, and so on. You do not need to register any personal details to access the jobs. The ETeach website (www.eteach.com) also features jobs in education. Again, you can use a combination of various search criteria, such as subject, type of job, and so on.

The local authority

Depending on how efficient your local education authority (LA) is, it may be worth contacting them directly to check on the jobs situation locally. Many local authorities also send a booklet with current jobs to the schools in their area. If you are already in post and looking for a new job in a nearby location, this could prove useful. Some LAs advertise for NQTs in the *TES*, particularly in the First Appointments supplement, which is published several times a year and included with the main sections of the paper.

Your local authority will have a 'recruitment strategy manager' (RSM) who may be able to help you in your search for a post. Again, much will depend on the efficiency of your local LA. Look on the website of the local council in the area where you wish to teach to find more information and contact details.

Supply agencies

If you are interested in working as a supply teacher, or if you need to take supply work until you find a permanent post, you will find a huge number of supply agencies vying for your services. Many of these agencies advertise in the publications listed in this chapter, and on the internet. Agencies range from the small, local operation, perhaps run by ex-teachers, to the larger national operations with branches in many different locations.

You can find a list of supply agencies in the Directory, pages 353–4. You will also find a lot more information about supply work in Chapter 14. It is also possible to register for supply work via your LA. This route is in fact recommended by some teaching unions, but again the reality of doing supply via an LA will vary a great deal across the country. In Scotland, applying to an LA is the accepted way of finding supply work.

Working overseas

In my experience, working abroad as a teacher is a wonderful experience, and one that can only enhance both your personal and professional life. You have the chance to teach a very different group of students, to see a bit of the world and to experience another culture. However, there are pitfalls out there for the unwary, and do bear in mind that your employment rights will probably be less well protected than they are in the UK. Most international schools are looking for teachers who already have at least a year or two's teaching experience. For an insight into what teaching abroad is really like, see Chapter 13 (pp. 231–4).

If you are thinking about working overseas, your best bet is to work at a school which belongs to an accredited organization. The European Council of International Schools (ECIS) and the Council of International Schools (CIS) are both good starting points. You can find more information about these organizations at their websites – www.ecis.org and www.cois.org. The CIS holds teacher 'Recruitment Centres' internationally, and school representatives attend these to find recruits. The London Recruitment Centres take place in February and May. For more information see www.cois.org/Recruitment/lrc.htm. Overseas teaching jobs can also be found in the *TES* jobs section.

The independent sector

When you're looking for your first (or subsequent) teaching job, you may want to consider working at an independent school. If you are interested, look at the Independent Schools' Council website (www.isis.org.uk). When considering a job in the independent sector, there are a number of differences of which you need to be aware:

- Many private schools operate a different pay scale to those in the state sector. This may be more, or less, than the nationally agreed pay rates.
- Your working terms and conditions may differ to those agreed by the government with state sector teachers.
- Similarly, your pension arrangements may not be the same as for state sector workers.
- If you are just starting teaching, and need to take induction, you should check that the school is able to offer and support this.

There are a number of factors for and against working in private education. At the end of the day, the decision about which sector to work in will be an entirely personal matter.

For

- Smaller class sizes
- Better resources and more funding
- Better school buildings and facilities
- Generally speaking, discipline is likely to be better
- On the whole, higher academic standards (especially in schools that select by academic ability)
- Some independent schools will accept graduates without traditional teaching qualifications

Against

- There is often greater pressure from parents and the school to demonstrate academic success
- There can be a higher demand on teachers' time outside of the classroom, for instance in extracurricular activities
- It may be hard to move back into the state sector
- Personal considerations, such as your own stance on private education

Types of state school

State schools fall into different 'types' according to who runs the school and the way that admissions are handled. Nine out of ten children in England go to a state school. The following are considered 'mainstream' state schools:

- *Community schools*: These are provided by the LA, which also decides on admissions. They do not adhere to a specific form of religious education.

- *Foundation schools*: These are provided by the LA, but the school manages its own admissions, and can select criteria for this. As with community schools, they have no particular religious affiliation.
- *Voluntary aided schools*: These schools are partly maintained by voluntary organizations. The religious teaching will be based on the denomination of the school as originally set up.
- *Voluntary controlled schools*: As with voluntary aided these schools have a particular religious affiliation, but they are fully funded by the LA.

In addition to these mainstream schools, there are a number of other types. The admissions process to these schools is run in the same way as mainstream schools, but there may be extra admission criteria.

- *Community special schools and foundation special schools*: These provide education for children who have specific, special educational needs or learning difficulties.
- *Faith schools*: While these are similar to other mainstream state schools, they usually follow a much more religious and spiritual curriculum than non-faith schools.
- *Grammar schools*: These aim to cater for high achievers and select all or most of their students based on their academic ability.
- *City Technology Colleges (CTCs)*: These are non-fee-paying schools in urban areas for pupils of all abilities aged 11 to 18. They are managed independently and their curriculum has a strong focus on science and technology. These schools often offer a wide range of vocational qualifications as well as A levels.
- *Academies*: These are independently managed schools for pupils of all abilities. They are set up by sponsors from business, faith or voluntary groups in partnership with the DfES and LA.
- *Maintained boarding schools*: Tuition is free, but a fee is charged to cover board and lodging costs.

Trust Schools

'Trust Schools' are the government's latest big idea, as described in a White Paper in October 2005 (*Higher Standards, Better Schools for All*). The idea is for a new type of school, which would be government-funded but which (like academies) would receive additional funds from local businesses, universities or charities. Governors would be appointed to help run the school, some of these being the parents of children at the school. The idea behind Trust Schools is to give schools more independence and freedom.

'Specialist' schools

In England, a recent innovation has been the 'specialist' school or college, and there are now over 2,000 schools with this status. There are ten areas in which schools can specialize: arts, business and enterprise, engineering, humanities, languages, mathematics and computing, music, science, sports and technology. For more information on this programme, see www.standards.dfes.gov.uk/specialistschools.

When using a school's specialist status as the basis for taking a teaching post, make sure you look into how 'deep' the special interest goes. Anecdotal evidence suggests that some schools have applied for specialist status simply to attract additional funding for equipment, for instance for extra computers.

Applying for jobs

Because the majority of teaching jobs are in the public sector, the application process is, generally speaking, very similar from school to school, or from LA to LA. Those of you who have previously applied for jobs and worked in the private sector may find the whole application process mystifyingly long-winded and complex.

Application forms

Most LAs use a fairly standard application form, and you can see an example of this in the Teacher's Toolkit (Part Six, pp. 287–9). You will probably be asked to provide a 'letter of application' or 'supporting statement' (see below) to accompany this. There is usually a small space on the application form, where you can write your supporting statement. Normally, this is far too small to suffice, and it is fine to simply put 'see attached' in the box, and staple or paperclip your statement to the application form.

You should fill out the application form in black ink and, it goes without saying, take great care not to make mistakes. Filling out these forms is a frustratingly time-consuming process, but sadly there is no way around it. Some schools simply ask for a CV and a letter of application.

> **TOP TIP**
>
> I really wish someone had advised me to do this when I first started teaching …
>
> Make sure you keep a note of all those little 'extras' that you do outside your normal job, perhaps in a small notebook. For instance, you might have acted as ICT rep, directed the school play or organized a trip. Keep a note, too, of all the training courses you go on. All these things should be included with your application, either on the form itself or in your supporting statement. So, when you next have to fill in an application, you can refer to your notebook rather than racking your brains trying to remember what you did a year or two ago.

Referees

When you apply for a teaching post, you will usually be asked to provide the names of two people who can give a reference. For a trainee, this might be your university tutor and a TP supervisory teacher. For a working teacher, this will probably be your current headteacher and perhaps a head of department or other manager. Do, please, make sure that you ask your referees before naming them on an application. If you are lucky, your referees may show you a copy of what they have written about you, although this is by no means guaranteed.

Many schools will only apply for references once you have been shortlisted or actually offered the job. There will usually be an option on the application form to say whether the school may apply for references before interview. (If you are already working as a teacher, but don't wish your school to know that you are job hunting, this lets you apply for jobs without alerting them to the fact.)

Letters of application

The 'letter of application' (sometimes also called a 'personal statement') is peculiar to the teaching profession. If you're a mature entrant to teaching who has worked in the commercial sector previously, you may find this aspect of the process rather puzzling. The letter of application allows the candidate to demonstrate how his or her experience, skills, abilities and personality match the post being advertised. Your letter of application will be used, in addition to your application form, to decide whether to invite you for interview.

You can find some sample letters of application in Chapter 17. Here are some thoughts and tips to help you write a successful letter of application.

- *Fit it to the job description*: Match your description of your abilities and experiences to the post for which you're applying. Look carefully at the job description before you start, and ensure that what you say about yourself fits with what the school wants. This might call for some 'creative writing', but don't tell any outright fibs. You'll only get caught out at the interview.

- *Echo the language of the advert*: The language you use should echo that of the school's advert. They will have thought carefully about the wording, designing it to attract the appropriate candidates, and you should consider it closely too. Take time to look under the surface at what they are really saying. For instance, a school that describes its students as 'challenging' will be looking for a teacher who is enthusiastic about working with more difficult children. In this case, you might comment that you 'relish a challenge'. A school which notes that its intake includes 'children with a wide range of abilities' will be looking for a teacher who is able to differentiate his or her teaching and planning, to suit students of all abilities. Again, comment on how your previous experiences fit you to a post at this type of school.

- *Make the most of the experience you have*: If you're a trainee with little or no work experience, talk about your teaching practices and any other voluntary or part-time work you have done, especially that which involved working with children. Talk, too, about what you have contributed to university life. Perhaps you've been involved with the student union, or have helped to put on student drama productions? What have you learnt from these experiences? How might these help you contribute to the extracurricular aspects of school life, as well as in your day to day teaching? Which skills did you develop that might help you in your work in the classroom?

- *Don't be shy!* This is no time to be a retiring daisy. Describe your abilities and skills, and how they match the post. Talk about your talents, but try to do so in a reasonably self-deprecating way. Use phrases such as 'I feel that I am' or 'I believe myself to be'. That way, you won't sound as though you're boasting.

- *Structure it properly*: Although you don't want the letter of application to be excessively long, do include a brief introduction and conclusion, just as you would when writing an essay. Your introduction might give an overview of you and your style and philosophy as a teacher. Your conclusion could summarize the ways in which you meet the requirements of the post.

- *Check how it should be written*: Some schools like your letter of application to be handwritten, so check whether this is the case before you start. Unfortunately, handwriting application letters can be very time-consuming, especially if you make a mistake halfway through. If you do have to handwrite your application, it's a good idea to type it out on a computer first, to make sure that you have it word perfect before you start. In this way, you will also have a copy of the letter, in case you need to use something similar in the future. If you do get halfway through and make a mistake, remember that the excessive use of Tipp-Ex is not going to go down well. Obviously, you should also ensure that your handwriting is as neat as possible.

- *Create a 'standard letter'*: Use a computer to create a standardized letter which you can then tailor to the different jobs for which you apply. This standard letter should include all the essential information about yourself and your skills and experiences. You can then add in some comments that are personalized to each individual post.
- *Make it readable*: If you do send a computerized letter of application, use a normal font such as Arial or Times New Roman, rather than a fancy, pretty looking one that is liable to irritate the reader. Ensure that the type size is large enough to be easily read (12 point is usually perfect). If possible, stick to one page of A4, or an absolute maximum of two pages. If you do use a second sheet, ensure that you staple the two pages together, including your name and the post on each one in case they get split up.

Job interviews

One of the drawbacks of a teaching job is that you only really find out what a school is like after you've actually started teaching there. Although this applies to all jobs, in education the ethos and management of a school can have a huge impact on the quality of your experience as an employee. In addition, if you do make a mistake in the post you take on, there is nothing you can do about it once you've agreed to take the job. In most cases you will be looking at a reasonably long-term commitment to the post.

On the day of the interview you're likely to be nervous, and this could stop you from getting a realistic view of what the school is really like. In addition, the headteacher will want you to get the best impression possible. After all, they need to fill that vacancy. It's unlikely, therefore, that they'll take you to visit that nightmare Year 9 group whose horrendous behaviour forced the previous teacher to quit. On the other hand, you may be looking for a school which presents you with a challenge, rather than one at which all the children behave in an exemplary fashion.

Unlike some other professional jobs, teaching appointments are generally made on the basis of a single interview (although the 'interview' may be only part of a long day at the school), along with references. Also unusual is the fact that teachers are typically made to decide whether or not they will take the job on the day that the interview takes place. This puts you in a difficult situation if you're unsure about whether or not this is the job for you. In the following sections you'll find some useful checklists to help you make your decision.

Pre-interview checklist

Before you even attend the interview, make sure that you are well prepared. This will also help you feel more confident on the day, as you will be going into a situation about which you have some prior knowledge. Here is a checklist with some ideas for preparing yourself for the ordeal ahead:

- *Look at school information*: Read the school prospectus or brochure carefully, and any details sent to you with your application form. Try to read between the lines. Remember: a school brochure is designed to encourage parents to send their children to that school, and it will by its very nature be showing the best side of the organization.
- *Look at inspection reports*: Check the school's latest Ofsted report (available at www.ofsted.gov.uk). Again, read between the lines, but bear in mind that some of these reports will be a good few years out of date, and much may have changed at the school since the inspection was done.
- *Look at government information*: Look at the school's vital statistics in the government performance tables. These give you information about exam results, absence rates and so on. They will also show you whether the school is improving or not. You can find this information at www.dfes.gov.uk/performancetables/.
- *Don't be too judgemental*: Remember that Ofsted reports can never tell you the full story about a school, and they are not necessarily up to date. Even though the children are weak academically, or come from disadvantaged backgrounds, they may still be hard-working and rewarding to teach.
- *Check the school's popularity*: Find out whether the school is under- or oversubscribed. This will tell you whether the school is popular with its local community. Undersubscribed schools may have to take on students who have been permanently excluded from a previous school, and this can have a serious impact on the overall behaviour and atmosphere.

- *Check the school's location*: Take a look at the local area, especially if you are not familiar with this part of the world. Are you looking for a 'cushy' job in a leafy suburb? Or would you be more interested in a busy and vibrant multicultural community? If possible, visit the area just as the schools are kicking out their students for the day: watch to see what behaviour is like outside of school hours, as this will give you a rough indicator of attitudes during school time.
- *If possible, visit the school*: Ask to visit the school before your interview – many schools will be happy to accommodate such a request. This visit will give you the chance to take a realistic look around, at a time when you are not feeling stressed or nervous. It will also demonstrate how enthusiastic you are about the post, and could well have a beneficial impact on your chances of getting the job.
- *Ask around*: If you live locally, ask around among your friends and family to get a general view of the reputation of the school. If you can find someone whose child attends the school, this would give you a really good perspective on how things really are in the classrooms.
- *Prepare yourself*: Make sure that you have some questions prepared to ask during the interview. There is no harm in writing these down if you wish, and referring to your notes. There's no need to go overboard, but do show that you've thought about what you want to know in advance. See the section below, 'The interview questions' (pp.63–4) for more ideas.

Teaching at an interview

Some schools will ask you to prepare a lesson, or an activity, to teach to a class on the day of the interview. In my opinion, this should be an essential requirement of teaching interviews – after all, we're being employed for our ability to teach, rather than how well we come across in an interview. Try not to panic if you are asked to teach at interview: it is unlikely that the school will give you a nightmare class to work with – they won't want to put you off. Also, the presence of another member of staff observing you (probably a senior teacher) should ensure that the children behave themselves, which will allow you to teach to the best of your ability. When you're planning what and how to teach, take into consideration the following points:

- *Do what they ask you to*: Follow any guidelines that the school have given you very closely: for instance a primary school teacher may be asked to prepare a literacy lesson that fulfils the requirements of the NLS. Although a splash of inspiration will always go down well, this is not the time to demonstrate your individuality by deviating from the set task.

- *Give it energy*: Deliver your lesson with a good sense of pace and energy, and make sure that you show how enthusiastic you are about teaching and about children.
- *Make it engaging*: Find ways to really engage and interest the children (and the teacher observing you). This might mean bringing in an unusual resource, or simply using a really irresistible activity.
- *Use the time effectively*: Don't try to cram too much into the time you are allocated. It is far better to give a decent amount of time to each activity, rather than feeling that you have to rush the students to fit in everything that you've planned. If you do have some time available at the end of the lesson, spend it on a review with the students, making sure you praise their work (if, of course, they deserve it).
- *Don't forget to show that you like kids*: Don't be so busy worrying about how the lesson's going, that you forget to show how much you like children, and how much enjoy working with them. At the end of the day, that's what teaching is all about.

The format of the day

Teaching interviews normally follow a reasonably similar format, although this will depend on the type of school, the number of candidates, the post being filled and so on. You are likely to encounter some or all of the following:

- A tour of the school
- A visit to observe a (well-behaved) class
- An introduction to the department or current year group teacher
- Teaching a lesson
- A lunch break, sometimes in the school canteen
- The interview
- Waiting for the results

Pointers to a 'good' or 'bad' school

The pointers in this section cover factors that are reasonably easy to judge on the day of an interview, perhaps by keeping your eyes open as you're shown around the school. Alternatively, they are ones that you can assess for yourself by asking questions, either in the interview, or of the teachers you meet during the day. When using these pointers to assess whether or not this is the school for you, do consider the following factors:

- The school will be out to make a good impression, and you should try to look beyond your initial reactions.

- Even the most challenging children will be far easier to teach in a school that is supportive and well run.
- A school with impeccably behaved children can still be a nightmare to work in if the management are useless.
- The actual structure and buildings of the school may be in need of repair, but the school itself could still be well managed.
- Be very wary of a school that does not allow you to observe at least one lesson during the day of your interview. What are they trying to hide?

The pointers and questions below focus on the structure, set-up and staffing of the school, and on the attitudes of the students to their education. The way that your children behave and work in class will have a great deal to do with the overall ethos of the school. These pointers should help you discover what that ethos is:

- *The environment*: The way that children and teachers treat the environment can be a powerful indicator of their feelings about and opinions of the school. Are the entrance hall, corridor and classroom displays colourful and reasonably neat (not just the front reception area)? Is there evidence that these displays are changed regularly, and that they relate to the learning that is going on in the school? Alternatively, does the school environment show evidence of vandalism, with graffiti on the corridor walls and in the toilets?
- *Staff relationships*: In my experience teachers can be incredibly supportive of each other, and good staff relationships will make the difference between a good or bad working environment. Look to see how many teachers are in the staffroom at break and lunch time, and how they interact with each other. If there are only a few staff there, why is this? It could be because they are giving detentions and dealing with incidents of poor behaviour. On the other hand they might all be busy running extracurricular clubs for the children, because they enjoy their work so much.
- *Movement around the school*: The way that the children go from lesson to lesson, or come into lessons from break and lunch, is a good indicator of their attitude to their learning. Is there a sense of urgency but not aggression, or do you notice pushing and shoving or a total lack of enthusiasm? Is the focus on getting to the learning, and do the children have smiles on their faces and look keen to start work? Or do groups of students loiter in doorways and toilets or linger in the playground and have to be chased into class?
- *Treatment of staff*: When they interact with teachers or other staff, how do the students treat them? Are all staff are treated with respect by the children, including teaching assistants, office workers, lunchtime

supervisors, caretakers and catering staff? Alternatively, do the students only show respect to the headteacher and other senior staff?

- *Student relationships*: The way that the students mix with each other, both inside and outside the classroom, can be a good indicator of the ethos of the school. Is there evidence of bullying or gangs? Do the children play together cooperatively in the playground or not?
- *Staff turnover*: This is a tricky one to check up on, but well worth doing if you possibly can, perhaps via a subtle chat with a current member of staff. A high turnover of staff does tend to indicate a school with low morale or poor support structures.
- *Extracurricular activities*: If the school has lots of after-school clubs, or other extracurricular activities, this suggests that the staff are enthusiastic and keen to get involved.
- *Support for NQTs*: If you're joining a school for your induction year, make sure to ask how NQTs are supported and developed. Promises made in the formal setting of an interview are more likely to be kept.

The interview

The interview itself will probably take place in a formal setting, such as the head's office, or a meeting room. You are likely to be interviewed by a panel made up of a number of people. This might include the headteacher, a school governor and a manager (probably the head of faculty or department for a secondary post). Depending on the job for which you are being interviewed, the interview may last around half an hour to an hour. If you have already decided that this is definitely not the school or the job for you, then it is best to tell the panel that you have decided to withdraw before the interview starts.

The interview questions

Below are just a few of the questions that you could be asked in your interview. It's worth considering what your answers would be if you were to be asked any of these questions. Although there's no point in preparing an off-pat answer, which you're unlikely to remember anyway, it is certainly useful to have some familiarity with the types of points that you might raise. If you're asked a question that you don't understand, ask the panel to clarify what they mean, rather than waffling vaguely around the issue.

- 'How would you describe yourself as a teacher?'
- 'What do you feel are the most important attributes of an effective teacher?'
- 'What skills and abilities would you bring to this school?'

- 'What would you do if you witnessed one child bullying another?'
- 'What can you offer our school outside the classroom?'
- 'Please describe a lesson that you felt was particularly successful.'
- 'How do you incorporate the National Literacy Strategy into your teaching?'
- 'How do you differentiate work for different children and abilities within your class?'
- 'How could you contribute to extracurricular activities at our school?'

At the end of your interview, it is likely that the panel will say: *'Is there anything that you'd like to ask us?'* At this point, you may well find that your mind goes completely blank because of the stress of the interview situation. For this reason it's a very good idea to work out in advance some questions that you want to ask. There is no harm in writing these questions down and referring to your notes in the interview. This shows that you are well prepared and professional.

On the other hand, don't overdo things at this point. It's best to stick to what you feel are the really important issues, and not to ask lots of questions just for the sake of it. Bear in mind that queue of other nervous interviewees waiting in the staffroom. It's unlikely that the panel will have scheduled loads of extra time just to answer your long list of queries.

The final interview question will often be: 'If we offered you this post, would you accept?' This makes it easier for the panel to decide whether or not to offer you the job. It can be very tempting to accept any job that you're offered, and so you may feel like saying 'yes' despite any misgivings you have. However, it does pay to be honest – if you're not sure at this point what your answer would be, then say so. If you would turn the job down even if offered it, admit this and you can then go home.

Questions about salary

If you have experience outside the teaching profession, or in another role within education, you might want to ask whether additional money would be available, should you be offered the job. This is an awkward one. The school will have to find extra money for your salary out of the budget, and this can make a 'cheaper' teacher seem a tempting option. On the other hand, if they employ an experienced teacher, he or she will automatically start at a higher point on the scale. So, it is a difficult balancing act between actually getting the job and being paid what you know you're worth.

Do feel free to check on your salary at this point, before making a verbal agreement to take the job. It is relatively easy for schools to go back on a vague discussion during the day, but far harder if you have actually specified what you expect in the interview, before accepting the post.

Succeeding at interview

Success at teaching interviews relies on a whole range of factors, some of which will be outside your control. If you're not successful in getting a job from your first interview, don't assume that this is because you're not good enough, or that you're rubbish at interviews. Bear in mind, too, that every interview provides useful experience for the next one (and the one after that, if required). If you don't succeed, it might have been as a result of one or more of the following factors:

- *Your previous experience*: Unfair as it might seem, a school could invite a few trainee teachers to interview alongside more experienced candidates, perhaps to make up the numbers.
- *How much you 'cost'*: A teacher with a good length of service will be far more expensive than an NQT, and consequently the newer teacher might prove tempting.
- *An internal candidate*: It is sometimes the case that interviewees are put up against an internal candidate, who has already practically got the job in the bag
- *The competition*: Some posts are simply more competitive than others. This is both as a result of the number of people with that subject entering the profession, and also the number of posts actually available (i.e. a school will have more English teachers than art teachers). If you are qualified in a shortage subject, such as secondary physics, you are likely to have the pick of the jobs. At the moment, there is a surfeit of primary trained teachers in some areas, and this makes competition really tough for these posts.
- *The area*: Similarly, some areas of the country have far more jobs than candidates. This is especially the case in the costly inner cities such as London.

Despite all this, it is of course still worth doing your absolute best at interview. The following areas will help increase your chances of being offered a job:

- *Your appearance*: Teaching is a graduate profession, despite the relatively low pay levels compared to areas such as law or accountancy. You should aim to look professional at interview, although there is some flexibility given the active nature of the job. There is no doubt that the way that you dress will affect your chances. Your interviewers will make snap judgements about you based on your appearance, and this will have an influence on your chances of getting the job. It might sound blatantly obvious, but do wear a smart outfit, put your hair into a neat style, and remember to polish your shoes.

- *Your body language*: Being able to use your body effectively is a crucial part of being a teacher. You will hopefully have learned how to appear confident in front of your children, and you need to transfer this ability to the interview situation. Sit up straight, with your head held high, and try not to fidget nervously throughout the interview.
- *Your facial expressions*: Similarly, the way that you use your face and eyes is all part of the skill of the teacher. So, put some animation in your face while you're talking, and look the interviewers in the eye, both when they question you and when you answer.
- *Your responses to questions*: Nerves can play a huge part in making you clam up, or alternatively waffle on endlessly. Make sure that you answer the question that you've been asked; this can be surprisingly hard when you're under stress. Keep your responses clear and reasonably brief, although with sufficient detail to make your points clear. Give specific examples from your own school experience whenever possible. With practice you will find it easier to judge exactly how much to say.

Choosing the right job

With only one day to get a feel for the school, it is often very difficult to decide whether or not it is the right job for you. Take time *before* the interview to get some background information and ideas about the school (using the 'pre-interview checklist' on pp. 59–60). During the day, use the pointers given earlier (pp. 61-3) to get a better feel for the place. Finally, go with your gut instincts, bearing in mind that you are committing yourself to this job for a substantial period of time.

After the interview

When your interview is completed, you will probably be asked to wait in a room for all the other interviews to take place. After this, the panel will discuss the relative merits of all the candidates, and this can take a long (and very nerve-racking) time. In some schools, the candidates will be sent home after they have been interviewed, and a telephone offer will be made either later that day or on the following day. When the panel have reached their decision, one of them will come back to the room and ask a person to come with them. In most cases, this is the person who has got the job. If you don't get the post, ask for feedback if this is not freely offered. This feedback may take place on the day, or may be by telephone after the event.

Job offers

Job offers in teaching work in a rather unusual way. If you've worked in the commercial sector before moving into teaching, you will find this approach very different. Basically, you will be invited into the room, offered the job, then asked for a response on the spot. Once you have accepted a job, you must go through with your acceptance. You will have made a verbal contract and you may be sued or even 'blacklisted' from all the schools in the area if you decide to pull out. If you are unsure, tell the panel. In some situations (perhaps where there are no other suitable candidates), you may be given 24 hours to come to a decision.

Police checks and medicals

After you have been offered the job, you will be asked to take a police check. Anyone with substantial access to children must not have a criminal record or offences that would render them unsuitable for such work. All ITT students and newly appointed teachers are required to apply for a Criminal Records Bureau (CRB) Enhanced Disclosure before commencing their course or position of employment. These checks are organized via the DfES.

You will also be checked against information held under Section 142 of the Education Act 2002, previously known as 'List 99'. This is a list of teachers who are barred from employment because of medical or misconduct issues. If you do have a criminal conviction, much will depend on what the offence itself was. For instance, it's unlikely that a school will refuse you employment because of a speeding offence.

Some schools and LEAs also insist on a medical examination, in which you will be asked to demonstrate that you are fit to teach.

Part Two
BEING A TEACHER

5

The first year

This chapter gives you advice, information and strategies for getting through that crucial and difficult first year as a teacher. It looks in detail at the induction arrangements, including answers to some commonly asked questions. You can also read some interviews with NQTs, and hear about their experiences of the first year in teaching.

What's it really like?

I can still remember vividly the days leading up to the start of my own first year in teaching. After the academic pressures of qualifying to be a teacher, and the stress of searching for my first job, I was filled with a mixture of overwhelming excitement and a feeling of almost total dread. There really is nothing that can truly prepare you for that first day in front of your very own class: that first moment when you really become a proper teacher. Hopefully, though, you'll find answers below to some of the biggest concerns that face you before you start work, and in your first few weeks in the job.

> What if I've forgotten how to do it?
>
> Will the kids riot?
>
> Why is it so hard?
>
> What if I can't cope?
>
> How do I fit everything in?
>
> Will I pass my induction?

- *What if I've forgotten how to do it?* When you're new to the job, or when you've been out of the classroom for a while, you might be struck by the awful feeling that you have somehow 'forgotten' how to teach. But teaching is like riding a bicycle – once you've done it, you'll never really forget how. As soon as you stand in front of the children, it will all come flooding back to you (honestly). And after a few days, or perhaps even hours, it'll feel like you've been doing it for ever.

- *Will the kids riot?* Managing behaviour is, for many of us, one of the biggest concerns in our professional lives. I'm not going to promise you that your kids won't misbehave, because it probably won't be true. On the other hand, it is unlikely that there will actually be a full-scale riot in your classroom on your first day of teaching. This is as much to do with external factors as it is to do with your own classroom-management skills. Bear the following points in mind to give you comfort:
  - Many children look up to teachers as figures of authority.
  - The students will normally give you a few lessons' grace while they decide whether or not to behave for you.
  - Although a small minority may make life hard for you, many children will never or rarely misbehave.
  - The children will be aware of the school rules, and what might happen to them if they mess around.
  - There are plenty of people ready and willing to support you in achieving good discipline.
  - If things go badly wrong, your school will hopefully have some sort of emergency procedure in place.
  - If the worst comes to the worst, send a trustworthy child to get help.
- *Why is it so hard?* Unless you're some kind of superhuman, you will find the first few days and weeks in teaching incredibly hard. One of the main reasons for this is that your body is adapting to the life of a working teacher, and the intellectual, physical and emotional input that your new job requires. You might find yourself physically exhausted at the end of the day, or emotionally drained by poor behaviour. Hopefully, you'll also be enthused and excited about finally being a teacher. When things seem particularly hard in your first year, remember that it'll never be this difficult again.
- *What if I can't cope?* The feeling that you simply can't cope is actually quite normal for a teacher. This state of affairs can be brought about by a whole variety of things: difficult behaviour, excessive workload, trying to mark all the books. As an NQT, learn to turn for support to other members of staff – we were all new teachers once, so we know exactly how you feel. Teachers really are wonderful at supporting each other. Please don't suffer alone.
- *How do I fit everything in?* Prioritizing, and knowing when to stop work, is perhaps one of the hardest tasks that faces the teacher, whether he or

she is new to the job or very experienced. You want to do the best that you possibly can, but the job expands to meet the amount of time that you're willing to devote to it. The answer to this problem is that you must work out what really matters, and which bits of the job you should spend less time on. In your first year, put 'teaching well' right at the top of the agenda, followed by 'getting to know the kids'. Writing overly detailed lesson plans and doing filing really is not essential.

- *Will I pass my induction?* If you're a good teacher, the answer to this question is (barring unforeseen disasters) 'yes'. Instead of worrying about induction, try to focus on doing the job to the best of your ability. Find out the facts about the induction year (see pages 80–90 below) but don't let thoughts of passing or failing prey on your mind.

Top tips for surviving your first year

Pace yourself: Don't use up all your energy at the start of the term or year.

Don't take on too much: Make your classroom teaching the main priority.

Balance your planning: Give yourself 'quiet times' during the school day/week.

Don't reinvent the wheel: Use pre-existing plans and resources.

Don't suffer alone: Ask for help and support when you need it.

The first week

The first week of any school year is a busy and exciting time for teachers; your first week as a 'real' teacher is bound to be a stressful experience. You should have at least one INSET day at the start of term, with the staff in school before the students arrive. Much of this time will probably be given over to meetings and training, but you should hopefully be given at least some time to yourself to get prepared. Use this opportunity wisely – you'll soon realize that spare time is a very valuable commodity! The tips and advice below will help you prepare for, and survive, the first week in your new job:

- *Make an impact in your room*: The children will be making judgements about you as a teacher from the first moment that they meet you. The way your room appears is vital in making that important first impression a good one. Making changes to your room (or rooms) helps you mark out the classroom as 'your' space, and can increase your confidence. The children will often have had a previous experience of this space, not necessarily a positive one. It is now yours, and doing some preparation will help indicate to the children the type of learning experience they can expect from you. For more thoughts on setting up your room, see Chapter 6 (pp. 124–7).

- *Get your room organized*: Aim to be an efficient teacher, who knows where everything is and can access resources, equipment and materials easily. This will help you appear well-prepared, and ensure that you do not waste time or get flustered when the children need something. Consider the kind of jobs that your students can do for you, especially when it comes to handing out materials. Take time to consider how you will organize and delegate routine jobs for the children, ahead of their arrival in your classroom.
- *Keep important papers together*: In your first week, it's inevitable that you'll be given lots of bits of paper. Some of these will be more important than others. For the time being, it's a good idea to have one folder in which you keep every piece of paper that you need to refer to on a daily basis. This might include class lists, lesson plans, timetables and so on.
- *Don't be too organized*: This might seem like a strange tip to give. However, it can prove very tempting to start writing your class lists or timetable into your teacher's planner or mark book during the first week, but being this organized is actually a mistake so early on. The information you're given may not be fully accurate yet, for instance there may be changes to the school roll in the first week or so. It's far better to wait for a couple of weeks before you finalize your planner.
- *Get hold of resources early*: Exercise books and paper can be like gold dust at the start of term, especially if orders have not yet arrived at school. If possible use the INSET day or days to collect the resources that you need. Don't feel guilty about this – I can assure you that the 'old hands' will grab the resources they need early on as well.
- *Don't aim to do too much in your first few lessons*: There tend to be lots of administrative tasks to take care of in the first week, such as handing out exercise books, checking names, and so on. There will often also be changes to the timetable, for instance special assemblies, and these can eat into your class time. In addition, it's crucial to spend some time talking through your expectations, rules and boundaries with your class or classes. Although it's important to have lessons planned, don't feel any pressure to get through huge quantities of work in the first week of school.
- *Set the standards now*: In the battle to get good order and discipline, the first week is a crucial time. Think carefully, in advance of meeting your students, about how you are going to run your class and your lessons. What expectations do you have of the students' behaviour? What standard and quantity of work do you want to see? What will

happen if misbehaviour does occur? Take time out in the first week to talk all this through with your children. Show them that you know exactly how your class will be run, and that you have high expectations of what they can achieve.

'First lines' for greeting a class

One of the biggest stresses for new teachers is often the very first few minutes with a class, when you are setting the tone for what will follow. Here are a few useful and tactical 'first lines' for meeting and greeting your students at the start of the year, with a brief explanation of how and why each one might work.

The triple command

- 'Before we go in the room I want you all lined up, facing front and standing in silence, please.'
- 'I want everyone sitting in their seats, completely silent and looking at me, please.'

Use a command or statement ('I want'), rather than a question ('Would you all ...'). This lets the children know exactly what is required of them and suggests a teacher who is sure about and confident in what he or she wants. Don't waffle endlessly – focus on what is really crucial instead. Three instructions is normally the maximum amount of information that children can take in at any one time.

The target + reward

- 'Let's see who's sitting silently, ready to work and deserves a merit mark.'
- 'That's fantastic, Jimmy, you're obviously ready to work because you're sitting silently in your seat. Well done!'

By giving the children a target, and a reason for aiming to achieve that target, you set a positive atmosphere in the lesson right from the start. In the second example, the teacher focuses on one individual who is doing what she wants, thereby setting a target for the others to follow. The reward in this case is verbal praise.

> ### The target + avoided sanction
>
> - 'Let's see who's ready to work and wants to go to break on time?'
> - 'Hmmm, I'm a bit surprised that so many of you aren't silent yet. Can it *really* be that you want me to give you a detention?'
>
> The great thing about this approach is that the sanction is only hinted at vaguely, rather than actually threatened. It is almost as though the children will be 'rewarded' for good behaviour by missing out on the sanction, rather than being 'punished' for bad behaviour by receiving it. In the second example, the teacher's surprise that the children might 'want' a sanction makes his wishes very clear.

Survival tactics

In your first year as a teacher, it can often seem as though your first priority is actually to survive each day, let alone enjoy your work. The tips below will help you survive as an NQT: physically, emotionally and psychologically. And please don't worry, in your second and subsequent years as a teacher, life really does become much, much easier.

Physical survival

Teaching is a surprisingly physical profession. This is true not just for teachers of physically active subjects such as PE and dance, but for every classroom teacher. Teachers spend a huge amount of time involved in verbal communication, and this can put a considerable strain on your voice. We also move around the classroom helping individuals, handing out books, and so on. For some teachers, particularly those without a classroom of their own, there will also be a lot of carrying equipment around the school.

Looking after your voice

The following tips will help you take care of your voice, in the first year and beyond. If you get the chance, it is worth taking some specialist INSET training in voice usage.

- *Avoid shouting at all costs*: As well as putting a terrible strain on your voice, and potentially doing long-term damage, shouting simply doesn't work as a strategy in the classroom. Teachers who resort to shouting are demonstrating a loss of control to their students. Stay calm, and keep the sound of your voice low and calm as far as humanly possible.

- *Be a 'quiet' teacher*: The quieter you are as a teacher, the quieter your students will have to be to hear you. This method really does help in getting children to be more attentive to what you are saying. Think of the image of a volume control button on a stereo, and learn to lower the volume of your own voice just as you would with a piece of music.
- *Learn to 'hear' yourself*: I can remember listening to my mum teaching her students when I was a child, and thinking that she sounded very different to the mum that I knew. Often our voices will betray the tension and strain of controlling a class, but these are the very messages that we don't want to send, because we want to appear calm and in control. Take a moment on occasions to step back and hear yourself as you appear to others. You may be surprised at how loud or tense your voice actually sounds.
- *Don't rely on 'chalk and talk' methods*: It can be tempting to focus on teacher led work in your first year, as this gives a sense of control over the class. However, this type of strategy is very heavy duty in terms of voice usage. Let your children do the talking whenever possible, for instance during group work or question and answer sessions. Ask a child to 'be teacher' and explain the work to the class when your voice needs a rest.

Looking after your body

As well as taking care of our voices, we also need to limit the strain we put on our bodies. Here are some tips to help you:

- *Delegate!* Many physical jobs can be delegated. If you've got books to hand out or equipment to carry between rooms, ask for a couple of student volunteers to help. (Ensure, though, that you don't put a child's health and safety at risk when you do this.) It's very worthwhile fostering a good relationship with the school caretaker. That way, if you need the chairs set out in the hall, you can get help with the task.
- *Dress sensibly*: Nurses spend much of the day on their feet, and the shoes that they wear reflect this. The same applies for teachers: if you decide to wear that pair of high-heeled stilettos, your back and feet are bound to suffer for it.
- *Sit down when you get the chance*: As an eager new teacher, you will probably find yourself bounding around the classroom, explaining work and enthusing about the subject. Remember to sit down occasionally to give yourself a rest, perhaps getting the children to come to your desk for help, rather than you going to them.
- *Take your breaks*: I can't stress enough how important it is to go to the staff room at break and lunchtime if at all possible. The chance to sit

down and have a quick cup of tea or coffee will help you relax and recharge yourself for the rest of the day. It may seem like a hassle at the start of term, especially if the staff room is a long way from your classroom, but in the long run taking your breaks will really pay off.

- *Pace yourself*: If you know you've got a particularly heavy-duty or very physically active lesson during the week, balance it out with some opportunities to sit and rest. This rest might be setting a class test, watching a video, or doing some silent reading.

Emotional survival

As well as the physical demands made by teaching, there will also be many times when you feel emotionally drained and exhausted. Long-term survival as a teacher is about learning how to cope with the emotional stresses of the job, such as dealing with students who are abusive towards you. The following tips should help you cope and brave the emotional storms of your first year as a teacher:

- *Learn to deflect insults*: An insult from a child is only a problem if you allow it to get to you and hurt your feelings. (Of course, I'm not saying that you shouldn't address the behaviour, but rather that you should deal with it in a calm and rational way.) The natural reaction to being insulted is an emotional response. If you work with difficult children you will need to find a way of overcoming this, or you could end up in floods of tears every other lesson. One approach for deflecting low-level insults is to simply agree with everything that the child says. This leaves the student feeling silly, with nowhere to go, and no reaction to feed off. So, if a child says 'you're really fat/ugly/stupid, miss', simply answer 'yes, I know, isn't it wonderful/awful/amazing?'
- *Put up a 'wall'*: If you can learn to put up a metaphorical 'wall' between yourself and difficult behaviour, this will help you keep your emotions in check. Like the deflector shield on the Starship Enterprise in *Star Trek,* try simply to let the rudeness 'bounce off' your defences.
- *Remind yourself that it is the child who has the problem*: A child who is rude or abusive towards an adult generally has a problem of some sort. After all, this really is not normal behaviour. Remind yourself that it is the child who has the issue – perhaps his or her parents are unable to keep control and set boundaries in the home? Feel sorry for, instead of angry with, the child.
- *Don't be afraid to let it all out*: Having said that you should try to block out your emotional responses in the classroom, there will be times when you are tired or fed up and you cannot simply intellectualize the situation. When this does happen, get yourself to the staff room or

somewhere private, find a sympathetic shoulder and have a good old cry or rant.

- *Don't get overly involved*: Some of the children with whom you work may have very unhappy lives outside of school. Although you will obviously become emotionally involved with these young people, if you are to survive teaching in the long term you need to keep a separation between your working life and your home life. A teacher told me recently that, for him, 'the caring stops at 5 o'clock'. This might sound harsh right now, but it's a great approach for keeping yourself sane.
- *Build up your support networks*: There are many people who can support you: your colleagues, family, friends, the unions and so on. Build up a network of support to get you through the tough times, especially during your NQT year. If possible, spend time sharing your worries with other NQTs – having a good old moan with others who are experiencing the same as you can provide a very useful safety valve.

Psychological survival

To survive psychologically as a teacher, one of the main criteria is that you simply cannot be a perfectionist. The job really is as big and as difficult as you allow it to be. Even the teacher who worked 24 hours a day, seven days a week would still not be able to do the job perfectly. Here are some strategies that will help you keep in tip-top psychological condition:

- *Learn to prioritize*: One of the crucial factors in finding a balance as a teacher is learning to prioritize. You must accept that you simply cannot do everything, and instead work out what you feel is most important. This applies both in terms of the parts of the job that you see as vital, and also in finding a balance between work and your normal life. For instance, on a Friday night is it more important to get that set of books marked, or to go home, put your feet up and watch TV?
- *Know when to say 'no'*: The temptation in your first year is to agree to do everything that you are asked. It can be very difficult to say no, especially when you are full of enthusiasm for the job. However, a teacher who spreads him or herself too thinly may be able to do a little bit of everything, but will do nothing properly, especially the teaching.
- *Keep a home/school divide*: Teachers do have a tendency to take their work home with them, both literally and metaphorically. It can be incredibly difficult to switch off at the end of the school day, especially when you've been through a particularly difficult incident. However, achieving this home/school divide is crucial for your own sanity, so find your own best ways to achieve it.

- *Don't expect to get it right always*: Even the most experienced teachers have days when their classroom or behaviour management falls apart, or when they teach an awful lesson. If you set your standards too high, you are lining yourself up for failure. Accept that you will make mistakes, try to learn from them, and then put them behind you.
- *Develop your confidence*: The most effective teachers are very confident in what they do, and this confidence communicates itself to the students. Build up your confidence by celebrating your own successes: in a difficult school, simply getting the children to stay in their seats may be a huge achievement. Learn to pat yourself on the back: use a positive philosophy of rewards rather than sanctions on yourself as well as on your students.

The induction process

Although you will have spent plenty of time on teaching practice, your first year in the profession is the time at which you really become a teacher. It's during this tough period that you learn about the reality of life at the chalkface: the ups and downs, the stresses and strains, the shortcuts and strategies essential for survival. Not so long ago, the first year was known as the 'probation year'. Along with the name change to 'induction' has come a more rigorous and rigid system of testing. This 'induction' is described in detail in the sections below.

Although the guidelines are fairly clear cut in what should happen during your induction year, schools will vary in how good they are at following them. Much will depend on how effective (or not) your induction tutor or mentor proves to be. It can be hard as a new teacher to make a fuss if things aren't progressing as they should, but do make sure you know your rights. After all, it is you who passes or fails at the end of the year.

At the most basic level, induction is made up of both support and testing. The idea is both to help you become the most effective teacher you can be, and to test whether you are suitable for the profession. As an NQT, you will (or should) receive:

- Support from experienced teachers
- Non-contact time to help you cope with and adapt to the workload
- Observations of your work
- Informal and formal assessments of your teaching
- Target setting and objectives on which to work
- Further professional development

Induction arrangements vary from country to country within the UK. It's important to understand the particular requirements of the place in which you find your first job. The following sections will help you do this.

> ### Something to remember
>
> In the darkest hours, don't forget:
>
> - Nobody expects you to be 100% perfect yet
> - Induction is designed to help, not hurt, you
> - The overwhelming majority of teachers do pass

Induction in Scotland

The Scottish induction process was changed in August 2002. Previously, the induction period was two years of teaching service. However, there were often problems for teachers in completing their probation. All eligible teachers working in Scotland are now entitled to a one-year 'training post' with a Scottish LEA immediately after they qualify. During this year, they undertake their 'probation' (induction).

NQTs should teach only 70 per cent of a full timetable, and should have 30 per cent non-contact time in which to work on their professional development. They also have an 'induction tutor' to help and support them (an experienced teacher within the school where they are working). Once the probation year has been completed successfully, teachers qualify for full registration with the GTCS. Scotland also offers a financial incentive of £6,000 to those NQTs who agree to complete their induction year in a remote area of Scotland.

Induction in Northern Ireland

Northern Ireland has an 'induction stage' in teacher education. Teachers who have completed this are exempt from induction in English schools.

Induction in England and Wales

In this section, you can find straightforward and easy to understand answers to some of the more common questions about induction. It really is well worth equipping yourself with all the information you can about induction – that way if something goes wrong, or if your school is not meeting its obligations, you will know about it. You will also know who you are meant to turn to for help. You can download the current Induction Guidelines from the internet from the TDA website:

www.tda.gov.uk/teachers/induction.aspx, and from Teachernet: www.teachernet.gov.uk/professionaldevelopment/induction/

[Please note: in most circumstances, the 'appropriate body' referred to in the Guidelines is the LEA, and I have used the term 'LEA' to indicate this. In certain situations (see the Induction Guidelines for details), the 'appropriate body' will be different.]

Q. Who has to complete induction?

A. The DfES introduced a compulsory period of induction for newly qualified teachers (NQTs) in September 1999. All teachers who gained QTS after 7 May 1999, and who want to work in a maintained (i.e. state) primary or secondary school (or non-maintained special school) in England must complete induction. New induction standards came into force on 1 September 2003. NQTs who gained their QTS after this date are required to follow the updated standards. These standards are directly linked to those you must meet to gain your QTS.

Q. How long is induction?

A. Induction takes one academic year, which in most cases is still three terms, although at some schools it may be four or five. If you move schools during induction, and your new school operates a different term structure, the induction period becomes one calendar year. If you are working part time, the induction is done on a pro rata basis. In other words, if you only work half a full timetable, your induction will take two academic years. Note: the induction period does not have to be continuous.

Q. Do I have to start induction immediately on qualifying?

A. No, there is no time limit for starting induction, although you would normally be expected to complete induction within five years of starting it. Of course, it's probably best to get it over and done with straight away. If you choose to postpone your entry into teaching, you will need to show that you have kept up to date with new developments in education and continued to use your teaching skills. You should also check the time limits of any incentive payments you may be entitled to as a shortage-subject teacher.

Q. Where can I do my induction?

A. You can complete your induction at any state school or non-maintained special school. Sixth-form colleges are also able to offer induction if the LEA agrees. It is also possible to take induction at an independent school if the school fulfils certain criteria and liaises with the LEA.

Q. What types of schools cannot provide induction?

A. The following schools cannot provide induction training for an NQT:

- Schools that are in 'special measures'. NQTs may continue to work at the school, providing they were appointed before the school entered special measures.
- Pupil referral units.
- Independent schools that do not have an arranged Appropriate Body, and are unable to provide adequate support and assessment.
- Outdoor and other educational centres that are not 'proper' schools.

Q. Who is responsible for my training during my NQT year?

A. Responsibility is shared between:

- The headteacher
- The induction tutor
- The 'Appropriate Body', usually the LEA. (You should be provided with the name of someone you can contact at the LEA if you have any concerns about your induction.)
- Governing bodies should also monitor the school's provision of adequate monitoring, assessment and support for NQTs

These people also have a responsibility to give you the support that you need to pass induction. Your induction tutor is responsible for keeping records of your lesson observations, meetings and so on. At the end of induction, the GTCE is sent lists of those who have passed and failed induction. Any appeals are made to the GTCE.

Q. How much teaching should I be doing during my induction year?

A. You should be teaching for no more than 90 per cent of normal average teaching time. It is a statutory (i.e. legal) requirement that the headteacher ensures this, so make sure you get your entitlement! The time created by this reduced teaching load is meant to be a proper part of your programme for development activities, and not just viewed as 'non- contact' time. It is well worth remembering that this 10 per cent reduction is on top of the 10 per cent PPA time to which all teachers are entitled.

Q. Who will my induction tutor be?
A. The guidelines say that this should be your line manager, a senior member of staff, or other experienced teacher with whom you have considerable contact. Your headteacher may also act as your induction tutor, although in reality this is probably relatively uncommon.

Q. What about my Career Entry and Development Profile (CEDP)? What role does that play?
A. The CEDP is designed to help NQTs progress with their professional development. You should show your CEDP to your headteacher and induction tutor as soon as possible after you start your job. It remains yours, but it is meant to be used when setting your objectives. You can find lots of useful information about the CEDP online at www.tda.gov.uk/teachers/induction/cedp.aspx.

Q. What should I expect in terms of who and what I have to teach?
A. In theory, you should be teaching within the age group and subject that you trained to teach. You should not be given a class or classes that have particularly bad discipline problems. You should teach the same class or classes on a regular basis, and undertake the same type of planning, teaching and assessment as other similar teachers at your school. Finally, you shouldn't be given extra, non-teaching responsibilities without being properly prepared and supported.

Q. What other help can I expect?
A. You should also be given advice on various aspects of your role as a teacher. This would include being given a formal schedule of when your assessments will take place, and being given information about sick pay, salary and pensions. This sort of advice and information is similar to what any new employee would be given.

In addition, you should be given information about the school itself, and how your induction programme will work. You should have the chance to take part in any training that is going on at your school. You might also get the opportunity to spend time talking to the school's SENCo about SEN issues, and this can be a very valuable and worthwhile experience for an NQT.

Q. What will the induction programme be like?
A. The programme is meant to be 'tailored to your individual needs'. It should also be designed actually to help you pass induction. The programme should build on your ITT training and your CEDP, setting

objectives and giving you regular assessment of your progress. It should also help you develop your self-evaluation skills and prepare you to develop your career further.

The guidelines suggest that you are actively involved in planning the programme. You should also have complete access to records of observations and the outcomes of meetings about your progress. In reality, the quality of the programme you receive will vary widely from school to school. Much will depend on how effective, efficient and supportive your headteacher and induction tutor prove to be.

Q. How often should I be observed and receive reviews of my progress?

A. You should receive at least one observation in your first four weeks in the job. You can then expect to receive one observation every six to eight weeks, which basically means every half-term. The same applies to reviews of your progress, which should take place once every half-term. You'll find an overview of the observation, review and assessment process in the following section.

Q. What sort of things will my tutor be observing?

A. The observations should focus on specific aspects of your teaching and will be linked to the requirements for passing induction, and the objectives that have been identified for your development. You can find out more about the 'induction standards' at the end of this section.

Q. What should happen after the observation?

A. You should have a discussion with your induction tutor about the lesson, and you should also have access to a short written report on the observation. This is meant to focus on your objectives, showing where any action needs to be taken, and whether any changes have been made to the objectives. Schools are busy places and it may be that you need to 'chase' your tutor to ensure that the discussion takes place, and that you receive the written report.

Q. Do I get the chance to watch other teachers in the classroom?

A. Yes, you are meant to get this opportunity. These observations might take place in your own school, or they could take place in a school nearby that has been shown to be a particularly effective one. If nobody offers you the chance to observe, then ask! Watching other teachers in action really is an invaluable way of learning.

Q. How many formal assessment meetings will I have and when will they be?

A. You should receive three formal, or 'summative' assessments during your induction year. In a school that works on the three-term system, these will probably take place towards the end of the term. In other situations, such as a five-term school or a teacher working part time, the formal assessment meetings should be spread evenly over the induction period. Again, see the overview in the following section to see how this works.

Q. What will happen at these formal meetings?

A. The meetings will be with either the headteacher or your induction tutor. At the first meeting you will look at how you are beginning to meet the induction standards; the second meeting will look at how well you are progressing; the final meeting will confirm whether or not you have actually met the standards required. In this final meeting, if you've been successful, you might set some objectives for your second year in teaching.

Q. What evidence will be used to check on my progress at the assessment meetings?

A. A variety of forms of evidence should be used. These will include notes from at least two observations and progress review meetings that have take place during the term. The meetings might also look at your assessment records of students (including exam results) and your lesson planning and self-evaluations. You should be given copies of all written records about your induction.

Q. What happens after the summative assessment meeting?

A. After the meetings, you will be asked to sign the summative assessment forms. There is also a space on the form for you to write any comments of your own. The forms are then returned to the LEA within ten days of the meeting (or at the end of your induction period after the third meeting).

After the final meeting, your headteacher will write to tell the LEA whether or not you have completed induction satisfactorily. You should receive a copy of this notification.

Q. What happens if my progress is unsatisfactory during the induction period?

A. There should be early intervention and you should be given support and advice to help you improve. Your weaknesses should be identified, and a programme of support should be put in place to help you. If your headteacher is not your induction tutor, he or she should come in to observe some of your lessons, to check that the induction tutor's evidence is correct.

The headteacher should also formally notify you that you are at risk of not passing induction, and he or she should send you a copy of the formal report identifying where your weaknesses are, what objectives have been set, and what support will be given.

If you feel that your progress is being impeded because the school is not fulfilling its responsibilities, you should notify the named person at the LEA. This information may be important if you fail induction and then decide to appeal the decision.

Q. What do I do if I'm not happy with my induction?

A. This is an awkward situation in which to find yourself. According to the guidelines, your first line of action should be to make use of your school's internal procedures, including going to the governing body. If that doesn't work, you should then contact your LEA. In practice, though, this might prove very hard for an NQT to do. Your best first step is to try and talk things through with your induction tutor, assuming that you get on with him or her. As an experienced teacher, your tutor may well be able to advise you further.

Q. What if I'm working as a supply teacher?

A. If your supply post is going to be longer than a term, the headteacher must agree that it will count towards induction. If you're employed for periods shorter than a term, you are exempt from induction. However, this only applies for the first year and one term that you're working as a teacher. It's not possible to 'collect' short-term periods of supply (of less than a term) and add them together to make up your induction.

Q. What if I don't pass my induction?

A. If you don't pass induction, you won't be able to teach in the state sector. However, you will be given the chance to appeal against the decision, and if you do go to appeal, your school does not have to dismiss you. If you're going to appeal you should do so by sending a 'notice of appeal' to the GTCE within 20 working days. Details of what must be included in this notice can be found in the induction guidelines.

Q. What if I'm off school for a long time during induction?

A. If your absence is due to sickness, and this is for more than 30 days, the induction period will be extended by the total of your absences. If you are off school because you're on maternity leave, you do not have to have your induction period extended, unless you want to. In this situation, your final assessment won't take place until you return to work, and have been given the opportunity to receive an extension.

Q. What if I did my probationary period outside England?

You don't have to do induction in England if you completed the equivalent probation period in Scotland, Northern Ireland or Wales. Note: Teachers who trained in these areas are also exempt from taking the QTS Skills Tests.

Any UK-trained teacher who successfully completes a one-year induction programme (after 1 September 1999) in the Isle of Man, Guernsey, Jersey or Gibraltar, or a Service Children's Education (SCE) school in Cyprus or Germany, is exempt from requirements to serve induction in England.

Q. How is my induction paid for?

A. Schools are given money within the Standards Fund to pay for the costs of your induction. Bear this in mind if you're not being properly supported!

Q. What are the induction standards?

A. As well as continuing to meeting the standards for QTS, you'll also be expected to meet the 'induction standards' in your NQT year. These cover all the 'basics' of being a good teacher, such as planning, teaching, classroom management, assessment and so on. You can find a detailed outline in the induction guidelines. The standards cover a range of areas:

- Target setting
- Teaching strategies
- Planning for all abilities
- Getting good behaviour
- Dealing with SEN
- Multicultural approaches
- Assessment
- Liaising with and reporting to parents
- Implementing school policies
- Professional development

Induction – a brief overview

The diagram below gives a brief outline of the timings of observations, reviews and formal assessments in your induction year. There are standard assessment forms that need to be completed after every formal assessment. These should be signed by the headteacher, induction tutor and the NQT. Always ensure you receive and retain a copy of these induction assessment forms for your own records.

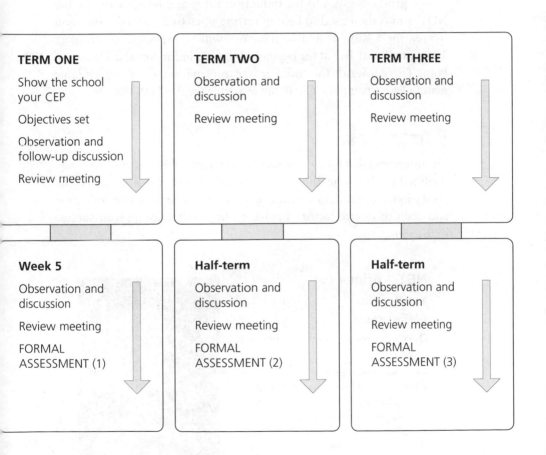

TERM ONE

Show the school your CEP

Objectives set

Observation and follow-up discussion

Review meeting

TERM TWO

Observation and discussion

Review meeting

TERM THREE

Observation and discussion

Review meeting

Week 5

Observation and discussion

Review meeting

FORMAL ASSESSMENT (1)

Half-term

Observation and discussion

Review meeting

FORMAL ASSESSMENT (2)

Half-term

Observation and discussion

Review meeting

FORMAL ASSESSMENT (3)

Career entry and development profile

On qualification, trainee teachers are given a 'Career Entry and Development Profile' (CEDP). This profile gives information about the strengths that a teacher already has, and also about the type of professional development they might need. At the end of your ITT you will be asked to complete Transition Point One. This asks you to reflect on your achievements as a trainee teacher and consider your continued professional development process.

The profile is given to the induction tutor and headteacher by the NQT, and is then used to help in setting objectives for induction and in creating a suitable action plan. You will be expected to complete Transition Point Two at the beginning of your induction and Transition Point Three towards the end. Further information and downloadable materials regarding the CEDP are available on the TDA website.

Starting out

The interviews that follow give you a glimpse into the lives of some newly qualified teachers, tackling the ups and downs of that first year in the profession. From each of my interviewees comes a sense of determination and dedication: two factors that have a huge influence on your success in the job.

NQT – primary

Year 2 teacher

Gemma Horton

Q. What made you decide to become a teacher?

Gemma – I first decided I wanted to be a teacher when I was ten years old, much to my parents' surprise. It took them a long time to picture me in that role because as a child I was never really around younger children – all my relatives and friends were older. It was just something I knew I wanted to do and I never thought about doing anything else.

The main thing which still grabs me is seeing the children develop and knowing that I had a big role in that development, whether it is academically or socially. I had good teachers throughout primary school. Some of them have been in the back of my mind throughout my teacher training and during my NQT year as I develop into the teacher I aspire to be.

Q. What was your training like?

Gemma – I took the primary BEd route, which for me was the right course as I was certain that teaching was my career choice. It was a huge learning curve; I don't think I was fully prepared for what it was going to be like. In January of my first year I began my first primary placement which was a big wake-up call. Looking back to that I cringe at how awful my teaching probably was!

Between that February and the following March I was in university full time, which was good as it gave me a lot of time to learn and slowly get my head around various strategies and educational theories as well as develop personally. However, it was a long time out of the classroom and by the time the second placement came around I was becoming impatient and very much raring to go.

My second placement had a 'one step forward, two steps backward' feeling about it. I ended it feeling very confident and much more positive than after the first. The gap between my second and third placements was 13 months again, but this time I took on supply teaching to gain extra experience and as part of my course I took part in various projects in different schools and areas. My final placement was great. I left it with a great job in another school after being recommended by the head at my placement school. I felt fully prepared as a result.

Q. How have you found your first year of teaching?

Gemma – I've really enjoyed my first year and cannot believe how fast it has gone! The support I have had from my school has been great. I have had opportunities to observe other staff and have been on a range of courses to widen my knowledge and understanding.

My NQT mentor is also my parallel teacher. We get on really well and we have a good working relationship. We plan together, we speak at length on a daily basis, whether it is about the lessons I am teaching or just a general natter about other matters. She encourages me to have a life outside of the working day which I have realized is so important. On teaching practice, it is easy just to dive in and keep your head down working, because at the end of the seven or eight weeks you know that is it. But this is life now, this is the job I have chosen and I do not want to resent it by working every night and all weekend.

I have experienced so much this year and I'm proud that I have come out the other side smiling. In early November, we had a visit from the 'dreaded' Ofsted. It was the hardest couple of days of the year in terms of late nights at school, preparation and generally making sure the class ran smoothly very early in our working relationship. I completed Key Stage 1 SATs during the spring term. I was anxious about it but I did it, and realized if I can do that I can do anything. I pride myself on only having one tearful day, which out of the whole year is, I think, fantastic. Every other day I have left with a grin on my face.

Q. What's been the best thing about teaching for you so far?

Gemma – I think the best part was when we completed the SAT assessments and worked out the results and I realized just how far some children in my class had come. I cannot tell you how proud I am of some of the individuals in my class. That is a nice feeling, it makes you realize you are doing a good job. I also enjoyed having my first class photograph taken! I have also enjoyed working in a school where the staff just get on so well. We all work well together and there is a fun atmosphere which I think shows to the children.

Q. And what about the worst thing?

Gemma – The worst part for me was probably report writing. School gave us some extra time within the timetable to write them but it really did eat into my own time. I estimate I spent an extra 40 hours typing, proofreading, correcting and adding personal comments to them.

Q. What's the best thing about teaching in Key Stage 1?

Gemma – I like teaching Year 2 as it's a busy year! At first it was quite daunting seeing all the things my class would be involved in but despite the hard work I have come to enjoy it. As my school is a split-site infant and junior school my children play a lead role in many aspects of school such as productions, sports days and so on, as well as having the SATs assessments. I have also enjoyed the transition period as my children make the move to the junior department. I have really noticed them mature and show a readiness to leave.

Q. And the hardest thing?

Gemma – This year the SATs have been quite hard as a new teacher. I feel confident about doing them next year but it was initially quite difficult both administering them and then analysing them.

Q. What about classroom planning – how is that different now that you're a 'proper' teacher?

Gemma – It's better! I plan with my parallel teacher during our PPA time and I have learnt to get the job done a lot quicker. I was a 'faffer' before I started in September. I would spend hours searching for inspirational ideas or just staring blankly at a screen. I have learnt to be snappier with my ideas and have found that you don't always need to make or prepare time-consuming resources for lessons for them to be good. Often simple lesson ideas are the best.

Q. How about longer-term planning. How does this work at your school?

Gemma – This year the school has taken a more thematic approach and as the majority of us were new staff at the school we have all planned from scratch. It has been hard work getting it all in place and making it all link together, but the planning we have now is great. The best bit is our hard work will have paid off as next year we can just use our prepared planning with a few tweaks here and there.

Q. Any thoughts on all those government initiatives and strategies? How have they affected you as a classroom teacher?

Gemma – My planning has had a very thematic approach as a result of current initiatives. This has worked well and making links really does help the children retain and enjoy their learning.

Q. How do you feel about the induction process? How has it gone for you?

Gemma – I couldn't have asked for better support this year. My mentor has been fantastic and has been there for me in so many ways. Even at this end of the year I know I can go to her with any problems, questions or queries I may have and she will be there for me straight away. She is always encouraging and constantly reminds me that I am doing a good job. She also makes sure I go home on an evening which is always a good thing. I have had half-termly observations from her and also from my headteacher and their feedback has given me good points for development. I have been allowed to go on a number of different courses by my school which has helped me to develop my areas of weakness and also to develop areas I was particularly interested in.

Q. Can you recommend any good resources for NQTs?

Gemma – The *TES* message board forum (www.tes.co.uk/staffroom). I haven't used it for a while but initially it was a good place to go to talk to others in a similar situation. I found that I needed to get a wider picture of how other people in my situation were feeling and what they were doing.

Q. Would you recommend a teaching career to others?

Gemma – Yes, in my opinion it is the best job in the world. It is hard work and you certainly have to be dedicated but the rewards are so great in many ways. I know that I am given a lot more respect from people around me, both family and friends, now that they have seen just how much work is involved. Many people think it is an easy job with nice holidays but they don't see what happens at the weekend or on an evening at home.

Q. What could be done to improve teaching as a profession?

Gemma   Well, more money would be nice. My colleague worked out that if our salary was divided by our 'actual' working hours we would be working close to the minimum wage. That is a scary thought.

Q. Any tips for other NQTs, anything you wish you'd known at the start of the year?

Gemma – Yes, don't spend the whole summer before you start working. I spent a lot of last summer making things for displays, book labels and other random paraphernalia, which in all honesty I haven't used. Enjoy the break because September to Christmas is a long time and even that break doesn't feel like a break as it is so busy. The first real holiday I felt I had was Easter.

The best tip I can give to any NQT is to find out from an experienced teacher or from your school what 'little jobs' you could do before you start to help make things run smoothly. This might be simple things like making drawer labels, getting ideas for the first week, and creating a bank of time-filler activities.

Q. Finally, in your opinion, what makes someone a good teacher?

Gemma – A good teacher is someone who is patient, fun and not afraid to try new things. A good teacher never learns everything, the day I think I know all there is to know I will quit.

NQT – primary

Year 3/4 teacher

Katie Solen

Q. What made you decide to become a teacher?

Katie – I know it's what they all say but I really have always wanted to be a teacher, even since I was at school. The inspiring and influential teachers I had at primary school made me think 'I want to be like them'. I wanted a job that I would enjoy and that would reward me in some way (and I'm not talking about money). With the prospects of 40 years of work ahead of me I knew I couldn't handle a 9 to 5 office job.

After carrying out a variety of part-time and voluntary work in school and child environments I knew that teaching would meet all my expectations and more. I believe that a teacher is not simply someone who educates others. A teacher is a mentor, a friend and above all has a great impact upon an individual's life. This is why it has always been my dream and ambition to become a teacher, the teacher that you always remember for influencing your life and making a difference.

Q. What was your training like?

Katie – Having completed a BA Honours degree in history and sociology I decided that teaching was definitely something I wanted to go into, so I completed a PGCE in primary education. The training was very intense. A lot of the foundation subjects were rushed through in as few lessons as possible and didn't provide me with the necessary experience for my first year in teaching. However, I've attended lots of courses this year for my professional development. I've also observed experienced teachers to help build my confidence, experience and subject knowledge.

While my course provided me with the appropriate policies and procedural information, it failed to outline strategies for teaching, dealing with behaviour issues and general classroom management. My teaching practices were a great experience, and it was during the block placements that I learnt the most. Sharing the experiences with other trainee teachers was valuable and informative.

Q. How have you found your first year of teaching?

Katie – It's been a challenging yet exciting experience and has confirmed my determination to succeed as a teacher. There's no denying how daunting it is the first time you are faced with 30 or so faces waiting for you to say something, and you just want to dig a hole and hide in it. Yet the time when a child or a parent thanks you for your contribution to their education, and you can finally see progress, completely outweighs all the worries and negative days. It really is worth it.

My training didn't provide me with enough information on how to deal with serious behaviour issues. It was not until I was in the class on my own, right in the middle of a violent outburst, that I truly knew what to do. You have to trust your instincts.

My NQT year has not been as stressful as my PGCE year, apart from writing reports. It has been much more enjoyable and really worthwhile. I love having my 'own' class, and not having to report to anyone else before I make a decision. However, now that I'm coming to the end of my NQT year the daunting feeling is coming back. I will no longer have inexperience to fall back on for any mistakes made, and the reduced timetable will be sorely missed.

Q. What's been the best thing about teaching for you so far?

Katie – There have been many highlights. One of the best feelings comes towards the end of the year when you sit down with the test paper marks and assessment data and you can actually see that the children have made significant progress as a result of your teaching. You can see the change in the standard and quality of work and the children have something positive to say about being in your class. That really does make you feel on a high.

Those very rare times when a parent thanks you for educating their child can also be very satisfying. The other day I had a note from a parent explaining why their child had not handed in their homework on time. On the bottom of the letter it said 'My child is really enjoying being in your class. Thank you for all you are doing.' I kept that note and framed it! A comment like that makes you feel proud of all your hard work.

Another great thing about teaching is having an off-the-cuff lesson that you devise as you're going along and it goes so well that you wish you had CCTV in your room with someone watching your success.

Q. And what about the worst thing?

Katie – There aren't many 'bad' things about being a teacher. Ask me in my fifth year of teaching and I may have a different view. It's difficult dealing with irate parents who insist their child does not misbehave at home so could not possibly behave in an inappropriate way at school, unless you, the teacher, are doing something wrong. How do you convince them that their child is no angel?

Another thing I can't stand is marking the same piece of work 30 times – very monotonous. I'm still trying to find a solution to that problem. Also, writing reports. They are very time-consuming and I sometimes wonder if the parent actually understands what the levels and objective-based comments mean. I would rather hold an extended parents' meeting, showing the child's work as evidence to support my comments.

Q. What's the best thing about teaching at primary level?

Katie – I currently teach a mixed Year 3/4 class. They are old enough to be independent in their work (although every lesson I still get asked at least three times 'What do I have to do, Miss Solen?'). They don't rely too much on adult support for everyday things. They can go to the toilet on their own, tie their shoelaces and the majority can read and write. The quantity and quality of work expected is much higher than with younger children and, in my opinion, much more rewarding.

Q. And the hardest thing?

Katie – I still find it hard to believe how much attitude a child aged seven can have. Where do they get it from? When I was their age I would not have dreamt of talking to anyone in the way that some of the children in my class speak to me. I am often faced with the phrase 'am I bothered?' Abusive language and swear words can be heard in the playground. You have to remember not to take it personally, or it gets you down.

I also can't believe how much of a love life some of the children in my class have. They are always talking about who they fancy, or who they have fallen out with because of boyfriend/girlfriend issues. Another thing is, if you're quite short like me, then some children will be taller than you. This can make it hard to discipline them.

Q. What about classroom planning – how is that different now that you're a 'proper' teacher?

Katie – Planning is much less stressful now than when I was training. I complete a weekly plan for literacy and numeracy, sharing this with the other members of my team. I also produce a lesson outline for the foundation subjects; again I share this task with my Year group. This is nothing compared to the individual six-paged lesson plans I had to complete during my block placements, which I was expected to do for every subject. However, my time is still used up on all the other jobs you don't have to do when you are a student.

Q. How about longer-term planning. How does this work at your school?

Katie – In my school long-term planning is drafted and finalized by senior management so the classroom teachers know what topics they have to teach and when. The medium- and short-term plans are then completed by the teacher. Topics run on a two-year rolling rota because of the mixed-age classes. We follow QCA plans and schemes of work. This helps with objectives and ideas but they need to be adapted to suit your own class.

Q. Any thoughts on all those government initiatives and strategies? How have they affected you?

Katie – One of the big changes that has taken place is PPA (planning, preparation and assessment) time. This was put into practice when I started as a new teacher and I have benefited from it. It's a positive initiative if it is implemented efficiently. You can achieve a lot if you have the time in one block and the other teachers in your team have the same PPA time. My school will be organizing PPA time in this way next year.

Q. How do you feel about the induction process? How has it gone for you?

Katie – It's been a positive experience. However much I have worried about the observations, the feedback has always been constructive and assures you that you are on the right track. I would have liked to have observed some teaching in other schools, because not all schools use the same routines and approaches.

Q. What about support for you as an NQT? Where has that come from; who has helped you most and how?

Katie – My induction mentor has always been there to offer help and advice if I asked for it. We met up once a term to review my progress and think about targets for the next term. The other members of my teaching team have helped me the most, though. They have worked in the school for a while so knew all the rules and routines. This helped me a great deal being a new teacher and new to the school. We shared the work load where possible and had weekly meetings (aside from our planning meetings) to catch up and gossip.

Q. Can you recommend any good resources for NQTs?

Katie – During my training and NQT year I came across a multitude of valuable teaching resources. I have completely taken over the bookcase with these and I have masses of files at school containing worksheets, activities and ideas. The internet is a valuable resource – I've found the following websites particularly useful:

www.tes.co.uk – great to chat to other NQTs in the staffroom forum
www.primaryresources.co.uk
www.teachingideas.co.uk
www.coxhoe.durham.sch.uk – great online resources for children and
    teachers
www.ebay.co.uk – go to instant display shop and bid on cheap display
    resources

The only books I would buy are photocopiable resources. They are expensive, but well worth the money. It's great to have these to hand when you need to find some work quickly.

Q. Would you recommend a teaching career to others?

Katie – Without a doubt, although it's not a career that suits everyone. It can take over your life. You need to want career progression and be determined to succeed. You must be patient, you have to always give 100 per cent effort and even if you are having a bad day, you can't let the children know about it. You have to be prepared to take your work home with you; it's not a job you can forget about when you walk out of the door.

Q. What could be done to improve the teaching profession?

Katie – A lot of recent changes have been a positive step in the right direction. However, I feel that test results and league tables are taking over. They put schools, pupils and teaching staff under a lot of unnecessary pressure to succeed. They create competition between schools and parents are choosing the 'best' schools, which leads to some being oversubscribed with long waiting lists.

Q. Any tips for other NQTs, anything you wish you'd known at the start of the year?

Katie – Your teacher training will give you an insight into classroom management and you will pick up a lot of tips from the experienced teachers you observe. This is invaluable – make sure you see as many experienced teachers as you can. Use the summer holidays to relax and get things done at home; you won't have the time once you start the academic year.

In school be flexible about your timetable and teaching strategies. Be prepared to change your behaviour management strategies when the children start to become complacent about them and ignore them. Don't let the boundaries drop. Avoid school and staffroom politics. You have to work with these people the majority of the day – it's not good to get on the wrong side of them.

The NQT year is easier than your PGCE teacher training year. If you can get through that then you can get through your induction year easily. Most importantly, don't give up. When you succeed it's a great feeling.

Q. Finally, in your opinion, what makes someone a good teacher?

Katie – A good teacher must be hard-working, organized, knowledgeable and experienced in working with children. Children and staff appreciate someone who is patient, flexible and prepared to change and respectful to others.

NQT – secondary

Maths teacher, independent boarding school

Sarah-Jane Rhead

Q. Why did you decide to become a teacher?

Sarah-Jane – I've wanted to be a teacher for as long as I can remember. When I was little I apparently used to 'teach' my teddies. At first I was undecided as to whether I wanted to teach primary or secondary, but my love of mathematics won through.

Q. What was your training like?

Sarah-Jane – My training was very school based. We had two weeks in university at the start of September and then went straight into our first school. I was in the fortunate position of being in a different school each term. I had subject-specific training every Thursday afternoon and more days in university throughout the year. I also had projects to complete which filled the school holidays.

Q. How have you found your first year of teaching?

Sarah-Jane – Exhausting! I now live and teach in a boarding school so my first year has been pretty much 24/7, but I'm so pleased that I made that decision. There have been highs and lows but I can honestly say that I have loved it. I am in a department where we share ideas and try to observe one another whenever possible. I've written a lot less down than I did last year but that doesn't mean that I haven't spent the time planning, only that I'm learning to do it differently.

Q. Can you tell me a bit about why you decided to teach in an independent school?

Sarah-Jane – I had been to the school the previous summer when I volunteered for a charity that runs week-long residential camps for children and young people with cancer and other serious illnesses. As we drove home at the end of the week, I just happened to say that that would be a great place to work. It was fate because in the February they were advertising for a maths teacher.

Q. Are there any differences between your school now and the state schools where you trained?

Sarah-Jane – In terms of the curriculum, there are no differences because for Years 9, 10 and 11 they are working on GCSEs and Years 12 and 13 are studying for their A levels. Year 9 don't take SATs. I still don't have my own classroom, though! On paper I am only actually in the classroom for 10 hours a week, but on top of that there are individual correction periods with all of my Year 11 and 12 students, and as a department we run a maths clinic two afternoons a week which is basically a drop-in for any student with any maths question.

Q. And have you been able to get your QTS while working at the school?

Sarah-Jane – Yes. I've had to complete the same Induction standards and paperwork, as well as attending termly meetings.

Q. What's been the best thing about teaching for you so far?

Sarah-Jane – Teaching my sixth-form group – I've had a class of eight students and it has been a pleasure. They've all chosen to be there which is a good starting point. In my school we are fortunate to have timetabled individual correction periods with both Year 11 and sixth form so you get to know the students while you're working with them. The focus and determination that they had in the run up to their modules was fantastic.

Teaching my Year 11s comes a close second, though. Not all of them enjoy maths but they all want to try and beat their neighbours, even if only by 1 per cent. I've also been able to introduce an element of fun, whether it's using juggling to teach projectiles, paper hats to teach inequalities or magic tricks to teach algebra. I always try to make any subject fun.

Q. And what about the worst thing?

Sarah-Jane – The deadlines and the amount of paperwork that finds its way into my pigeonhole. I found the process of writing reports straightforward (once I'd learnt to work the computers!) but actually thinking what to say was tricky for a mathematician.

Q. What's the best thing about teaching your particular age range/subject?

Sarah-Jane – Maths is such a real-life subject and it's so satisfying to achieve the right answer. I teach 13–18 year olds and I think watching them grow more confident with the subject is the most enjoyable thing.

Q. And the hardest thing?

Sarah-Jane – Never being thanked! Well that's not strictly true because there are one or two students who do say 'thank you' or 'we've really enjoyed today's lesson', but on the whole these are the minority.

Q. What about classroom planning – how is that different now that you're a 'proper' teacher?

Sarah-Jane – I've been able to develop a long-term filing system. The planning itself has been less structured although all of the elements of the planning are still there. My lessons are only 35 minutes long so the three-part lesson is not always the optimum use of time.

Q. It must be hard to fit any meaningful learning into such a short time frame. What strategies have you used to manage that?

Sarah-Jane – I think that you'd be surprised how much you can fit in. I'd finished teaching my Year 11s by February so they had plenty of time to practise exam-style questions and brush up topic by topic as identified. The one strategy that I do miss is enabling students to discover ideas for themselves, there is time once in a while but not on a regular basis. My Year 9 class arrived with the expectation that they were going to be spoon-fed all of the information that they need and I do not teach like that. I will always put up the learning objective or outcome either on the board or on the top of their questions.

The students have long assignments – seventy minutes for years 9 to 11 and three hours for Year 12. This enables knowledge to be imparted during class and practice to be done outside the classroom.

Q. How about longer-term planning. How does this work at your school?

Sarah-Jane – At the start of the year I was given the outline of the scheme of work for the year so I know what I am teaching when and can plan ahead.

Q. How do you feel about the induction process? How has it gone for you?

Sarah-Jane – I've had termly NQT induction days where I have been able to meet other NQTs in the area. I have been observed and tried to observe as many other teachers as possible. I have asked my mentor and other members of the department and teachers in the staff room for advice.

Q. What about support for you as an NQT? Where has that come from; who has helped you most and how?

Sarah-Jane – My housemistress and matron have been superb and always been there to listen to me after a hard day. Other young teachers in the department have also been good as sounding boards and have offered suggestions.

Q. Can you recommend any good resources for NQTs?

Sarah-Jane – *The Teacher's Toolkit* (Paul Ginnis), *Getting the Buggers to Behave* (Sue Cowley), *Getting the Buggers to Add Up* (Mike Ollerton), the *TES* staffroom (online forum – www.tes.co.uk/staffroom).

Q. Would you recommend a teaching career to others?

Sarah-Jane – If you're prepared for hard work, for no two days to be the same and enjoy working with young people, then I'd certainly recommend it!

Q. What could be done to improve teaching as a profession?

Sarah-Jane – I think that teachers need to be recognized as professionals on a level with doctors and lawyers.

Q. Any tips for other NQTs? Anything you wish you'd known at the start of the year?

Sarah-Jane – Everyone has been there so don't be afraid to ask for help/advice or those trivial questions. It is easier than your PGCE/training year.

Q. Finally, in your opinion, what makes someone a good teacher?

Sarah-Jane – Someone with a good subject knowledge and the ability to communicate this to others. Someone who can enforce rules and discipline, but is fair and willing to listen to students. Someone who is patient.

NQT – secondary

RE and citizenship teacher

Louise Sutcliffe

Q. Why did you decide to become a teacher?

Louise – My main ambition had always been just to be brainy enough to get to university and get a political degree. When I got there (Bradford uni – BA peace studies) the world seemed to open up and I remember sitting in the pub with friends putting the world to rights and debating about the state of the country, the world, George Bush, 9/11, etc. I had a vodka-fuelled epiphany, decided I didn't fancy being a politician as I've too much baggage, and figured teaching would be a good way to sculpt the youth of today into political beasties, and begin a revolution from the grassroots of society. I still have this same naivety!

I didn't want to teach straight from university as I didn't feel like a proper adult. I managed to get interviews at MI6 and at the London School of Economics but I felt restricted by their demands and that I was expected to give up my life for Queen and Country when I'm a socialist. So I temped in the NHS while applying for a place on a PGCE course. I was so bored after a month that I applied to go back to my old school for a week to see if I felt comfortable back in the school environment. It was the best thing I ever did – scary but enthralling and enlightening at the same time. I stuck to temping to save up for a place on a course and managed to get on a SCITT in Herefordshire.

Q. Tell me a bit about your training?

Louise – Training is a fallacy. It is nothing like teaching and you should all be told this before you start a PGCE. Read Brian Viner's *Tales of the Country* and it will give you an insight into the warped world of countryside teaching in which I inadvertently found myself. Brian now runs holiday cottages at Docklow Manor, where I rented a cottage for a year with a couple of wonderful people from the PGCE … no shops in sight, only other cottages and a local pub.

The friends you make are friends for life; other brave soldiers who have battled through pointless essays on educational theorists. These people are the ones who have helped you to develop vices that allow you to teach effectively without getting stressed. Don't go into teaching if you don't have at least one vice from this list: drinking, smoking, drinking, smoking, sex. I saw too many fellow soldiers fall at the last trench of their PGCE by not having at least one of these.

The training itself was based around the fact that, being a large rural area, there were limited schools, so you had a 'mother' school where you spent the first full term. Many found themselves a good 50 miles away from where they had set up their new homes. I was sent to a lovely school: nice kids, big gobs, but a good 50 miles from home. Very early starts were managed by copious amounts of tea, bacon butties and the thought of how many pheasants I could flatten with my ten-year old Metro each day. I was teaching within the first week – a true baptism of fire which sorts the SAS marines from the puny cannon-fodder of the teaching army.

I learnt within my first fortnight how to register kids using the SIMS system, how to plan and teach using the three-part lesson, then the five-part lesson. I learned not to be scared of kids with ADHD and to laugh with them; not nervously at them. I learnt that I should not sit in established teachers' chairs as it causes great negativity in terms of the feng shui of the staffroom, and the two most important things of all – how to make tea in 30 seconds as you've no time to yourself at all, and who to make friends with on the teaching staff. These people are the ones who stay with you, mentor you in ways a mentor does not and ensure that any mistakes such as inadvertently saying 'f**k' in class get covered up.

The problem with training is that what is taught to you during the sessions at 'uni' bears little or no resemblance to what is required within a school. University course leaders appear to live in the same naive, rose-tinted liberal, bleeding-heart leftie planet I have lived on all my life; the reality of assessment for learning, the reality of differentiation and the reality of inclusion is very different within the school environment to that of the lecture theatre.

The second term was spent building on the lessons learnt and travelling to a school 75 miles away, and not getting home until 7pm. The third term I was back at my mother school completing yet more essays, personal-development folders and reflecting, reflecting, reflecting. Teaching was just a vehicle to practice strange theories on the kids. Training is about jumping through hoops successfully. The more hoops you get through, no matter how inappropriate or banal, the better a teacher you will become.

The main thing I learned during teacher training was not how to teach, but how to deal with so many different people in the space of a day and how to cope with professional criticism. If you can take people ripping your lessons to shreds and you can still get up in the morning full of beans waiting for the challenge, then you can cope with teaching. But remember, training is not teaching.

Q. How have you found your first year of teaching?

Louise – Crap. I'm not one to mince my words. I was the happiest bunny alive when I was offered a job teaching citizenship at a secondary school in London. I thought it strange that they did not ask me to teach. Lesson learnt – if a school does not ask you to teach during an interview, they're trying to hide something! Always go with your gut instinct. You will know if a school 'feels' right.

I started a week after completing my PGCE. I knew within a further week that I did not want to stay any longer than a year. Some staff were very unsupportive, my induction wasn't being managed as it should have been, and the pupils were very difficult. Chairs were thrown so regularly I grew accustomed to catching them without even looking. Threats were commonplace.

By my second term, I found myself weeping everyday before and after school, tired of the persistent violent behaviour of certain classes. As a pregnant NQT in a rough, apathetic, unsupportive school, I should have got out earlier.

The final straw came when I was told I had failed my second term. I challenged the report, doing my best Ally McBeal impression, giving counter-arguments with evidence to back them up. My union was incredibly supportive and eventually I was given a glowing reference with which to start a new school, plus the bonus of passing my second NQT term. Lesson learnt – always pay your union membership, fight hard if you think you are unfairly treated and don't ever give up and be defeated. The major thing I learnt here was that union work is a future vocation. Never enter a classroom without them.

Thankfully, after I left that school I got a fantastic one-term contract to complete my NQT induction period at a school in Rotherham. Here I found I could actually teach and the staff were ultra-supportive of NQTs. I learnt all is not lost if everything goes tits-up during your first year. The battle rages on in different guises.

Q. What's been the best thing about teaching for you so far?

Louise – I now have a permanent contract teaching RE at a mixed secondary school in Barnsley. It seems my experiences in London have paved the way for behaviour management here. I can actually teach a five-part lesson to most classes, the majority of pupils have respect for me and I have begun to turn them into political beasties. I've also set up a citizenship club which is proving quite popular – very little apathy.

Best of all, the staff are wonderful. If you're having a tough time, you just have to ask for help and you get it. It also means that when you see others pressurized, you feel able to help them. For the first time since leaving training, I can actually begin to put theories into practice and develop my style of teaching rather than thinking 'Oh crap, chair at 2 o'clock … quick duck down…'!

Q. And what about the worst thing?

Louise – I've never been so ill in my life. Kids bring germs into school and pass them on to new teachers via books, desks, pencils, etc. You need a constant supply of vitamin C to fight off colds and flu.

Q. What's the best thing about teaching RE and citizenship?

Louise – The variety of the day. You teach your Year 7s a beautifully constructed lesson comparing Che Guevara to Jesus for your performance-management observation. It goes down a storm. Year 7 think you're fantastic; so knowledgeable – such a well-organized, funny, friendly teacher. Your head of department is impressed. You believe you have finally come of age. You do break duty. Pupils offer you crisps to get past you to the toilet (they know I like pickled onion Space Raiders and could get through to Fort Knox if I was guarding it if they had these on them). You think that after lunch you are going to teach your Year 9 pupils about weapons of war and the morality of the Iraq war according to the Just War Criteria. Your year 9s enter the classroom with a brilliant plan to scupper this by asking you halfway through the lesson if you've ever licked someone's bum.

Q. And the hardest thing?

Louise – At the moment, trying to keep a straight face when berating pupils for their behaviour. Keeping up with marking 17 sets of books is also an art I have yet to master, as is writing assessment grades in the back of my planner. You can get away with being slack up to a point.

Q. What about classroom planning – how is that different now that you're a 'proper' teacher?

Louise – Planning now starts with looking at the pupils' behaviour, then what they're capable of and how you can push them to achieve the objective of the lesson. No class is the same and so you cannot use the same Year 8 lesson plan and activities from one group to the next as it creates behavioural problems. Having said that, you do feel more confident in walking into a classroom without a plan at all and just saying 'Turn to page 98, let's discuss the role of oppression in early Sikh history'. I've spent the past year trying different methods of teaching with different groups – experimentation has given me a greater confidence with planning.

Q. How about long-term planning. How does this work at your current school?

Louise – Long-term planning is done through a series of meetings once each term. Generally, I state if I find something a little dry to teach or downright boring, and my head of department, a wonderful, supportive woman, states that I can do what I like about it. I give ideas and they get taken on board. It makes you feel like a 'proper' teacher when that happens as you feel valued and that you're contributing to the school.

Q. Any thoughts on all those government initiatives and strategies? How have they affected you as a classroom teacher?

Louise – I've learnt to ignore the government on its education policy. I teach rather than think about implementing policy. Historically in education, what goes around comes around. Blackboards will resurface in approximately 15 years' time, when it's realized that it takes up too much expense and energy to have a school fully fitted with interactive whiteboards and laptops for each pupil.

I've also noticed that older members of staff huff with indignation at any government initiative, as in practice they are all rubbish and trying to implement them into a crammed timetable is impossible. I have a feeling they're hankering for the time before the national curriculum even existed, when they could teach relevant topics according to the ability of their pupils. And I have to say I'm on their side. We need an educational revolution where the government stops interfering with all these new-fangled policies and actually just lets us teach. Exams aren't easier, the pupils aren't any dumber or brighter; we just have different expectations now that we have league tables and inclusion – which sucks by the way. It's a fantastic way of holding back bright pupils – well done to the Tories on that one.

Q. How do you feel about the induction process? How has it gone for you?

Louise – Ridiculously laborious. Induction would be excellent if it were not for all the stupid bits of paper that you have to document everything on. There was far too much paperwork, and it's going to end up on the bonfire in a cleansing ritual over the summer – along with the essays on Vygotsky.

Q. What about support for you as an NQT? Where has that come from; who has helped you most and how?

Louise – Wine, family and friends have helped the most. Seriously. I would have left teaching within the first week had it not been for the support of wine, friends and family. Returning to Yorkshire was the best move I've made during my brief teaching career and the friends I've made through teaching really understand what you go through and what the pressures are as an NQT. They give you advice that actually works, they tell you where to go to get help and they back you up if you're feeling rough. You meet wonderful people when teaching and you learn to value them dearly.

Q. Can you recommend any good resources for NQTs?

Louise – The internet is full of rubbish in terms of resources. What NQTs need are good peer mentors in schools who have only just been NQTs themselves and so understand the workload and can give them ideas to form their own resources. Any good school will already have a stash of excellent resources. Don't try to reinvent things if there are already some excellent resources, just tweak them instead.

Q. Would you recommend a teaching career to others?

Louise – Only if they were mental and definitely bored of the day-to-day routine of office life.

Q. What could be done to improve teaching as a profession?

Louise – Scrap inclusion – it doesn't work. I'm not trained to teach Key Stage 1 material to 14 year olds. Scrap government interference with silly initiatives. Better still, scrap the government. Scrap the literacy and numeracy hours in primary as we get the majority of pupils in Year 7 being unable to write correctly anyway. Let them be creative instead.

Get rid of league tables – they mean too much pressure on schools to get grades rather than focusing on the strengths of the individual child. Let teachers teach. Put the onus back on parents to be responsible for the behaviour of their children, rather than it being a teacher's responsibility to discipline a child they only see for an hour once a week. Bring back decent school uniforms rather than polo shirts (lame but I'm a believer in the benefits of smart dress and its influence on self-respect). Have at least one 'Summerhill'-style school in each LEA. I like revolution!

Q. Any tips for other NQTs, anything you wish you'd known at the start of the year?

Louise – I wish I'd known to trust my gut instinct about taking that first job. If a school feels uneasy when you walk in, then make your excuses and walk straight back out again. Stick to your guns. It's hard, but you will get there, just ensure you have friends and family to support you and a local pub/Spar/off-licence that will give you a tab behind the counter for when you're skint as the pay's rubbish for the first couple of years.

Q. Finally, in your opinion, what makes someone a good teacher?

Louise – Someone who doesn't take themselves too seriously and can stick their head above the parapet on occasion and stand up for what they believe.

NQT – secondary

Maths teacher

Beth Dennis

Q. What made you decide to become a teacher?

Beth – I had spent nine years as a chartered accountant and was bored with the day-to-day job and had had enough of the pressure of working long hours in London. I wanted more variety and fewer hours. I have always loved my subject and enjoyed explaining things to people.

Q. What was your training like?

Beth – I did a PGCE. My placements were variable. In one, staff politics were almost unbearable but in the first I was really well accepted and supported. My university subject tutor was inspiring.

Q. How have you found your first year of teaching?

Beth – Easier and more enjoyable than expected! I am used to being organized which helps but I have found the workload manageable and it has become more so over the year.

Q. What's been the best thing about teaching for you so far?

Beth – Being told after an observation that the students had 'enjoyed me'.

The relationship that I have built with that group has been really satisfying and it has also been great to hear parents commenting on how their children have improved.

Q. And what about the worst thing?

Beth – The poor behaviour in one of my lower ability Key Stage 4 groups. This year has been an ongoing battle with this one group, who I know I will have again next year. After breaks for work experience or mock exams they return as bad as ever and I have to start working on behaviour again.

Q. What's the best thing about teaching secondary maths?

Beth – Teaching 11 to 18 year olds offers a lot of variety. In maths, how you deliver the same topic varies hugely on the ability of the students. Finding a way to make the different students understand each topic, at the right level for them, is an interesting challenge.

Q. And the hardest thing?

Beth – Lower ability groups in Key Stage 4. They have already been put off maths. Most of the GCSE covers material that they have already been taught and forgotten and it is very difficult to persuade them that it will be different with you.

Q. What about classroom planning – how is that different now that you're a 'proper' teacher?

Beth – My planning now is for me and not for evidence in a file. I rarely produce full lesson plans but I did start by planning each topic in advance. Now that I have done this once I have found that I do not need to spend as much time planning but can look back at previous topic plans. Setting work at the right standard is an important skill for teaching maths and I think I have improved at this dramatically over the year.

Q. Any thoughts on all those government initiatives and strategies?

Beth – Inclusion has an ongoing impact. It has offered benefits to me of learning to work with deaf and autistic students. There is a downside in that it is difficult for the school to get rid of students who behave persistently badly. My school has made one permanent exclusion in the last five years. This has an impact on behaviour across the board as all students perceive that there is a limit to what the school can and will do about their poor behaviour.

Q. How do you feel about the induction process? How has it gone for you?

Beth – I've found it useful and much less paperwork-intensive than my PGCE!

Q. What about support for you as an NQT? Where has that come from; who has helped you most and how?

Beth – My mentor has been my department head with support from an assistant headteacher. Both have been available for ad hoc help. The main help has been support from my head of department who is available for a chat whenever I need a bit of guidance. He has also provided back-up with behaviour problems.

Q. Can you recommend any good resources for NQTs?

Beth – Reading Louanne Johnson's *One part textbook, two parts love* was inspiring. Looking organized is important so have a box for your books from each class. This prevents any accusations of you having lost a student's book.

Q. Would you recommend a teaching career to others?

Beth – I would if they can deal with poor behaviour without taking it personally.

Q. What could be done to improve teaching as a profession?

Beth – Improved sanctions for poor behaviour would help. More PRU places and the potential for holding students down a year would be my initial suggestions.

Q. Any tips for other NQTs, anything you wish you'd known at the start of the year?

Beth – My top tip is to start every lesson standing at the door smiling. Let the students know that you have given them a clean slate so their behaviour is up to them.

Q. Finally, in your opinion, what makes someone a good teacher?

Beth – Enthusiasm.

Preparing to teach

6

In this chapter you'll find everything you need to know about getting ready to teach. There are lots of ideas about how to plan effectively. There's information about the statutory curriculum and about recent government initiatives that have changed the professional roles of the teacher. You'll learn about how to help children who have special educational needs. You'll also find information about how to organize resources and set up your classroom space.

The information, ideas and advice that you will find in this chapter will help you survive and succeed in your NQT year. There is also much here that will prove helpful to trainee teachers in getting ready for teaching practice, and in preparing for their first job.

Lesson planning

As a trainee teacher, lesson planning plays a central role in becoming an effective practitioner – it gives you a chance to think ahead, and to reflect on what has happened during the lessons. It is also, of course, vital for actually passing your course. However, once you take on a teaching job, and become more experienced (and busy), you start to realize that it is not important or indeed possible to plan every single lesson in the kind of detail that you used when you were a trainee. As you gain in experience, you will start to understand exactly what you need to put in a lesson plan that is going to work for you. In some cases your school or department will provide you with ready-made formats for schemes of work and lesson plans that you can or must use.

At times, for instance when your school is being inspected, or when managers ask you to produce paperwork, you may find yourself returning to a more detailed format. However, the majority of the time you will want to focus on finding a lesson plan that is simple, effective and not too time-intensive to prepare. For an experienced teacher, or for one who has taught a particular topic before, it may not even be necessary to have a plan at all. In fact, some of my most successful lessons ever have been ones where I entered the classroom with a topic in mind, but without all that much idea about how I was actually going to teach it.

This kind of spontaneous approach allows you to react to the particular children and their specific responses and moods right at that moment. It also allows for the kind of individuality and even (dare I say it?) inspiration that seems to have been knocked out of the teaching profession by the constraints of the National Curriculum. Of course it's not something that I would recommend doing all the time, but just occasionally you might like to experiment with a more relaxed approach to your lessons.

You can find lots more information about planning in Chapter 3 which deals with teaching practice. Part Six, Teacher's Toolkit, also offers you some blank lesson-planning formats to use or adapt.

'Good' and 'bad' lesson plans

What makes a 'good' lesson plan?

- It makes you feel happy and confident about what you're going to teach.
- It's easy to refer to and use in a real-life classroom situation.
- It's flexible enough to adapt on the spot if you find that the activities aren't working.
- There's enough information for you (or someone else) to re-use the plan at a later date.

What makes a 'bad' lesson plan?

- It is excessively prescriptive, and does not allow the individual teacher to have any input.
- The layout is complicated and cannot be easily referred to and read in a real-life classroom situation. (This can lead to a situation where the teacher spends more time reading the plan than teaching!)
- There is little flexibility and the teacher tends to stick to the plan, even though it isn't working.
- Alternatively, the plan is too vague or lacks sufficient detail.
- In these cases, there is not enough information for you (or someone else) to re-use it at a later date.

Planning time savers

Planning lessons can be as quick or as time-consuming as you want to make it, and there are plenty of things that you can do to save yourself some time, without compromising your teaching. The tips below should help you keep paperwork to a minimum:

- *Don't reinvent the wheel*: There are a huge range of different sources from which to find ready-made lesson plans: your colleagues at school, the internet, resource and text books, and so on. Using these will mean you don't have to repeat work that has already been done, and thus offer you a way of saving time.
- *Adapt what you've already got*: Many of us have lesson plans, for instance from our student days, that sit mouldering in a file. Take a look through what you've got at the moment, and see which bits you can adapt to use again.
- *Repeat work from year to year*: As the years go by, you'll find that you can repeat work that you have done in previous years, perhaps making small alterations to improve things, or simply to keep the teaching fresh for yourself.
- *Think on your feet*: Sometimes there simply isn't time to plan a lesson properly. In these circumstances, try going into a lesson with a general idea about what you might teach, perhaps with an interesting resource or two. Involve the children in working out exactly what questions they want answered, or which activities they wish to try.
- *Use a project*: Giving your students a project on which to work means that a single sheet of tasks or activities can be spread over a number of lessons. Projects are also an excellent way of motivating uninterested children, and can help you stretch those of higher ability.
- *Worksheets*: I'm not a huge fan of worksheets, because they can end up as an excuse for very little actual teaching to go on. However, they do offer a good stopgap for when you don't have time to plan. One important tip – make sure that you read the sheet through before you hand it to the students. Otherwise, you might find yourself with an unsuitable worksheet, which the children don't understand.

The teacher's planner

Many schools now provide their staff with a planner – a useful notebook that allows you to keep all your important records in one place. If your school doesn't automatically provide you with a teacher's planner, do ask if you can order one. The advantages of keeping all your information in one place really cannot be overemphasized. The teacher's planner comes in two sizes – A4 and A5. There is a huge range of information that you can keep in your teacher's planner, including:

- A yearly diary
- A daily diary with space for lesson outlines and homework
- Class registers
- Class assessment and marks
- Weekly timetable

For more information about teachers' planners, look at www.school-planners.com.

The National Curriculum

The National Curriculum sets out a framework for teaching and learning for all children in government-funded education from the ages of 3 to 16. It is organized in four Key Stages: Key Stages 1 and 2 cover the primary school years, while Key Stages 3 and 4 take place at secondary school. There is also a Foundation Stage, for children aged between 3 and 5.

Key Stage 1	Ages 5–7	Years 1–2
Key Stage 2	Ages 7–11	Years 3–6
Key Stage 3	Ages 11–14	Years 7–9
Key Stage 4	Ages 14–16	Years 10–11

The three statutory core subjects in the National Curriculum are English, maths and science. The other statutory non-core subjects are information and communication technology (ICT), physical education and religious education. Schools must also provide the non-statutory PSHE (personal, social and health education) framework for all Key Stages.

In addition to these required subjects, at Key Stages 1, 2 and 3 all pupils must study the non-core subjects: design technology, history, geography, art & design and music. At KS3 they must also study modern foreign languages. Students in Key Stages 3 and 4 must study citizenship, careers and sex education, with KS4 also taking a course of work-related learning.

Within the National Curriculum subjects, there are details of programmes of study (which say what pupils should be taught), and attainment targets and level descriptions (which set the expected standards that the students will achieve). You can find the National Curriculum online at www.nc.uk.net. For further details, see www.qca.org.uk/3.html.

The Foundation Stage

The 'Foundation Stage' was introduced into the National Curriculum in 2002. The 'Early Learning Goals' in this stage are an essential part of a child's education from the ages of three to five. There are six statutory areas of learning within the Foundation Stage: personal, social and emotional development; communication, language and literacy; mathematical development; knowledge and understanding of the world; physical development; creative development.

The Foundation Stage aims to provide learning opportunities that build on a child's knowledge and reflect his or her development. The idea is to ensure that all children feel valued and are included in the learning process. The goals are not meant to put any pressure on the child; to them, the activities should simply be a normal part of playing and having fun. The Foundation Stage also helps to build partnerships between parents and schools. The government is currently considering the implementation of an education framework for all children from birth to age five.

You can find lots more information about the Foundation Stage on the following websites:

- www.surestart.gov.uk/improvingquality/ensuringquality/foundationstage/
- www.direct.gov.uk/
- www.literacytrust.org.uk/Database/earlyyears.html
- www.qca.org.uk/160.html and www.qca.org.uk/10000.html

The National Literacy Strategy

The National Literacy Strategy (NLS) lays out how reading and writing should be taught in primary schools in England. You can find the NLS at www.standards.dfes.gov.uk/primary/literacy/. The idea behind it is (obviously) to improve literacy standards. Teachers are given word, sentence and text-level work, and specific areas are set that must be covered with each year group. The 'Literacy Hour' is a daily literacy lesson that has a recommended structure:

- Shared reading/writing (approx. 15 mins)
- Word-level work (approx. 15 mins)
- Guided group/independent work (approx. 20 mins)
- Plenary (approx. 10 mins)

Having originally been implemented in primary schools, the National Literacy Strategy (NLS) has now reached secondary schools as well, with the 'Framework for Teaching English' (see www.standards.dfes.gov.uk/primary/publications/literacy/63505/).

The National Numeracy Strategy

Similarly, the National Numeracy Strategy (NNS) provides a framework for helping children with maths work, initially at primary level but now moving into secondary schools. Students in Years R (Reception) to 6 are given a daily numeracy lesson of 45 minutes to an hour. As with literacy, a mixture of different strategies is to be used, such as individual and pair work, group work, whole-class work, and plenaries. The framework provides teaching programmes for primary school children, and again you can find much more information at the DfES 'Standards' site: www.standards.dfes.gov.uk/primary/mathematics/.

Social and Emotional Aspects of Learning (SEAL)

This programme is an innovation at primary level. It offers a way of teaching social, emotional and behavioural skills to young children. Anecdotal evidence from heads and teachers already suggests a very favourable response to this programme. You can find more information and access the new materials and resources at www.teachernet.gov.uk/teachingandlearning/socialandpastoral/sebs1/seal/.

Every Child Matters

In 2003, the DfES published a Green Paper called *Every Child Matters*. It's important that teachers are aware of the report and its impact on our professional role. The focus of the paper was making children's lives as fulfilling and happy as possible. It was published alongside the government's response to Lord Laming's report into the tragic death of Victoria Climbié. By 2004, the government had published *Every Child Matters: the Next Steps*, and passed the Children Act 2004, which looked at how better services could be developed for all. The paper was devised to benefit all young people from birth to the age of 19.

The main objective of *Every Child Matters* is to protect children. It also aims to provide opportunities for young people to encourage and empower them, and to help them improve their lives by reaching their full potential. The Green Paper looks at a number of areas, particularly those of those children who are at risk. It focuses on how best to improve parenting, fostering, activities for young people and the youth justice system. Its aim is to build on what has already been achieved, such as the Sure Start project and schemes for improving education.

Further information on the Green Paper and the Children Act 2004 can be found on the following websites:

- www.everychildmatters.gov.uk/
- www.ofsted.gov.uk/childrenandyoungpeople/
- www.literacytrust.org.uk/socialinclusion/youngpeople/greenpaper.html

Special educational needs

The number of children identified as having special educational needs (SEN) will vary widely from school to school. It is important to bear in mind, too, that not all children who actually have a special need will already have been identified when you meet them in the classroom. The students that you teach will have different levels of severity in their SEN. It might be that some of your children are 'statemented' (see 'What happens to children with SEN?' (pp. 116–17) and 'Statements' (p. 117)). If this is the case, it is possible, although by no means guaranteed, that you will be given additional support in your classroom to help you meet that child's needs.

There should be a register of special educational needs within your school (kept by the SENCo). You would normally expect to be informed about the children in your class or classes who do have a special need, although this does not necessarily always happen. If you are not given this information, make sure that you ask for it. It is helpful to make a coded note of children with SEN on your register or mark book. Bear in mind that all SEN information is highly confidential, and take account of this when dealing with the children, and the paperwork.

The classroom teacher and SEN

Although formalized assessments will play some part in identifying students with SEN, the classroom teacher also has a hugely important role. Some children do slip through the net, perhaps because they develop a special need later on in their school career, or alternatively because they have simply not been identified by their previous teachers or schools. If you suspect that a child has SEN, you should notify your school's SENCo or other relevant person as soon as possible, so that testing can take place.

What are special educational needs?

There are a huge range of different special needs: some which the classroom teacher may come across on a fairly regular basis, others for which children would often attend a specialist school. The National Association of Special Educational Needs is an excellent source of detailed information on identifying and dealing with children who have SEN (see the Directory (p. 361) for contact details). Some of the more commonly experienced difficulties are explained below:

- *Social, emotional and behavioural difficulties*: This is typically one of the major areas of concern for the teacher, and was previously often called simply 'EBD'. The term 'SEBD' is a catch-all name for a whole range of issues. Children with SEBD might present the teacher with confrontational, angry attitudes, or even with violence. They might also be withdrawn, or have social problems.

- *ADHD*: A condition that has only been defined in recent years. Children with attention deficit hyperactivity disorder can appear very clumsy and disorganized. They may have problems interacting socially with other children. Inattention to work is often a problem. Children with ADHD are sometimes treated with the drug Ritalin.
- *Specific learning difficulties*: This term covers special needs that involve a particular area of learning. If left unidentified, a child with a SpLD may exhibit bad behaviour, as they struggle with a particular area of the curriculum. Special needs such as dyslexia come under this heading.
- *Physical needs*: Some children will have a SEN with a clear physical origin, such as the child who has a visual impairment.

What happens to children with SEN?

The sooner a special need is identified, the better it is, both for the child and for the teacher. Once a problem has been noted, the teacher, SENCo, other specialists and also the parents, will work together to try and help the child. The Code of Practice for SEN gives full details about how teachers, SENCos and other agencies can work together in identifying and meeting a child's needs. Until fairly recently, five different 'stages' were used to show where a child was in the process of identification and support (these are shown below). These stages may still be in use in some schools, where you could be told that a child has SEN and is 'at stage 3'. The latest SEN Code of Practice can be downloaded from the internet – go to www.publications.teachernet.gov.uk.

- *Stage 1*: The child is identified as having a special need.
- *Stage 2*: The SENCo and teachers work to develop an individual educational plan (see below for more information).
- *Stage 3*: Support is given to the teachers and the SENCo by outside specialists.
- *Stage 4*: The LEA decides whether a statutory assessment is necessary.
- *Stage 5*: The LEA decides whether a statement of SEN is required.

Individual education plans

An individual education plan (IEP) is a plan that shows what is going to happen to help the child with SEN, and how this help will occur. When you teach a child with SEN for the first time, it is well worth getting hold of a copy of any IEP that the child has. This will help you deal with the child's specific needs, whether they are to do with behaviour or learning. The IEP should include a range of information, as listed below:

- What the child's SEN is
- What is going to happen to help deal with the child's needs, to include short-term targets, teaching strategies and so on
- Who will be involved in the process
- Details about the type of activities, resources, etc. that are needed
- How the parents or guardians can help
- What targets the child should aim to achieve, and by when
- Any particular pastoral or medical needs
- How the progress is going to be monitored and assessed
- When and how reviews are going to take place
- How it will be decided whether the support has been successful

All children at stages 2 and 3 of the model described above should have an IEP. After a review of the IEP, the child might stay at the same level, or might move up or down.

Statements
Only a relatively small number of children with special educational needs will be given a statement. The 'Statement of SEN' is given to children whose needs are such that they cannot reasonably be met by the resources available within the mainstream schools in that area. The school might consequently be given additional resources by the LEA, or the child may be entitled to provision in another, more specialized educational environment. The child with a statement may also be disapplied from certain aspects of the National Curriculum. You may find that you teach a child with a statement within a mainstream classroom, but that there is a specialist working alongside him or her to help facilitate learning.

Inclusion
Inclusion is about ensuring that all children, whatever their needs or background, have their entitlement to the same standard and quality of education fulfilled. In the past, children with special needs were often removed from the mainstream classroom. The 1981 Education Act began to move the emphasis towards educating all children within the mainstream state system. The National Curriculum (introduced in 1988) was designed to ensure that all children's needs were met with a broad and balanced curriculum. During the 1980s and 1990s there was also a great deal of legislation designed to help students with SEN to be effectively catered for within mainstream schools.

Schools and teachers have a responsibility for providing an inclusive education. This might involve adapting the way your classroom is set up, for instance ensuring that children with visual problems are able to see the board properly. It will also mean that you need to adapt the way that you teach, and the way that your lessons are organized, in order to allow all children to learn. You can find information on differentiation in Chapter 7 (p. 132).

Schemes of work

A scheme of work provides a medium-term overview of work planned for the classroom. It details the lessons that will take place to cover an entire topic or subject area, perhaps over a half or even a full term. Schemes of work do not include as much detail as lesson plans, but give a general outline of how the subject or topic will be approached, with a series of lessons listed in (usually chronological) order. You can see some examples of schemes of work in the case studies on planning (chapters 15 and 16, pp. 282–3). You can also find a blank medium-term plan in Part Six, Teacher's Toolkit (p. 298).

For the experienced teacher a scheme of work may provide sufficient detail actually to teach the lessons. This is especially the case when you have taught the lessons before, and in these instances the scheme of work acts simply as a reminder of the content. Primary (and some secondary) teachers will be working from a number of different schemes of work simultaneously, in a variety of different curriculum or topic areas.

Resources and equipment

Finding, setting up and organizing resources and equipment can be a time-consuming business for the teacher. This is especially so for the primary school teacher, dealing with the whole curriculum, or for the teacher of a secondary school subject that is resource or equipment intensive (such as art or PE).

On the other hand, resources can be an extremely effective tool for learning. They can help you motivate your children to work hard; provide a reward to encourage good behaviour; and also allow a tired teacher to step back from teacher-led work and take a well-deserved rest. The tips below will help you in finding and managing resources within your own classroom:

- *Everything in its place*: Schools are full of *stuff* (planning documents, worksheets, textbooks, exercise books, pens, pencils, etc. etc.). To avoid complete chaos, aim to find a suitable and set place for each type of resource or equipment. For a drama teacher this might mean organizing a costume and props cupboard. For a primary teacher it could mean labelling drawers that contain pencils, felt-tip pens, rulers, different types of paper, and so on.

- *Be well organized*: It really is best, if at all feasible, to get your resources or equipment organized before a lesson begins. This is especially so for the new or trainee teacher, as it helps prevent any last-minute panic. It is also crucial with resources that may cause problems, such as the TV and video.
- *Give the children responsibility*: I can remember 'tidying the stock cupboard' being viewed as a real treat when I was at primary school. Take advantage of your children's natural willingness to help out with adult tasks. At a signal from you they could divide into teams, each one responsible for tidying up or sorting a particular resource area.
- *Think laterally*: A resource is basically anything that the teacher or student brings into the classroom to inspire or assist the learning. Think laterally about resources, coming up with unusual and exciting ideas whenever possible. The sections that follow give some more original suggestions for resources, besides the traditional worksheet.

Using paper-based resources

Worksheets are a real boon for the hard-working teacher. They can be created on a computer and are consequently easy to differentiate for a variety of abilities. They are also a good-cop out when you feel that you just can't cope with any whole-class or teacher-led work. Of course, you should be wary of using too many worksheets, because students will quickly become bored with lesson after lesson of them.

Although on the face of it a simple task, when making or adapting a worksheet for your class you do need to think carefully about factors such as presentation, readability and so on. Consider the following points, to make sure that your worksheets are as effective as possible:

- For students with low levels of literacy, it can be difficult to read a worksheet that is heavily text based. Keep worksheets for these children clear and simple.
- Use a text box or other highlighting device to identify important instructions.
- If there are a number of tasks or activities for the children to complete, put a short summary of these at the top of the worksheet, then a more detailed description below.
- Pictures and other visual aspects are important. These will help motivate your children in their work, and can also help with the clarity of the tasks.

The joys of photocopying

With the worksheet comes the joy of having to make photocopies; getting enough copies for your class can be a stressful business. The following thoughts and comments about photocopying are based on my own experiences as a teacher. They are designed to be helpful but also slightly tongue in cheek:

- School photocopiers are not necessarily top-of-the-range machines, and the copies will not always be of the best quality. A badly copied worksheet which the children find hard to read is likely to lead to disinterest and confusion.
- The school photocopier is a busy machine. Sod's law says that it is likely to break down, jam or run out of toner when you are most in need of it. Alternatively, there will be a queue of five people ahead of you, all with equally urgent work to copy.
- Trying to photocopy a worksheet for the lesson following break at break time really is asking for trouble. Always do your photocopying well in advance of the actual lesson.
- Most schools have some sort of budgetary or other constraint on the amount of photocopying you're allowed to do. You may be given a code or a photocopying card, which will keep a check on the number of copies you or your department makes. It is best not to use up your allocation too early in the year; save some copying capacity for when you're exhausted and need a lesson off.
- With the advent of PPA time, teachers should no longer have to bulk photocoping.

As a useful alternative to photocopying, you could try a sneaky tip that I worked out early on in my teaching career. Open the document on a school computer, then send the number of copies you want to the school printer. That way you don't 'buy' the photocopies from your copying budget. In addition, each copy is clean and easily read. All this assumes of course that you don't have similar breakdown problems with your school printer.

Some sensible schools employ a technician to do photocopying, although you will have to remember to order copies well in advance. If this is the system at your school, it's well worth getting friendly with the relevant person, in case you do have a situation where you require a last-minute emergency copying job.

There will be (or should be) a copyright notice posted above your photocopier. As someone whose livelihood depends on copyright, I would urge you to read this notice, and to take account of it.

Using media resources

Media resources, such as DVD players and digital/video cameras, can be incredibly engaging and motivating for students. The stress involved in organization and set-up is usually more than worth the effort in terms of the enthusiasm elicited from your children.

The basic rule with electronic equipment seems to be 'if it can go wrong it will'. This is particularly so in schools, where machines are used frequently, and are moved around from room to room, generally being mistreated by students and teachers alike. A few tips, then, to make using media resources as stress-free as possible:

- *Check them first*: It can prove a real nightmare if you are teaching a difficult class and the pupils have to hang around while you attempt to repair the video or DVD player. Check any equipment you plan to use before the lesson begins.
- *Make it worthwhile*: Watching a film offers the teacher a 'time out' from the hard work of actually teaching. One proviso: make sure that the programme is one that will interest, engage and educate your students, otherwise they will become bored and restless.
- *Make it a reward*: When using a camera or other media resource with your class, frame it as a 'treat'; one that must be earned by good-quality behaviour or preparation in the run-up to the lesson. For instance, your students might spend several lessons scripting a piece of drama, finding costumes, props and different locations. The filming then becomes a reward for completing this work properly.
- *Hand over the reins*: If you are brave, and if it's appropriate with your children (i.e. they are old enough and trustworthy enough), let the students handle and use the media resources themselves.

Using the computer as a resource

Using computers and ICT in your teaching has a number of important benefits. As well as being a key aspect of a modern child's education, using computers also makes for a relatively easy, child-centred lesson for the teacher (and there's nothing wrong with that!). In my experience, the children's behaviour is often much better when they are sat in front of a computer. In addition, you can use the privilege of using a computer as a motivating factor to encourage hard work. Here are some factors to consider when using computers as a resource for your class:

- There will not necessarily be sufficient computers to go round the whole class; find strategies for dealing with this issue before the lesson begins.

- Some children will be far more advanced in their ICT skills than others (and more advanced than their teachers for that matter).
- There can be a tendency for children to stray off-task when faced with the myriad temptations of computers and the internet.
- Crashing computers can cause real heartache for children who have not learned to save their work.
- If using the internet, be aware that high traffic levels at certain times of the day can lead to a frustratingly slow experience.
- In some situations and some schools, the children may treat the machines with a complete lack of respect, and you will need to deal with this problem.

You can find lots more useful information about using computers as a teaching resource in Part Seven, ICT.

Using people as a resource

As well as the more traditional resources, don't forget to consider other people as a source of information, entertainment and motivation. Bringing somebody new into the classroom always seems to go down well with the children. For some (highly irritating) reason, children who normally misbehave in your lessons will become little angels when confronted by an adult who isn't a teacher.

The work inspired by a visitor to the classroom can be a surprisingly powerful motivator for the lessons that follow. And of course, another useful side effect of inviting other people into your classroom is that you get a lesson off. Here are just a few ideas for using people as a resource:

- *The parent/guardian as 'expert'*: Many of your children's parents or guardians will be 'experts' in a field of their own so, if they are willing, invite them in to share their interests and expertise. This might be connected to the work they do (a poet or astronomer); it could be to do with their hobbies (the keen amateur painter or potter); it might also be part of their cultural background (the Indian dancer or Welsh harpist).
- *Specialist agencies*: Some schools have an arrangement with local police officers who come in to do work with the children about crime-related issues. If not, consider setting up this type of scheme yourself, especially if you teach PSHE. Nurses may also come in to offer sex-education lessons, and so on.
- *Theatre groups*: For those children who have never gone to the theatre, watching a drama group perform, and perhaps doing a workshop afterwards, is a wonderful experience. Although there will be costs involved, it is usually well worth the money. Some secondary English

departments bring in a group to perform an abridged version of a Shakespeare play near SATs time.

- *Visiting artists*: There are opportunities to organize visits from many different types of artists – sculptors, musicians, poets, authors and so on. For instance, you may like to work with your school library in making contact with, and organizing an author visit, as a wonderful way to inspire children with their reading and writing. See www.booktrust.org.uk/writingtogether/ for a scheme which will help you organize a visit from a writer. See also www.artscape.org.uk for a directory of writers and other artists available to work with schools.

Unusual resources

Often, the more unusual a resource is, the better the children will respond. For some reason, seeing something in the classroom that would not normally be there can inspire high levels of interest and motivation in your students. Here are some ideas for unusual resources:

- *Objects*: You might bring in a beautiful shell to inspire some creative writing. A sealed cardboard box could prompt interesting discussions about exactly what is inside. Work on the senses will be much more inspiring with a range of different objects to smell, touch, taste and so on.
- *Props*: A prop that the children can use while pretending to be somebody else is a great way of stimulating the imagination. For instance, a handbag containing different objects that a character might use.
- *Costumes*: All children love dressing up (and this includes those disaffected teenagers in your Year 9 class, I promise). There is no need to limit the use of costume to a drama lesson. For instance, if you're teaching geography you could look at different clothes worn around the world, or in art you could do some work on different fashion designs.
- *Living things*: Bringing a plant or animal into your classroom can motivate and educate your children, and also teach them about taking responsibility for others.
- *Food*: Any child is going to be motivated by the idea of something as 'naughty' as eating in class. Using food in a lesson is especially good for subjects such as modern foreign languages. For instance, the children could set up a café and learn how to buy different types of meal.

Setting up your room

The way that you set up your room will have a big impact on how your children behave and learn. In teaching, there can be a tendency to maintain the status quo when it comes to classroom set-up. If you're an NQT, it's only natural for you to feel cautious about rearranging furniture in a room that has only just become your own. You might not have the time or the inclination for shifting desks, chairs and bookcases around. However, changing the way your room is set up can have a number of important consequences, especially for a teacher who is new to a school or a class:

- It helps you take charge of the space, to mark your territory and feel more confident within it.
- It will help you stamp your own personality on the room, and start to feel as though you belong there.
- It's actually good fun setting up the classroom exactly as you want it.
- Taking personal charge of the space in this way shows the children that you mean business.
- When the class first arrives at the room, it will be clear that this is a fresh start, with a new teacher who has different ways of doing things.
- It will allow you to organize resources, equipment, etc. in a way that best suits you and your class.
- You can become familiar with what is actually in the room. You will know where everything is, having moved it around yourself.
- You can take the opportunity to chuck out old papers, books, etc. or anything else that is not of use to you, thus freeing up space within the room.

If you are nervous about rearranging things in your room, check first with your line manager or induction tutor. You will probably find that he or she is more than happy for you to do this, and views it as a very positive sign of your initiative. One final tip about rearranging a room is to do it before the term starts, when you have a little time on your hands. (Alternatively, a mid-term rearranging session can inject a fresh impetus and atmosphere into your classroom and your teaching, for instance if you are having some behaviour problems with your class.)

How should I set up my room?

One of the most important decisions for secondary, and indeed primary, teachers to make is whether to put the desks in groups or rows. There are a number of factors that might influence your decision:

- *The attitudes and behaviour of the children*: Highly motivated and well-behaved children will generally find it easier to cope with desks placed in groups than their less well-behaved counterparts. A difficult or poorly motivated class may work better if the desks are set out in the more formal arrangement of rows facing the teacher.
- *The learning needs of the children*: If you teach a class or classes where the children have special needs (for instance, problems with literacy), it is very important that they are able to see the board clearly. This will have an influence on your preferred set up. It is also important for children with hearing problems to be able to see the teacher's face clearly when he or she is talking to the class.
- *Your preferred teaching styles*: A teacher who tends to use whole-class activities that involve a lot of board work will find desks placed in rows a more suitable arrangement. If much of the learning is based around group activities, the tables are best arranged so that the children can sit in groups.
- *The subject(s) you teach*: In the primary classroom, the whole range of subjects will be taught, and it may be that the desks need to be changed between rows and groups to suit the area of the curriculum being delivered. In the secondary classroom, subjects such as science will use specific furniture (i.e. lab tables) that are fixed in one particular format.
- *The space available*: Generally speaking, grouping desks takes up less room in the class than putting them in rows. If your room is small, think carefully about how you can maximize the available space for your students.

What's in the primary classroom?

Having worked with both the youngest primary school children and the oldest at secondary school, I'm well aware of just how different primary and secondary classrooms can be. For many secondary teachers, there is little in the room beyond desks, chairs, a whiteboard and some shelving. The primary classroom is generally a much more interesting and personalized space within which to work and learn.

When you are deciding how to lay out the furniture in your room, make yourself a paper plan first so that you can experiment. That way you can move the different elements around easily, to see what works best. You won't have to physically lug furniture around until you're sure where you want everything to go. If there are heavy items to be moved, enlist the help of the caretaker or another teacher if possible. Below is a list of some of the things that might be included in the primary classroom space, particularly at the lower end of the age ranges (i.e. nursery, Reception and Year 1 children):

- A carpet or mat on which the children can sit, for instance when taking the register or listening to stories.
- Small desks and chairs where the children can write.
- A flipchart, chalkboard or interactive whiteboard.
- A book box containing a range of different reading books.
- A cloakroom area for the children to store their coats and lunch boxes.
- A carpeted play area where children work on activities such as lego and model making.
- A listening area with tape recorders, headphones and musical instruments.
- A role-play area where the children can set up a shop, dress in different costumes, and so on.
- An art area with paint, brushes and a sink.
- A place for sand and water, and other messy work.
- Labelled drawers for each child's work and equipment.

Setting up the primary classroom

When you're looking at how you might set up a primary school classroom, there are a number of considerations to take into account:

- Matching the room layout to the age of children and the type of curriculum activities they will be doing.
- How you are planning to organize any ability or other groupings.
- What should be done for any children with particular special educational needs.
- How the children will access the resources.
- Keeping the children's movement through the space unimpeded as far as possible.
- Health and safety issues that may arise when the children move around.
- Keeping messy activities near the sink or the playground.
- Ensuring that all children can see the board, or using a flipchart that can be moved around from place to place.
- The noise levels that will be caused by different activities.

The diagram opposite shows one possible layout of a primary classroom for Reception year children.

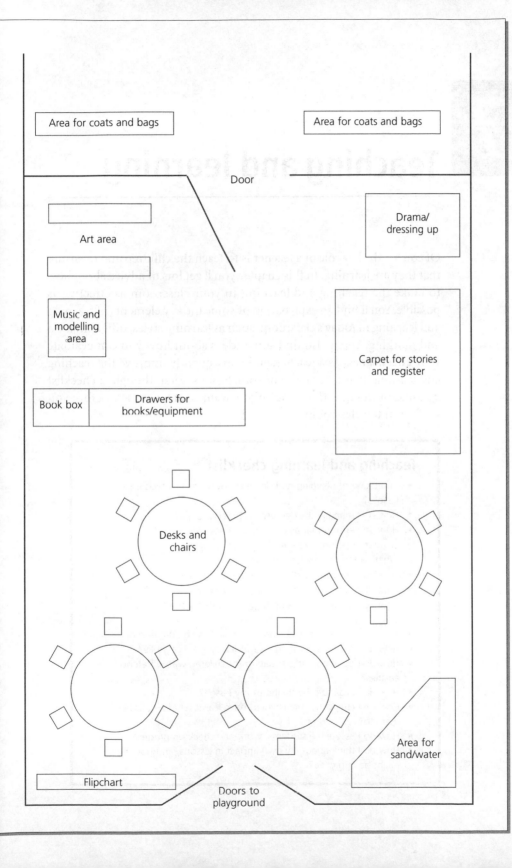

7 Teaching and learning

Of course, the key role of a teacher is to teach the children and to ensure that they are learning. In this chapter you'll get lots of advice about how to make the teaching and learning in your classroom as effective as possible. You'll find an explanation of some the key elements of teaching and learning in today's classroom, such as learning styles, differentiation and marking. You'll also find some ideas about how you can evaluate your effectiveness as a teacher, and consequently improve the teaching and learning that takes place in your lessons. First, though, a checklist of some of the questions you might want to ask yourself before you set foot in the classroom:

Teaching and learning checklist

- What kind of planning do I do, and how does this feed into my lessons?
- How do I manage the delivery of the curriculum?
- How do I ensure that all curriculum areas are covered?
- In what order do I teach each subject or topic?
- What pattern do my lessons take?
- How do I engage my students in their learning?
- What different styles of teaching and learning do I use?
- How do I go about working together with other adults in my classroom?
- What resources will I use, and how will these be organized?
- How do I help the child who is not learning successfully?
- How do I go about differentiating for children with different abilities?
- How do I organize the timing of my lesson?
- How do I check that the children have learnt what I intended them to?
- How do I assess the students' work and check on progress?
- How do I think about my own impact in lessons, and how this might be improved?

Types of lesson activities

The traditional lesson format of the teacher explaining a new subject to the class, then the children doing some writing or exercises on that subject, now seems very old-fashioned. There are countless different types of activities that you might use in your lessons: the more diverse your choice of exercises, the better your students will probably respond. Using a range of activities will:

- Help you keep the students engaged and motivated
- Appeal to a range of learning styles (see below)
- Encourage your children to develop a range of skills
- Add pace and interest to the lesson
- Make lessons interesting for you!

There are a vast number of different activities that you might use. Below are a few suggestions for when you need inspiration. You can also find lots of interesting suggestions at www.teachingideas.co.uk (these are aimed at primary teachers but many could be adapted to the secondary classroom).

- Group discussions
- Small-group presentations to the class
- Practical demonstrations or experiments
- Quizzes or tests
- Making a film
- Creating a collage using photos or magazine pictures
- Drawing, painting, modelling
- Going on an expedition around the school or playground
- Using props or costumes
- Sensory activities – tasting, smelling, etc.
- Listening to stories
- Writing in a range of formats – news reports, crosswords, recipes, as well as the more standard forms
- Whole-class 'in role' – creating a different place and set of characters in which to work

Starter activities

Starter activities can be useful to settle a class and to get the students in the mood to start work. They can usefully be linked to a topic you looked at in the last lesson, as a revision activity, or to a new topic, as an introduction. Alternatively they might simply provide a kind of mental or even physical warm-up for the children.

The ideal starter activity is short and does not require too much preparation from the teacher. Don't feel that you must begin every single lesson with a starter activity – whether or not it is appropriate will depend on the topic being studied and the kind of class you are teaching. Here are some suggestions for exercises you might use:

- quizzes
- name games
- memory games
- anagrams
- word games
- countdown
- a minute to talk about a topic
- odd one out
- brainstorming antonyms (words that mean the opposite)
- brainstorming synonyms (words that mean the same)
- mini crosswords
- word searches
- twenty questions

Try www.puzzlemaker.com for a tool that will help you make a quick word search and other useful starter activities.

Learning styles

The idea behind 'learning styles' is that students learn in different ways. Some prefer visual input (looking at the board, drawing diagrams), others prefer to learn through listening and talking (to the teacher, with their peers), while others like a hands-on approach (making models, doing practical exercises). These three approaches are often referred to as VAK – visual, auditory and kinaesthetic.

An American professor called Howard Gardner first proposed the idea that there are 'multiple intelligences' – that people have varying forms of intelligence. He suggested seven different types of intelligence: linguistic, logical-mathematical, bodily-kinaesthetic, spatial-visual, interpersonal and intrapersonal.

The idea that there are different learning styles has become a kind of educational Holy Grail. Alongside all their other work, there is now an expectation that teachers will differentiate or personalize their teaching to the preferred learning styles of their students. This would be all well and good if we had, say, ten students in a class. Unfortunately, with up to 30 (or even more) children to teach, it becomes an impossible task.

To my mind, the best way of appealing to different types of learner is to use a variety of activities in any one lesson. So, in a typical lesson, you might have:

- Teacher giving a verbal introduction to the topic to the class, backed up by showing some images on a whiteboard and discussing some props
- Students in small groups doing a brainstorm of what they already know
- Class pooling ideas together to create a brainstorm on the whiteboard
- Students doing a practical experiment based on the topic
- One group talking to the class about how they did the experiment
- Students writing up the experiment individually, drawing diagrams to show the various stages

Working with another adult

In many modern classrooms, particularly at primary level, there will now be one or more other adults working alongside the teacher. This other adult might be a teaching assistant, a learning support assistant, or perhaps a parent who has volunteered to help out. The following tips will help you get the best out of working with others:

- Whenever possible, spend at least some time planning together, allowing your TA or LSA to give his or her ideas on how you might approach a topic.
- Encourage your support staff to adapt exercises for specific children, for instance those with specific learning needs.
- Offer a team approach to the class. Show the children that you have the same expectations of work and behaviour, and that you will back each other up when your expectations are challenged.
- Draw on the expertise that another adult can bring – find out the kinds of experience your support staff have, and encourage them to give you advice and suggestions.
- Ask for advice from your support staff on those individual children with whom they work closely.
- Ask for feedback on your lesson delivery as well – were there parts of the lesson which the children struggled to understand and why was this?
- Where support staff are relatively new to the role, you might need to suggest strategies to them, for instance for managing difficult behaviour.
- Say 'thank you' regularly, and give specific praise for jobs done well.

Differentiation

Differentiation is about meeting the specific needs of the different students in your class or classes. It could be that you have some children with specific and severe learning needs, or simply that you teach a wide ability range within one group or class. In an ideal world, the work that we set would be matched exactly to each individual child. In this ideal world, we would of course be teaching classes with only ten children in them, and we would be given plenty of time each day to plan for their differing abilities. In the real world, differentiation tends to be a little more haphazard. There are a number of ways in which schools and teachers differentiate for their students.

- *By setting*: Organizing the children into sets gives the teacher a better chance of matching the work to the students' needs, because the majority of the class are working at the same or a similar level. Setting may take place in some subjects at primary level, by mixing children across the year groups. In the secondary school, children may be set from Year 7 (perhaps in the core subjects), at GCSE level, or not at all.
- *By activity*: Teachers may differentiate the work that they set by giving a range of activities to their class. These activities would offer differing levels of difficulty, and the children would be asked to complete the activity appropriate to their own level of ability.
- *By presentation*: Even when the activities are the same, it could be that some children need a different form of presentation in order to understand the work. For instance, children with literacy problems may need a simplified version of the class worksheet.
- *By amount completed*: Children will naturally differentiate their work because they will finish different amounts of work within the same timescale. In this case, the activity is much harder for some children than for others, and consequently the amount completed is far less. (This type of differentiation may lead to frustration and disaffection for the less able.)
- *By outcome*: Just as with differentiation by amount completed, this relies on a natural process of differentiation. With every piece of work, the end result or outcome produced will differ according to the abilities of the child completing it.

Homework

The setting, collection and marking of homework can add considerably to your workload. It's important, therefore, to think it through carefully:

to consider how it will help your children learn, what kind of activities you should set, and how you are going to find time to check them through and give feedback.

Those outside the teaching profession with a vested interest in homework (parents, government ministers) tend to view it as a vital part of the educational process. Certainly it can be helpful, where it is carefully constructed and linked to what is happening in class. In all honesty, though, teachers do sometimes conjure up a pretty meaningless homework activity from thin air, simply because it says on a timetable somewhere that today is the day it must be set.

Teachers will often set written homework, without considering the amount of time this is going to take to mark. Rather than always setting homework that involves writing, think laterally instead. For instance, you might ask your students to:

- learn some spellings (not just for English lessons or teachers – technical terms in other subjects could also be learnt)
- undertake some research
- tape-record an interview
- memorize some important information or facts
- design a poster
- make a model
- learn a poem to recite to the class
- bring in resources for the next lesson
- collect some photos or pictures
- collect some materials from the natural world

For ideas on making homework more interesting, successful and worthwhile, see the book *Getting the Buggers to do their Homework* by Julian Stern (Continuum, 2006).

Marking

Marking, like teaching, is a balancing act. Unless you are planning to work every available hour of the day and night, it really is not possible to mark every single piece of work in detail. At some point, you will need to make difficult decisions about exactly how you are going to do your marking. The temptation is to 'mark' everything very quickly, using the 'tick and flick' method described below, because this gives the impression of completeness. However, your choice of marking style should obviously be informed by the impact it will have on your children's learning. The benefits and drawbacks of some different marking styles are described below.

'Tick and flick'

Description

The teacher puts a big tick or cross on each paragraph or question, then flicks to the next page. At the end of the work a brief comment such as 'good work' or 'could do better' is written, and a grade or result is given.

Benefits

- The work 'looks' marked: both children and parents tend to appreciate this.
- The teacher gets an overall sense of how well the child is doing, and where his or her strengths and weaknesses lie.
- The resulting grade can be recorded in the teacher's mark book.
- It's the fastest way of marking.

Drawbacks

- The student gets little or no sense of why he or she is making mistakes, and how to put them right.
- Consequently, there is little real educational value in terms of improving the student's learning.
- For weak students, a series of crosses on a piece of work can be de-motivating.

'Close' marking

Description

With close marking the teacher corrects every error, making detailed comments about what the student is doing right/wrong and giving targets for improvement.

Benefits

- The student is given detailed information about the strengths and weakness of his or her work.
- The child also sees what the errors are, and what the correct piece of work would look like.
- This method offers good value in terms of improving work and developing learning.

Drawbacks

- This marking method is very time-consuming, especially where a large number of mistakes have been made.
- The weaker student will end up with a piece of work covered in the teacher's pen, and this is potentially very off-putting.
- Unless the child actually takes the time to read through the work carefully, and to understand his or her errors, this detailed marking is effectively wasted time.

Marking for specific errors

Description

With this marking style, the teacher highlights a particular area for which he or she will be marking with a specific piece of work. The focus or target might be set with the class as a whole, or with each individual. For instance, the teacher might decide to look closely at the use of punctuation, or at the content of the work, rather than the spelling or grammar.

Benefits

- The children and teacher work together to focus on a specific area of learning.
- The teacher can focus on the different strengths and weaknesses of each child. For instance, asking the weak speller to focus on his or her spelling, while the child with poor punctuation skills focuses on using full stops and commas correctly.
- This method offers a compromise between the speed of 'tick and flick' and the slowness of 'close' marking.

Drawbacks

- Not all the errors in every piece of work will be corrected. This can sometimes lead to complaints from parents (e.g. that the teacher is not correcting spelling).
- The teacher has to take time to set targets and to focus carefully on the chosen area.

You can find some samples of different types of marked work in Chapter 17 Teacher's Toolkit (pp. 299–301).

Marking: some time-saving tips

There are a number of ways that the enterprising teacher can save time with his or her marking. Many of the tips given below also offer benefits in terms of your children's learning:

- *Do it yourself*: Ask the children to review and mark their own work before it is handed in. This is a very effective way of encouraging your students to reflect on what they have done. This self review also gives the teacher a starting point for his or her own marking. For instance, you might ask the child to write comments at the end of a piece on different areas of the work, such as spelling, punctuation, content and so on.
- *Swap and mark*: This method is useful for tests with factual answers, for instance a maths or spelling test. The children swap their work with a partner and the teacher (or a child) reads out the answers as the students mark each other's work.
- *Marking during lessons*: It is possible, just sometimes, to find a lesson in which you can actually do some marking. This might be a period of silent reading, perhaps last thing on a Friday when the class is too tired to misbehave.
- *Marking non-written work*: There can be a tendency to focus on the marking and assessment of what our children write. Oral and practical work also needs to be marked, and these assessments are usually best done when the work is actually taking place, thus saving the teacher time. For instance, a group of children might give a talk to the class, and you could mark their contributions as they do this.

Assessment

The effective teacher carries out a process of more or less continuous assessment of his or her students, whether this is on a formal or informal basis. There are a number of very good reasons why teachers assess their students, and also some 'not so good' reasons for assessment:

- So that you know where the children are at a certain point in their learning, in terms of skills, understanding and so on.
- To inform the work that you give the class in the future, both the content, and the level of difficulty involved.
- So that you can check how far the children have progressed in their learning.
- In order to understand the differing levels of ability and understanding within the class.

- To find out what the class do and do not know about a particular subject or topic.
- To encourage the children to learn more about a topic, or to memorize specific details (for instance in the spelling or times tables test).
- To check whether the students have understood or learnt the work set (for a test or in class).
- To check for special educational needs or other individual learning requirements.
- To help you differentiate the work for children who have different learning needs.
- To prove what the teacher or school is adding in terms of 'value'.
- To prove the 'high' standards that a child, class or school has achieved.

Informal assessment

Much of the assessment that we do as teachers is actually subconscious, or performed in an informal way. For instance, during a class discussion you might be forming opinions about how well each individual within the class contributes, and consequently making an informal assessment of their oral work. Similarly, when a child shows you a piece of work, you will immediately judge whether or not it is up to the standard which you know that child can achieve. When you mark a child's exercise book, you may not give or record a score or grade for each individual piece of work. However, you will be assimilating the standard achieved into your overall understanding of the student's ability and the amount of progress he or she is making.

Formal assessment

Formal assessments will generally involve the recording of a grade or mark, and perhaps a comparison of how each child has fared across a class or year group. Formal assessments include class tests, 'baseline' assessments, examinations such as SATs, GCSEs, and so on. Some teachers might use a weekly spelling test to check their children's progress and to ensure that they are memorizing a number of words each week.

Formal assessments in the shape of exams can have their benefits for the classroom teacher, beyond the actual information that they provide on how well each child has fared. For instance, many teachers will notice how forthcoming SATs exams encourage a greater focus and motivation from many of their students. Formal ('baseline') assessments at the beginning of primary or secondary school can be a useful diagnostic tool in discovering what point the children have reached, and who might need additional help with specific subject areas.

Assessment is often described as being either 'summative' or 'formative'. Summative assessment provides a summary of the point that the individual child has reached at the end of a topic, Year or Key Stage, for instance a final grade in the GCSE exams. Formative assessment is used on a day to day basis. It is designed to inform the teacher about the child's current level of progress, and show where the teacher and student need to go next, for instance informing the work that the teacher plans for the next lesson.

For some useful ideas on making more of assessment in your classroom, see Tabatha Rayment's book, *101 Essential Lists on Assessment* (Continuum, 2006).

The downsides of assessment

It is easy to imagine that assessment is always a helpful and informative tool within the classroom. However, this is not always the case, and it is important for the teacher to be aware of the downsides of assessment for his or her students. The main two problems are the potential for de-motivation, and the stress that formal assessments can cause.

- *De-motivation*: For the weakest students in a class or year group, it can be very demoralizing and de-motivating to undergo formal assessments. This is particularly true for those assessments that make comparisons between children of the same age. It cannot ever be particularly pleasant to know that you are way behind your peers in the work that you do.
- *Stress*: In our high-pressure world, children are beginning to suffer high levels of stress from an increasingly early age. An awareness that an exam or assessment is very important, and a sense that you are going to 'pass' or 'fail', is potentially very stressful for the young person. This is perhaps especially so for those children whose parents are extremely keen for them to do well, and also for children who do not tend to do well in exams.

There are a number of ways in which teachers can help their children cope with assessment, both in the classroom and in the more formal setting of exams:

- *Keep the results private*: Although it might save you time, don't read out the results of a test in front of the whole class. If you wish to do this, offer individual children a choice of whether or not you read their results out loud.
- *Teach them revision techniques*: The effective teacher lets his or her children know how to revise, how to memorize facts or organize their time and so on.

- *Teach them 'how to pass' exams*: Children also need to know the best way of approaching an exam: for instance using their time wisely, how marks are awarded, how to plan their essays effectively, etc.
- *Talk to them after the assessment*: It really is worth sparing the time to talk through results of an assessment, especially with any children who are particularly anxious, or who have underachieved. Explain to the children why they got the results they did (whether this was poor technique or lack of effort), and how they can improve next time.
- *Let them know you still care*: Our primary aim is not getting the 'top' results, but about getting the best that we can out of our children, and helping to grow and develop as people. We need to show them that the marks they achieve do not affect our opinion of them – they are all still important individuals to us, irrespective of their exam grades.

Self-evaluation

Being able to evaluate yourself as a teacher is part and parcel of effective teaching and learning. It will help you adapt your classroom practice so that you constantly improve your lessons; it will also help you develop as a professional. When we first start out in teaching, as a student or an NQT, we are actively encouraged to evaluate ourselves and our teaching on a regular basis. We are also subjected to regular observations and evaluations from our tutors and our colleagues.

However, as you become more experienced, you may find yourself evaluating the work you do in a far less conscious way, or perhaps not at all. With all the other pressures of the job, all the issues to worry about outside of our teaching, the tendency is for us to just to get on with it in the classroom. And when we do have a bad lesson, or a bad day, it is very tempting to just say 'forget about it' and try to put it behind us without much further consideration.

In my opinion, this lack of continuing reflection is (although perfectly understandable), a real shame. Self-evaluation and reflection is a crucial part of being a professional, and of continuing to develop your teaching skills. On the other hand, no teacher needs or wants to be continually evaluating him or herself. Stick, perhaps, to the times when something has gone particularly well or particularly badly wrong.

Why should I evaluate myself?

You will find a list below that gives some of the reasons why it is it so crucial to evaluate yourself, and to reflect on what happens in your classroom. Bear in mind that evaluation is not just about looking at and analysing yourself and the way that you work, it is also about looking at how a certain situation might have led to problems in your classroom, and understanding why this was.

- *Identifying weak spots*: Even for the best teachers, sometimes something does go wrong in a lesson, whether with the work that you've set, or the behaviour that you received. When this happens, it's important to work out what it was that went wrong, and think about how it might be fixed so that it doesn't happen again.
- *Dealing with emotional fallout*: In the situation where you are suddenly faced with serious misbehaviour, there will inevitably be an emotional factor for you as a teacher, and as a human being. If a child turns on you and throws a stream of abuse at you, you need to consider why this happened. When you evaluate the situation, it could be that the behaviour had nothing at all to do with you as a teacher, but simply that the child was having a particularly difficult day. Alternatively, it could be that you made a contribution, that you somehow set them off. By analysing the situation in detail, you will gain a better understanding of what occurred, and help yourself deal with the emotions involved.
- *Identifying strengths*: As well as looking at the negative side of your classroom practice, evaluating yourself also allows you to understand what your strengths are. Perhaps you conceived and delivered a lesson that worked particularly well. If this is the case, try to understand *why* it was so good, so that you can create similar lessons in the future. Maybe you dealt with a difficult incident of behaviour in a way that defused and resolved the situation instantly. As well as the importance of understanding how and why these things work, it is also a wonderful idea to share your successes and the strategies behind them with your colleagues.
- *Giving yourself a pat on the back*: Taking the time to consider that fantastic lesson you taught allows you the opportunity to congratulate yourself, to revel in your own abilities as a teacher. Although everyone tells us that rewards and praise are crucial in our work with our children, it's not all that often that we are praised as teachers, so we need to learn to do it for ourselves.

How do I evaluate myself?

The following tips and advice give you some ideas about how you might undertake a self-evaluation, and the areas of your work that you could consider. As well as looking back on a lesson that has gone well (or badly), you might also select a particular lesson to evaluate, before it takes place.

- *Narrow the focus*: Rather than trying to evaluate everything you do in a particular lesson, try instead to focus on one area of your practice. This might be behaviour management, lesson planning, or timing and organization.
- *Consider yourself as a teacher*: As well as thinking about the external aspects of your work, such as lesson planning, look too at your own skills as a teacher. Consider particularly the verbal and non-verbal signals that you use with your children, how effective (or not) these are, and why they do or do not work.
- *Put yourself in their shoes*: Although it is difficult, do try to see yourself as the children see you. Often, we will focus on what we see as our students' bad behaviour, rather than thinking about what we might have done to provoke the situation. For instance, is the work we have set too easy or difficult, leading to boredom or frustration?
- *Use a video or tape*: If you can bear to, videoing or taping yourself is an invaluable way of seeing your teaching as the children see it. Be warned, though, it is never pretty looking at yourself in action!
- *Get some feedback*: Your students are the 'consumers' of the educational product that you offer, so why not ask them for some feedback on what you do, and don't, do well? It can be tough hearing the criticisms of your students, but you can be sure that they will pick up on those tiny faults and mannerisms of which you are totally unaware. (You may also find that they give you some lovely positive feedback.)
- *Look at incidents from start to finish*: If you are evaluating the way in which you dealt with a problematic incident, think about the time leading up to the event, and what happened afterwards, as well as the actual incident itself. Often, there are clues here as to why the problem occurred.

8 Classroom and behaviour management

Of course it is never as easy as simply standing up in front of a class and teaching (and in any case, where's the challenge in that?). For effective teaching and learning to take place, the classroom needs to feel like a safe, controlled environment. It is your skill as a teacher to create this peaceful haven of learning. This chapter focuses on ways of organizing your classroom and managing your interactions with students, so that nothing need come between you and the real job of being a teacher – getting your children to learn.

What is 'classroom management'?

The term 'classroom management' covers the whole spectrum of organizational issues that a teacher has to deal with in his or her classroom. There's a surprising amount to consider, and the way that you manage your classroom will have a powerful influence on how effectively your children learn and also on how well they behave. The key purpose of good classroom management is to create a calm, orderly environment in which proper learning can take place. This, it has to be said, is far harder than it might sound.

There is much advice throughout this book that could come under the heading 'classroom management'. As you gain in experience, you will get into an instinctive pattern of setting up your classroom and your lessons without too much thinking or stress. If you are new to teaching, the checklist questions below will help you to consider some of the different areas involved in managing your own classroom. The tips that follow this cover three important areas of classroom management – managing the beginning and end of lessons, and organizing a seating plan.

Classroom management checklist

- How do I manage the way that my class enters and leaves the room?
- How do I organize the timings of my lessons or my day?
- How do I control the way that the children use the space?
- How do I organize the furniture, equipment and students within the room?
- What happens when the children need to access equipment?
- What sort of displays do I have, and how do these contribute to learning?
- How do I make the environment as comfortable as possible?
- How do I manage external factors, such as the noise of other classes?

Managing the start of lessons

The way that your lessons begin sets the tone for what is to follow. An effective opening can be enough to create a positive, hard-working environment throughout the lesson; a disorganized start can be enough to make your time together chaotic and stressful. Many of the tips below about starting and finishing lessons can also be applied to the beginning and end of the day in the primary school.

- If at all possible, station yourself just outside the classroom door as your students arrive. This indicates that the room is 'your territory' and will help you manage their entrance into the room.
- Welcome your students by name as they enter, and pick up on any minor infringements of the school code, such as incorrect uniform. Where students are incorrectly dressed, ask them to step to one side to sort out their clothing before they enter.
- Make a few positive comments too – perhaps about good work or behaviour in a previous lesson ('That was a great assignment you did last lesson, Jade'), or more personal ('You look really smart today, James').
- Once the majority of the students have entered the room, come inside and position yourself so that everyone can see you (probably at your 'teaching spot' right at the front of the room).
- Decide, in advance, where the students will sit and what they will do when they get to their desks. If you are using a seating plan, get this organized in advance (see below for some tips).
- Have a clear rule about 'stuff' – bags, equipment, mobile phones, etc. Let your class know whether or not you wish them to get books and pens ready on their desks before the lesson starts. Be aware that too much 'stuff' can lead to a lot of fiddling – a clear-desk policy is sometimes best, particularly if you wish to talk with the students first.

- Be ruthlessly well organized. It's a great idea to create 'kit boxes' of all the equipment the students might need during the lesson, one to each table. If the students are going to need loose paper and pens for the first exercise, then have this already on the tables before you begin, rather than wasting time (and losing momentum) by handing it out.
- Begin your lessons punctually – preferably within five minutes of the timetabled start. Have a 'cut-off' time beyond which students are marked as officially late, and decide on an appropriate sanction for lateness.
- Adapt the way that lessons begin to the kind of class you are teaching. For some students, a quick starter activity on the desk will make for an effective beginning. Other classes will respond well to a lesson that begins with a 'bang' – with the teacher doing something to grab the attention. With other classes you may be able to get away with taking the register in silence at the beginning of the lesson.
- When the actual lesson begins, inject a strong sense of pace, energy and focus. Keep your eyes scanning the room, making eye contact with as many students as you can. Use an upbeat, interesting vocal tone to suggest that they will be doing lots of exciting things with you.

Managing the end of lessons

Similarly, the way that your lessons end is a very important part of your classroom management. If the bell or buzzer goes, and the students rush off in an unruly bundle, this will set the tone for the next time that they are in a lesson with you. In addition, you may well be left with a lot of tidying up to do all by yourself. Stay in control right up to the end of your lesson time by taking the following advice on board:

- Leave plenty of time for finishing off the lesson – about twice as much as you might think you need. You can always string it out, but if the bell goes before you have finished the students will (justifiably) want to leave, and may do so despite your protests.
- Have a mental bank of short, fun activities that you can use just in case your lesson finishes early. Look at any good drama book for plenty of ideas. Name games are always useful and a great way of learning what your students are called.
- Consider how you want the furniture to be left at the end of your time together with the students. Do you want chairs tucked in or up on tables at the end of the day? Getting your children to stand behind their chairs gives a good 'finishing point' to the lesson.

- Have a few moments of silence at the end of lesson time, so that you can give any final words of praise or homework instructions to the class. It creates a good sense of completion if you can find the time to do this.
- Spend a bit of time referring back to the original objectives of the class – talk with the students about what they have achieved during the lesson. This will help send them away with a good positive feeling of success.
- Dismiss your students a few at a time, rather than letting them all rush out the door at once. Choose those students who have worked or behaved best to go first. If it's a break time or the end of the day, keep any tricky students behind to have a private word with them.
- Wherever possible, don't detain an entire class for the misdemeanours of a few.
- With a particularly tricky class, it can be wise to position yourself by the door to back up the idea that they are not going to leave until you say so. However, do not physically block students from leaving, as this can lead to confrontations. If they wish to run off, let them do so, but make sure you chase up on it afterwards.

Organizing a seating plan

A seating plan is a really effective way of organizing your classroom and controlling your children's behaviour. It also offers you a useful way of learning your students' names as quickly as possible. If and when you do start to use a seating plan, you will need to get the organizational side of things completely right. If you don't, you are likely to find that your students sense your uncertainty and begin to play up.

- Choose an appropriate 'fresh start' moment to instigate a seating plan – preferably the beginning of term or just after a half-term break. Make it part of how you do things in your classroom, rather than introducing it as a sanction when things are going wrong.
- If any students question you or claim you are being unfair, use 'learning your names' as your justification.
- Focus on the positive, perhaps giving the students a reward for sitting where you ask quickly and without any fuss.
- Stick to your guns – if the students start to play up, know what kind of sanctions you will use to get them to comply.
- Seating the children alphabetically is a useful approach, for several reasons. It is relatively easy to organize and makes it easy to learn names as you take the register. It will often result in a good mix of genders, and because it is a random method, the children cannot complain about where they end up being seated.

- When the students arrive at your lesson, make sure you are at the door to stop them coming in and sitting where they wish. Ask them to line up outside, if there is space. Get the class silent then explain to them that they will be sitting according to your plan.
- Consider how you are going to let the students know where they should sit. There are various options:
  - Get the class to line up in alphabetical order before allowing them to enter one by one.
  - Draw a large picture of your seating plan and stick several copies up – one outside the room, and one on each classroom wall. Challenge the children to find 'their' place as quickly as possible.
  - Create name tags to place on each desk – this is also a useful way of learning names in the first few lessons with a class.
- Use the promise of 'free choice of seating' as a reward for several lessons of good work and behaviour.

What is 'behaviour management'?

Some teachers find that they are instinctively rather good at managing the behaviour of their students; for other teachers this is an area of real concern. Most of us do find behaviour management to be an issue right at the start of our teaching careers, while we are still learning the ropes. After all, it is never going to be a straightforward task to be asked to stand in front of a large group of children or teenagers and get them to listen to you.

In many ways, the management of your classroom and the management of your students' behaviour are inextricably linked. If you have effective control of the environment, and of the children within that environment, you will be well on your way to managing their behaviour.

Good behaviour management is, at its heart, about developing positive relationships between you and your students – about creating a bond of trust and caring. It is a complex skill and one that comes more easily as you gain in experience. The overall aim of behaviour management is to ensure that behaviour never becomes an issue – any misbehaviour is dealt with quickly and effectively, so that it doesn't get in the way of the learning. Again, here are some checklist questions to get you started on thinking about managing behaviour:

Behaviour management checklist

- How do I explain my expectations of behaviour to the class?
- How do I manage the setting of rules and boundaries?
- How do I manage behaviour issues at the beginning and end of lessons?
- What teaching strategies do I use to manage behaviour?
- How do I manage my own behaviour, and its influence on the way my children behave?
- How and when do I apply sanctions and rewards?
- How do I manage low-level disruption?
- What do I do if a serious incident occurs?
- How do I manage the aftermath of a serious incident?
- How do I manage the stress that poor behaviour causes me?

What makes a good manager of behaviour?

Even if you feel that maintaining discipline is not something that comes naturally to you, it is certainly possible to learn how to be a good manager of behaviour. The diagram below gives you a 'mini guide' to successful behaviour management:

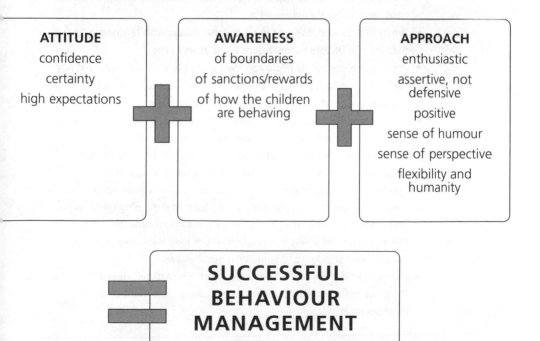

ATTITUDE
confidence
certainty
high expectations

AWARENESS
of boundaries
of sanctions/rewards
of how the children
are behaving

APPROACH
enthusiastic
assertive, not
defensive
positive
sense of humour
sense of perspective
flexibility and
humanity

SUCCESSFUL BEHAVIOUR MANAGEMENT

Whole-school behaviour policies

A whole-school behaviour policy is a document that sets out the school's intended approach to behaviour. The policy is meant to be enforced by all staff at the school, and your managers will (rightly) see consistency of application as a vital tool in creating a positive whole-school ethos. Some schools will now call this document a 'Behaviour Curriculum' or a 'Behaviour for Learning' policy.

The policy might begin by listing the school's expectations of its students, staff and parents. This will probably take the form of a list of 'school rules', or alternatively perhaps a 'charter' that sets out what the school views as the appropriate approach to learning and discipline. The policy will also give details of what will happen to students who behave and work well, and to those students who choose to misbehave rather than conform to what the school requires of them.

What makes a good behaviour policy?

There is a huge difference for the teacher between simply having a whole-school behaviour policy on paper, and having one that actually works well in practice. Here are some factors that go towards making a policy really work for the classroom teacher:

- The policy is not just a 'paper exercise', but is used effectively on a daily basis, and across the whole school.
- When first devised, this was done in consultation with teachers, rather than in spite of their views, feelings and experiences.
- The policy is constantly being reviewed and updated, to ensure that any parts which do not work are altered. The policy is able to adapt as the children, the teachers and the school change over time.
- The contents and application of the policy are made 100 per cent clear to students, parents (and staff). Everyone knows where they stand.
- The policy sets out exactly what the school expects from its students (and teachers) in terms of attitude, effort, behaviour and work.
- The policy is a clear and effective part of the whole-school ethos.
- It puts the emphasis on positive aspects, such as rewarding good work and behaviour, rather than on excessive use of punishments.
- The policy puts teachers in a position where they know exactly what to do, and who to turn to, if students do misbehave.
- When sanctions do have to be given, there are methods of ensuring that these are enforced and followed through every time (right up to the most senior level).

- It asks the students to make an informed choice about the way that they behave, and puts the decision-making in the child's hands, rather than the teacher's.
- The policy is seen to support the teacher as a professional, and to trust in his or her judgement.
- It encourages consistency, but also allows for individual approaches to discipline.
- The students view the policy as fair and reasonable, and as fairly and consistently applied by all staff.

Rewards and behaviour

One of the most effective methods of managing behaviour is to take a positive and enthusiastic approach, in which good work is expected and rewarded. The aim is to create an ethos where hard work is the norm, and misbehaviour is dealt with quickly, consistently and effectively. As far as possible, try to see rewards as your first line of attack, for instance greeting a class by asking 'Let's see who wants to earn a merit mark today'. The box below gives you lots of ideas for rewarding your students:

Some different types of reward

A smile!
Verbal praise
Written praise
Merits and commendations
Certificates
Positive referrals to tutor
Positive phone calls home
Letters or postcards home
School awards
Marbles in a jar
Raffle tickets
'Golden time'
Lucky bags/Treasure bags
Stickers
Star charts
'Student of the week' awards
Celebration assemblies

Top 10 strategies for encouraging good behaviour

It is far more effective to encourage good behaviour (and work), rather than having to deal with misbehaviour as it arises. I do fully understand how difficult this is with some classes, and at some schools. However, even in the worst-case scenario it is worth trying lots of strategies to see if you can make a difference

The ten strategies explained below are designed to help you encourage your children to behave well, so that you can hopefully avoid having to deal with misbehaviour. See the section that follows for what to do if they don't behave as you wish.

Top 10 strategies for encouraging good behaviour

1. Wait for silence.
2. Expect the best.
3. Tell them what you want.
4. Give them 'the choice'.
5. Use the 'deadly stare'.
6. Control your voice.
7. Praise one, encourage all.
8. Set the boundaries.
9. Set them targets.
10. Learn to laugh!

- *Wait for silence*: I repeat this strategy in every book that I write, and for a very good reason: because it is the single most effective thing that a teacher can do to get his or her classes to behave and learn properly. Whatever it takes (and however long you have to struggle), *never ever* address a class until they are sitting in silence, looking at you and ready to listen to what you say. I promise you, it's crucial. Depending on the children you teach, to achieve silence from your class, you might try:
  - simply waiting for them
  - giving a 'silence command', such as 'I want everyone looking at me and listening, please'
  - using sanctions for chatty individuals or whole classes
  - giving them a 'shock', e.g. pretending to bang your head on the desk, storming out of the room theatrically, etc., etc.
- *Expect the best*: Children will generally live up, or down, to what you expect of them. Always expect your students to work and behave impeccably, and express surprise (rather than anger) if they don't.

- *Tell them what you want*: Our students need to know where they stand, so tell them exactly what it is you want. One good way of doing this is to use 'I expect' statements right from the word go. Let them know that 'I expect you to listen in silence when I am talking' and 'I expect you to stay in your seats unless you have permission to get up'.
- *Give them 'the choice'*: Pass the responsibility for behaving appropriately over to your students – it is, after all, their decision to make. Essentially, the children have a choice between (a) doing as you ask and being rewarded, or (b) refusing to comply and accepting the consequences of this.
- *Use the deadly stare*: Non-verbal messages are a very powerful tool in getting good behaviour. Learn to perfect the 'deadly stare', so that a single look will silence an individual or a class.
- *Control your voice*: Our voices give away our inner state of mind, and can also influence the way that our students behave. Learn to keep your voice calm and relaxed, and this will help you control your class.
- *Praise one, encourage all*: A quick word of praise to a student who is doing what you want, rather than a snap of annoyance at those messing around, will encourage the rest of the class to behave in the appropriate way.
- *Set the boundaries*: When you first meet your class or classes, let them know where your boundaries are – what you will and will not accept. A good way to visualize boundaries is to think of them as a box within which your students must stay. Make it clear to the children which behaviours are inside and outside the box, and be consistent in your adherence to these standards.
- *Set them targets*: We all like to have something to aim for. Set targets for how your children should behave, as well as how they should work. A quick target of 'I want everyone to work silently for ten minutes, starting from now' can prove very effective.
- *Learn to laugh!* Using humour in the classroom will show your students that you are human, and consequently encourage them to respect you. Being able to laugh at yourself when you make a mistake offers a good counterbalance to the moments when you must be strict, and so helps lighten the classroom atmosphere.

Sanctions and behaviour

Sanctions vary widely from school to school. In some schools, the sanctions will be a prescriptive part of a whole-school behaviour policy. In other schools, much will be left to the discretion of the individual teacher. In fact, the clearer the policy is about exactly what sanctions should be used, and when they should be applied, the easier life will be for you. The students cannot claim that you are being unfair, because you are simply following the policy that is laid out by the school, exactly as every other teacher does. Here are some of the sanctions that you might have at your disposal:

Some different types of sanction

Verbal warnings
Written warnings
Time out
Red cards
Detentions
Referrals to manager
Phone calls home
Letters home
Being put 'on report'
Exclusion

Detentions

The detention is perhaps the most commonly used type of sanction. In some schools detentions work very well as a deterrent; in others they do not work at all. Much depends on factors such as the school ethos, and the way that the children view detentions as a sanction. For instance, in a school where going outside at break times feels quite threatening, a break-time detention might be seen as a reward rather than a punishment. When a detention is given, it must be followed through if it is going to work in the future, and this can prove exhaustingly time-consuming. Here are some general points about detentions:

- Detentions might be imposed on an individual, on a group of children, or on the whole class. Take great care when using whole-class detentions, as they can be seen (often correctly) as unfair. If you do have to detain a whole class, it works well to let the children leave gradually, letting the better behaved ones go first.
- The short 'same-day' detention is often served during break time, lunch time or after school, and is usually taken by the class teacher who imposed the punishment.
- 'Same-day' detentions are legally allowed to be no longer than 15 minutes.

- If a longer detention is to be served, 24 hours' notice must be given to the child's parents or guardians.
- As well as short, 'same-day' detentions, longer departmental or faculty detentions might take place in the secondary school, perhaps once a week. These could be used for the child who has failed to serve a short detention.
- Some schools also offer senior management or school detentions, and indeed some will make a repeat offender serve detentions on Saturdays.

Applying sanctions

Although rewards and other strategies are very important, this is not to say that sanctions are unnecessary, but rather that they should be viewed as a last resort. A classroom in which sanctions are constantly in use has the potential to become a very negative and confrontational place. The teacher who intervenes quickly when misbehaviour occurs, and who then applies sanctions consistently and fairly, will generally have to use them far less than a teacher who does not really understand how they work. Here is a 'quick guide' to how you might intervene with misbehaviour and then apply sanctions in an effective way:

Quick guide to applying sanctions

Misbehaviour
Intervention 1: The 'deadly stare'
Teacher gives 'deadly' look in direction of child
Unspoken message: *'Are you sure you want to mess with me!?'*

Misbehaviour repeated or ... Child decides to behave
Intervention 2: The 'choice' is made clear
Teacher beckons child to side of room
Teacher explains 'choice':
'You decide. Behave as I expect or accept the consequences. If you do that again, you will force me to use sanction x.'

Misbehaviour repeated or ... Child decides to behave
Sanction Level 1: e.g. written warning
Teacher explains child's 'decision':
'You decided to continue the misbehaviour. That misbehaviour earns this sanction. Make the right choice now, please.'

Misbehaviour repeated or ... Child decides to behave
Sanction Level 2: e.g. short detention
Teacher repeats explanation of child's 'decision'

Misbehaviour repeated or ... Child decides to behave
Sanction Level 3: e.g. long detention
Teacher repeats explanation of child's 'decision'

Misbehaviour repeated or ... Child decides to behave
Sanction Level 4: e.g. child sent out
Teacher explains why child has received the 'ultimate' punishment

Top 10 strategies for dealing with misbehaviour

Most teachers are, of course, faced with at least some misbehaviour in every lesson they teach. The key to preventing, or at least lessening, the stress that this misbehaviour causes is to have a number of strategies for dealing with any problems. In addition to helping you cope with stress, these strategies will also make it less likely that the misbehaviour recurs in the future. When the child sees you dealing fairly and rationally with their actions, they quickly come to realize that it is not worth messing with you.

Top 10 strategies for dealing with misbehaviour

1 Use 'I want' statements.
2 Stay calm.
3 Remove the audience.
4 Defuse, don't escalate.
5 Don't rise to the bait.
6 Build a 'wall'.
7 Make them decide.
8 Sanction the behaviour.
9 Follow it through.
10 Make the sanction count.

- *Use 'I want' statements*: The effective teacher tells the child exactly what he or she wants. Rather than asking little Sammy 'Would you mind stopping that chatter now?', use the more assertive statement 'I want you to stop talking right now and listen to me, please.'

- *Stay calm*: However natural it is to get wound up by poor behaviour, this will only ever add to your problems. A calm teacher will deal more effectively with the problem, and will also encourage the child to stay calm too.
- *Remove the audience*: It can be tempting to address a child's poor behaviour in front of the whole class (the classic 'Would you like to explain why you did that to the rest of us?'). However, this makes it far more likely that the situation will escalate into a confrontation. Instead, take the child to one side, or even out of the room, before you have a chat.
- *Defuse, don't escalate*: It is an instinctive reaction, when faced with rudeness or confrontation, to start a 'tit for tat' battle with the student concerned. However, a relentlessly calm and polite approach will be far more likely to cool down the situation, and it will also demonstrate appropriate behaviour to the child. Bring your vocal tone and volume right down, until you are speaking with an almost hypnotic calm.
- *Don't rise to the bait*: Much misbehaviour is designed to get a rise out of the teacher. If your refuse to rise to the bait of a child whose aim it is to wind you up, the tactic becomes meaningless and a waste of time.
- *Build a 'wall'*: A very good way to avoid rising to the bait is to build a metaphorical 'wall' between you and the behaviour. Imagine that a barrier stands between you and the child. However badly he or she misbehaves, you are completely impervious to its effects. That way you are in a far better position to deal calmly and rationally with the situation.
- *Make them decide*: When you do have to use sanctions, keep reminding your children that they have a choice at every stage. They can start to behave, accepting the current level of sanctions. Alternatively, if they decide to repeat the misbehaviour, they will earn a higher level of punishment.
- *Sanction the behaviour*: If a child feels that the punishment is a personal attack, this is far more likely to create a confrontation. Make it clear that it's the behaviour, and not the child, that is being sanctioned. In addition, keep the whole situation as depersonalized as possible. You can do this by blaming 'the school rules' for the fact that you have to impose a sanction.
- *Follow it through*: Every time you apply a sanction, you *must* follow it through, for example chasing the child to serve the detention. Otherwise, the sanction is meaningless and not worth imposing in the first place.
- *Make the sanction count*: If you set a detention, spend time during that detention actually talking to the child about his or her misbehaviour. Often,

children don't really understand why they are being punished, and they need things explained clearly. Hopefully, this discussion will prevent a recurrence of the behaviour that earned the sanction in the first place.

Serious incidents

Although thankfully still reasonably rare, you should be aware that serious incidents can and do occur in schools. For the most part, the teacher will prevent extreme behaviour by the way that he or she handles the children within the classroom. However, there will be times when (often for reasons outside your control) a student 'goes off on one' and completely loses control over his or her behaviour. At this point, if it is appropriate, you are entitled to make a physical intervention. See the sections below (pp. 157–8) for more detail about what 'reasonable force' is, and when it might be used.

Examples of a serious incident could include a physical attack by one student on another, a fight between two students in your classroom, or a physical attack on you as a teacher. Other serious offences include catching a student with a weapon, with drugs, or in the process of committing a crime. As well as experiencing serious incidents within your classroom, you may also be faced with a serious incident happening in the corridor or the playground.

Dealing with the serious incident

In any serious situation, your first priority is ensuring the safety of the children (both those involved and others in the vicinity) and of course of yourself. With some incidents, the situation may actually require you to use physical intervention, but always view this as a last resort. In all instances, if you feel that physical intervention is going to put you at risk of injury, for instance from a student who is bigger than you, then do not intervene yourself but call for help instead. The guidance from the Education Act states that teachers are allowed to use 'reasonable force' in a 'wide variety of situations'. These situations fall into three main categories:

- Where a student might injure him or herself or others.
- Where a student is causing damage to property (including his or her own).
- Where the child is behaving in a way that prevents 'good order and discipline' from being maintained (both inside the classroom and in the school as a whole).

As soon as a serious incident begins, take the following steps:

Dealing with the serious incident

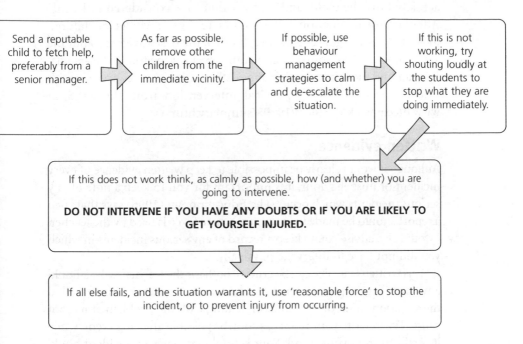

Send a reputable child to fetch help, preferably from a senior manager.

As far as possible, remove other children from the immediate vicinity.

If possible, use behaviour management strategies to calm and de-escalate the situation.

If this is not working, try shouting loudly at the students to stop what they are doing immediately.

If this does not work think, as calmly as possible, how (and whether) you are going to intervene.
DO NOT INTERVENE IF YOU HAVE ANY DOUBTS OR IF YOU ARE LIKELY TO GET YOURSELF INJURED.

If all else fails, and the situation warrants it, use 'reasonable force' to stop the incident, or to prevent injury from occurring.

What is reasonable force?

The Education Act guidance helpfully states that 'there is no legal definition' of this term, and that it must depend on the individual circumstances of each case. The advice is to use reasonable force only when the situation really warrants it, and also when all other avenues of resolution have been tried. (Of course, when two students are at each other's throats, the natural reaction is to try and prevent them from hurting each other.) If it is required, the reasonable force that you use would normally take some form of physical intervention.

What is 'physical intervention'?

The government's guidance suggests that you might use some of the following strategies to intervene:

- Putting yourself physically between the students.
- Standing in front of the child to block his or her way.
- Holding the child.
- Pushing or pulling the child.
- Leading the student by the hand or arm.
- Moving the child using a hand on his or her back.
- Using a more 'restrictive hold' (but only in extreme circumstances).

At all times you should ensure that your physical intervention doesn't actually hurt the child, and that it cannot be 'considered indecent'. Although the temptation will always be to dive in when two children look like they are going to hurt each other, the best advice is to put the safety of your class, yourself (and your career) at the top of the agenda. You can find more information about all the legal issues concerned with teachers and the use of physical intervention from the DfES, at www.dfee.gov.uk/circulars/10_98/summary.htm.

Written evidence

Although it would clearly be impossible to keep written evidence of every incident of misbehaviour, it is important for you to keep a note of any serious incidents which occur. The Education Act (1996) says that such a report should be made in every case where force is used by the teacher. I would also advise you to keep a record of any serious incidents in which you did not have to intervene physically.

This written evidence can be crucial, both for the teacher's sake (should any complications arise, such as an accusation that you mishandled the situation) and for the child, in dealing with the problem at its root cause. Try to write your report as soon as possible after the event, while it is still fresh in your mind. Your school may have an 'incident book' in which you can make a note of what happened. Do ensure that you keep a copy when you write in the incident book, or pass on a written report to somebody else. There are a number of very good reasons why this written record is important, especially in the case of serious incidents such as those described in the sections below.

- An accumulation of written evidence will allow a child with serious behavioural issues to receive the help that he or she needs.
- Although it is increasingly difficult for schools to exclude very poorly behaved students, this type of written evidence is essential in creating a case against such a child.
- If there is any comeback from the incident on you as a teacher, it is vital to have written evidence of what actually happened.
- It is very easy for the memory to distort an incident after the fact. It is also relatively easy for a child to bend the truth to get a teacher into trouble.
- Writing a report about the misbehaviour that occurred is all part of acting as a professional.
- The written report can be copied and passed on to the relevant people, for instance the head of year or other manager responsible for behaviour issues.

- Writing down the details of an incident can be cathartic – a good way of dealing with the stress that the incident might have caused you as a teacher.

What should be included in the report?

It is a good idea to include the following details in your written report of the incident:

Written report of serious behaviour incident

Your name
The child's name
The child's class and/or form
Any other children who were involved, e.g. as victims or witnesses
The date that the incident occurred
Where the incident took place
Details of exactly what happened
What you did to try to de-escalate the situation
How the incident was dealt with at the time
How the incident was followed through afterwards
Who else helped to deal with the problem
Any injuries that occurred, to children or staff
Any other damage that occurred
If force did have to be used, what this was and why it was necessary

---

9 Beyond the classroom

There are, of course, a million and one jobs that the teacher has to do beyond the confines of the classroom walls: paperwork, report writing, parents' evenings, pastoral responsibilities and so on. Some of these jobs feel rather mundane and pointless (any meaningless form-filling, for instance). Others play a vital part in creating positive relationships between yourself, your children and their parents or guardians. In this chapter you'll find lots of advice about minimizing the boring aspects of the job, rising to the challenge of the trickier ones, and developing your skills beyond the classroom walls.

Admin

Paperwork can cause a lot of stress, and get in the way of the 'real job' of helping your children to learn. Some paperwork is important and meaningful and will have a valuable impact on your work as a teacher; other paperwork is simply something that must be done, typically because someone no longer in the classroom has decided it is a good idea. Best, then, to learn how to get your admin done efficiently and effectively, using time spent on it in the most productive way possible.

Teachers come into the job with widely varying levels of organizational ability. Some are naturally tidy, and take to all the paperwork like a duck to water. Others are destined to face a huge pile of papers on their desk throughout their teaching careers. Here are some top tips for dealing with admin effectively, without allowing it to become an issue:

- *Empty your pigeonhole regularly*: When you first start teaching, it can make you feel rather special having a slot with your very own name on it. However, before long, the pigeonhole can become a source of misery and heartache. The problem is that both highly important and completely meaningless bits of paper will get shoved into your pigeonhole. If you fail to empty it for a few days, it will be stuffed full of forms to fill, urgent memos, etc. Get into a routine of checking your pigeonhole each day, perhaps first thing in the morning or straight after the school day finishes.

- *Deal with it immediately*: As far as is humanly possible, deal with every piece of paper you receive straight away, especially those which can be passed on or back to somebody else. If you're given a form to fill out, fill it in right away so that it is no longer your problem.
- *Be ruthless*: Never hang onto a piece of paper just because you 'might need it again'. There is far too much paper in the teaching profession: only by being completely ruthless will you ensure that you can actually find those bits of paper that you really need.
- *Keep vital information in one place*: There are some really important bits of paper, such as class lists, which you will need to keep close to hand, particularly at the start of the year. Keep it in a cardboard folder or slipped inside your teacher's planner.
- *Have a yearly chuck-out*: About once a year, find the time to go through all your bits of paper and throw out anything that is no longer required.
- *Know your rights*: See the list of tasks you should no longer have to do at www.teachernet.gov.uk/wholeschool/remodelling/cuttingburdens/toolkit/tkannex/tkannexc.

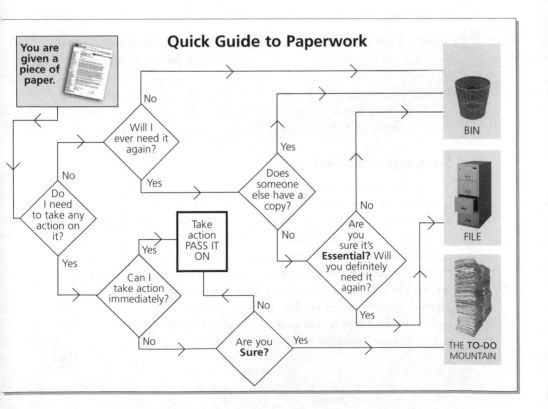

Quick Guide to Paperwork

You are given a piece of paper.

Will I ever need it again? — No

Do I need to take any action on it? — No

Can I take action immediately? — Yes → Take action PASS IT ON

Will I ever need it again? — Yes → Does someone else have a copy?

Does someone else have a copy? — No → Are you sure it's **Essential?** Will you definitely need it again?

Are you sure it's **Essential?** Will you definitely need it again? — No → BIN

Are you sure it's **Essential?** Will you definitely need it again? — Yes → FILE

Can I take action immediately? — No → Are you **Sure?**

Are you **Sure?** — Yes → THE **TO-DO** MOUNTAIN

BIN

FILE

THE **TO-DO** MOUNTAIN

Recording and reporting

The areas of recording and reporting are closely linked to your assessment of your students, which was dealt with in Chapter 7 (see pp. 136–9). The teacher's mark book is a vital part of his or her teaching materials. The mark book allows you to keep a record of all marks that your students have achieved. These records will help inform your planning, report writing, overall assessment grades and so on. You can find a sample page from a mark book in Chapter 17 (p. 301).

Top tip

Sometimes a student will claim to have been absent from class on a day that homework was set. It can be difficult to know if he or she is telling the truth.

Avoid this problem by keeping your class register (i.e. absent/present) together with the marks for the class.

When you set homework, leave a blank line for the marks alongside the class register for that lesson. (See the mark book sample for an example of how this works.)

Reports come in many shapes and sizes. The handwritten reports that were the 'norm' until relatively recently are increasingly being replaced by typed or even computerized formats, such as SIMs (see below). Reports offer the teacher an excellent opportunity to communicate with the home, and thus it is important that they are written well. You can find a number of different tips below for writing good reports.

SIMs report format

The SIMs reporting format is very similar to the SIMs registers, with which you may already be familiar. The registers are sheets on which the teacher marks a student present or absent by filling in a lozenge-shaped mark. The register is then read by a computer software programme. SIMs reports work in a similar way – the teacher places a series of marks on the sheet to indicate which comments will be included in each student's report. The computer then selects the relevant comments from a 'bank' created by the teacher or department, and puts them together into each individual report. The main downside to SIMs reports is that they can seem very impersonal and 'samey' (which, of course, they are).

Tips for report writing

Below you will find some general tips for report writing, as well as some examples of how to write, and not write, a report:

- Start each report with a general sentence which summarizes the child's progress and overall achievement in your class, then proceed to more detailed comments.
- Use a formal writing style and take great care with spelling, particularly of children's names. Avoid unnecessarily 'fancy' vocabulary – you are trying to communicate effectively, not to impress with technical terminology.
- Although I normally prefer to call a spade a spade, when it comes to writing reports, you need to learn the art of euphemism. Being brutally honest might make you feel better, but it is likely to de-motivate the children you most need to encourage.
- In the light of this, aim to frame your comments in a positive, rather than a negative way. The two examples below show the difference between the two approaches:
  - Negative: 'Charlie just can't keep quiet. He's always chatting with his friends when he should be doing his work.'
  - Positive (using euphemisms): 'Charlie finds it difficult to work in silence. He needs to concentrate on his own learning at all times.'
- Give comments on a range of areas: include the child's learning in the subject or subjects, his or her current levels of achievement, the child's attitude to the work, behaviour in class, emotional and social skills, and so on.
- Even for your most difficult students, try to comment on at least one or two things that the child does well. For instance, even for a child who is underachieving, you could include a positive comment about his or her potential (see the 'good example' below).
- Don't let your own emotions about a child shine through in a report. While it may be tempting to let off steam about a kid who's been winding you up all year, your professional duty is to report accurately, effectively and dispassionately on each individual.
- Bear in mind the potential parental reaction to the reports that you write. With the 'very difficult' child, a very negative report may have the opposite effect to that intended. Instead of encouraging the child to do better, with the support of his or her parents, a negative report may simply exacerbate a difficult home situation. (Alternatively, the child may decide that it is safer to 'lose' the report on the way home, and it might never even be seen by the parents.)

- Finish the report by setting clear targets for future improvements. These targets can then be referred to in class with the student, and in subsequent meetings and contacts with the parents or guardians.

Report writing

The two examples below show how a secondary English report might be written. The general principles of report writing that are shown here can be adapted to different subject areas and to primary aged children.

A 'good example'

Charlie is an able and creative student who has the potential to do very well in this subject. He has an imaginative approach to the tasks set, and his oral work is always confident and clearly expressed. At the moment, Charlie finds it difficult when he is asked to work in silence. He needs to concentrate on his own learning at all times, rather than allowing others to distract him.

Charlie's written work would benefit from much more attention to detail, particularly when checking for spelling errors. He needs to write at greater length, especially when preparing coursework assignments. Charlie is a fluent reader, and he has shown a particular talent for working with the Shakespeare texts we have studied this term. He should now aim to develop his concentration in class so that he can succeed to the best of his ability.

A 'bad example'

Charlie is a weak student who has a poor approach to this subject. He just can't seem to keep quiet and is always chatting with his friends when he should be doing his work. His writing is always full of mistakes, and his spelling is very bad. He doesn't put enough time or effort into writing his coursework assignments, and this means that his grades are not going to be good. Charlie does like to read out loud in class, it's just a shame he doesn't put the same amount of effort into his written work.

Examinations

A series of statutory examinations now punctuate the child's school career. Alongside these externally assessed exams, many schools will run annual 'school exams' of their own. These are normally held during the summer term. Secondary schools will also run 'mocks' for their GCSE and A level students in the run-up to the real examinations. A brief run-down of when formal, externally assessed exams take place is given below:

Exam type	Usually taken in	Subject areas
SATs	Year 2	English, maths
	Year 6	English, maths, science
	Year 9	English, maths, science
GCSEs	Year 11	a wide range
NVQs	varies, post-16	vocational subjects
AS levels	Year 12	a wide range
A Levels	Year 13	a wide range

Preparing for exams

To help your students succeed in their exams, it is worth putting in some time helping them to prepare. Although I would not advocate 'teaching to the test', you can certainly give your children some valuable advice about how to approach exams. The tips below give you a range of ideas about how you might do this:

- Let them know what to expect. If children go into an exam without any idea of what is going to happen, they are bound to suffer from nerves. Talk them through the whole process: how long the exam will be, where it will take place, what equipment they might need to have with them, and so on.
- Give your children plenty of practice with old papers, looking carefully at the format of the paper, the way the questions are worded, how the marks are allocated, etc.
- Talk with your students about how and why marks are awarded. Some children find it hard to understand the relationship between the marks available for a question, the amount of time which they should spend on it, and the level of detail that they should include.
- Teach your children 'exam technique', looking at the importance of timing, deciding which questions to answer, how to ensure that they answer the question, and so on.

Pastoral work

The 'pastoral' side of a teacher's job can be extremely rewarding, and it can also be time-consuming and emotionally draining. As teachers, we have a special role to play in the care of the 'whole' child. Although our principal responsibility is for educating our students, the teacher is often the main (or only) adult outside the home who will have contact with a child in a professional context.

Some of the children with whom you work will be under the care of a social worker or other specialist outside the school, but the majority will not. Some of the problems that your children bring to you may be connected solely to the school environment, while for others the teacher offers a dependable adult with whom to share their fears and concerns about life outside the school gates. An important part of our role, then, is to care for the social well-being of our charges, as well as for their educational welfare.

Depending on how well you relate to your students, you could find yourself acting as a sounding board for large numbers of young people. This is perhaps especially so at the difficult transition times: the first move into mainstream schooling, the transfer from primary to secondary school, and the change from childhood into adolescence. The list below gives you an idea of the type of concerns you may have to deal with, and is followed by some tips on how to resolve the issues:

- *Bullying*: This may take the form of verbal or physical abuse. Bullying should be taken seriously, both by the teacher and by the school: make sure you find out whether your school has an anti-bullying policy, and what this involves.
- *Friendship issues*: Some children find it hard to socialize and make friends, while others will have traumatic rifts with a particular friendship group.
- *Problems at home*: Students may approach you to talk about a situation at home that is worrying them, for instance a problem with a sibling.
- *Serious issues*: When a problem raised by a child involves child-protection issues, it is very important that you know what steps to take. See the sections below on child protection and serious issues for more information (p. 168).

When your students do approach you with problems that they want to discuss, follow these tips to help resolve the issue in a professional manner:

- *Let them talk*: Sometimes a child will simply need a shoulder to cry on. Try to find the time to let them talk out the issue with you, however trivial you might feel it to be. If necessary, suggest that the child books a time with you after school.
- *Don't get overly involved*: There is something rather pleasing about a child choosing to confide in you, and the temptation can be to see yourself as a bit of an agony aunt or uncle. However, unless you are

a professionally trained counsellor, you will not have the proper experience to undertake this role. Do try to keep your emotions out of any pastoral discussions. Getting overly involved with a child can make your day-to-day teaching job difficult.

- *Never promise confidentiality*: Sometimes a student will try to make you promise that you won't tell anyone else before revealing the problem. Never promise confidentiality, because if the issue turns out to be serious, your first duty will be to inform the Child Protection Officer (CPO) of the conversation.
- *Make a record*: Keep a record of any discussion you feel is of a sufficiently serious nature. Make a note of the child's name, when he or she came to see you, what the problem was and so on. If necessary, pass a copy of this information to a senior colleague.
- *Pass on your concerns*: In the secondary school, the child's form tutor should be informed about pastoral issues which concern their tutees. In the primary school, if the child is not in your class, you should inform their classroom teacher of what has been said. Depending on the seriousness of the issue, you might also inform the Head of Year, your line manager, or in serious cases the CPO. These people will take the responsibility for informing the parents as necessary. In some schools a trained counsellor is also available to talk with troubled children.
- *Take them seriously*: Don't try to shrug off a problem which a child chooses to share with you, even when you see it as trivial. You will get children who regularly 'bend your ear', but this in itself could be a symptom of something more serious.

In the primary school, the pastoral care of a particular group falls mainly to the class teacher, who works with one class for the majority (or all) of the time. In the secondary school, the form tutor takes on responsibility for the pastoral care of one particular group of students. He or she may or may not actually teach this 'tutor group'. See below for more information about the role of the form tutor.

The form tutor

In the primary school, the class teacher is able to develop a close relationship with the children, because he or she sees them all day every day. In addition, many parents or guardians drop their children off and collect them from school, and it is possible for them to maintain relatively close contact with the class teacher on a day to day basis. Parents know who their child's class teacher is, and it is not overly difficult to make arrangements for a quick chat about progress, or to air a particular concern.

On the other hand, in the secondary school a child will be only one of perhaps hundreds whom the subject teacher sees in the course of the week. Because of this, the form tutor takes responsibility for the pastoral care of the children in their form or tutor group. In Part Three, Anatomy of a School, you can find a detailed description of the role of the tutor (pp. 203–4).

Child protection

Depending on the type of person you are, and the relationship that you have with your students, you may find that a number of children approach you seeking help. Often, these children will be raising less serious concerns with you, such as those to do with friendship, worries about work and so on. Of course, these concerns should be dealt with sympathetically, and taken seriously.

However, from time to time you may find that students bring serious pastoral issues to you, and it's vital that you know what should be done in these circumstances. It may be the case that you have serious concerns about the welfare of a particular child in your form or class, even though the child has not spoken to you about his or her problem. Again it is your professional (and indeed personal) responsibility to ensure that these are dealt with in the proper manner. Just a few of the serious issues that you may encounter are listed below:

- Unexplained injuries that suggest physical abuse, for instance frequent bruising.
- A student fears that his friend is becoming addicted to drugs.
- A child tells you that her parents beat her when she does badly in a test.
- A teenage student is worried that she may be pregnant.

What should I do about a serious issue?

Schools must have a designated person responsible for dealing with child protection issues (often called the Child Protection Officer – CPO). It is to this person that you should pass on your concerns. As soon as possible after the child has approached you, document your discussion in full detail, including the child's name, the date, what the child said and so on. You should then go in person to see the CPO, giving him or her a copy of your notes, and keeping one for yourself. The CPO will then take over responsibility for the problem, and liaise with other agencies as necessary.

The parents' evening

[Note: The term 'parents' is used below to include the child's guardians. For some children this may be brothers or sisters, foster carers and so on.]

Parents' evenings can be stressful and tiring occasions. However, the majority of teachers also find them a very valuable and important event. In the primary school, teachers may have regular contact with parents or guardians, for instance if they drop younger children off at school. For the secondary school teacher, the parents' evening is often the only form of contact with their students' guardians during the year. Sadly, it is often the case that the parents you most need or want to see at the evening will not attend.

In the run-up to the parents' evening, you will probably be given an 'appointments' sheet so that you can book individual time slots for each child. If you are a secondary school teacher with a large number of students, it may be that you need to double-book the children within each time slot. If this is the case, you should ensure that you keep each discussion very short and focused (see the section below for ideas about how to do this). There are a number of very positive aspects about the parents' evening:

- The evening provides a way of creating an initial contact with the home, particularly if the student is experiencing problems.
- Teachers are able to pass on information about the student's strengths and weaknesses.
- The teacher is able to highlight any particular concerns, for instance about weak literacy skills or problematic behaviour.
- Many parents are very happy to support the work that their children do in the classroom, but are unsure about how to do this. The parents' evening allows us to explain more about the role they can play.
- If the child attends with his or her parents, the teacher can extract promises about future effort, work, behaviour and so on.
- The teacher can check with the parents whether they are happy to be contacted directly in the event of any problems occurring.

You can find ten tips for 'surviving' the parents' evening in Chapter 18 (pp. 311–2).

What should be in the discussion?

If you only have to see a limited number of parents, you can spend quite a substantial amount of time over each discussion. However, if you do have a large number of parents to see, you will need to be concise and very focused in order to fit everybody in. Here are some ideas about the format that your discussion might take:

- A summary of where the child is now, in terms of work, progression, behaviour, attitude and so on.
- Details of the individual child's strengths and weaknesses within the subject (secondary) or the curriculum (primary).
- Information about any specific concerns, or areas of weakness that need further work.
- Targets on which the child should work.
- Ways in which the parents can help you as a teacher.
- Details of forthcoming assessments, for instance SATs, GCSEs, and how the parents can help the child prepare.
- Any questions that the parents may need answered.

Extracurricular activities

Extracurricular activities are those which take place outside the normal timetable and curriculum. These activities might be run before school, at lunchtimes, after school or at the weekends. Teachers can get involved in a huge range of different activities, depending on their personal expertise in an area, or simply on what they enjoy doing. Teachers may become involved in actually running and supervising an activity, or they may offer their assistance in a more peripheral way, for instance organizing the props or costumes for a school play.

For some secondary teachers, the subject that they teach involves extracurricular work almost as a matter of course. This includes teachers of music/drama (the school production) and teachers of PE (the school sports teams). Speaking from personal experience, those teachers who run large-scale after-school activities are only too happy for their colleagues to help them out. There are a huge range of activities with which you might like to get involved, from the computer club to the sports team, the school production to the Duke of Edinburgh Award.

Unless you are teaching drama or PE, running extracurricular activities would not generally be part of your job description as a classroom teacher. For posts in some independent schools, great importance is placed on a willingness to contribute to this aspect of school life. In any case, although participating in extracurricular activities is obviously hard work and time-consuming, there are a number of valuable reasons for getting involved:

- These activities offer a great way of developing relationships with students outside the classroom environment.
- Your students get the chance to see you as a 'real person', and consequently build respect for you.
- You get to meet children whom you don't actually teach yet. If you do teach these children in the future, you will already have developed a good relationship.
- You can help children develop skills outside the normal curriculum.
- You can also develop your own skills beyond those required for the day to day job.
- Active participation in these activities looks great on your CV!

Just one quick word of warning: beware of doing too much as an NQT. In the first year, your classroom practice will take up all or most of your energy. Save the more time-consuming extracurricular activities for your second and subsequent years in teaching.

Trips

A school trip can be a very positive experience, both for the students participating, and for the teachers involved. For many children a trip is a rare opportunity for a day out of school, doing something completely different, or seeing somewhere new. Teachers are, however, perhaps becoming more wary about the implications of taking children on a trip. We certainly need to be fully aware of the extent of our responsibilities, and about the 'duty of care' which we owe to our students both on and off site.

A school trip might take place during the school day, for instance a visit to a museum. Alternatively, it could be an evening event, such as going to the theatre. Some trips are longer, for instance the popular 'residential' which is sometimes held in the early years of secondary school. In some cases, a school trip will be to an overseas destination, and this would include the skiing trip and MFL visit or exchange.

There are a wide range of health and safety considerations involved in setting up a trip. Before the event, a detailed risk assessment should be done, by a person trained in what to do. Parental consent must also be given. If you are an inexperienced teacher who wishes to arrange a trip, get help from a senior and experienced member of staff who is aware of all the legal niceties. You might like to look at www.teachernet.gov.uk/wholeschool/healthandsafety/visits/for some useful advice and links.

Part Three
ANATOMY OF A SCHOOL

School management

10

This section of the book offers you the 'anatomy' of a school: details of the wide spectrum of different people, jobs and roles that go to make up an educational establishment. For each post you'll find a brief description of what the role involves. You'll also find some interviews with people doing some of these jobs, to give you an insight into exactly what is involved.

Schools vary greatly in their size and structure: from the secondary school with thousands of students and literally hundreds of staff, to the small village primary school with only a few employees. Whatever the kind of job you have, getting to know what the other staff at your school do is a vital part of working as an effective team.

Typical management structure of a primary school	Typical management structure of a secondary school
Headteacher	Headteacher

Typical management structure of a primary school

Headteacher

Deputy headteacher

Subject coordinators

Classroom teachers

Learning support assistants /
Classroom assistants

Typical management structure of a secondary school

Headteacher

Deputy headteacher(s)

Assistant headteacher(s)

Curriculum   *Pastoral*

Heads of faculty/   Heads of year
Heads of department

Deputy HoDs/   Deputy heads of year
Subject coordinators

Classroom teachers   Form tutors
(subject specialists)

Headteacher

The role of the head can seem a bit of a mystery to classroom teachers. In a large school you may have little contact with the man or woman at the top, and little real idea of exactly what it is that your headteacher does on a day to day basis. Although you will not necessarily be aware of what is actually involved in being a headteacher, you will certainly feel the impact of a good (or bad) leader at your school.

If you're interested in moving up the promotion ladder to become a head in an LEA-maintained school, you will need to gain a qualification called the 'National Professional Qualification for Headship' (NPQH). This was first introduced in 1997, and is designed to be a practical, professional qualification for prospective headteachers.

Anyone with good experience of whole-school leadership can apply for a place on the NPQH; around 5,000 candidates enrol on the programme each year. The course can take between six months and two years to complete, depending on your experience and expertise. Further information can be found through the National College of School Leadership (NCSL) at www.ncsl.org.uk/programmes/npqh/.

This site also gives the 'National Standards for Headteachers', published by the DfES. Within these standards are 'key areas' of headship which give an outline of the key roles involved in being a headteacher. These are:

- strategic direction and development of the school
- teaching and learning
- leading and managing staff
- efficient and effective deployment of staff and resources
- accountability

Headteacher (secondary)

Tuxford School, Nottinghamshire

Chris Pickering

Q. Why did you become a teacher in the first place?

Chris – Because we didn't get any formal careers guidance in school, and I fell into it. Fortunately, I took to it like a duck to water, and now I wouldn't do anything else.

Q. And how did you originally qualify and in what subjects?

Chris – I did a teaching certificate which took three years, followed by a

BEd for one year. Then I took two diplomas in education after I'd been teaching a couple of years. I trained as a geography/PE teacher originally. I taught both on teaching practices, but I've never taught PE since.

Q. What are your feelings about the way that teachers are trained nowadays?

Chris – I think we've got some much better trained teachers, because the training establishments have got their acts together. Student teachers are being trained to teach, and trained in the art of teaching, as opposed to being trained academically.

Q. And what are your thoughts about a teaching degree versus the PGCE route?

Chris – I think we have better trained teachers who come through the specialist teaching degree course. That's not to say that you don't get good teachers with PGCEs, but I would far prefer to see somebody trained to do the job than be swayed by the offer of money after doing a first degree.

Q. How would you describe yourself as a teacher, when you were a full-time classroom practitioner?

Chris – I was determined to get the best results out of those children, but I was not necessarily the greatest risk taker. Fifteen years ago, that wasn't high priority on people's lists. I was quite didactic. Essentially in those days it was about getting people through their O levels. Things have changed away from knowledge-based learning to the development of skills and concepts, which needs different methods of teaching. In the classroom now I'm completely different to what I was like as a full-time teacher. I've had to adapt like everyone else.

Q. Could you tell me about the route that you took to become a headteacher?

Chris – My first teaching post was in Doncaster in a large comprehensive school. I was there for five years. I went for my first promotion after two years, to become a second in the geography department. I left there to become head of geography at a school in Derbyshire. After two years there I was promoted again to head of upper school and head of department. After five years there I went to a boys' school in Buxton. When the boys' school amalgamated with the girls' school, I got the deputy headship. In my last year there I was acting head, before getting a permanent headship at a school in Sheffield. After three years there I got the headship at Tuxford and this is my sixth year here.

Q. When you originally came into teaching, did you plan to become a headteacher?

Chris – No. I've not actually had a plan in my career at all. I basically tried to do my best at every level and that's how I get satisfaction, by doing my best and people recognizing that what I do is good. Then the opportunities just came along, or I suddenly felt that it was time to go for something else.

Q. As a headteacher, how are you involved in the classroom now?

Chris – I'm intimately involved in all the different initiatives and developments that impact in the classroom. I do a little bit of teaching, but I don't think it's absolutely essential for headteachers to teach in the classroom. I think it's essential for headteachers to keep in contact with the classroom and have the ability to teach, but I find that every hour that I spend in the classroom has to be matched with an hour for marking and preparation, which basically reduces my working week. We're moving into an era now where it's increasingly hard to combine classroom teaching, leadership and management responsibility with quality delivery in the classroom. I would always ensure that I had the skills to step into the classroom and do a good job, if ever I was called on to do it, though.

Q. Would you recommend your job to teachers just starting out on their careers, or would it be too stressful for some?

Chris – The stresses and strains of headship are immense, but there are stresses and strains at all levels. When people say, '*I could never become a head, it's too stressful*', then my response is '*Well, if you find that you can cope as a teacher, then you'd be able to cope with headship too.*'

Q. What sort of person does a headteacher need to be?

Chris – It takes the sort of person who is happy never to be praised, who is happy to carry the can, and to bail people out, and who can bite their tongue, and still remain positive and enthusiastic. You also have to be the sort of person who doesn't wear their heart on their sleeve. No matter how frustrated or angry or stressed I am, that has to stay with me. Otherwise you can have a terrible effect on other people.

Q. What skills does a headteacher need to have?

Chris – Multi-tasking, having many things on the go all at once. Having the capacity to switch from something that is very mentally demanding, which is high-powered in respect of the impact the decisions you make will have, to something which may be very trivial to you, but which to other people is very important. You get that all day. I don't think you get that sort of pressure in industry. You can never be sure that things are going to go well for any longer than a few minutes. I can come in and something will happen which is a real success, then in the next five minutes something happens which brings you straight down into the trough. It's crest, trough, crest, trough, that sort of roller-coaster ride all the time.

Q. What's your approach to dealing with your staff?

Chris – My attitude is that teachers are your most valuable resource and therefore they need to be treated as such. My philosophy is to invest as much as I possibly can in the staff – in their training, their morale, their working conditions, in the way I treat them personally. I think that time and money invested in that way reaps its rewards in terms of good work. That's why this school puts its Investors in People status at the heart of things. I'm talking about all staff, too, not just teachers.

Q. What sort of person would be your 'ideal' teacher?

Chris – Someone with energy, enthusiasm, a desire to make a difference with children. A really first-class classroom practitioner with a sense of humour and a sense of perspective.

Q. And how do teachers keep that energy up in the long term?

Chris – A lot of how teachers react isn't just about life in the classroom, it's about how the school as a whole is managed and run. The stresses and pressures on teachers can be multiplied many-fold if the working conditions and the atmosphere in the school are not good. I passionately believe that. The morale here is such that for 90 per cent of the teachers it alleviates the downsides of the job, and helps them to retain the energy and enthusiasm.

Q. When you're looking to promote someone, what sort of person are you looking for?

Chris – Somebody who has vision, who appreciates what it is to plan, set targets, achieve targets. Somebody who can manage people – who can challenge poor performance, who monitors and evaluates, analyses and brings the best out of people. Who can build and lead teams. Someone with initiative, vision, ideas and the capacity to carry them through and make a difference. There're not many people around in middle management positions who've got those qualities. There are lots of middle managers who believe it's all about the administrative aspects, and who shy away from the real, hard-nosed bits of the job.

Q. Could you describe for me one of the best moments of your career, something that really sticks in your mind as making it all worthwhile?

Chris – It's difficult to pick one out. I doubt that one moment would make it all worthwhile. I have received some excellent feedback from parents on a number of occasions. People who have bothered to put pen to paper and pass on their thanks and gratitude. Achieving the best ever GCSE results, gaining technology status and perhaps above all the accolade paid to the school after our last Investors in People assessment stand out above most things. Our assessment report began 'Tuxford is a model organization, one which has people (staff and pupils) and their development at its core'. This tells me that we are on the right lines.

Q. Could you tell me a bit about what's happening at Tuxford School at the moment – I understand you're moving into a new building in the next academic year?

Chris – It is a very exciting time. The new school is in the final stages of construction and we are due to move in March 2007. We have just undergone a very successful Ofsted inspection which confirmed the school to be outstanding in its provision for Student Support and Guidance and Welfare and Development, in addition to many other examples of outstanding practice. We are currently in the process of applying for specialist school re-designation and have recently been invited to apply for a second specialism. Lots on the go!!

Q. What about all those government initiatives – what kind of impact do they have on your day-to-day work?

Chris – They don't make life any easier that is for sure! However, we have established an excellent infrastructure for sustaining school improvement. This enables us to create the capacity within the school to manage initiatives effectively, build them into our planning processes and ensure that the students in the school benefit.

Q. Any thoughts on behaviour (a particular interest of mine)? Is student behaviour getting worse? If it is, what are the reasons and what can we do to combat this kind of problem on a school-wide basis?

Chris – Student behaviour is not getting worse, but is certainly more challenging as teachers have to learn how to respond to behaviour which is in itself a response by pupils to the world they live in. Today's hi-tech world cannot easily be recreated in every classroom every lesson! It is vitally important to be constantly seeking new techniques to manage behaviour and to train and develop teachers accordingly.

Q. What would you say to teachers who are interested in moving into a management position in a school?

Chris – Get as much experience as you can leading projects and working with teams in your own school. Access the NCSL programmes and start to build up your leadership skills. Develop your leadership styles and raise your awareness of the debate surrounding emotional intelligence.

Deputy headteacher/assistant headteacher

The role of the deputy headteacher, and the type of management responsibilities that he or she may have varies widely from school to school. Some large schools may have a number of deputy heads, while others may only have a single deputy, and then a number of assistant headteachers. In a school with a number of deputies (perhaps two or three), one may perhaps be responsible for curriculum issues, another might look after the pastoral aspects of school life, while a third deals with timetabling and behavioural issues. Again, the way that these responsibilities are organized varies very widely between schools.

The 'professional duties' of a deputy headteacher include taking over the role of the head if he or she is away. The deputy is expected to carry out the duties of a teacher and also any management responsibilities that the head assigns. Deputy heads are expected to play a major role in working out the aims and policies of the school. As with the headteacher, there is no limit on the number of working hours that the deputy headteacher must do.

The position of 'assistant headteacher' is a fairly recent innovation, and is designed to replace the previous post of 'senior teacher'. As with the deputy headteacher, the assistant head may take responsibility for a particular area within the school.

Deputy headteacher (primary)

Tracey Dunn

Q. Why did you decide to become a teacher?

Tracey – I left school at 16 following my O levels and went into the banking profession. At the time I was involved in scouting. I realized that I was really dissatisfied with work but that I really enjoyed cub-scouting. I started thinking about what else I could do. A fellow cub scout leader put me in touch with a local headteacher and I spent some time helping out in her school. It made me realize that this was what I wanted to do, and the head encouraged me to apply to university. I had completed a BTEC at night school which gave me the equivalent of A levels. At the grand old age of 22 I left work and became a student.

Q. Please describe your training.

Tracey I completed a Bachelor of Education course at the University of Wolverhampton. My main subject was religious studies and my minor was geography. It was a four-year course with core teaching studies and the option to diversify, for example to take more SEN or PE. I did both of these and focused the PE on swimming, gaining my swimming teacher's certificate. I spent quite a lot of time in school either on placement or as part of the core teaching we had.

Q. How long have you been in the teaching profession?

Tracey – Eleven years.

Q. Please describe your teaching career so far.

Tracey – I spent my NQT year in a junior school, working in a Year 3/4 team. I then moved to a primary school where I spent six years. At that school I had additional responsibilities as literacy coordinator, library coordinator and RE coordinator. I brought in the NLS to the school, I worked alongside literacy consultants for the authority to develop literacy medium-term plans that could be used as a scheme of work for the schools in the local authority. I also ran family learning sessions. While at the school I taught Years 1, 3, 4 and 5 in various combinations. I was also a teacher governor.

I've been in my current primary school for four years, and have taught in Years 3, 5 and 6. I have taken on additional posts as literacy coordinator, educational visit coordinator, multicultural coordinator, and assessment and curriculum coordinator. I organize trainees from the local teacher training institution. I also act as the SENCo and as a teacher governor. I'm currently the deputy head and have spent a couple of terms as acting head.

Q. Why did you choose to move into management?

Tracey – I was beginning to lack challenge. The feedback I was receiving from those who observed me indicated that I was a good classroom teacher and

I was well respected by my headteacher and within the authority. However, I was frustrated and wanted to be able to have a greater influence on the decisions made within school. We were relocating to a different area of the country and there were no Key Stage co ordinator jobs, so my head encouraged me to apply for deputy positions. Many different people I have worked with have told me that I will be a head – I always disagreed but the move to management changed that!

Q. How did you move up the scale to become a deputy?

Tracey – The head I was working for encouraged me to participate fully wherever I could in management decisions. I took every opportunity that came my way, often without extra pay because I felt that it would provide me with the experiences I needed to progress.

Q. Could you tell me a bit more about your role as a deputy head?

Tracey – It's about being a good classroom teacher, conducting myself as a model for the rest of the staff. It also involves working alongside staff to implement good practice across the school and to enable colleagues to develop their skills. You have to be a communicator between the staff and the headteacher. I have to keep the head grounded with what is achievable and work alongside him ensuring that policy becomes practice. I am the main point of contact for day-to-day behaviour management issues. I am also involved in the strategic management of the school.

Q. What are some of the positive aspects for a teacher of moving into management? How do you find combining classroom teaching with a management role?

Tracey – It's challenging! There's the opportunity to be fully involved in the direction and development of the school while retaining the contact with the children. Being organized as a teacher is essential as your day never goes as you plan it, something to do with management always crops up, even if it is just covering the absent teacher's playground duty. Being able to prioritize and working to deadlines is essential. You have to be willing to put the hours and effort in when it is needed; it will be redressed but not always straight away.

Q. What would you say are some of the best things about being a teacher and a deputy head? What gives you satisfaction personally?

Tracey – Being able to teach children and have daily contact with them, while being able to influence the strategic development of the school. Being able to ensure that policy is there for a positive reason and enhances children's learning. Personal satisfaction comes from knowing that I am helping to give children the best possible education, and enabling them to realize that there is another way of being successful at school.

Q. And what about the downsides?

Tracey – Having to do a full management role and a full teaching role without adequate time to do either, but having to do both really well. Constant indigestion.

Q. In your opinion, what makes a 'good' teacher? What do you look for in applicants to the school?

Tracey – Commitment, a willingness to work over and above, seeing the children as their driving force/passion. Someone who is in teaching for the children, who wants to make learning individual, positive, FUN. Someone who is willing to take risks and is able to model this to children, someone who will listen and ask questions. Someone who is driven by the lifelong learning journey themselves.

Q. What could be done to make teaching a 'better', more attractive profession?

Tracey – Restoring the professional status of teachers. Recognizing us for our value and ending the continual criticism. Removal of league tables and tests to measure school performance against – stopping treating children as piece-work – that's what factories are for! Re-evaluating pay against what we actually do and how we work (compared with other professions), continuing to improve our work/life balance. Make teachers truly accountable, run performance management as it is done in companies – make the pay rise mean something and be able to sack those that don't come up to the standard. Make sure teacher-training agencies are actually up to date and not leaving it to the schools.

Q. And, finally, what about the future? What does that hold for you?

Tracey – My experiences as acting head gave me the realization that I could run a school and I earned the confidence of other local heads and the LEA advisor. It was exceedingly hard work, but that was due to the circumstances I found myself and the school in. I found it gave me new challenges and I did enjoy it. I found it quite hard going back into the classroom and back to deputy role especially after the acting headship last summer. Despite this and continually overstepping the mark as I kept forgetting I was back to deputy, I have managed to develop a positive relationship with the new head. Together, along with the rest of the staff, we are moving the school forwards.

The experience has led me to realize that I have to do NPQH. I want to complete this at my current school because I want to leave in a couple of years once the transformation has been complete. I also want to complete my MA.

The second acting headship was quite different from the first. The first time, I was effectively caretaking as the head was on sick leave for a specified period of time and I knew he was coming back. The second time he had retired and I was the interim before the new headteacher took up post in the September. I had decided that I didn't want the headship and hadn't applied for the post.

I was allocated an excellent mentor who supported me really well through the steepest learning curve of my life. This was because of the local circumstances of the school and what I discovered once I had taken over. Each day was a new experience and I had to deal with many things that heads who have been heads for a long time haven't had to deal with; for example, I had an 'outbreak control' meeting with the director of communicable diseases and the head of the primary care trust, occupational health and the school nurse because we had a potential epidemic of Parvo virus (commonly known as slapped cheek). It's a fairly common childhood illness that isn't harmful, except for pregnant women and I had a pregnant member of staff!

I also found myself visited by the health and safety executive for an inspection, triggered by an accident where a teacher fell off a chair and broke her arm while putting up a display. This lead to an in-depth inspection of 'working at height' issues and of all health and safety at the school. The LEA were also involved because this could have led to issues with the whole of the LEA.

I learnt about building work as I triggered a major window replacement. I had a child sever her fingers in a gate (almost to the bone) and a resulting request for compensation. I had to learn about redundancy, as a teacher and a teaching assistant had to be made redundant.

It was a very eventful term but one that made me realize that if I could do all this and begin to turn behaviour around, then I could maybe do it 'for real'! I haven't yet started NPQH because just as I was about to apply my personal circumstances changed (I'm expecting my first baby) but I do intend to do NPQH in the next few intakes.

Head of department or faculty

In the secondary school, the different subjects are divided into departments or faculties. A department is a smaller unit, in which each subject or subject area has its own management team, meetings, area of the school buildings and so on. In some cases, a single department might have responsibility for more than one related area: for instance, an English department might include media studies and drama; a Humanities department would include both history and geography teachers. In many cases, teachers in a department which covers different curriculum areas would teach each of those subjects.

With the faculty system, each faculty includes a number of different but related subjects grouped together. These groupings vary from school to school, depending on management decisions about which subjects 'work best' when placed together. For instance, in one school art, music, dance and drama may be grouped together as a 'Performing Arts Faculty', while in another school dance, drama and PE may be put under the same umbrella.

Alongside the responsibilities of the 'normal' classroom teachers, as listed in the section on classroom teachers (pp. 188–9), managers also have a huge range of other duties, including those listed below:

- Organizing the planning and delivery of the curriculum
- Managing assessment, recording and reporting within the subject
- Helping to select and interview teachers and non-teaching staff for the department
- Helping to provide professional development

- Helping with the induction and assessment of NQTs
- Managing the work of other teachers
- Taking part in reviewing, developing and managing activities related to the curriculum and to whole-school issues

Head of Department (English)

Caroline Forgeron

Q. Why did you decide to become a teacher?

Caroline – It was something I'd always wanted to do. To start with I wanted to teach abroad. That didn't work out, but I found teaching in England was just as good. It's probably more of a challenge too, which is very rewarding.

Q. Could you tell me about your career so far?

Caroline – I started out in London as a classroom teacher of English and French. I did that for two years. Then I dropped the English to teach A level psychology. After that I took a promotion as assistant exam secretary. Finally, I moved to my current post of head of English, which I've been doing for four years now.

Q. Why did you decide to move into management?

Caroline – It seemed a logical step for me. I wasn't satisfied with the way things were being organized in my department when I was a classroom teacher. I constantly felt I could do things better. To me there wasn't enough emphasis on basic skills or continuity within the department, so moving to HoD meant I could choose how I organized schemes of work, etc. and allowed me to develop the ethos I wanted. I've been lucky at my current school in that the department has grown a great deal since I've been here. We started with only three English teachers and now there are seven full-time teachers and also several part-timers. Most of these teachers were NQTs which meant, although they didn't have lots of experience, they had lots of new and exciting ideas. This also meant I was able to do lots of the training within the department myself. We are now a very strong and united team.

Q. What do you see as the main roles and responsibilities of an HoD?

Caroline – The role of HoD means you have to be very organized – that was the first thing I learnt when I took up the post. You have to manage all the stress of exams – Key Stage 3, SATs, GCSEs, the new A levels. In addition, there are further exams such as the Year 7 progress tests and internal school exams to deal with. Another responsibility which seems to take up lots of time is schemes of work – especially with the new literacy strategy which means all our current schemes of work need to be reorganized! The GCSE syllabus also has this effect. Then there are things such as stock, stationery, discipline issues, coursework moderation, exam moderation, evaluating baseline data to predict next year's results.

I really enjoy deciding on schemes of work and finding new resources which I know will motivate the boys. I've always been interested in reading so this tends to influence me, I suppose. Being a head of English also means I'm involved in whole-school literacy initiatives and so I've had to deliver INSET to the whole school on training days about reading, writing and spelling. Although this was quite nerve-racking it was also quite exciting knowing you could be helping the whole school take on a more consistent approach to basic literacy skills.

Q. What sort of advantages and disadvantages are there in running your own department?

Caroline – I think this is a very personal thing. For me, lack of time is always a disadvantage. I only get one extra free day a week for running a large department – other smaller subjects get the same which has always seemed unfair. Advantages are things like having more power and control over issues in the school. As an HoD you are asked for your opinion (sometimes) about new initiatives. As a classroom teacher your voice would often go unheard.

Q. And what are the best and worst things about the role?

Caroline – I have always liked the fact I'm in charge! The trouble is that also means carrying the can when things go wrong. I'm very lucky in that my department are a good team – we all get on really well not just in school but socially too. Making decisions about things is never hard work – the main problem is usually that we have too many ideas.

Q. What sort of qualities do you feel make a 'good' teacher. What do you look for in applicants to your department?

Caroline – For me the main ingredients for a good teacher have to be enthusiasm and confidence. They need to have a sound knowledge of their subject but more importantly love what they are doing.

Q. Could you describe one of your best moments as a teacher?

Caroline – The best moment for me is when a student who has always seemed very weak or under-confident makes some monumental step. It might be a very small step but they suddenly realize that they can achieve it. That is very rewarding.

Q. And what about your worst moment?

Caroline – That's a very difficult one. It's probably not anything to do with the teaching in the classroom. It would have to be something like watching a very ineffective teacher giving INSET on a training day and thinking the whole time about what you could be doing with your time instead.

Q. Finally, what sort of changes do you feel need to be made for teaching to become a more attractive career choice?

Caroline – More time and more money would definitely give anyone a bigger incentive to join the profession. Also the constant bombardment of new initiatives doesn't really inspire anyone – as soon as you think you've got it all organized they change it again. It used to be every few years, which was acceptable – now it seems to be every year. Most of us just can't keep up with it all – however hard you work.

Subject coordinator

Subject coordinators are found at both primary and secondary level. In the primary school, a subject coordinator would help with planning the curriculum and delivery of their 'own' area (often their specialism at degree level). The coordinator might help create lesson plans and resources for the whole school, and could also hold seminars or training sessions covering the latest ideas and developments within their subject. There may also be coordinators with special responsibility for literacy and numeracy.

In the secondary school, a subject (or Key Stage) coordinator might work within a department or faculty, focusing on one smaller area of that subject. For instance, within a science department there might be subject coordinators for biology, chemistry and physics. Alternatively, there could be Key Stage coordinators, one for KS3 and another for KS4.

Head of year/house

In a secondary school, the head of year is responsible for the pastoral care of an entire year group. This might mean, in a large school, the responsibility for 200 or more students. Often, the head of year 'stays with' his or her year group as they progress up the school, getting to know the students in that year very well in the process. There are sometimes separate posts for the heads of Year 7 and sixth form, to take into account the additional responsibilities that these jobs might entail (for instance the induction of new students into the school for a head of Year 7). Some schools use a 'house' rather than a year group system.

A head of year undertakes a wide range of pastoral and administrative responsibilities, just a few of which are listed below:

- Ensuring that registers are taken correctly, absence notes received and so on.
- Meeting with form tutors on a regular basis to discuss relevant issues.
- Dealing with the behaviour issues within the year group. This would include meeting with individual students, keeping records of incidents, meeting with parents and so on.
- Taking Year assemblies.
- Planning trips and rewards for the year group.
- Dealing with examination-related issues, e.g. SATs in Year 9, GCSEs in Year 11.

11 Classroom posts

As well as the traditional role of the classroom teacher, nowadays there will often be one or more other adults in the room working alongside the teacher. In this chapter you can get lots of information about what being a classroom teacher is like, and exactly what the job entails. You will find details of the different options for progression, for those teachers who wish to stay in a classroom role. You can also gain an insight into the role and responsibilities of some support staff.

Classroom teacher

The classroom teacher has a surprisingly wide remit when it comes to his or her duties. You are responsible for a lot more than simply teaching – you must also take care of the pastoral well-being of your students and get involved in the administrative aspects of the school. The list below details the different jobs that you must do:

1 Teaching
  • Planning and preparing lessons
  • Teaching students according to their educational needs
  • Setting and marking work for school and homework
  • Assessing, recording and reporting on how the students are progressing, and what their attainment is
2 Other activities
  • Looking after the students' progress and well-being
  • Offering advice on issues related to students' education, social matters, further education and careers
  • Recording and reporting about students' personal and social needs
  • Liaising with parents and other bodies outside the school
  • Taking part in meetings related to any of the above
3 Assessment
  • Giving or taking part in spoken and written assessments about individuals and groups of students

4 Appraisal
  - Taking part in appraisal (of yourself and others) as set out in the regulations
5 Review
  - Reviewing your teaching methods and planning
  - Taking part in training or other professional development
6 Educational methods
  - Working with others to prepare and develop plans, schemes, resources, etc.
7 Discipline, health and safety
  - Keeping discipline and looking after student health and safety, both at school and during school activities (e.g. trips) elsewhere
8 Staff meetings
  - Taking part in meetings about the curriculum or about the running of the school as a whole
9 Cover
  - Supervising and, if possible, teaching students whose teacher is away (with some exceptions)
10. Public exams
  - Preparing your students for exams, and assessing them for exams
  - Recording and reporting on the assessments you have made
11 Admin
  - Doing admin and organization as required for the tasks described above
  - Organizing equipment and resources
  - Going to assemblies, registering and supervising students

Below you'll find interviews with classroom teachers working with different age groups and in very different kinds of settings. These interviews will give you an insight into what the role of classroom teacher involves. The final interviewee in this section, Tabatha Rayment, also explains what it is like teaching with a disability.

Classroom teacher

Primary

Steph Leach

Q. Why did you decide to become a teacher?

Steph – After graduating from university with no idea of what I wanted to do, I spent a year doing administrative work in various educational establishments. I craved a job that had variety, excitement and where I felt valued. I got a job delivering the ALS (additional literacy support) scheme in my local school and realized that teaching would bring me all these things and much more.

Q. What was your training like?

Steph – I took a PGCE at the Institute of Education in London. It was a bit of a whirlwind year. They cram so much in, sometimes it all felt too much, but now I realize that it was the best grounding for my career. Teaching is a bit like driving: you only really learn once you are left to get on with it. Although my training was incredibly useful and prepared me for teaching full-time, I have learnt more from actually teaching.

Q. Tell me about your career so far.

Steph – I started my teaching career at a junior school in Hertfordshire. I was teaching Year 3 in a two-form entry school. Overall the staff were very supportive and made my transition into full-time teaching enjoyable. I stayed there for three years, becoming the history coordinator and also the school's assessment coordinator.

After that I moved to Lincolnshire to get on the property ladder and I secured a temporary contract teaching Years 3 and 4 at a primary school. The following year I accepted a one-year contract and became the school's literacy and history coordinator. I also had the Year 2 children join my class in February. I left this post because it was too far from my home to travel every day. I've found myself a job starting in November teaching Year 2 at an infant school in Lincoln. I'm looking to do supply until then.

Q. What's been the best thing for you about teaching?

Steph – Interacting with the children every day. I love to see them excited about something I have planned and I love to see them enjoying themselves and getting something out of being in my class.

Q. And the worst thing?

Steph – Dealing with behaviour issues and playground problems. It just wears you down dealing with petty squabbles and low-level disruption all the time. It's not fair on the other children who do want to learn and it's every day (especially at the beginning and end of the year).

Q. What's the best thing about teaching at primary?

Steph – I like Year 3/4 because they are still very much children and do not yet have the teenage attitude you see further up the school. They are mostly hard-working and independent, respect adults and want to listen.

Q. And the hardest thing?

Steph – Dealing with friendship problems and playground issues. You have to spend a lot of time teaching new skills and helping them find ways to solve their own conflicts without telling a teacher all the time.

Q. Tell me how you go about planning. What kind of approaches do you use?

Steph – I do all my planning on a Sunday afternoon and, unlike some teachers, I like to plan thoroughly and produce computerized detailed plans. The way I plan has changed little since I was an NQT as I find it works for me. The more detailed I plan something, the clearer I am about it when I am delivering it.

I block all my foundation subjects except PE, so each week has a topic that we do every afternoon. I try to link this topic with literacy and numeracy too, but that is not always possible. For example, the next two weeks will see us focus on history and the Vikings, with some linked literacy.

Q. What about a typical lesson – how would that go?

Steph – I always start my lessons 'on the carpet' with an introductory whole-class session. The length of this varies depending on the lesson, but I feel it is the best way to get the children focused and generating ideas. Then lessons usually have an activity for the children to do at the tables. Depending on the lesson, this may be done individually, in pairs or in groups. I then finish each lesson with a session on the carpet to recap or to develop ideas further.

I enjoy teaching practical activities the most, as I feel the children benefit from the 'doing' aspect of these lessons. I also find that you get the best ideas from children when there is no pressure for them to write anything down that will be kept.

Q. How do you feel about all those government initiatives and strategies? How have they affected you as a teacher?

Steph – As an NQT you feel overwhelmed by all the initiatives and almost don't know where to start. However, once you get into your own rhythm of planning and teaching you feel more confident in using them (or not!). When something new arrives in school, everyone is so busy getting on with whatever it is that they normally do, that they are mostly ignored. It is only when you are sent on a course for a particular initiative that you have the time to reflect on it and incorporate it into your lessons.

Q. Can you recommend any good resources for teachers?

Steph – Abacus is excellent for numeracy, but expensive. The Hamilton Trust (www.hamilton-trust.org.uk) has excellent mixed-year literacy and numeracy plans for every week of the year. I find the unit plans for numeracy useful too (there are single year groups and mixed which is useful). The site www.bbc.co.uk/schools/scienceclips is great for all science topics. Coxhoe School in Durham has a wonderful website with links to all sorts of things categorized by subject, year group and then by topic (www.coxhoe.durham.sch.uk).

Q. Would you recommend a teaching career to others?

Steph – Definitely, but I realize it's not for everyone. You need to be a certain sort of person. It's a vocation I think.

Q. What could be done to improve teaching as a profession?

Steph – Pay us more! Only joking! I think the government needs to stop asking for the impossible and take the pressure off us. Sometimes children are never going to get a Level 4 no matter how many ALS, ELS, Owl schemes and booster sessions you throw at them. The government needs to accept this and just let us get on with our job without us having to worry about targets and league tables.

I think teachers need to know that they are doing OK. We are only ever told that what we are doing is not quite good enough and that we could do better next year. We always feel like we are failing some children and it would be nice to hear that we are doing the best possible for those kids.

Q. Any tips for other teachers, anything you wish you'd known when you first started teaching?

Steph – A teacher friend of mine told me when I was an NQT that there is no point trying to cut corners in your first year. You have to accept that you will have to do everything the long way first and everything will take you five times as long as your colleagues. After that, everything becomes easier.

The other thing I would like to have known at the beginning of my teaching career is that, however bad things get, whatever it is that you have done/not done, someone else has been there before and made the same mistake. Getting support from fellow teachers is invaluable when you feel like you don't know what to do.

Q. Finally, in your opinion, what makes someone a good teacher?

Steph – A good teacher is flexible, a great listener and a good speaker. They can multi-task and have the memory of an elephant (or a book of long lists like me). They are organized, professional and can think on their feet. They have the patience of a saint and are creative and open to new ideas.

Classroom teacher

Primary, special school

Nichola Beech

Q. Tell me a bit about how and why you became a teacher.

Nichola – I've always wanted to be a teacher, for as long as I can remember; I thought about it all the way through my school life. After passing my GCSEs and going to college to do my A levels, I took the opportunity to do one afternoon a week in my old primary school. I realized that it was definitely what I wanted to do – to follow in my mum's footsteps and become a primary school teacher. After passing my A levels I went straight to Manchester Metropolitan University on the 4-year BEd (Hons) 3–11 primary education degree. I qualified with a 2.2 in 2002.

Q. What happened after you qualified?

Nichola – In September 2002 I started my NQT year in a Reception class in a seven-class infant school. I worked alongside another, very experienced teacher who taught me lots about good Foundation Stage teaching. I'm forever grateful to her. Unfortunately, that was only a one-year contract and I was sad to leave.

I didn't manage to get a job for the following September, despite numerous good interviews. (I was told several times I was a close second, although that means nothing when you're second and not the successful one!) I decided to try my hand at supply teaching till something more long-term came up. Although it was quite daunting the first time I went to a new school, I really enjoyed my time on supply. It gave me the chance to see how different schools worked, to get lots of great ideas from other teachers and to gain experience teaching different age groups. I did this for a term and then just before Christmas, I was offered a two-term post as a Reception/Year 1 teacher to replace someone who had got a promotion and was leaving on quick notice.

It was here that my experience in teaching children with SEN started. Alongside 29 others (the class was 10 Reception Years and 20 Year 1s) was a boy with a statement for autism. I learnt a lot from him and the 2 TAs who were employed as full-time support. After the two terms I was successful at interview in gaining the permanent post. Again I worked with those two great TAs and with another boy with autism. He was totally different to the first and he opened my eyes to the range of abilities within a diagnosed difficulty.

After a while I realized it wasn't the right school for me and I started my search for a new job closer to home. Sadly, I ended up having to take some time off due to work-related stress and I decided that it would be best to resign. It was a very difficult decision to make, especially with no job to go to and a wedding fast approaching. I knew, through discussion with my family, my fiancé and my doctor that it was the right thing to do and I would go back to doing supply if nothing came up.

The last few weeks of the summer term were approaching and I was getting disheartened with things. I was chatting online one night to a group of teachers about jobs and they asked me if I'd ever been interested in special education. I said I'd considered it but hadn't really thought about it since qualifying, as there never seemed to be any vacancies around and back then I knew I needed some mainstream experience. My friends said I should keep my eye out on the Special Ed sections and lo and behold the next day there was one for a local SLD/PMLD school. I was shortlisted for it and the rest as they say is history. September 2005 saw me start at this school with so much to learn, but so willing to learn.

Q. What would you say are some of the difficulties of being a teacher?

Nichola – Teaching is a rewarding profession, but you do have to be willing to put up with all the work that you bring home at the end of the day. It is not a Monday to Friday, 9 to 5 job and yes, it does come home with you. Paperwork makes your life hard sometimes and I wish there was some we could just stop doing. When I talk to those such as my mum who have been teaching for longer than I have I can see how things used to be simpler and less directed. The government seems to want to tell teachers what to do every minute of every day and doesn't give us the credit for being professionals. They don't go around telling doctors how to do their work, so why should they tell teachers?

Behaviour is also a problem. So many of my friends are teachers in primary, secondary, mainstream and special and they all speak of increasing difficulties with managing behaviour and a general lack of respect for teachers.

Q. Tell me about what it's like to work in a special school. How is it different from the mainstream classroom?

Nichola – I'm really enjoying life in special education. It's such a friendly, supportive environment and such a different way of teaching to the way I was used to. The kids are great, all so different and they each have their own little ways.

The major difference between special ed and mainstream is the adult to child ratio. In my last class there were eight children and four adults including me and sometimes that was just not enough! I never thought I'd say that, having spent time in mainstream with 30 children and just me for most of the week, but the needs of my class are so wide and varied and they require such support in so many different ways that those adults are really needed. This obviously presents its own problems, as I wasn't used to working in such large staff teams. Luckily, I've worked with a great team who have helped me so much to settle into the ways of the school and they know the kids really well, having worked with most of them in previous years.

Medical and therapy staff are also frequent visitors in class. We have physio support for some time nearly every day and speech therapy help once a fortnight. Obviously working in such a multi-professional environment has increased my own knowledge and has an impact on everything we do. The way we teach the kids is different to mainstream education, although I find the foundation stage principles apply in so many ways to my class, even though at the moment I'm teaching lower Key Stage 2 and my class have access to things that others don't such as weekly hydrotherapy sessions.

A major difference is I feel I can give my class such quality one-to-one time and I know them really well. All too often in mainstream I was worried about seeing all my class and working with them all. A class of eight is so different to a class of 30.

Q. What are your plans for the future? Do you see yourself staying within special education?

Nichola – Yes, I think I have found my place within education in the special education system. I hope that I can stay in my current job for years to come, although who knows how many as I'm still only young and life has a habit of bringing things to challenge us. I also wish to start a family in the future so obviously that will have a huge impact too. I don't have any desires to go into the world of deputies and heads. I enjoy being in the classroom too much for that, but never say never as they say!

Classroom teacher

Secondary drama

Colin Ward

Q. Why did you decide to become a teacher?

Colin – Besides my subject interest, and experience working with children before training to teach, I work on a simple ethos: I have been successful, and I will continue to grow in success, so I must provide my pupils with the best opportunity to achieve success for themselves.

Q. What was your training like?

Colin – My PGCE in secondary drama was excellent! The training I received both in my subject and as a teacher had me feeling very prepared for a career in teaching – equipping me with skills in planning and assessment that were some of the most up to date in my subject. I was so impressed with my course I intend to train as a mentor for the university and continue working with them.

Q. Could you tell me about some of the things you've done in your teaching career so far?

Colin – I've taken on a very active role in raising standards in my subject, bringing from my training and experience a new Key Stage 3 curriculum and assessment scheme. I worked on the 'School Improvement Group' for my first two years, looking at raising standards across the school in teaching and learning. Aside from these, I am a regular writer for *Teaching Drama* 'Rhinegold'.

Q. What's been the best thing about teaching for you so far?

Colin – The pupils! My pupils are wonderful young people with energy, enthusiasm and humour. They make the job worth doing. I teach in an inner-city, comprehensive school, where academic grades seldom truly reflect how great our kids are. Having a very good relationship with the pupils I teach makes my job a little less stressful. Getting to know them as individuals has a profoundly positive effect on the day-to-day routines in school.

Q. And what about the worst thing?

Colin – A lack of support from some managers – at times it's had me considering whether I am in fact in the right job. There is often no real recognition for what you achieve as classroom teacher, despite being equipped with expertise and experience that really could be better utilized by the more experienced and 'mature' members of staff.

Q. What's the best thing about teaching secondary drama?

Colin – I have a very strong belief that *anyone* can 'do' drama, but that it takes time, effort and determination to be truly great at it. However, all of my pupils can achieve that, and I have enjoyed designing a curriculum that is fun and exciting, but very challenging.

Also, I really enjoy teaching secondary age for their potential to really achieve great heights in my subject that primary pupils would not – mainly due to time. Also, as a drama teacher in a smaller school I teach the vast majority of pupils at some point in their school career, which gives a really good feeling that I play a role in the school as a whole.

Q. And what's the hardest thing?

Colin – It is very difficult to remain enthusiastic sometimes, with so many things thrown your way in teaching that feel almost like a conspiracy of negativity. Nevertheless, keeping yourself focused on why you are a teacher is one way to survive!

Q. Could you tell me about your approaches to planning and lesson delivery?

Colin – I have always found that the most effective way to plan a lesson is to begin with what you want the pupils to 'learn', and then go on to decide 'how' you will facilitate this. The learning objectives should be differentiated and the tasks designed to target all these groups. The plan must focus on learning and make this overt rather than hidden, no matter what the subject is. However, formulas for lesson deliveries are dangerous grounds. For example, always starting with the learning objectives on the whiteboard may not be the best way to go. I like to include the elements of mystery, surprise and discovery in my lessons – the kinds of things that make pupils *want* to learn.

As a drama teacher I constantly battle with people who say that my subject is 'easier' than other subjects … until they see the lesson that starts with a cross, a tree and some smoke, and hear the pupils leave the room talking about semiotics!

Q. Any thoughts on all those government initiatives and strategies? How have they affected you as a teacher?

Colin – 'Government initiative' is in many ways oxymoronic. I do believe that we should strive to improve standards, but so many things we do as teachers are undermined by the government's tick-box culture. Initiatives are churned out year upon year, with no real time to see if they actually work. The biggest killer, however, is the whole culture of the 'C grade'. In many ways this is treated as a 'pass' and anything below is a 'fail'. I have lost pupils from my GCSE to 'focus on core subjects' … simply because they were projected a 'D' in drama. The fact that a 'D' would have been a superb achievement (their success) was immaterial as the whole education culture is now so geared to the 'C' grade. The biggest effect is that we focus on grades and numbers, excel spreadsheets with pretty colours, CATs results and SATs tests – the one thing the government are actually neglecting is education.

Q. Can you recommend any good resources for teachers?

Colin – As a drama teacher I can certainly recommend *Teaching Drama*. Aside from this I could list books or references, but I have found much solace and support in the *TES* Staffroom section of their website. Here you'll find fellow teachers (and some random 'trolls') sharing ideas and stories, and supporting each other.

Q. Would you recommend a teaching career to others?

Colin – Yes – but only if they really want to be a 'teacher'. I have found myself at times saying 'I love *teaching*, I just hate being *a teacher*!' It is a very difficult job indeed, and there really isn't a financial gain, nor one of status for most teachers. However, if the reward of being one piece in a huge jigsaw of all your pupils' lives is what inspires you, then why not? But get some experience in schools before you make any decisions!

Q. What could be done to improve teaching as a profession?

Colin – Fewer initiatives, less grade-snatching … less politics. More excellent teachers being made to feel that the job they do is valued and respected.

Q. Any tips for other teachers, anything you wish you'd known when you first started out?

Colin – Make sure you find your way of teaching and dealing with pupils – there isn't a right-and-wrong with this, but there are ways that are more effective than others, so make the effort to find out what they are (e.g. 'don't smile until Christmas' is one of the most useless pieces of 'advice' I have ever heard … and ignored).

Above all, make the effort to know your pupils and their parents – positive relationships promote a good atmosphere and more success. Remember that you are NOT the most important person in your pupils' lives, but you are an incredible influence.

Q. Finally, in your opinion, what makes someone a good teacher?

Colin – Genuinely wanting your pupils to do the best *they* can; taking an interest in them; and being able to feel proud of what you achieve with them.

Classroom teacher

Secondary English

Teaching with a disability

Tabatha Rayment

Q. Why did you decide to become a teacher?

Tabby – To be honest, I sort of fell into teaching. It was always a career I'd had in mind, but after I'd finished my BA at university I wanted to get out into the job market and start earning some cash!

I worked as a library assistant at two FE colleges over the course of two and a half years before finding myself thinking more and more about teaching. I loved working with the kids at the college, and I was getting the most fun out of 'teaching' them rather than just helping with their library enquiries. I decided to change my career path and go back to university to do a PGCE in secondary English.

Q. I understand you have a disability. Did you have any concerns about how this might affect you as a teacher?

Tabby – I have nerve deafness in both ears and have to wear hearing aids to get by on a day-to-day basis. Despite not being able to hear an awful lot without them, I never think of myself as 'disabled', and I don't seem disabled to others. My speech isn't affected and my hearing aids aren't obvious unless I want them to be. I honestly didn't know what to expect in terms of how people would view my disability and decided to just give it my best shot. I was confident that whatever hurdles I might come up against I would be able to work around them.

Q. What was your training like? How well do you feel your university catered for your disability?

Tabby – It was a very mixed experience. My hearing loss did have an impact on my training. I found that people were very surprised I was even considering it as a career, and the staff at the university were a little unsure as to how to approach the issue at first. Towards the end of my course I met up with one of the senior members of university staff and helped her come up with an action plan should they ever get any more deaf teacher trainees joining the university.

However, that aside, the actual training was really good. It was tiring and stressful and one heck of a challenge at times, especially in my main placement where I was put in a much more 'challenging' school than my diagnostic one, but it challenged me in a good way. In the end I found that I enjoyed the challenge much more than the 'easy' school, and really started taking an interest in underachievement issues and behaviour management. There *were* times when I felt like I couldn't do it, that I wasn't good enough, and I'll admit I did have times when I came home and cried a lot, but as clichéd as it might sound, it toughened me up. I made it through the training, and got a brilliant result on my essay work, not to mention a super reference from my MTP. I was even offered a job at my MTP, which I wish now that I could have taken, but I had already found another position elsewhere.

Q. Did you encounter any particular problems while on teaching practice due to your disability?

Tabby – I had a bit of a bad time of it at first as my diagnostic placement school wasn't told about my deafness, which made things a bit difficult. Some members of staff were worried about what kind of impact it might have on my teaching ability and if they needed to make any changes to assist me. They didn't need to worry: I developed my own ways of coping in difficult situations.

I had student volunteers who acted as my 'ears' who would alert me to people at the door or alarms going off. I used a lot of non-verbal, visual signals to 'control' the class, and ensured every student knew the importance of communicating loudly and clearly. I carried on these classroom-management strategies into my main teaching practice and adapted them as necessary.

The most important thing for me was to ensure that people were aware of my deafness but didn't make a big deal out of it. Sometimes not appearing obviously deaf was a double-edged sword for me as people forgot I couldn't hear them! I still rely a lot on lip-reading and sometimes people would forget to face me and I would miss what they said. Assemblies and staff meetings were particularly difficult for me, as were break duties and helping to manage behaviour in the canteen or yard.

Q. What would you say is the best thing about teaching for you so far?

Tabby – Being able to look at a student's work, seeing that they understood what you've taught them and done really well. You suddenly realize, 'Wow! I did that! I helped this kid get a greater understanding about something and I've made a positive impact on his education.' When a student says 'thank you' or takes the time to come and talk to you and involve you in their lives, that's brilliant too. I really think that to be a great teacher you have to love kids, more than the subject you teach, more than your own career – you have to really value children and be prepared to stick your neck out for them. They're the reason that teaching comes alive, and it's the little moments that make teaching wonderful.

Q. And what would you say is the worst thing about teaching for you so far?

Tabby – The lack of support I have received from other members of staff in some jobs. It sounds quite daft, but if you don't feel like you're one of the team, or if others aren't helping and supporting you, the job is very lonely and isolating. It is too easy to start thinking, as a trainee or an NQT, that you must not be very good, or that you won't ever fit in with your teaching peers. That makes the job so much harder.

I have to say it's one of the things that makes me very cross about teacher training and induction – there is this whole idea that new teachers should 'sink or swim' and that if they can't toughen up then they might as well get out of the profession. It's ridiculous, and completely unfair. I've seen colleagues teach amazing lessons and be brilliant teachers, who are still knocked down by senior members of staff for whatever reason. There is an element present of needing to get a bit of thick skin, but there should also be credit where credit is due. I sometimes wonder if some teachers have been in the profession so long, the 'playground' mentality of their students has rubbed off on them.

Q. Have you ever had any negative reactions, or difficult moments, with your students because of your disability?

Tabby – There have been a few, although usually from staff rather than students. I think some teachers were concerned about how my deafness might impact on my teaching ability – whether I would miss what students said to me or not have good classroom control. The students never saw my deafness as a problem, in fact I think they saw it as a little quirk that made me different from other teachers and wanted to know more about it. Only a few students tried to use it to their advantage and play up, but I never took it personally and simply disciplined them accordingly.

I don't try to hide my hearing aids (I put coloured beads on them to match my outfits!) and most students are fascinated by this. I think it helps to show students that just because you might be 'different' it doesn't have to hold you back.

Q. What's the best thing about teaching English at secondary level?

Tabby – For me, it's because I'm passionate about English, so I can't really imagine teaching anything else. I enjoy the grammar and analytical side of the subject just as much as the creative. I've also taught a bit of drama in conjunction with English, which is great fun, and appeals to my daft and flamboyant side! It doesn't matter what the actual topic *is* as long as I can make it fun in some way. As for the age range, well, I seem to understand and bond with older students better than the little ones; I'm not sure I have the patience to teach primary.

Q. And the hardest thing?

Tabby – The poor behaviour – but that's obvious really, teaching at secondary level. Once those hormones kick in, a student who was a little angel last term can be an absolute horror the next. I just have to keep remembering not to take it personally and that it's not like they *want* to make my life hell. Well, I hope they don't anyway. In all fairness, behaviour management isn't hard, it's just complicated sometimes. It doesn't matter how much you think you know, and how prepared you are, there will always be some times when you lose your temper and have a bit of a rant. It's not good, but I suspect that if teachers didn't do that occasionally they'd go a bit mad.

Q. Do you think having a hearing disability has made it harder for you to deal with difficult behaviour? Do the students ever take advantage?

Tabby – Because I need a well-controlled classroom with minimal background noise in order to hear properly, I think my lessons are often better controlled than many other teachers'. My classroom management is based on mutual respect – I respect my students and they (hopefully) respect me. I make sure that I never portray my deafness as a negative or difficult thing, it is simply a part of who I am, and this seems to discourage students from taking advantage.

Having one sense dulled makes the other senses more active, so I am very observant of what is going on in my classroom. My students soon become aware that I am a very 'alert' teacher, and bad behaviour is dealt with very quickly. I have zero tolerance of students who try to use my deafness as an excuse to muck about, and not many students have made the same mistake twice.

Q. Tell me a bit about your planning and lesson delivery. What approaches work best for you?

Tabby – I do have a habit of over-planning sometimes, working out every detail and trying to fit everything into a set time-plan, but the reality is the lesson usually doesn't follow that plan to the letter. There are times when I've had to pull a lesson 'out of a hat', so to speak, as I've been asked to cover, or my planned lesson hasn't been quite right, but I wouldn't advise any teacher to make a habit of it. During your training you are required to plan meticulously, which seems tedious at the time, but if you stay in that habit you can actually make life easier for yourself. I've got records of pretty much all the lessons I've ever taught, which means I can track back and re-use resources and information.

With lesson delivery, the best advice I can give any teacher is be enthusiastic. You have to be interested in what you're teaching, even if the subject is as dull as ditchwater! If you can't get a bit excited about it, then your students definitely won't. If you can, make things into games, which is great for teaching more 'stale' topics. For example, trying to explain adjectives and adverbs to a class of fairly low-ability students could have been a total nightmare, but instead I used the 'Traffic Lights' game where each student had a red, green and orange card. (Red = no, orange = not sure, green = yes.) That way I could ask questions about a sentence and they could respond with their cards. It made it fun, engaged them, and they actually understood the principle behind it at the end.

Q. Do you have any advice for teachers who have a student with a disability in their classes? How can they cater better for children with physical difficulties, such as hearing loss or visual impairment?

Tabby – Personally, I hate being pigeon-holed, or treated differently just because I'm deaf. The important thing is that people are aware of my disability, but they don't need to give me special treatment because of it. When I was at school I was petrified of being involved in group discussions or speaking in front of the class – not because I was nervous of speaking in front of other people, but that they might say something I didn't hear and I would embarrass myself in front of them.

Teachers do need to consider the implications a disability or special need has on the student and put themselves in their shoes. If they don't know what kind of changes they need to make, ask the student. At whatever age, students are able to identify the kind of support they need; from simply sitting them at the front of the class to making handouts in a bigger typesize. It doesn't help to make a big deal out of it though; most disabled or SEN students are already acutely aware that they are 'different' in some way and it is far better for teachers to help them integrate with their peers instead of singling them out.

Q. Can you recommend any good resources for teachers?

Tabby – Can I recommend the books I have written? *grin* No, seriously, probably a really good starting point for any teacher would be Teachernet.gov.uk. I spent a lot of time on that site while doing my training. For an English teacher, Teachit (www.teachit.co.uk/) is indispensable, and Andrew Moore's teaching resource site (www.universalteacher.org.uk/default.htm) has some super links.

Q. Would you recommend a teaching career to others?

Tabby – Definitely, but they have to be committed to it. I've seen too many people enter the profession with naive attitudes, or they're only doing it for the cash. Some people are just born to be teachers. My good friend Melanie is one of these people; she's an amazing teacher and has such a wonderful relationship with the kids.

You have to enter teaching with your eyes open and be prepared to find it hard sometimes. It *is* a gruelling career; you spend a lot of your free time sorting things out, and planning and marking and getting all that pesky paperwork done. But as for the rewards you get in the classroom, you won't find them in any other job. If you're prepared to put a lot into it, you will get a lot out of it, but if you're not then you're likely just to end up bitter and cynical and hating it.

Q. And would you advise other people who have a disability to go into teaching?

Tabby – Having a disability of any kind shouldn't stop you from doing what you want to do. You need to know your limits, be flexible and prepared to adapt, but you should never, ever give up. There are lots of organizations that are specifically designed to help you if you need help, such as 'Access To Work' through Jobcentre Plus, and you can even get a grant to buy any equipment you need to help you do your job.

It is important to realize that teaching can be hard work for anyone, and if you have a disability it *can* make it even harder, but if you are determined and focused there is no reason why it should stop you achieving your goals. I actually think it's good for students to be taught by people with disabilities as it teaches them awareness, understanding and respect for all, regardless of their differences.

Q. Anything you wish you'd known or done when you first started teaching?

Tabby – You don't have to know all the answers; you just have to know where to look for them. Never be too proud to admit that you're struggling or having a bad time of things, and don't beat yourself up if you have a bad lesson. It's no big deal in the grand scheme of things, and even the best and most experienced teachers have bad days (just because you never seem to *catch* them having a bad day doesn't mean they don't get them).

Above all, enjoy your job, and don't let it consume you. Yes, it might be tough, but would you enjoy it so much or get as good a feeling of satisfaction out of it if it were too easy? I wish I'd been more assertive when I first started teaching; I didn't give myself enough credit and I didn't recognize my own achievements. You have to put everything in perspective, but make sure you are proud of yourself as well – not everyone has the skills to be a teacher.

Q. And any advice for others with a disability who are going into teaching? What tips can you give them?

Tabby – Most importantly: If you need support, ask for it! Check out the university and your placement schools and write down any concerns you have so you can broach them with your mentor or course leader. Similarly, find out what kind of support systems are in place such as: loop systems, ramps, modified classrooms, interpreters, etc. Don't 'play up' your disability but don't ignore it either if it is likely to affect your teaching ability. Be confident in yourself and your skills – don't let people put you down or try to convince you that teaching isn't right for you, you won't know until you've given it a go.

Make sure you have a good support network from a variety of sources and ensure you know where to go if you're finding things hard. Most universities have special needs or disability coordinators who can help you get the most out of your course. Remember, there is no shame in asking for help if you think your disability is holding you back in some way.

Q. Finally, in your opinion, what makes someone a good teacher?

Tabby – A good teacher is someone who loves their job and loves the kids. A really great teacher gains the respect and trust of their students without even trying, and they make learning fun. We forget that, while we've gone through our education and have proved ourselves to some degree, the students we teach are still taking their first steps, finding out about the world and trying to make sense of it and themselves. A good teacher doesn't just teach their subject, but teaches about life as well.

Form tutor

In a secondary school, the form tutor is responsible for the pastoral care of his or her form or tutor group. Although not every teacher in the school will necessarily be a form tutor as well, in the majority of cases a secondary school teacher will, at some point, also be expected to fulfil this role. The form tutor undertakes a number of responsibilities, some of which are listed below:

- Giving out various routine paperwork, such as school diaries (at the start of the year), parents' evening timetables, detention reminders, etc.
- Managing the form group during registration (some schools set specific activities to be done during form time, such as private reading)
- Taking the register
- Checking that students are wearing the correct uniform, and dealing with them appropriately if they are not
- Passing on information to the tutor group
- Assisting with option choices in Year 9
- Helping with other career or further education decisions
- Checking school diaries on a regular basis
- Collating information on tutees from subject teachers, e.g. about behaviour and rewards
- Talking to individual students about problems/issues
- Meeting with parents as necessary
- Preparing presentations for Year assemblies

In addition to the responsibilities listed above, the form tutor might also undertake a number of additional jobs under their own volition. These could include activities designed to cement a positive feeling within the tutor group, such as those listed below:

- Creating a 'form notice board' for the group, which might contain:
  - The names of the tutees
  - Pictures, messages or other personal contributions
  - Jobs rota (e.g. collecting the register).
- Keeping a chart of merits/commendations received
- Giving birthday cards
- Giving individual 'tutor certificates' for good work or behaviour
- Collecting money for presents, and getting cards signed, e.g. when a member of the tutor group leaves the school

Advanced skills teacher

Becoming an advanced skills teacher (AST) allows teachers who want to stay in the classroom, rather than moving into management, to further their careers (and get paid a higher salary). The government provides various 'signs of excellence' for those wishing to become ASTs. These include high-level teaching, classroom-management and behaviour-management skills, as well as quality of planning and assessment, and relationships with students.

An AST is expected to spend 80 per cent of time teaching his or her own classes. For the remaining 20 per cent, additional 'outreach' responsibilities would be undertaken, so that good practice is shared with the wider community. Typically, the AST would spend four days a week in his or her own school, then one day working with others.

Additional responsibilities might include:

- giving demonstration and 'model' lessons
- helping schools in special measures
- supporting lessons of other teachers
- helping with induction and mentoring
- developing quality resources

For more information, see www.teachernet.gov.uk/professional development/ast/and www.standards.dfes.gov.uk/ast/. For some useful documents about the scheme, see also www.teachernet.gov.uk/professionaldevelopment/ast/guidance/.

Excellent teacher scheme

This new scheme was introduced from September 2006. For more information, see www.teachernet.gov.uk/management/payand performance/pay/excellent_teacher_scheme/.

Teaching assistant (TA)

Teaching assistants (TAs) work with teachers in the classroom, helping pupils with their learning on an individual and/or group basis. TAs often specialize in key curriculum areas such as literacy, numeracy or special educational needs. You don't have to have formal qualifications to become a TA. The skills, experience and qualifications needed to get a post as a TA will vary from school to school.

The LEA should provide induction training for their TAs: induction programmes will include sessions on literacy, numeracy, behaviour management, inclusion, role and context, and special educational needs.

TAs usually have some form of vocational qualification, often an NVQ. In the same way as teachers, all TAs have to pass police and criminal records checks before they are appointed. There are no national pay scales for TAs and higher-level teaching assistants (HLTAs). Salaries vary dramatically across the UK.

Higher-level teaching assistant (HLTA)

TAs with a high level of skills and experience can apply for HLTA status. This involves additional training and also an assessment to ensure that the 31 HLTA professional standards are being met. These standards come under three headings – professional values and practice, knowledge and understanding, and teaching and learning activities. The role of an HLTA will obviously be much more complex, diverse and demanding than that of a 'regular' TA.

You can find much more information about becoming a TA and HLTA on the Teachernet website at www.teachernet.gov.uk/teachingassistants, and from the TDA at www.tda.gov.uk/support.

The interview below with Janet Kay clarifies exactly what the role of classroom assistant is all about. It should be of interest both to the classroom teacher working with a teaching assistant, and also to those interested in working in a classroom-support role.

Programme Leader, BA (Hons) Early Childhood Studies

Sheffield Hallam University

Author, *Teaching Assistant's Handbook*' 2nd edn (Continuum, 2005)

Janet Kay

Q. First, could you tell me a little bit about your background and current work in education?

Janet – I'm a qualified social worker and I worked in social services for children and families for many years, specifically in child protection. My second career was in further education, teaching and managing in the early years, health and social care programme areas. I'm currently the Course Leader for the BA (Hons) Early Childhood Studies course at the Sheffield Hallam University.

Q. Could you explain exactly what a 'teaching assistant' is?

Janet – It depends on the definition used. The DfES use the term 'teaching assistant' to describe a whole range of classroom support roles. Under the DfES definition, teaching assistants can support individual pupils, or support the teacher, the curriculum or the whole school. In local authorities the term is used to describe more specific roles, but these can vary between LAs. Overall there are literally dozens of terms used to describe the roles of non-teachers in the classroom.

Q. What sort of things would a teaching assistant do on a daily basis?

Janet – Teaching assistants may be employed to work with an individual child or children, usually with SEN, EAL or any issues that may delay learning or create learning difficulties. They might support a class in more general ways, such as working with small groups, or supporting specific core curriculum subjects. They could also be helping a teacher with routine tasks such as escorting children, setting up materials and equipment or demonstrating activities.

Some teaching assistants are also involved in planning and assessment, and devising differentiated activities for individuals or small groups. They may work with one class or a range of classes, groups or individual children. They are also involved in school-wide activities such as organizing events (sports day, trips out) and contributing to whole-school developments. Many teaching assistants have a number of varying roles throughout the week. For example, they might be supporting a single child for part of the week, supporting the reception class for another period of time, and supporting literacy and numeracy hours at Key Stage 1 for the rest. HLTAs tend to have more of a role in planning and delivering the curriculum, and assessing work with support and direction from the teacher. They may at times supervise whole classes doing work set by the teacher.

Q. Now that the post of teaching assistant has been around for a while, how has the role changed over the last few years?

Janet – Teaching assistants have more of a role in supporting the curriculum and are seen as more directly involved in learning delivery and support in some cases. There are still big variations in the role but teaching assistants are more likely to have relevant qualifications and the role has become more professional and respected in its own right.

Q. What sort of qualifications do teaching assistants have?

Janet – Not all teaching assistants have qualifications. Some have childcare qualifications such as NNEB, CACHE Diploma in Childcare and Education, BTEC National Diploma in Early Years or relevant childcare and education NVQs. Others have qualifications gained 'on the job' such as the CACHE Specialist Teaching Assistants Award or NCFE Initial Training for Classroom Assistants qualification. There are now a whole range of different types of qualifications for teaching assistants including NVQs for classroom/teaching assistants and foundation degrees, which can lead to Senior Practitioner status in the early years, where they are sector-endorsed. Sector-endorsed means that the Foundation Degree meets the 'Statement of Requirement' for Early Years Sector-Endorsed Foundation Degrees published by the DfES Early Years and Childcare Unit. As such, the Foundation Degree confers Senior Practitioner status on those who pass it. This denotes a higher level of competence in the practitioner. Six per cent of teaching assistants have degrees. Some teaching assistants have demonstrated competencies to achieve HLTA status, which can lead to a higher level of pay and more responsibility.

Q. What kind of qualities does a person need to make a good teaching assistant?

Janet – They need knowledge and understanding of a wide range of children's needs, including SEN, child development and how children learn. Also, strategies for promoting learning and supporting the growth of confidence, independence and good self-esteem. Patience, good teamwork skills, excellent interpersonal and communication skills are very important. Also, the ability to work flexibly and to learn new skills and knowledge as required.

The ability to recognize parents as partners and work with them is vital, as is good knowledge of the curriculum, how schools work and health and safety issues. Finally, teaching assistants need to work with a wide range of other professionals and to understand other's roles and responsibilities within multi-agency and multi-disciplinary teams. For example, the teaching assistant may work with an educational psychologist, a speech therapist, an advisory teacher, the class teacher, SENCo and a physiotherapist, all involved in supporting the learning and development of one child.

Q. Can a teaching assistant become a qualified classroom teacher? How would they go about doing this?

Janet – Yes, they can, and there are different ways that they might achieve this. There are employment-based routes into teaching which particularly suit mature experienced students who wish to work while they train. The graduate teacher programme (GTP) lasts one year and is for graduates who are working in schools. The registered teacher programme (RTP) lasts for two years and is for students who have completed the equivalent of two years of higher education and have a place to complete their degree while training, and who are also working in a school. For example, a teaching assistant who had considerable experience and was employed in a primary school started a part-time BA in Early Childhood Studies. After completing the equivalent of two years' higher education she applied for the RTP and over the next 2 years, completed her degree and the RTP to become a qualified teacher. In both cases, the student needs to be supported by the school and by a recommending body, for example a school, university or LEA.

Other routes include the PGCE, which requires a degree in a relevant subject and one year full-time or two years' part-time study including teaching practice. Teaching assistants with Level 3 qualifications such as A levels, or BTEC or CACHE diplomas can use these as entry to a BEd, which will lead to qualified teacher status, or to get onto a BA Early Childhood Studies course, which could be used to go on to a PGCE. Access courses can be used as entry to teaching in some cases, especially where they offer English, maths and science GCSE equivalence.

Q. What are the main differences between being a teaching assistant and a qualified classroom teacher?

Janet – At present, teaching assistants do not normally have sole responsibility for all aspects of classes. HLTAs may take whole classes on occasion but the work and assessment is still the overall responsibility of the class teacher. Teaching assistants may have a role in planning and assessment, but the overall responsibility for this lies with the teacher. The teaching assistant works within plans developed and agreed with the teacher and they have responsibility for some of the learning and assessment within these. However, they work under the direction of the teacher to achieve their agreed aims. Basically, the class is the teacher's responsibility and the teaching assistant works under his or her direction.

Q. Could you tell me a bit about your book, *Teaching Assistant's Handbook*. How would it help people training to be or already working as teaching assistants?

Janet – The book is a very practical guide to the sort of knowledge and skills a teaching assistant may need across the range of roles they may be expected to perform. It's designed to support teaching assistants at all stages of their development including those doing courses. It provides the knowledge base for the NVQs and other relevant courses. It gives a clearly written introduction for new teaching assistants and a handbook for reference for those already doing the job.

The book covers a whole range of issues: the role of the teaching assistant in supporting core curriculum subjects at Key Stage 1 and in supporting groups and individual children; how children learn and the role of the primary school; assessment; working with others; behaviour management; professional development; and good-practice issues including child protection, equal opportunities, health and safety and bullying. The book includes case studies, discussion points and exercises to promote reflective practice and deeper understanding or to be used as teaching tools on relevant courses. The style is simple and straightforward, in order to be accessible to a range of readers, including those who have not as yet accessed training courses as yet. The second edition has updated information about the teaching assistant's role and responsibility and the HLTA's role.

Q. Finally, any other comments that you'd like to add about the work that teaching assistants do?

Janet – During my research for the *Teaching Assistant's Handbook* I spent a lot of time talking to teaching assistants and looking into what they actually do. I am filled with admiration for this group of workers who have a huge range of skills and talents, who don't always get paid much or have much status or recognition outside their school, but who really are the 'glue' that keeps many a primary school together. They deserve wider recognition and more opportunity and support for their contributions, rather than some of the negative comments that occasionally come their way. There are some new and exciting developments coming and, hopefully, their role will continue to be developed and extended in ways that benefit schools, children and the teaching assistants themselves.

12

Beyond the classroom

There are many jobs outside the classroom that will have a direct impact on you as a member of the teaching staff. These posts are very varied – from staff whose role is to help with the children's welfare, to those who deal with the administrative functions of the school. Getting to know what these staff do, and indeed to know the individuals themselves, will be a great help in your day to day dealings at work.

Special educational needs coordinator (SENCo)

The role of the SENCo (in Scotland the Principal Teacher, Support for Learning) is a complex and crucial one within the school. You can find a huge amount of information about SENCos, and about SEN, from the National Association for Special Educational Needs (see the Directory for contact details). It really is worth getting to know your special needs staff properly, and turning to them for expert advice when you need it, especially if you are working in a school with 'challenging' children. An experienced special needs teacher may be able to give you some background information, or make a simple suggestion, that transforms your relationship with a particularly difficult child. SENCos have a number of different responsibilities within a school, and these include the following roles:

- *Entitlement*: Making sure students with SEN get full access to the curriculum.
- *Inclusion*: Making sure students with SEN can access the same opportunities as others.
- *Meeting with parents*: For instance, agreeing targets for the student and ways that the guardians can help at home.
- *Working with other agencies*: Helping to encourage links between different types of support for the student with SEN.

Educational psychologist

Educational psychologists are highly qualified individuals. To become an educational psychologist, you must have a degree in psychology (or equivalent), at least two years' teaching experience, and also a postgraduate degree in educational psychology. Schools have a 'link' with a named educational psychologist, who will help with assessment of children who have SEN, for instance in diagnosing dyslexia.

The psychologist would normally be called in after the child's IEP has been drawn up, and if the SENCo feels that additional help or advice is required for the individual. The educational psychologist may observe the child in class, work with the child individually, and use tests to check on their skills. A consultation meeting may also be held, at which various professionals discuss how best to proceed. As well as working with children, educational psychologists also help with training work, advising teachers about SEN, and so on. For more information on educational psychology, see www.aep.org.uk.

Educational welfare officer (EWO)

The EWO deals with issues connected to the educational welfare of the children, ensuring that they benefit fully from their education. The EWO helps with issues such as truancy and absence, for instance checking registers, monitoring attendance, talking with children and making home visits. Some schools have an EWO who works 'on site', while many others have a visiting EWO from the LEA.

School librarian

The role of the school librarian, or learning resource centre manager, is being seen as increasingly important within schools. He or she may be a 'chartered librarian'. This involves a graduate or postgraduate level training, and membership of the Chartered Institute of Library and Information Professionals (CILIP). School librarians undertake a number of different responsibilities:

- Helping school managers to create policies about providing learning resources.
- Assisting students in accessing the resources they need for their learning.
- Teaching core skills, such as ways of accessing knowledge.
- Managing and promoting the library resources, which include books, ICT and so on.

- Helping to promote literacy skills and to increase students' enjoyment of reading.
- Managing the library environment.
- Managing the library budget.
- Passing on relevant advice and information to teaching staff.

School librarian

Clevedon Community School

Mélanie McGilloway

Q. How did you become a librarian?

Mélanie – To become a qualified librarian, you can either do a degree, or a Master's. I did an English degree in France, then I did a Master's in library and information studies in Aberystwyth. Then you become chartered after a few years' experience.

Q. And why did you decide to become a librarian?

Mélanie – I knew I wanted to work with books and it was either publishing or librarianship.

Q. What are attitudes like towards school libraries? Are they generally well funded, and run by well-qualified staff?

Mélanie – It depends on what they think of the library. If the head is interested in the library, they give it money. The same goes for the librarian's wages as well. CILIP, the Chartered Institute for Library and Information Professionals, recommends that qualified school librarians should be paid between £20,000 and £22,000 a year and chartered school librarians between £22,000 and £26,000. Unfortunately, there are not many school librarians paid at that level! Some librarians, for example, are on the same scale as technicians.

It really depends on what people think of their librarian and the library. I've been lucky in my jobs, where I've been paid reasonably well and I've always been treated well. A lot of school libraries employ non-qualified librarians. It doesn't mean they can't do the job, but it makes it easier not to pay them much money. In Scotland, though, all the school libraries have a qualified librarian.

However, in the last couple of years there have been a few initiatives by the government and a new report by Ofsted (*Good School Libraries: Making a Difference to Learning*) which are trying to raise the profile of libraries and librarians in schools.

Q. What was your first post as a librarian?

Mélanie – It was in a secondary school in Glasgow. The kids were rough but nice. There were a lot of social problems, they really had a hard time, and you did feel sorry for them. It was my first job and I learned a lot, but it wasn't too daunting because the numbers at the school were quite small.

Q. What sort of resources did you have there?

Mélanie – Hardly anything. Everything was over 20 years old, because there wasn't any money. There were no computers, and I had a budget of £50.

The kids were enthusiastic, and I managed to do some things, like having an author in.

Q. What about your second post? What were things like there?

Mélanie – I worked at a big secondary school in Berkshire. There were about 1,300 children including a sixth form. The school had quite a big library, and I had an assistant. There were loads of computers in the library. That was the year when the government gave extra money to schools to buy computers. There was a big stock and a reasonable budget of about £6,000 a year. I was there for three years. I did things like writing a whole reading unit, and organizing all the lesson plans and activities. That's the part of the job that I really enjoy.

Q. And your current job?

Mélanie – I'm at Clevedon Community School which is a semi-rural community school, with a sixth form, in the south-west of England.

Q. What sort of different things do you do in your current post?

Mélanie – I do everything that needs to be done in the library! I buy, process, catalogue, issue, return and shelve the books, supervise students during lessons and breaks. I help teachers with lessons in the library, and also deliver lessons myself, such as the Year 7 library induction (delivered through English, history and PSHCE). I am in the process of creating a 'Reading for Enjoyment' unit for Year 7s too.

The long-term plan is to create and deliver an information literacy programme which is delivered across the curriculum and across the year groups (this was identified by Ofsted in the report mentioned earlier as being vital but missing in most schools). I also organize activities for events such as Book Week and World Book Day.

Q. What sort of things do you spend your budget on, and how do you decide where the money goes?

Mélanie – When I started in the school, I did a stock evaluation. I had a look to see what different areas of stock were like, and I found a few where the books were really old. I try to do this once a year now and tackle a few subject groups every year, often those which are being updated in the National Curriculum. Then, when you get reps in, you see books that are good and you know that the kids will use them, so you buy those too.

I buy a lot of fiction, obviously, there are always authors who are popular. I subscribe to a few magazines that do reviews to keep in touch with things. There are so many children's books published now. It's the new thing, since Harry Potter it's just gone mad. I also buy newspapers. We get the *Telegraph* free – they give it free to all schools who've got a sixth form. We also get the *Guardian* (who also offer a money-saving scheme to schools), the *Daily Mirror*, and local papers.

Q. What ideas do you have for getting your students more interested in reading?

Mélanie – If you want the kids to come and read, you have to give them what they want to read, so for example, we stock magazines such as Simpsons comics. With fiction, there are some excellent authors around who write really well, but if the kids prefer to read a Point Horror surely it's better for them to read that than nothing? I tend to be open-minded. They love series, the comfort of knowing what they're reading, of knowing what they're getting. So it is our job to have what they want on offer, but it is also our job to try to move them on to something a bit more challenging when they are ready. Of course, there are also some really good readers at my school, and they'll read anything you give them.

It's a matter of how you present it as well. A lot of libraries (public and school) now present their stock the same way as bookshops do (cover facing, using tables for display, etc.) and it works well. I also use categorization by genre, which makes it easier for students to choose books. Basically, most students tend to be a bit lazy so if there are just shelves of books, they won't bother. Therefore presentation is very important.

A lot of the students pick up books that are much too easy for their reading level. They read in tutor time once a week, and a lot of them just want something quick to read, especially boys, something quick and painless!

We also have reading club which meets every Tuesday lunchtime during which we do lots of activities around reading. The members get points every time they take a book out, or write a review or take part in shadowing a book prize. Once they gain a certain amount of points, they get a prize. I am hoping eventually to do that across the school and to fit it in our new house point-system.

I have also started to produce a newsletter for the library in which all the reviews are written by students. Peer recommendation is what works best so we need to emphasize that.

Q. Do you enjoy the teaching aspects of your role?

Mélanie – Yes, I do. Being a school librarian is a bit like being a teacher but without the extra pressure of marking, target setting and report writing. It's hard at first – behaviour management, how to conduct a lesson, things like that, as we don't get any training at university, unlike teachers. But when you feel you've really grasped it, and the kids actually listen to you, that's great. The first time I actually said 'quiet' to a Year 8 and the kids actually listened to me, I was like 'Wow'. I love that bit. I'd also love to design textbooks, and schoolbooks in general.

Q. How do you go about getting teachers more involved with the library?

Mélanie – There are teachers I can go to, and they'll always be open-minded about things. It's really hard to get to the ones who're not interested. A lot of the time, teachers haven't got time to get involved, but I try to push it. Every so often I put stuff in their pigeon-holes, like lists of websites or lists of books I have bought that might interest them. Teachers ask me for information, and I do research for them, for instance on the internet.

Q. If a teacher is planning a visit to the library what can they do to help you, and what do you do to assist them?

Mélanie – It's important for me to know the year group and subject, and if you're in a school with sets, to know what level the kids are at. A lot of the time I do a book box, so if the teacher wants the kids to get on with their work straight away, I can have the books ready. I also need to know whether or not they're going to use the computers, and if they are, whether they want me to find some websites. The kids get 'lost' on the internet and sidetracked very easily. If you give them a list of websites they get on task more quickly.

If a teacher wants to use the resources, but they don't want to come to the library, I do them a book box which they can take away. They can then use these in the classroom. Sometimes they book the computer room and the kids have the computers and the books as well.

Q. What sort of hours is the library open?

Mélanie – We're open all day, including breaks and lunch. We start at 8.15am and go through until 4.15pm.

Q. How do your students view the library? What sort of behaviour do you see, and how do you deal with misbehaviour?

Mélanie – Some of them see it as a place to hang out. A lot of the kids do come just for the computers, which is annoying. I was thinking about doing a non-computer day at least once a month. When the computers don't work, it's amazing how the atmosphere changes in the library. Then the pupils that come in are the ones that want to read or study. When it's raining, it's particularly busy. If the weather's nice, the kids go in the field to sit down. We're much more popular on a rainy day!

The pupils are usually quite good. They're noisy, but not really bad. I don't think in a normal comprehensive it's possible to have complete silence. I don't think you can expect 13 year olds to be totally silent. On the other hand, during lesson time, if it's only the sixth formers or small groups of students in, I expect them to get on with their work quietly. If students do misbehave, we can send them out and they do go when they're asked. We like to keep the use of the library as a privilege, rather than as a right.

Q. And finally, do you also have books for teachers?

Mélanie – That's an area we are trying to develop. I weeded the staff collection which was in the staff room and was very out of date and the assistant headteacher in charge of teaching & learning is building up a new collection. We will then decide where it will go; I would quite like to have it down in the library, as it is supposed to be a 'whole-school' resource. We've got the *TES* in the library, and that's a big attraction!

Office staff

In my experience, it really is worth spending time getting to know the office staff in your school. They play an invaluable role in the day to day running of the school, although their work is not always understood or acknowledged by hard-working teachers. Having the office staff 'on your side' will make life much easier for you, in small but numerous ways. For instance, when the photocopier breaks down in the middle of that vital run of exam papers, the office staff will often be far more knowledgeable and skilled in fixing it than you are. Alternatively, when you're waiting for that important phone call from a particularly troublesome parent, a receptionist who likes and respects you is far more likely to ensure that the call gets through, or that a proper message is taken and passed to you.

The headteacher's secretary is often one of the most powerful people in the school. She (or he) has access to a surprising amount of information, and will generally have a very good idea of exactly what is going on. Again, keep on the right side of the head's secretary, and he or she may ease your path when you do need an emergency meeting with the head!

Bursar

The school bursar is responsible for the accountancy functions of the school, and he or she will report to the headteacher. Some bursars are also given additional administrative responsibilities. The bursar's job might include areas such as maintaining financial records, paying invoices and staff expenses, preparing contracts for teachers and other staff, and reporting to the school governors about the finances of the school.

In smaller schools, the bursar may take on the whole range of administrative roles, in addition to the finance function. In larger schools, the bursar may have other administrative staff working for him or her. In the very large secondary school, with a complex budget, there may also be a finance manager.

Caretaker

The caretaker is responsible for running and maintaining the physical environment of the school. This might include general upkeep and repairs, dealing with the boiler, managing the setting up of chairs for assemblies, keeping master copies of school keys, organizing the school for lettings, and many other jobs. It really is well worth the classroom teacher getting to know the caretaker, and taking the time to thank him or her for any help, for instance in setting up the hall.

School governor

School governors come from a huge range of backgrounds. Some governors will be parents of children at the school, who are appointed by the parental body. Others will be teacher governors, appointed by other teachers at the school. There may also be governors from the non-teaching staff of the school, lay governors, people appointed by the church to be governors in a religious school, and so on.

Governors work as a team, attending meetings perhaps once or twice a month. They will play a variety of roles in the running of the school, including agreeing the budget, helping to interview new staff, appointing the headteacher, ensuring that the curriculum is broad and balanced, and so on. You can find lots more information about school governors from the DfES, at www.dfes.gov.uk/governor.

Inspector

An inspector might work for an LEA, as part of an advisory team who go into schools to help them improve. These 'general inspectors' might have responsibility for a specific subject area, e.g. RE, or for a particular phase, e.g. primary. Another option is to qualify to be a 'registered inspector', working as part of an Ofsted team. The interview below with Gordon Wallace will give you an insight into what the job of an inspector involves.

General Inspector (Primary Links)

Nottinghamshire County Council

School Improvement Service

Gordon Wallace

Q. Could you explain what your job as an inspector involves?

Gordon – My main role is that of 'linking' with 15 primary schools with a brief to 'challenge and support' them. The main purpose is to give the Local Authority a full picture about how well the schools are doing in terms of attainment, teaching and learning, and leadership and management. I do this through regular visits, analysis of outcomes data, target setting, classroom observations, analysis of school documentation and discussions with staff and children. I also support governing bodies in the appointment of headteachers and deputy headteachers.

This role will change progressively, and by September 2007 all schools nationally will be allocated a 'School Improvement Partner' and link inspectors/advisers will cease to exist as such.

Q. Please tell me more about the new School Improvement Partners. What will they be doing, and how will this help schools?

Gordon – This is a government initiative, targeted at the drive to raise standards, to enable schools to be 'supported and challenged' by a person who has undergone national accreditation. The aim is to encourage successful headteachers to take on the support of a number of other schools on a part-time basis. It is too early to judge how successful this will be so it is almost certain that in the primary field the majority of school improvement partners are likely to be re-invented inspectors and advisers.

Q. What else does the job entail?

Gordon – I also organize conferences and courses and manage our headteacher induction programme. I deliver training to individual schools, groups of governors or open-access courses. I'm a trained and experienced Ofsted inspector, although that element of my work is currently taking a back seat.

Q. Could you tell me how the new Ofsted framework has affected your work – how are you helping schools in dealing with the new-style inspections?

Gordon – Of course, the Ofsted regime continues to change and the latest framework, on a three-year cycle, came into operation in September 2005 with shorter inspections and only 48 hours' notice! The new emphasis is on school self-evaluation – the better a school knows itself and responds to that knowledge, the 'easier' the inspection process will be. Despite the fact that at the time of writing the framework has been operational for only ten months there are now moves towards 'proportional inspection' where successful schools get an even lighter touch and 'satisfactory' schools may be visited one year on to check how they are doing. I help schools to develop their self-evaluation processes so that they can be secure in their own judgements. Generally schools like the short notice of the new framework. However, this can work against some schools who know that they are due for an inspection but it doesn't seem to happen. This can end up as a potential two-year notice period!

Q. How does a teacher get into advisory/inspection work? How did you move into the job?

Gordon – Most inspectors, particularly at primary level, come through the route of having been successful headteachers. My route was a little different. I started teaching in a middle school, then moved to a high school, then I looked for a job which would involve development and training, but which would also get me into a wide range of mainstream schools. I ended up opening a new teachers' centre just outside Nottingham, then moved to run the main teachers' centre in the middle of the city. After that I had a succession of jobs which involved developing training and support activities for schools in different areas of Nottinghamshire.

In 1993 I was appointed as Inspector for Consultancy and Training. In 1998 we were reorganized and all inspectors had to take on a 'link' function and as most of my previous work had been with primary schools I became a primary link inspector but still hung onto some of the training and development function. It is unclear how the route will look in the future with advent of the School Improvement Partner initiative. Most headteachers are reluctant to leave their schools for significant parts of the week and, currently, any full-time roles in this field are not seen as secure and generally don't pay as well as headship!

Q. What are some of the best things about working as an inspector? What really satisfies you about your job?

Gordon – The best things are working with enthusiasts and seeing improvements in schools as a result of things I've said or done. Also, the variety in the job. There's a significant amount of personal autonomy within an agreed structure. I get satisfaction through knowing that I've done a good job – people tell you! I also enjoy seeing children getting a better deal as a result of my work. Plus, people saying things like, 'You know that course you ran two years ago which I thought was crap! Recently I dug out the notes and it has been really useful.' Also, knowing that, sometimes, I make a difference.

Q. There must be difficult parts to the job as well. What's hard about your job as an inspector and how do you deal with it?

Gordon – The most difficult things are giving hard messages and the frustration of knowing what is needed without the power to insist. I deal with this by constantly reminding myself that *schools* carry the responsibility for what they do. My responsibility is to know about the quality of what they do and advise. I can't do it for them!

Q. How do the teachers you meet react to you, especially in your work as an Ofsted inspector?

Gordon – Reactions vary. In the Ofsted context teachers have reacted in many different ways – defensive, assertive, aggressive, crying, compliant, cooperative, uncooperative… etc., etc. I always respond by being polite, pleasant, understanding, showing a sense of humour, but not prepared to accept or condone a situation where children are not receiving their entitlements. In my link role where I've developed long-term relationships with schools I usually get very friendly and positive reactions.

Q. What do you feel makes a 'good' teacher?

Gordon – Qualities like empathy, patience, humour, sense of fun, understanding, resilience, optimism, intelligence, self-knowledge, credibility, creativity…etc., are crucial.

Q. What about a 'good' headteacher?

Gordon – The original National Standards for Headteachers published in 1998 suggested that heads need a number of qualities. Personal impact and presence; resilience; adaptability to changing circumstances and ideas; energy, vigour and perseverance; self-confidence; reliability; enthusiasm; intellectual ability; integrity; commitment. The 2004 revision detailed 'Professional Qualities' which implied many of the above. I would suggest that teachers need all these as well!!

Q. And what makes a 'good' school?

Gordon – I would say that a 'good' school has dynamic and creative leadership, and the staff are valued and developed. A school with good teaching which challenges *all* children and provides enjoyment, where children are cared about, respected and their views taken into account. Also, where children learn effectively and enjoy coming to school. The Ofsted criteria spell it out very clearly!

Q. What tips or advice would you give to an NQT just starting out in the job?

Gordon – I'd suggest that they read a good book on the first year in teaching! Plus, be highly organized, but not afraid to ask for help and advice. Set yourself small steps as targets – you can't change the world in a day. Also, remember to listen and contribute. Make the learning challenging and enjoyable – a sense of fun is crucial. And, of course, get to know all the children well.

Q. Would you recommend teaching to young people making decisions about a career?

Gordon – Probably not, unless they exhibited the personality and attributes mentioned above and were prepared to work harder and earn less than most graduates. If they met these criteria it would be a great profession for them.

Q. What could be done, then, to make teaching a 'better' and more attractive career?

Gordon – I have a theory about primary schools. One of the biggest problems and frustrations is finding time to do the job properly. If every primary class teacher had a four-day contact week with a day for planning, records, assessment, monitoring and evaluating, their lives would be changed overnight. Also, if every class had a classroom assistant to support the teacher with learning, behaviour issues and time-consuming classroom chores, the job would also be improved significantly.

Recent initiatives in relation to workforce reform have started on this process. All teachers now have time for planning, preparation and assessment; many classroom assistants are taking on new roles and responsibilities which are very supportive of both teachers and children. There are still teething troubles with this, but it is a step in the right direction.

Q. Now, what's on the horizon, the next big initiative?

Gordon – The big initiative – here and now, not on the horizon! – is the 'Every Child Matters' agenda. From a Local Authority point of view, this is bringing together all the services – education, leisure, social services – which impact on children's life chances into one department, a Children and Young People's Department. As this rolls out it will impact on every Local Authority employee who either directly or indirectly works with young people. Very exciting, but very challenging!

Part Four
YOU AND YOUR CAREER

Pay, promotion and career development

13

This chapter deals with some of the more technical aspects of your career as a teacher. It gives details about how much you will be paid, some options for promotion and advancement, and also information about the kind of professional development you might expect. You will also get some ideas about how you might develop your career within and beyond the profession.

Teachers' pay

Salaries vary widely in teaching according to where you teach, the type of post you hold and the school you work in. In addition, teachers' salaries are reviewed and raised on a yearly basis. Changes to teachers' salaries reflect a number of factors, including the difficulty of recruiting and retaining staff, how highly teachers are valued by the society in which they work, union negotiations and so on. The following comments are designed to give a generalized overview of how teachers' pay works:

- There are different pay 'spines' or scales, e.g. for leadership, ASTs, qualified and unqualified teachers. In Scotland there are different scales for main grade, chartered and principal teachers.
- Headteachers are paid according to the size and type of school in which they work.
- Teachers are paid their salary according to the number of 'points' they have on a particular spine.
- Classroom teachers move up one point on the spine for each year's experience, until they reach the top of the main pay scale (M6).
- At this stage, they may (or may not) move onto the next spine, for instance passing the 'threshold'.
- Additional allowances or points are given for:
  - Management responsibilities, e.g. heads of department
  - Number of years' experience (not just teaching, also 'life skills')

- Recruitment and retention
- SEN responsibilities
- Teachers in particular areas of the country, e.g. in and around London

Salary scales

Teaching pays reasonably well in comparison with other graduate professions. Teachers enter the profession on a respectable starting salary, there is a good rate of progression and many other benefits are available, such as a generous pension scheme. There are some variations in salaries between England and Wales, Scotland and Northern Ireland.

More information about teachers' pay can be found on www.teachernet.gov.uk/pay and on the TDA website www.tda.gov.uk. The teaching unions NASUWT (www.nasuwt.org.uk) and ATL (www.atl.org.uk) also have some excellent information about teaching salaries on their websites.

Pay scales in England and Wales

Qualified teachers

Classroom teachers start on the main pay scale. There are separate pay scales for England and Wales, inner London, outer London and the fringe. Qualified teachers who reach the top of the main pay scale may apply to pass the threshold (see below for more information). Teachers on the main pay scale move to the next point on the scale every September, subject to satisfactory performance. Teachers whose performance has been judged to be excellent can advance by two points. Other payments may be available to teachers who take on additional roles and responsibilities, such as SEN or management duties. Advanced skills teachers are paid on a separate, 27-point pay scale.

Unqualified teachers

Unqualified teachers are paid on a 10-point scale, with the governing body deciding exactly where on the scale they should start. Some teachers receive an additional allowance on top of this basic salary. Trainee teachers who follow an employment-based route to QTS are usually paid on the unqualified teachers' pay scale.

Pay scales in Scotland

In Scotland there are different scales for main grade, chartered and principal teachers. All teachers are placed on point 0 for their first (probationary) year in teaching. If you are successful in becoming a fully registered teacher, you should go up the pay scale by one increment each year. Teachers with relevant career experience can potentially jump up to four points after the probation year, subject to the employer's discretion.

There are additional financial incentives available for teachers who work in remote areas of Scotland, in the form of an allowance on top of the normal salary. These are a 'distant island allowance' of £1,536 and a 'remote schools allowance' of £957 or £1,791. There is further information on Scottish pay scales on the Teach In Scotland website – www.teachinginscotland.com – and from the Professional Association of Teachers (Scotland) – www.pat.org.uk.

Pay scales in Northern Ireland

Pay scales in Northern Ireland are the same as those in England and Wales, with classroom teachers starting on the main pay scale. The rules for passing the threshold are the same. Teachers rise up the pay scale by one point every September, pending satisfactory performance. Further information can be found at the Department of Education for Northern Ireland website www.deni.gov.uk/index/teachers_pg.htm.

Working conditions

Working conditions (Scotland)

Teachers in Scotland were guaranteed a 35-hour working week from 1 August 2001, thanks to a government enquiry into teachers' pay and conditions known as the 'McCrone Agreement'. They were also promised the introduction of a maximum contact time (in the classroom) of 22.5 hours per week. However, there are still some concerns about this agreement, and further changes may be made.

Working conditions (England and Wales)

The 'School Teachers' Pay and Working Conditions Document' explains your conditions of employment, i.e. your pay and professional duties. In January 2003 a National Agreement was signed between the government, employers and school workforce unions. This document has dramatically altered teachers' working conditions. The points below summarize details about the amount of time that you are actually required to work under your contract:

- Teachers working full time have to be available to work 195 days in the school year. Of this time, 190 days are those on which you actually have to teach students. The remaining 5 days would normally be used for whole-school and INSET activities (note: these conditions don't apply to heads, deputies, ASTs or part-time staff).

- You are required to work 1,265 hours during the school year.
- You cannot be made to supervise at lunchtimes, and you must be given a break 'of reasonable length' between school sessions or at lunchtime (i.e. between noon and 2pm).
- You are also required to work extra hours so that you can fulfil your professional duties, which include marking work, writing reports, preparing lessons and so on. This time is not specified, and is not included within the 1,265 hours.
- All teachers are now entitled to a minimum of 10 per cent planning, preparation and assessment time as part of their teaching timetable.
- The cover of absent colleagues should be limited to an initial 38 hours per year.
- Clerical and administrative tasks are no longer the routine duty of teachers and should be transferred to appropriate support staff. There are 21 tasks listed in the agreement which should not be the responsibility of teachers.

For more details about what the National Agreement includes, see www.remodelling.org/remodelling/nationalagreement.aspx.

Promotion

After a year or more as a teacher, you may well be looking for your first promoted post. Sometimes, in the larger secondary schools, the post will actually come looking for you! For instance, a vacancy could arise and you may find yourself in the enviable position where one of your managers asks you to apply. In smaller schools, and in the primary environment, it could be that you need to move on to another school in order to find a promotion opportunity. If you are interested in promotion, and in managerial posts, do take a look at the interviews with managers in Part Three, Chapter 10 (School management). These will give you a good idea of both the ups and downs of promoted posts.

If you take a promotion within your current school, bear in mind that it can be quite difficult to adapt the relationship you already have with your colleagues. Once you become their manager instead of just a fellow member of staff, this will alter the nature of the way that you work with them. On the other hand, taking a promotion can be hard work, and it is doubtless easier to adapt to a new job in a school where you already know all about the way things are run.

For some great advice on promotions, career development and other related issues, look at Hazel Bennett's book *The Ultimate Teacher's Handbook* (Continuum, 2005).

Moving schools

Some teachers are happy to spend a long period of time in one school, while others are keen to move on every few years. Much will depend on you as an individual, and also on the type of career path you hope to take. Below is a list of points 'for' and 'against' moving schools for you to consider if you are thinking of taking this step:

'For'

- Gaining a greater breadth of experience, which could be useful for your future career path, and which will certainly help you develop your teaching skills.
- Facing new challenges in a new environment can help prevent you becoming stale or bored with your job.
- Working with a different group of students, perhaps moving from the 'easy' to the 'challenging' school, and consequently developing new classroom-management skills.
- Shaking up your world a little. Teaching can become very easy and safe if you work at one school for a long time.
- Finding out how your students (and the staff) really feel about you when you listen to the farewell speeches and read the cards.
- Hopefully getting lots of presents!
- A chance to make a complete change to your image as a teacher. For instance, a relaxed teacher can choose to come across as strict at a new school.

'Against'

- Having to learn the ropes all over again. This can prove very stressful for the first term or so.
- Working with different policies, rules and so on, and getting used to new systems.
- Having to find your way around a completely new environment.
- Getting to know large numbers of new names and people, both staff and students.
- Potentially, students 'trying you out' and misbehaving to test a new member of staff.

Passing the threshold

The 'threshold' was introduced to give a financial reward and incentive to good classroom teachers who prefer to stay in the classroom, rather than move into management. The performance threshold gives experienced teachers at the top of the classroom pay scale (M6) a chance to access the upper pay scale. Teachers are assessed against eight 'national threshold standards of effective teaching'. These are grouped into 5 areas:

- knowledge and understanding (1 standard)
- teaching and assessment (3 standards)
- pupil progress (1 standard)
- wider professional effectiveness (2 standards)
- professional characteristics (1 standard)

If they pass the threshold, teachers move onto a new, higher pay scale. Once on this higher scale, progression upwards is not automatic each year, but depends on the teacher's performance within the school. To apply to pass the threshold, you need to fill in an application form and pass this to your headteacher. The head then writes his or her comments on the form, before it is passed to an assessor. For more details, see www.teachernet.gov.uk/management/payandperformance/performancethreshold/.

Fast Track

The Fast Track scheme is aimed at qualified teachers in the early stages of their careers. It gives them the opportunity to progress their career at a faster rate. Fast Track encourages teachers to take on positions of more responsibility, providing support and training to help them do this. The programme is designed so that teachers can achieve a senior leadership role within five years of beginning the course. To apply for Fast Track you should:

- normally be in the first two or three years of your teaching career
- have qualified teacher status
- be registered with the GTC
- have a university degree classified at 2.1 or above, or a 2.2 plus a postgraduate degree
- not have passed the threshold (you must be earning a salary on the main pay scale)
- get a reference from a member of your senior management, commenting on your suitability for the course
- be committed to developing your professional skills

- have a keen interest in progressing through your career
- be interested in improving your school's educational provision
- be capable of being an active school leader

You can find out more, including your eligibility and how to apply, from the DfES Fast Track website www.fasttrackteaching.gov.uk.

INSET

The training that you undergo while working as a teacher is known as INSET, or in service training. INSET generally falls into two different categories: school-based training, which is usually provided for a number of staff at one time (often the whole staff), and training for which you are given a day out of school to attend a course, often at a hotel or other training venue. Schools will generally have one or more INSET days at the start of term, when the teachers and other staff gather together to be 'trained'. (In reality, these days are often used for whole-school meetings, departmental time in a secondary school, and other focused activities, in addition to actual training.)

School-based INSET

The school-based training that is done during the academic year will be linked to aspects of the school development plan. For instance, the headteacher might feel that a focus is needed on one specific issue (such as behaviour), and he or she might spend a large part of the training budget for the year on that particular topic.

As mentioned above, many schools have one or more INSET days at the start of the school year. There are a total of five statutory INSET days within the academic year when the students are not at school, and the teachers gather for 'training'. In-school training may also be called 'twilight', which is training done after the students have gone home for the day. Some of the more common subjects for INSET are listed below:

- Behaviour management – creating and developing school policies, strategies for managing behaviour, focus on specific students and what can be done to help them.
- SEN – developing policies, differentiation, inclusion.
- Curriculum-based work – training for a new syllabus, developing schemes of work, moderation.
- Ofsted inspections – preparing for an Ofsted visit, feedback and whole-school review after the event.
- New initiatives – national literacy and numeracy strategies, and so on.

Training outside the school

In addition to school-based training, teachers should also get the chance to take training courses at other venues (often during school time). For instance, a newly promoted subject coordinator or head of department might undertake training to help prepare for this new role; an NQT might be given INSET on classroom and behaviour management. Some out-of-school training days are actually moderation meetings, where teachers of a subject get together to cross-check their grades against those given by their colleagues.

It is the teachers who can be bothered to book their places and fill in the relevant forms who get the chance to go on INSET outside school. In some schools you will need to push to get the opportunities to which you should be entitled. It really is worthwhile taking up every opportunity for training that comes your way. There are a number of reasons why this is so:

- Typically the training is useful and valuable (although it has to be said that the quality of courses can be a bit 'hit and miss').
- You will be adding to your own continuing professional development.
- You can get new ideas, develop new skills and find out about new ways of approaching a subject or area.
- You get the chance to mix with teachers from other schools, and to make a useful network of contacts.
- Attending INSET days looks good on your CV, or on a job application form.
- You get the chance for a day out of school. If possible, book a course for a time when you know you are going to be tired and in need of a break, for instance the middle of the second term.

In addition to general INSET, some schools offer finance or other forms of support for teachers who wish to take a further qualification, such as an MA, MEd or MBA. Again, if you are offered this opportunity, do consider taking it, although bear in mind the time commitment and additional workload involved.

Teaching and other careers

The skills that you develop as a teacher, and the experiences which you undergo, naturally lend themselves to a number of other related fields. Some teachers, after a few years in the profession, find themselves increasingly interested in a particular area of education, such as child psychology or special educational needs. Alternatively, some teachers will simply find themselves exhausted by the job, and unwilling to continue working as full-time teachers. Below are some ideas about careers into which the teacher might move:

- Educational psychology
- LEA advisory and inspection services
- Counselling and mentoring work
- Educational consultancy and training
- Writing curriculum materials and books for teachers

In addition to these areas closely related to teaching, think also about the type of skills you have that might be applicable out in the wider world. It is worth doing a brief 'skills audit' of the skills that you have developed, so that you can emphasize these when applying for other posts. For instance, the classroom teacher will have developed a huge range of abilities, including the following areas:

- Managing large groups of people
- Organizing paperwork and work time
- Forward planning
- Assessing and recording performance and progression
- Target setting

Private tutoring

Working as a private tutor can offer the teacher a useful source of additional income. Teachers may take on tutoring work via an agency, or may organize their own work, perhaps via small ads in local shops and papers. You may also find that parents at your school ask you to tutor their children. Generally speaking, it is best not to tutor children in your own class. The problem is that the divide between teacher/student is harder to maintain, and you may find parents expect you to treat their child differently, because they are paying you as a tutor. It is also inadvisable to set up tutor sessions on your own school premises, because of insurance and legal issues.

Teaching overseas

Teaching is a very mobile career, and for those who want to, there are plenty of opportunities to work overseas. Working in a foreign school offers teachers a wonderful way of seeing the world, of experiencing different cultures and also a great way of adding to the range and quality of their teaching skills. However, there are also pitfalls in teaching overseas for the unwary.

Many schools in Europe and beyond will teach a different syllabus to that which is common in UK schools. This may be IGCSEs (international GCSEs), or it could be the International Baccalaureate (IB) syllabus. You can find full details of the IB programme at the IBO's website: www.ibo.org. In brief, the IB programme is divided into three sections – primary years (PYP), middle years (MYP) and diploma. These correspond in age groups to KS1 and 2 (PYP), KS3 and 4 (MYP) and A levels (diploma). The IB programme is, generally speaking, much broader in scope than the system followed in the UK. There is an emphasis on a fully rounded education, and the programme is far less orientated towards formal, statutory assessments.

The interview below gives you an insight into what it is like to work overseas, and some of the advantages and disadvantages of moving to a different country to teach.

Teaching working overseas

Mike Bryan

Kaitaia College, Kaitaia, New Zealand

Q. Why did you decide to become a teacher?

Mike – Because I was not using my degree in my current work as an untrained social worker. I wanted to work with mainstream adolescents instead of people with learning disabilities

Q. What was your training like?

Mike – Excellent! I did a nine-month PGCE in Lancaster. It was a different experience to doing my first degree as the learning was directed to the job at the end and I was more mature and focused.

Q. Tell me about your career so far.

Mike – I worked at a high school in Blackpool for just over two years and a term. I was a teacher of science at a fairly tough school. There wasn't much relevant professional development. The local advisor was pushing a project on primary to secondary school science transition, so I volunteered myself for that. I became Key Stage 3 coordinator in my second year at the school.

We decided to emigrate to New Zealand because it seemed to be a better environment to raise three boys. I got a job over the internet at Kaitaia College, where I began teaching science to Years 9, 10 and 12. I was appointed Dean of Year 9 this year. I'm still teaching four classes of science and I'm getting professional development to help me develop my role as Dean. Deaning takes up lots of time.

Q. How have you found it, working overseas as a teacher?

Mike – It's going well. It's a fantastic living environment. The culture is interesting: the Maori are strong here in the north and they have a distinctive culture that infects all aspects of life. I have learnt a bit of the language: Te Reo. It comes in handy at school to talk a little with the disaffected ones. I say 'E pai ana koe?' 'How are you doing?' as they come into class and this does wonders for my relationship with them, especially when they are mistrustful of white teachers.

Q. What's been the best thing about teaching overseas for you so far?

Mike – Being able to combine a similar job to the one I had in the UK with a fantastic lifestyle. We have three acres to play with and can get our boys involved in raising sheep and poultry.

Q. And what about the worst thing?

Mike – Being a long way from family, especially difficult when my mum broke her hip recently and we were too far away to help.

Q. What's the best thing about teaching secondary science?

Mike – Science is a great subject to teach as I am learning so much myself by teaching it. I like teaching adolescents especially when they get caught up in enthusiasm for what they are learning.

Q. And the hardest thing?

Mike – Having enough time to prepare decent lessons and make the work suitable for different abilities.

Q. Could you tell me a bit about your approach to planning and lesson delivery?

Mike – I plan less than I used to and find that winging it can make the lessons more responsive to the needs of the kids sat in front of me. I enjoy doing practicals once all the gear is in the room; getting it all together in time can be a nightmare. I also enjoy doing role-plays where the kinaesthetic ones get to show off and demonstrate concepts.

Q. Can you recommend any good resources for teachers, particularly those who might want to work abroad?

Mike – The *TES* website has put me onto loads of stuff. Just collect stuff wherever you go. Nick ideas from other departments, especially language teachers. They have some neat games and science is basically another language.

Q. Would you recommend a teaching career to others? Would you recommend teaching overseas to others?

Mike – It's a good career for the right person. You have to like children. You have to be adaptable and generous with your time. Be prepared to be an adult in your dealings with poorly parented kids and not a grown-up kid yourself. If you can say 'yes' to those then I'd recommend it. If 'no', you will find it difficult.

Teaching overseas is going to depend on where you are. I can only speak from my experience. New Zealand is a good environment to teach in if you are adaptable.

Q. What could be done to improve teaching as a profession?

Mike – Good question! I'm not sure. We are different from doctors and lawyers – we're not taken as seriously, or paid as well. Perhaps teachers have to be more professional, we get very public exposure to a lot of people in a way that other professionals do not. The bad eggs don't help our case. Perhaps we could do with more support staff, like nurses or legal secretaries to do all the tedious non-professional work, leaving us free to do the parts of the job that actually are professional.

Q. Any tips for other teachers, anything you wish you'd known when you first started teaching?

Mike – Get your relationships right with your pupils. Be yourself and discover your own style. Make the job sustainable as soon as you can, don't become a workaholic.

Q. Finally, in your opinion, what makes someone a good teacher?

Mike – Enthusiasm for the subject and the ability to convey it to the MTV generation. You need tolerance for and enjoyment of the company of young people (the last being the most important). A sense of humour to cope with the regular insanity helps too.

Educational shows

Educational shows offer teachers a chance to view new resources and curriculum materials; to attend seminars, INSET sessions and talks by leading educationalists; and also to try out new products, such as educational software. There are three large shows during the academic year:

- BETT, Olympia, London
- The Education Show, NEC, Birmingham
- SETT, SECC, Glasgow

For more details see www.bettshow.com and www.besanet.org.uk.

Other issues **14**

This chapter provides a round-up of some of the other issues related to your career. There are details here about working as a supply teacher, including plenty of tips about surviving in what can be a difficult and demanding role. There is also information about what an Ofsted inspection involves, how the teachers' pension scheme works and how and why you might join a union. You will also find an in-depth interview with Carol Adams, former Chief Executive of the GTCE.

Supply teaching

There are a number of times in a teacher's career when he or she might turn to supply teaching. It could be that you are having trouble finding a permanent job, or in finding the right job or school for you. Perhaps you are an overseas-trained teacher, wishing to combine teaching with travel around the UK and Europe. It might be that you wish to continue teaching, but that you need to combine part-time supply teaching with other work or family commitments. Or maybe you simply enjoy the flexibility and experience of working at a range of different schools. Before you consider full- or part-time work as a supply teacher, think carefully about all the potential benefits and drawbacks. You'll find some points below that you might like to consider:

The benefits

- Supply teaching is relatively well paid
- Supply teachers have less paperwork to deal with than permanent teachers
- Although you may be involved in doing some planning and marking, this will certainly be less than for a permanent teacher
- You won't be required to attend after-school meetings or parents' evenings

- You won't have to run extracurricular activities
- You get to see a whole range of different schools, and learn more about how they work
- You get to teach a huge variety of children
- If you really don't enjoy working at a particular school, you're not stuck there for longer than one day at a time

Please note, though, that many of these benefits do not apply to a situation where a supply teacher takes a long-term contract. In these cases, you would certainly be expected to do planning/marking and attend meetings.

The drawbacks

- Students do tend to try and take advantage when they have a supply teacher (it's only natural, after all)
- It can be a lot harder to discipline children who don't know you, but who do know that you're a supply teacher
- You will be moving around from school to school, and for some people this lack of continuity is unsettling
- You may have to travel a fair distance to some assignments
- Some people (other teachers included) have a negative image or experience of supply teachers
- You are not guaranteed work
- Some times of the year are busy, while other times are relatively quiet
- You won't get paid if you're sick, or during your holidays, although some agencies do offer sickness and holiday benefits
- You don't get to develop long-lasting or in-depth relationships with the children, or with the other teachers at a school

Again, please note that many of these drawbacks do not apply to supply teachers working on a long-term contract.

Supply agencies

In the Directory at the back of this book, you'll find details of a number of different agencies. These agencies differ a great deal. Some are national chains, which cover the whole of the UK. Others are local, small-scale operations, perhaps set up by a group of ex-teachers to serve their local area. When choosing an agency (or agencies) for which to work, there are a number of issues to take into account:

- Whether the interview process seems professionally organized and handled.

- The type of benefits and support they offer.
- Whether they provide training, illness and holiday pay, pensions advice and so on.
- How well you get on with the consultant for whom you would work.
- Whether the agency takes account of your preferences about schools and areas in which you would like to work.
- If you're an NQT, how clued up they seem about the induction process.

Supply work via an LEA

In Scotland, the standard route for working as a supply teacher is via the LEA. Elsewhere, there are opportunities to work for your LEA, but the efficiency of the arrangement will depend a great deal on where you live, and how well your local authority is run. If you are interested in working via the LEA, you should contact your local authority or RSM (recruitment strategy manager) direct.

Tips for supply teachers

It can be tough being a supply teacher – I know because I've done it myself. But it can also be great fun, so long as you follow some basic rules. The tips that I give below will be particularly useful to those teachers doing supply for the very first time. They should help you to impress the schools that you visit, enjoy the assignments that you take and survive even when the kids do decide to put you through hell.

- *Never arrive late*: Always, always try to arrive on time for assignments, even if this means leaving home earlier than you think is necessary. When you get to the school, report to reception – most schools have some form of 'security' nowadays, and will want you to sign in and probably to wear a pass.
- *Get the information you need*: Many schools will give you a 'supply teacher's pack' when you arrive, which should include the information listed below. If you are not given this before the school day starts, do make sure that you get hold of:
  - a map showing the school layout
  - a copy of the school's behaviour policy, or at the very least some information about the sanctions that you can use
  - information about the rewards system at the school
  - the timings of tutor time (at secondary), lesson times and breaks
  - the name of someone to whom you can refer badly behaved students if things go wrong
- *Make contacts*: If possible, introduce yourself to the head of department (in a secondary school) or to a management figure (such as a deputy

head) in a primary school. These people will often prove very useful points of reference if you experience problems.

- *Come equipped*: Take your own tea or coffee, mug and milk. Although some schools provide these free of charge, you will often find that there are no refreshment facilities.
- *Find out about routines*: Before the day starts, try to find out what the usual routine is for the subject or class you are teaching. For instance, what are the children used to doing when they arrive at the lesson? Do they normally line up outside? Is the register taken at the start of the session? In a practical subject, what arrangements are made for changing clothes or organizing equipment?
- *First impressions are crucial*: Start your lessons tough, especially if you are unsure what type of children you are going to be teaching. With a nice class a teacher who gives a tough impression to begin with will do no harm to their reputation. With a difficult class it can make the difference between a nightmare lesson or day, and a good one.
- *Start as you mean to go on*: The first three minutes are crucial in setting the tone and letting the children know what you expect. Often, just the knowledge that they have a supply teacher will be enough to persuade them to try it on. So, aim to be in the classroom when the class arrive, and focus on the basics first. This includes commands such as 'coats off', 'ties on', 'go straight to your seats', 'books out', and so on (all leavened with the word 'please' of course). If it seems appropriate for the situation and the location, ask the class to line up outside the room before you allow them in. This helps give the impression that you are not to be messed with.
- *Lay down the basics*: Set down some ground rules and expectations right at the start of the lesson. For instance, I like to give my classes 'two choices'. They can behave appropriately and do as I say (and see the 'nice' side of me), or they can mess me around, try it on (and consequently see the 'nasty' side).
- *Be positive*: Aim to stay positive and friendly. Use comments such as 'You're already making a really good impression on me' if the class enter the room in an appropriate manner. That way, you will set up the expectation of a positive and fun lesson or day.
- *Be 'hard to fool'*: Don't believe everything that the children tell you! For instance, if they try to persuade you that 'we normally wear our coats in class', you can be 99.9 per cent certain that they are trying it on. Often, a class will inform you that 'we've already done this work'. If they do try to use this excuse, simply tell them that they'll be able to do it extra well second time around.

- *Do your 'admin'*: Make sure you get your timesheets signed and in to your agency if you want to get paid. If you are working at the same school all week, you might find that the school are willing to fax a copy of your timesheet to your agency on the Friday, to ensure that it arrives on time.

Getting the best out of your supply teacher

How well a supply teacher gets on depends a great deal on how the school or department treats him or her. If you are in a position where you use supply teachers, and you want them to be as successful as possible, here are some tips that you might find useful:

- *Good planning is still vital*: Please don't leave work that the children will find boring, or that they will finish before the end of the lesson. When you're heading off on a course, it can be very tempting to rush off a few photocopied worksheets – I confess that I've done this myself. However, if the lesson does not suit the class, you are not giving the supply teacher the opportunity to work successfully with them.
- *Give them the info they need*: Take the time to explain the basic patterns and routines to the supply teacher, as these often differ widely from school to school. For instance, does the class normally line up outside the room before the lesson starts? Is the register taken at the start of the lesson, or at the end? Are the children expected to work in silence or is low-level chat permitted?
- *Keep changes to a minimum*: Try to minimize disruption to the class, for instance avoid combining a room change with a visit from a supply teacher. Children typically react badly to unexpected changes in routine, and not having their normal teacher is already an unusual situation.
- *Offer your support*: A brief visit by the head of department or other manager at the start of the lesson can really settle down the class and allow the supply teacher a chance to succeed. A comment that you will be returning to check up on the class later, and ensuring that the teacher has not had any problems, will really help out.

Ofsted

Ofsted is designed to give an independent overview of the school being inspected. Under recent changes to the system, an inspection will take place at least once every three years. Schools now only receive about two days' notice that an inspection is going to take place. Ofsted looks at the standards a school is achieving, and also at their progress (or lack of it) since the last inspection. After an inspection has taken place, Ofsted gives a written report on what the school is doing well, and also on where its weaknesses are. These reports can be a useful source of information for parents and also for teachers looking to move to a new school.

The exact set-up of the inspection will vary according to the size of the school. There will be between one and five inspectors inspecting the school over a period of no longer than two days. To prepare for the inspection, the inspectors will use the school's self-evaluation form (SEF) and Performance and Assessment report (PANDA), as well as the report from any previous evaluation.

It is important to remember that Ofsted can only really provide a 'snapshot' of the true situation in a school, because despite all the changes inspections still take place in what is essentially an artificial environment. It is of course inevitable that staff try their best to impress when Ofsted appear. Teachers will plan in great detail, perhaps far more than usual; displays will be beautifully presented; graffiti will be scrubbed from the walls. There are even anecdotal stories of schools suspending their 'worst' students for the time when Ofsted is in.

An impending Ofsted inspection can be a source of great stress for teachers. It is natural to worry about whether your lesson planning will be viewed as up to scratch, and how your students will behave when the inspectors are around. You may find that your children behave perfectly when an inspector is in the room; alternatively you may find they turn into little horrors to show you up. Much will depend on the relationship you have with the class.

If you've not yet been through an inspection, you will probably have heard many horror stories about what the inspection will involve, of teachers 'failing' and schools being closed. In the (now-brief) run-up to the inspection you will certainly have an additional workload: writing detailed lesson plans, getting books marked up to date, and so on. Many thanks to Kirsty for her wonderful description of Ofsted as the 'Office for Stress, Tension and Endless Distress'. I think this sums up many teachers' feelings about the whole process!

You can find a 'bank' of Ofsted reports at the organization's website: www.ofsted.gov.uk. It is well worth taking a look at these, because they give you a very good idea about the type of areas that Ofsted will be inspecting. You can find some ideas about surviving Ofsted in the checklists in Chapter 18.

What is Ofsted looking for?

Around two thirds of the inspectors' time will be used to observe what actually goes on in the classroom. The inspectors evaluate each lesson that they see and give grades from 1 (poor) to 7 (excellent). While they're observing your work, the inspectors are looking for a whole range of different things:

- The type and quality of planning you do.
- How good your teaching is.
- What you're actually teaching.
- How well your students are learning.
- The type and quality of evaluation you do.
- How well the students apply themselves to the lesson.
- The attitude and behaviour shown by your students.

What should I do to prepare for Ofsted?

Essentially, preparations for Ofsted are simply the things that a good teacher would normally try to do in the course of his or her working life (if we weren't always so busy). If you spend a little bit of time ensuring that you have covered all the bases, then you can give the best impression possible and show what you are really capable of as a teacher. While accepting that an inspection creates an artificial situation, you will most likely feel under pressure to 'play the game'. In any case, you may as well demonstrate what a great teacher you are. The list below gives you some factors to consider in the time leading up to inspection:

Planning

- Plan your lessons carefully, and in sufficient detail. You may find that your school has a standard format that fulfils Ofsted criteria, which they ask you to use during the inspection. Take advantage of this if it's offered.
- Take special needs into account. Show that you know which children have specific learning needs and what these are. Demonstrate that you are planning for these needs.
- Differentiate the work carefully.
- Think about equal opportunities, cross-curricular possibilities, and multi-cultural issues.
- If you can find the time, talk your plans through with a colleague. This might be your head of department in a secondary school, or a teacher experienced in working with your year group in a primary school.
- Have a copy of your lesson plan available to hand to an inspector if s/he does arrive at your room.

Teaching

- Write the learning objectives on the board before each lesson begins, and refer to these in your teaching and review work.

- Make sure you use a variety of tasks and activities within each lesson. Employ different teaching and learning styles: whole-class teaching, class discussions, individual, paired and group work, and so on.
- Give your lessons pace, energy and enthusiasm.
- Set work that will engage the students, especially if the children in your school have low motivation.

Classroom management

- Think about how your class enters the room, and how quickly and well they settle to work.
- Ensure that any resources required are easily accessible, and consider how the children are going to access these.
- Use calm and purposeful strategies to deal with any behaviour issues that arise.
- Consider how well the end of your lesson is managed. Leave plenty of time to finish off the lesson and to get the children sensibly and safely out of the room.

General issues

- Make sure that the children's exercise books are marked up to date.
- Check that your displays are neat, interesting and linked to the children's work.
- Think about potential health-and-safety issues in the classroom: for instance where the children put their school bags and whether there are any hazards around, such as trailing wires.
- Know what the school policies are, and put them into use in your classroom, for instance the whole-school behaviour policy.

What other evidence do Ofsted use?

As well as observing lessons, the inspectors will also look at the paperwork that the school, its teachers and departments use. This will include school policies, schemes of work and lesson plans, departmental or curriculum handbooks and so on. The inspectors will also talk to the students and their parents. A questionnaire will be sent out to the parents, and a meeting held at which their views can be expressed.

After the inspection

The grading scale used for inspecting schools is as follows:

Grade 1	Outstanding
Grade 2	Good
Grade 3	Satisfactory
Grade 4	Inadequate

Most schools make it through the inspection with no real problems. However, if an inspector judges a school's performance to be inadequate, it may be put into 'special measures' or given a 'notice to improve'. Schools who receive these notices will be subject to more frequent inspections than those that are deemed satisfactory.

After the inspection is complete, the inspectors must communicate their findings to senior managers and, if possible, the chair of the governing body. After the initial oral feedback, a written report will be given to the school. A copy of this report is put on the Ofsted website, and paper copies are sent to the headteacher, the LEA and other relevant bodies. The report must be made available to the parents and carers of every pupil attending the school within five days of receiving it, and also to the general public.

You can find lots of useful detail about exactly what an inspection involves at www.teachernet.gov.uk/management/curriculumdelivery/ ofstedinspections/.

Pensions

Pensions (England and Wales)

Teaching pensions are administered by 'Teachers' Pensions'. You will automatically be part of the scheme if you are aged between 18 and 70 years, you work full time in a state school, or independent school that is part of the scheme, and you have not opted out. Pensions and financial arrangements are complex issues, but the overall view is generally that the teachers' pension offers a very good deal compared to other pension providers. Below is some general information about the scheme. Further details can be found at www.teacherspensions.co.uk.

- On retirement, the scheme pays you an annual pension and also a tax-free lump sum.
- Your pension is index-linked, and will not be reduced by the effects of inflation.
- You pay 6 per cent of your gross annual salary towards the scheme. Your employer contributes a further 13.5 per cent, making a total of 19.5 per cent. This is deducted before tax, which means you get tax relief on your contributions.

- The normal retirement age is 60 for both men and women. However, this is currently under review as part of the modernization of public sector pensions. Recent proposals suggest changing the normal retirement age to 65.
- The TP is a 'final salary' scheme, which means that it is based on your final salary, not on your contributions while working.
- If you are working part time, or as a supply teacher, you need to complete a form and apply to have your work recognized as pensionable.
- You can opt to pay additional voluntary contributions (AVCs) into the scheme.

Pensions (Scotland and Northern Ireland)

You can find more details about teachers' pensions in Scotland from the Teachers' Benefits Section of the Scottish Public Pensions Agency (see the Directory for contact details). Teachers in Northern Ireland should contact the Teachers' Pensions Branch of the Department of Education (again, see the Directory).

Support systems

With all its varied demands, teaching is a stressful job, and at times all teachers need to turn to others for support. This is especially true at the beginning of your teaching career, but it also holds true throughout the years you spend in the job. There are a wide variety of support systems that you as a teacher can use:

- Your family and friends can offer a shoulder to cry on when times are tough. However, those who are not teachers themselves may find it hard to understand fully the strains of the job.
- Your teaching colleagues will often be the most wonderful source of support that you can find. In my experience, this is especially so in the tougher schools where I have worked. Perhaps the sense of a shared, difficult experience makes us feel like more of a team, and consequently more inclined to help each other out.
- Your managers and, if you're an NQT, your induction tutor have a responsibility to ensure your welfare. A good line manager or head of department can make the difference between feeling properly supported and feeling completely alone.
- Government helplines for teachers may offer an additional source of support, and one which is confidential if you do have particular issues.

'Teacherline' is one such phone support line, jointly run by charity and government (see the Directory for contact details).

- The unions have support services that can help you at times of need. They also offer an invaluable source of legal advice and assistance. (See the following section for more information about the teaching unions.)

The teaching unions

There are a number of different teaching unions. You can find contact details for each of these unions in the Directory section at the back of this book. The unions are, in alphabetical order:

- Association of Teachers and Lecturers (ATL)
- National Association of Headteachers (NAHT)
- National Association of Schoolmasters Union of Women Teachers (NASUWT)
- National Association of Teachers in Further and Higher Education (NATFHE)
- National Union of Teachers (NUT)
- Professional Association of Teachers (PAT)
- Scottish Secondary Teachers' Association (SSTA)
- Secondary Heads' Association (SHA)

Which union you choose depends entirely on your own personal preference. It could be that you find one particular union more responsive and efficient in dealing with your initial enquiries; it might be that you have a particular stance on an issue connected to teaching (such as whether strike action is or is not acceptable), and you feel that one of the unions best represents your own philosophy; it could be that you want to join either a big or a small organization; alternatively, it might just be that you get on well with a particular union rep in your school.

There is absolutely no obligation for teachers to join a union. However, there are a number of very good reasons why you might consider union membership:

- *Legal advice*: The legal representation that the unions offer is becoming increasingly important for teachers, with the threat of legal action ever present.
- *Support*: The unions offer a useful support service and many have help lines that members can call with any questions that they have.
- *Getting your voice heard*: Membership of a union gives you a chance to have your say in debates about the teaching profession.

- *Campaigning for teachers*: The unions do important campaigning work to try and make conditions better for teachers.
- *Discounts*: There are many discounted services on offer, such as cheap car and travel insurance.

The unions are very keen to get you to join them while you are a student: the feeling seems to be that once you've joined a particular union, you will stay with them throughout your teaching career. As a trainee, you will be offered free union membership, and often a reduced rate during your NQT year and perhaps your second year in teaching. You can see an interview below with the PAT, one of the more recently formed, smaller organizations.

PAT

Professional Association of Teachers

Website: www.pat.org.uk

Q. When was PAT set up and why?

A. In 1970 by a group of teachers who, having seen the effects of teachers' strike action on pupils, wished to commit themselves to the principle of not striking.

Q. How is PAT looking to raise its profile as a teachers' union?

A. By increased media coverage, through advertising, exhibitions and seminars, and on the internet.

Q. What makes PAT special?

A. Its:

- no-industrial action rule – putting children and students first
- independence from the TUC/STUC and all political parties
- UK-wide representation
- commitment to representing the whole team from nursery to tertiary – teachers, heads and support staff, as well as lecturers, nursery nurses, nannies and other child carers in the public and private sectors
- more personal approach

Q. What does PAT feel is the main role of a teaching union, and how does it fulfil this role?

A. Looking after the interests of its members and helping and advising them individually as well as representing them nationally. It fulfils this role through its network of local officials and head office staff in Derby and Edinburgh.

Q. What is the organizational structure of PAT and how can members get more involved in their union?

A. PAT is run by an elected General Secretary, National Council and Committees, section committees, and local Federations and Branches. Members can go to local meetings and stand in elections for local and national posts. There is more information in the 'About the Association' page on the PAT website.

Q. What benefits could a teacher expect on joining the union?

A. These are wide-ranging. You can see full details at the Membership Benefits page of the website.

Q. What forms of ongoing support does PAT offer to its members?

A. Help, advice and representation on practice, pay and conditions nationally and locally, plus information in journals, advice publications and on the website.

Q. Which educational issues does PAT feel are of most importance to the profession?

A. A national register of childcarers; commitment to improved working conditions for all in childcare and education; a rationalization of salaries and career structures for the 'Whole Team' in education (teachers, headteachers, teaching assistants and other support staff); funding to be provided to maintain: staff and pupil ratios, the use of mentors, continued staff development and links with training agencies; national funding for a National Curriculum; and consideration of the effects of assessments on pupils.; successful implementation of the Workforce Agreement, the effects of Single Status, pupil behaviour, class sizes (particularly in Scotland), false accusations against school staff and lack of anonymity for those accused, implementation of the Every Child Matters agenda and Extended Schools, parity of pay with teachers for FE lecturers in England, the role of classroom assistants (Scotland) and implementation of McCrone (Scotland).

General Teaching Councils

There are separate GTCs for Scotland, Wales, England and Northern Ireland. These councils are responsible for promoting the profession, and for ensuring high professional standards. The GTCs also hold a register of people who are qualified to work as teachers. You can find out a lot more about the role of the GTC in England in the interview below with Carol Adams.

Chief Executive
General Teaching Council for England

Carol Adams

This interview was conducted with Carol Adams during the autumn of 2006. Sadly, Carol died in January 2007, but we have decided to carry her interview because it gives such a vivid picture of Carol's commitment to supporting teaching and teachers, We dedicate it to her memory.

Q. Could you tell me about your first few years in teaching?

Carol – I went into teaching because I loved my subject, history. I'd have spent all my time out at historic sites and castles if I could! The more history you can do for real, onsite, the better. I taught history in inner London comprehensives for six years – these were large, very challenging schools. I taught the whole range from Year 7 to A level, and I taught large numbers of children who were being failed by the system. I found inner London children fantastic, I loved the challenge of teaching children who didn't want to be there. There was a very strong bond between people who taught together in those days. This was in the early 1970s.

Q. How was the job of a teacher different at that time?

Carol – I would say that the expectations of the children were lower in general, and poor behaviour was more likely to be tolerated than now. Individual teachers had to organize their own discipline within a school structure that fundamentally didn't set sufficient boundaries. Also, we decided what to teach. It was pre-National Curriculum and you taught based on your enthusiasms, on the material available in the stock cupboard and on your team of colleagues.

Q. Do you think it's a shame that the curriculum is much more prescriptive now than it was when you started teaching?

Carol – I do in a way. I think the balance has swung too far and teachers need to have the flexibility to teach what enthuses them but this is now changing again, with lots more flexibility being introduced at Key Stage 3. With a lot of teaching, I believe it doesn't actually matter what the content is, so long as you can enthuse children with a love for the subject and they acquire specific skills and gain confidence. I think that having that choice of subject matter enabled us to be very creative and it inspired us to work phenomenally hard outside of school because we wanted to.

Q. And will we ever return to a situation where there's less prescription about what teachers have to do?

Carol – Yes, there are significant opportunities now for greater flexibility. It's part of a wider debate about accountability, which is of course, fundamental to working in the public service. Accountability has gone in a direction where it's linked to external controls and checklists. If you go down that route, it's very hard to avoid total prescription. If you don't trust professionals, then you've got to prescribe everything they do. We've got to return to a better balance, in which professionals' judgements are trusted more, with systems in place for effective evaluation which enables them to do the very best job. We're in danger of going down a path where all the emphasis is on people being seen to do the right thing, rather than asking what the right thing is.

Q. What path did your career in education take after your time as a teacher?

Carol – I worked for four years as an education officer in the Tower of London. It was marvellous: we had a load of artefacts; we did lectures, trails, study visits, dramas and all sorts. It was living history. The children loved it – the visits gave them a shift in their understanding about history. After that I managed the ILEA History and Social Sciences Teacher Centre. We ran professional development for teachers and trainee teachers and produced teaching materials. Then I became an ILEA Inspector for Equal Opportunities Gender. I published a book called *The Gender Trap* with a colleague and I was also involved with teacher colleagues in a series of books called *Women in History*. After that I was the Assistant Chief Education officer in Haringey for two years. Then I worked in Wolverhampton and Shropshire for ten years as a Chief Education Officer. In 1999 I came to work at GTC. They've all been fantastic jobs, every single one of them.

Q. What do you think makes a 'good' teacher?

Carol – A combination of expert knowledge and commitment to your students. You need to be honest, to have total integrity in what you're doing. A good teacher has enthusiasm, passion and creativity, and with that goes humour. It's also about really recognizing the students as human beings, having great respect for them. That means caring about them in an unsentimental sense and having high expectations of them.

Q. And how can we recruit more 'good' teachers, and retain those we already have in the profession?

Carol – In essence, it's about enabling teachers to feel they are doing a really good job, to give them maximum job satisfaction. They need to know that they've succeeded and that their pupils have, too, often in very adverse circumstances. At the heart of what gets to teachers and reduces morale is the feeling that they can't do a good job. In my experience, teachers actually like teaching, but many of them no longer love the job of being a teacher. Teaching can be the most satisfying, rewarding, wonderful job. I think we're very hypocritical as a society when we say that but then we don't actually enable teachers to enjoy the job by pressuring them and blaming them.

Q. What sort of things prevents teachers from getting job satisfaction?

Carol – It's partly to do with over-accountability, where the focus is on filling in detailed lesson plans, assessments and so on, spending more time *proving* what you're doing than actually doing it. For instance, inspection is perceived by teachers as all about people being *seen* to do something, rather than looking at what they're actually doing. There are many confident leaders who manage to avoid the pressure, but you need outstanding leadership to enable the whole school to stay focused on their agenda.

There's undoubtedly been too much initiative and change. Politics has come before education and governments have been badly advised about the capacity of human beings to absorb and implement change. People can only take on so much at once. If you throw too much at people, they feel like they're failing, they feel that they're not doing a good job.

The workload's got bigger. I don't think it's so much the volume of the work, but the nature of the work. Tasks imposed and not undertaken willingly are burdensome. I don't think teachers have ever had any problem working long hours. When you first become a teacher you recognize that you're either going to go insane and work twenty-four hours a day, seven days a week, or you're going to strike a balance. Potentially, every lesson could be a dynamic multimedia show, but you can't do that. So, you're sensible, you work hard on the things that really matter and have impact. But what is getting to teachers is that they're spending long hours doing things they don't particularly value. Doing someone else's task, not the one you've set yourself.

The less you trust people, the less they feel trusted, the less willing they're going to be to invest in their own judgement, their own professionalism. They're going to say, 'Fine, I'll tick the box!'

Q. Could you explain the role of the GTC?

Carol – The GTC was established by the Teaching and Higher Education Act 1998; the first Council began its work on 1 September 2000. The 1998 Act set the Council two aims: 'to contribute to improving standards of teaching and the quality of learning, and to maintain and improve standards of professional conduct among teachers, in the interests of the public.' This gives us three principal functions: we maintain a Register of qualified teachers in England; we enable the profession to regulate itself; we provide advice to government and other agencies on the key issues affecting the quality of teaching and learning.

Q. How does the GTC have an influence? How can you actually help to change teachers' working lives for the better?

Carol – All our policy advice is based on evidence from teachers, researchers and experts in the field. We present advice to ministers; we talk to partner organizations and work to change attitudes and the climate of opinion on teaching and learning issues. For example, we've developed policies on teacher retention, professional development and assessment and accountability.

Policies don't change overnight; it takes time, persistence and focusing on what will improve learning, since that is what really matters.

Q. Do you feel that you're actually starting to have an impact on what happens and, if so, in what way?

Carol – In lots of policy areas, I can see the GTC's influence over the past five years – professional development is now seen as central to raising standards, assessment is becoming more flexible and accountability has a lighter touch. Teacher retention is also taken more seriously. These are all areas on which we have focused and produced evidence-based policy advice.

Q. Please could you explain how the GTC is involved in disciplining teachers who fail to meet the professional standards? What would you say to teachers who feel that this has become one of your main roles?

Carol – As I've said, the Council's role is to help maintain existing high standards and improve standards of teaching and the quality of learning. The GTC does this through three functions:

- Registration, which ensures that teachers are qualified and fit to practice
- Advice on effective teaching and learning based on identifying and supporting good practice
- Regulation, which means addressing that tiny minority of teachers who have been dismissed on grounds of conduct or competency

Like other professional bodies, the GTC's role is to decide if these teachers have fallen below acceptable professional standards and if they should continue to teach. It is only better known than our other work because it attracts more press interest – negative news always does!

Q. How does the GTC find out what teachers really think, and how does this influence your work?

Carol – We do that through continuous interaction with teachers: a constant process of building up a strong evidence base and networks. GTC Staff and Members speak at headteacher and teacher conferences, and in schools and Local Authorities. We also hold regular meetings with teachers throughout the country on a range of topics and we take careful note of what teachers say. Over the past three years, we have seconded a team of experienced teachers who work locally to develop the two new areas of our policy work: the Teacher Learning Academy, and Achieve, Engage and Connect, the GTC's professional networks.

The Teacher Learning Academy offers public and professional recognition for teachers' learning, development and improvement work. Through the Academy, the learning which occurs in the daily professional lives of teachers can be recognized and celebrated through a national, portable system.

Our professional networks offer teachers access to research, case studies, project groups and conferences and events, each with a specialist focus: *Achieve* promotes race equality and diversity issues in schools; it shares, stimulates and supports good practice in curriculum, school workforce and pupil achievement. *Connect* is the network for those who lead CPD in schools; it offers opportunities to inform national policy work, share good practice and hear the latest research and initiatives in CPD. *Engage* is for teachers starting their careers and those who support them (such as teacher mentors) and it aims to give teachers in their first five years of teaching good-quality support so that talented teachers choose to stay in teaching.

Q. What will the GTC do for teachers in the longer term?

Carol – If we're successful, we will continue to improve standards of teaching and learning in schools – our strapline is 'for children, through teachers'. Both our regulatory work and policy support are about improving what happens in the classroom. Also, we'll contribute to teachers being better understood by the public, being better regarded and having better support and resources to do the job. The GTC is a long-term project, if we're going to bring about recognizable improvement across the whole system. I don't believe in quick fixes: change has got to be sustainable in the long term.

Q. What about the relationship between the GTC and the unions?

Carol – We work very well with them in many areas. They do our training for members on regulatory work. We work in collaboration with most of them on areas of policy, e.g. equality and diversity, assessment and on teachers' professional development. There is only one teacher union that opposes the GTC.

Q. Could we talk about the 'thorny issue' of fees? That's caused a lot of resentment right at the start, hasn't it?

Carol – The ground was never laid to prepare teachers for an independent professional body, supported and funded by the profession. The fee is the price of independence and it came as a shock to many teachers. Several years ago, teachers were given a special allowance of £33, paid as an addition to their salaries, in recognition of the fee. This included part-time teachers. We now get virtually no opposition to the fee, although a number of teachers ask, quite rightly, what it is spent on.

Q. And what about supply teachers?

Carol – Those employed by Local Authorities also get the full amount as an allowance on top of their pay. The only teachers who don't necessarily get it are those who work for agencies, but we work hard to encourage the agencies to pay it, and many of them do. Employers are responsible for making sure that everyone they employ is registered, and it's also the responsibility of teachers as professionals to do so.

Q. What would you say to teachers who feel that the GTC is just another imposition from above?

Carol – Log onto our website, look at our Research of the Month, read our termly mailing, come to a meeting, join one of our networks to support effective practice, email or write to us! You will find that our role is to help improve standards of teaching and the quality of learning and we do much of this by working with and through teachers, and responding to their needs and suggestions.

Q. The GTC has been operating for over five years now. What do you feel your main achievements are during that time? What are you most proud of?

Carol – The work we are doing with thousands of teachers all over the country to develop their practice, especially through the Teacher Learning Academy, which provides a framework for teachers based on classroom practice for recognition and accreditation of their change and improvement activities. I'm also very proud of the high standards of our customer services – staff are passionate about working to help and support teachers, whatever the enquiry or issue.

Q. What do you feel are the most important things that the GTC can achieve over the next five years? Where is the organization going now?

Carol – The GTC is a well-established and developing organization committed to constant improvement of our services and functions and that must continue. I see the most important development as moving our work to support improved practice through professional development and networks from pilot stage to national roll-out, available to every teacher. We will only achieve this through further collaboration with other agencies. Eventually I believe continuing professional development to a recognized standard should be a requirement of teachers to continue to practice, as in many other professions. But for this to happen we first need systems in place in every school so that every teacher has opportunity, time and structured support such as mentoring and coaching.

There is a huge agenda for all those concerned with enabling teachers to improve standards, and my job is to make sure the GTC plays the fullest possible role in this endeavour.

Q. And finally, anything else that you'd like to add?

Carol – Teachers do a fantastic job – they're very committed, highly professional and they work long hours. That needs to be said without qualification or equivocation. Sometimes you have to stop and think: at this moment there are around 25,000 schools in England in which children are learning in an orderly fashion. It's astonishing, really, that teachers do that so well.

I'm more interested in what happens to the profession, than with the success of the GTC. The GTC is just a vehicle for improving education. The key question is how can we contribute, through teachers, to improve learning and how we can help to achieve improvements for all children, to make teaching a better job, more creative and rewarding and continue to raise standards? That's the challenge.

Disciplinary procedures

The governing body of your school is responsible for deciding on disciplinary rules and procedures, and making it clear to all the staff what is and is not acceptable behaviour. You should be given a copy of your school's grievance and disciplinary procedures (perhaps within a school handbook). Teachers may be disciplined for 'misconduct', and in order for this to lead to dismissal it has to be very serious, or repeated on a number of occasions. For instance, this might include being late on repeated occasions, being absent from school without authorization or not meeting the standards of work that are required. Teachers may also be charged with 'gross misconduct', and this can lead to instant dismissal. These sorts of charges would be for serious contractual breaches, such as theft, physical violence or incapacity due to drink or drugs.

Where teachers are charged with 'gross misconduct', they will be suspended on full pay while an investigation is undertaken. With any disciplinary charges, you are entitled to receive full details of the offence, and to have a colleague or union rep with you at any meetings. You also have a right of appeal once a decision has been made.

The General Teaching Council can act as a regulatory body when assessing gross misconduct charges. The GTC has been responsible for investigating and hearing cases regarding serious allegations of unprofessional conduct or serious professional incompetence against registered teachers since June 2001. In some very serious cases a teacher can be removed from the GTC register for a minimum of two years, and may not return to teaching as a profession within that time. Cases that involve the welfare and safety of a child are the responsibility of the DfES.

Disciplinary procedures would normally have a number of stages: at each stage it should be made completely clear what the offence is, and why the warning has been given. A first, oral warning would be given for a less serious offence, followed by a written warning for further offences, or for more serious misconduct. After this, the teacher should then receive a final written warning that they will be dismissed if they do not comply/improve.

A record of written warnings is kept by the school, and these should be kept completely confidential. The Advisory, Conciliation and Arbitration Service (ACAS) recommend that these warnings are disregarded after a certain amount of time has gone by. (Six months for minor offences, a year for a final warning.)

You can find further information about disciplinary procedures on the GTCE website – www.gtce.org.uk/code and through publications on the DfES website – www.dfes.gov.uk/publications.

Part Five
LIFE AT THE CHALKFACE

Primary 15

Primary school teacher

Harefield Primary School, Southampton

Karen Garner

Q. Why did you decide to become a teacher?

Karen – I knew I wanted a job where I could make a difference, but after A levels I wasn't quite sure what that might be. My parents were both psychiatric nurses, and didn't really have any other expectation for me, or any other encouragement apart from suggesting I follow their career path. I tried it, I did make a difference, I listened to many sad stories and helped many people but it wasn't the 'difference' I'd imagined.

I realized I might need to go to university, if I were to find a career where I could make a difference, but there were so many choices, I was overwhelmed. I was also 20 with an 18-month old daughter, I needed a university and course that would fit with childcare and travel arrangements. I decided to do a degree in subjects I was interested in at A level – so I opted for a literature and history degree at Staffordshire University. The course sounded interesting, they had a crèche and I could get there by bus. Throughout my degree, my mind would often dwell on my future career: I wanted a challenge, to be creative, for every day to be different and to be able to see what 'make a difference' looked like.

During my final year, I volunteered to help at the local secondary school which my sisters attended. I really enjoyed talking to the teachers and I quickly realized that I was making a difference and each visit was a different experience. I had a dilemma though: English or history teacher? I talked to teachers of both subjects, and settled on English. I applied for a PGCE in English with history as a second subject at Keele University.

Q. What was your training like?

Karen – I remember being in lectures by Tim Brighouse, I was urged to attend a special session by Chris Woodhead – I didn't have a clue who they were!

Keele was a great place to do my PGCE, it had great resources, useful seminars and I felt well prepared when I did my first placement with Year 2. It was really enjoyable, the classroom was exciting and creative, the teacher was always smiling and I loved it. I knew I'd found IT – she was making a difference.

When we returned to Keele, and were asked if any of us wanted to switch to primary, I didn't put up my hand. I didn't talk over my concerns with my tutor but I knew they were there. I was so in love with literature, I wanted to inspire children to love books and reading, so thought I'd be best in secondary.

My main teaching placement was in Stafford, I remember being quite adamant that I wanted to teach the Year 10 GCSE drama class, the Year 9 history class, and Year 7 English. I was also given the opportunity to teach Year 10 GCSE English, Year 9 SEN drama, and lower-sixth A-level literature. Everything I was interested in! I had a fabulous mentor, Sue Lord, who was patient, knowledgeable and had an answer or response to everything – an inspiration to me.

At my second placement I put my foot down again about what I wanted to do. I asked to work in the SEN department and to carry out a bullying survey as part of my final assignment. Their deputy head described me as the best student teacher they'd ever had – it still makes me glow red!

Q. Could you tell me about your first teaching job?

Karen – I got a job in a secondary school in the West Midlands. It had over 1,200 pupils, and the English department had as many staff as my current primary school. I taught there for three years, passing my probation year with no problems. I worked closely with the head of department on implementing the drama curriculum at Key Stage 3 and at GCSE level. It was an exciting time: there was a new head of department who was buzzing with ideas and enthusiasm. I enjoyed my first two years there but my third year was a real drudge. I taught three Year 8 classes which was hard work during tracking times, and quite dull as I had to teach the same lessons three times a week. I just wasn't enjoying teaching any more, the GCSE groups I had made it obvious they hated the subject and seemed so switched off.

After a while I didn't feel I was making a difference in the secondary system. If you had a lower-set English GCSE, they hated the subject: something somewhere had stopped them loving what I loved so much. The children who opted for drama GCSE often thought they were there for a 'doss' – it was such a shame. I finally admitted to myself that I was teaching the wrong age group. Having a primary aged daughter clinched it for me – I enjoyed teaching her in the evenings and helping her to grasp the basics.

Q. How did you go about moving into primary, then?

Karen – I resigned from my post and went to my daughter's primary school for experience. We moved house and I had an interview with a supply agency. With the reference from my daughter's headteacher they accepted me for work as a primary supply teacher. I did supply work on a day to day basis for a few months. It was a very valuable experience.

I had an interview through the agency for a Year 5 post. I got the job, met the children on the Thursday and the Ofsted inspectors on the Monday! The inspection went well, and after the birth of my son, I went back to the school for two more terms.

Q. It must have been tough combining teaching with being a mum. What happened next?

Karen – My husband and I decided to take a break from the rat race. We wanted to live 'the good life'. We had allotments, grew our own fruit and vegetables, kept chickens and ducks and involved ourselves in raising money for the local schools. We sold plants, hanging baskets and home-grown vegetables. My husband used his woodworking skills to make bird boxes, dolls' houses and he even worked on an organic farm getting paid in potatoes which we sold on. It was a great experience.

The work we did at our daughter's junior school led to us being the leading force in the creation of a school garden and improvements to the school grounds. I became a parent governor and realized that making a difference was still very important to me. I threw myself into school governance. I decided that after the first birthday of our fifth child I would go back to supply teaching.

I made myself available five days a week, while my husband looked after the children and took a leading role in the house. I quickly got regular schools and one in particular became my favourite – Sinclair Primary School, in Southampton. I became a regular visitor, teaching across the two Key Stages. It was a recently amalgamated school, and headteacher Debbie Adamson was a real inspiration. All the staff there were working together to provide a creative and inspiring curriculum.

Then I was offered a full-time position at the school where I now teach – Harefield Junior School, Southampton. I began teaching Year 3. The following year I was moved to work with a tricky Year 5 group, because of my background in English.

Q. Can you tell me about the opportunities you've had so far for continuing professional development?

Karen – Gary our headteacher has helped me greatly with guidance and targets following lesson observations. I have become a more efficient and effective teacher under his leadership at Harefield. Over the past year I have worked on my questioning, lesson structure and pace. I've also written the Key Stage 2 RE curriculum using the 'Living Difference' agreed syllabus for Hampshire. RE Primary News was an absolute inspiration. I attended a course on assessment for learning and levelling in RE which was extremely useful.

I also chose to work on developing a reading culture and worked with the literacy coordinator on a Year 5 'Reading is Fundamental'. As part of this, I ran a staff INSET on reading difficulties and miscue analysis. In the next academic year I hope to undertake the Professional Diploma in Teaching and Learning run by the Institute of Education. This is worth 30 credits towards an MA. I also want to take the Hampshire Dyslexia certificate.

Q. What are your plans and hopes for the future? Where do you see your career going in the longer term?

Karen – I've been told that I would be a very efficient SENCo, and this is an area I'd like to move towards. I have spoken to the head about it and while there may not be a chance for me to be SENCo at Harefield he has said he will give me professional support and the right CPD opportunities. This year I hope to work closely with Rosie, our SENCo, as part of my CPD.

I am also very interested in the pastoral side, and am going to be working alongside the PSHE coordinator in developing PSHE and SEAL in our school. I will continue being RE coordinator and hope to work on establishing the link between RE and literacy.

I do enjoy being a classroom teacher – the thought of not having my own class fills me with dread – but I'm not sure I'm making the big difference I'd dreamed of. I suppose my long-term ambitions would possibly stop at deputy head but I think I'll know when the right job comes along. The excellent teacher scheme is very interesting as an incentive to keep good teachers in the classroom but with the tight budgets faced by many schools I don't think it will work in all schools.

Q. I understand that it's been a challenging year with your Year 5 class. Could you tell me a bit about them? What were they like when you began? What strategies have you used to help them progress?

Karen – When we started together in September, it was obvious that they were underachieving. Many children had made no progress since Year 2 and there were lots of self-esteem issues. There was only one child who had finished Year 4 at age-expected levels for writing, and there were many children who had failed to make any progress since Infant school.

It was clear that a previous year in mixed-age classes of 37 had not enabled these children to make progress. Many felt very insecure when a new area was introduced, and there seemed to be a fear of learning. The children with SEN had spent considerable energy in Year 4 on work-avoidance activities instead of concentrating on learning. Many had behaviour problems. A substantial number of the children had spent Year 4 retreating to their safety zones, rather than explaining to the teacher that they had not understood something. With the SEN children there had been an over-reliance on staff and an expectation that the TA would scribe for them. I knew that my first task was to create a secure and safe classroom where making a mistake or error was not a problem and just part of the learning journey.

The children were very shy orally and any new learning took a very long time to sink in. The literacy teaching needed to be adapted when new tasks and challenges were introduced. We worked in two-week blocks – a reading week leading into a writing week. The children needed to feel a positive sense of academic success.

Q. Could you tell me a bit more about some of the strategies you've used to achieve this positive feeling?

Karen – I introduced the idea of a 'poppadom bites' answer, clapping a child who gave a great answer and encouraging the children to join in. This was adopted very quickly by the children – they enjoyed catching others being clever. I also created a 'clever board'. During circle time the children described themselves using a positive adjective. I used these words to make badges in

Microsoft publisher, and printed and laminated these to keep on each child's desk. When they were caught being clever they got to put themselves on the bottom of the clever board. The goal was to climb to the top of the board first and be given a raffle ticket.

We talked openly about how we like to work, agreeing that we preferred a quiet yet purposeful atmosphere. The children identified aspects of their previous learning that stopped them making progress. They decided that last year it was too noisy; they worked best in a quiet classroom.

The reply 'no' has been eliminated and replaced with 'good try'. Children are clapped for good effort. Some children will remind others that they missed a previous answer and need to improve their listening skills. Children now position themselves so they can make eye contact with me. At other times they turn and make eye contact with whoever is contributing. Praising now comes naturally.

Q. Tell me a bit about how you organize your classroom. What kind of routines do you use? How do you organize your resources? What is the environment like?

Karen – I use plenty of structure in my classroom. Children are encouraged to stay in their seats and to put up their hands to ask or answer a question. Calling out is discouraged and the children know the procedures. When I ask a question the children understand that the question is asked of the class. I expect an answer from anyone, not just the children with hands up. They are offered opportunities for controlling some part of their lives – looking after their textbooks, table tidies, plants and so on. We constantly encourage them to take pride in their classroom and to help keep it a safe learning environment.

I have literacy kit boxes, and numeracy kit boxes on desks during lessons. These have the equipment that will be needed for the lesson stored inside. I have to get these organized before the lesson, but it's a great time saver, and keeps the classroom looking tidy.

I have found plants aid the environment, especially lavender, the smell creates a calm atmosphere. I also try to keep a constant temperature and will open windows to ensure fresh air is circulated. My children are also encouraged to take water and brain gym breaks.

Q. Please tell me about how you plan. How much detail do you include in your daily, weekly and longer-term plans?

Karen – When I worked with Martyn Bisset in Year 3 he hated my planning, he complained that it was far too detailed! I used to put everything down but have since improved. I now use the planning format developed by Martyn and Zoe Winfield that encourages assessment for learning (AFL).

I start with a medium-term plan and produce short-term daily planning for all subjects. Writing a lesson plan is like mentally rehearsing the lesson in your head, and I find that sometimes I don't need the plan in the lesson because I've written it and gone through it the night before, and first thing in the morning. Because I have planned the key questions I can ensure the lesson progresses and learning takes place. You get peace of mind if you have planned properly.

Planning is difficult at the start of the year, particularly with literacy and numeracy, because you don't know the children yet. I would only plan the first two weeks and am ready to change the planning as I get to know the children and their abilities. I have really enjoyed planning for SEAL New Beginnings, as it fitted in very nicely with the RE Community & Belonging, and the resources provided are excellent. The thinking behind SEAL is extremely valuable.

As RE coordinator I had to write all the medium-term plans due to the change in the new agreed syllabus. I'm looking forward to working with the foundation stage and Key Stage 1 teachers on the RE curriculum now Harefield is a combined primary/middle school.

Q. Can you describe the format of a typical lesson?

Karen – I always begin with a recap of the previous lesson or prior learning, then I give an introduction and establish the WALT ('we are learning to'). Throughout the lesson I make at least five or more references to the WALT and success criteria. Then it is lesson input and modelling, formulating the success criteria with the children where possible. I then move on to setting the task, repeating the success criteria as I teach. I finish with a plenary: a chance through self-evaluation or peer evaluation for the children to reflect on their work. I also get them to examine whether they have met all of the success criteria (must, should and could).

Q. Could you tell me a bit more about what 'success criteria' are?

Karen – The success criteria enable the children to receive support and guidance so they can achieve the learning objective. It is differentiated: 'must' is the work that everybody must do, and will be your expectation for your SEN group; 'should' is for your middle group; your high achievers are extended because they are expected to achieve all three – 'must, should and could'. However, the criteria are accessible to all and if the lesson is progressing well all the children should be able to attempt and achieve them.

Q. Can I see an example of some of your planning?

Karen – Here's an example of a numeracy lesson observation plan (*see the end of this chapter*).

Q. Tell me a bit about how you use assessment in your classroom.

Karen – Our school has worked a lot on assessment for learning this year: following these principles Harefield children are much more focused, engaged and interested in their learning. An AFL lesson involves sharing the goal with the pupils, helping them to understand where they are going and the steps they will take along the journey. Praise and encouragement are vital. The skills learnt in previous lessons are referred to and built on as each lesson progresses.

I devised an effective learner tick list that my TA Sue uses to observe the children. Through this we target children and then let children understand that any question the teacher asks is for all to answer. Listening to children in partner talk is very interesting and you can pick up quite quickly if there are any errors and misconceptions.

Pupil evaluation, either self-evaluation or peer evaluation, is a very useful tool. I use a simple technique of thumbs up – I understand it, thumbs straight

– I sort of understand it and thumbs down – I don't get it. This gives you a quick snapshot of the levels of understanding when introducing a new concept. I always make note on my planning of any children with their thumbs down. If they've all got it I usually draw a big smiley face.

I photocopy whiteboards in numeracy and literacy, as evidence of the child meeting a key objective. I keep these in an assessment folder as part of my teacher assessment. We also carry out pupil interviews in numeracy, listening to children as they work out a problem. This has been a great help and can show where a child has a misconception.

Since using AFL children can comment on what they have been learning. I have seen children grow in confidence and become more effective learners. I have also seen my own assessment of the learning improve. I can identify and question children to find out what they know, understand and do.

Q. What kinds of ICT and other interesting resources do you use in your teaching?

Karen – I love my Smartboard, and use it in every lesson. You can create some really exciting and inspiring resources using notebook. I also use PowerPoint presentations: they help create a context for the lesson, and the children love using it too. I regularly use Microsoft publisher to make posters for my room, and I hope that my displays are inspiring and help to create an effective and stimulating environment that makes children want to learn. I have also used finger puppets, and would love to have more story sacks available (a set of props and puppets that help get the children involved in storytelling).

Q. Tell me a bit about the relationship you have with your children. What kind of approaches do you use to help them develop both academically and emotionally?

Karen – When children feel that the teacher values their opinions, wants them to be safe and would miss them if they were away, they are more likely to develop a feeling of self-worth. My TA and I always make an effort of mentioning if a child is away, 'Shame Matthew isn't here, he would have known the answer.' One of the children will mention to Matthew during the recap that he was missed yesterday. This has made a real difference, because children who've been away will ask what work we have been doing and whether they need to catch up. My class has won our school-attendance Oscar five times.

Children need to be treated with respect, to be told when they are doing well, and to be encouraged to praise and to experience praise from their peers. This has an impact on how they see themselves and how they feel others see them. We have seen a remarkable development in the confidence of our SEN children. Two of them have been removed from the register, and another should be taken off the register at the end of the academic year. All SEN children have made progress in all subject areas, and have increased self-confidence.

We aim to be aware of the child in the 'big picture'. We take an interest in their lives outside of school. On Fridays we ask who is doing something interesting at the weekend; on Monday we follow up, and share any successes. We've also looked at how what they are learning now is part of the foundations for the future. I got the children to identify some careers that they thought might be interesting and I made some cards with a picture of their career and a bullet-point list of skills needed. We then discussed how what they learn in the classroom will help them achieve the skills needed for their job.

I've also provided the opportunity for all children to lead a classroom activity. The children have gained confidence by doing weekly feedbacks and presentations to the whole class.

Q. Could you tell me a bit about how you and your TA work together?

Karen – Children need to observe adults being enthusiastic toward education and coping positively with setbacks. For instance, I use my TA to talk about my 'modelled writing', asking her about how I can improve. I also use her to model writing as well. This helps me to listen to and observe the children, instead of having my back turned to the class.

We had a discussion about having positive and purposeful talk in the classroom. I involved my TA in the discussion, explaining that the classroom was our working environment too, and we worked best when it was quiet, so we could think, and if we needed to talk we talked about the work. I explained that it would be very bad if my TA and I started chatting in the middle of a lesson about last night's edition of *EastEnders*, so too it would be very bad for them to do that too. My TA and I have a very effective relationship, during modelling we both contribute and so show children what purposeful talk 'looks' like.

Q. Tell me about your relationship with your children – are there any pupils that particularly stick in your mind?

Karen – Jack has an attention disorder and low self-esteem, and he has had outside agency involvement. I decided to start 'Jack Patrol', as a strategy for improving his motivation. He chooses two children daily to be on 'Jack Patrol', they then record all the times they can catch Jack doing the right thing and being good. Jack has now moved away from having his own work station and can now work effectively in pairs and groups. He has made real progress this year, and can now explain his feelings, and communicate with other children and adults.

Q. Please describe your typical school day.

Karen – I try to walk to work, leaving my husband to handle the children and the school run. I aim to leave the house by 7.30am – walking to school means I can go over the day ahead and iron out any problems or niggles that I have. I pop into the staff room to look at the noticeboard while the kettle boils and I make a cup of tea. I go up to my room, set up the laptop, open some windows and get ready for the day.

I try to have resources prepared the night before so I just have to get the kit boxes ready, and get the first lesson organized. I have two monitors who come in ten minutes early to organize tables and water the plants. My TA Sue arrives, and we chat about the day ahead. Five minutes before the bell I go down to the playground so parents can talk to me if they want.

The children line up when they hear the bell, and I make sure they go safely upstairs. I take the register while the children get on with some early morning work. On Mondays we have a whole-school assembly and while this takes place I discuss the week's literacy and numeracy planning with my TA. We do literacy and numeracy work in the mornings, with a break of fifteen minutes mid-morning. At 11.30am we go back into class groups and have a 45-minute lesson, for instance RE on a Monday.

Lunchtime is at 12.15pm, and this is when my TA Sue goes home. It would be nice to have a full-time TA but I think Sue is a great asset and I really appreciate her. For lunch, I usually have a school dinner. It's really important to eat with the children, so you can talk to them and you are also able to model good eating habits that some children may need. Afterwards I have another cup of tea and a chat with the staff. Then I'll pop to my room and get ready for the afternoon's lessons.

Lessons start again at 1.05pm, and we usually have two sessions in the afternoon. On Mondays Year 5 have the laptops for the afternoon, so each class has an hour's ICT lesson. The last five or ten minutes of the day I usually read to the class. When the children leave my room I always do a high five and tell them to aim high. I go downstairs and walk the class out, again being available if a parent needs to see me.

Once the children are gone I get organized for the next day: marking, sorting out resources, doing some photocopying. I try to leave by 4 or 4.30pm, although Mark does understand if I work a little later. I like to find out what my own children have done and enjoy spending time with them in the evening.

Q. What kind of support networks do you have at school? Which other staff would you be in contact with during a typical school day?

Karen – We were very fortunate to have Suzy Brook join us last year as teaching and learning manager (she's now our acting deputy head). She's a real inspiration and very influential on me. She is an approachable person, and if I had a problem I would go to her. Zoe Winfield was upper school leader, and my Year 5 colleague so I would chat to Zoe on a daily basis and we'd support each other.

I think Harefield is that kind of school where everyone is friendly and approachable. When I was suffering from performance anxiety both Suzy and Martyn helped me, from support in planning to letting me just run through a lesson with them. Naturally, as a year team Zoe and I had weekly planning meetings and would go over any problems then.

Of course, there's always Sue, my TA. I always ask her how she thought a lesson went and now she even annotates my lesson plans too which means I get a good impression of how much learning took place: who didn't have their glasses on, who was answering lots of questions, who was really engaged.

Q. How often do you have to take work home with you?

Karen – I'm terrible, I love making resources and Smartboard files so will do those at home with a big grin on my face. I don't like taking marking home, with five children my house is not the quiet environment that you need for effective marking. Plus it is very important to have down time – my father-in-law has all the children overnight on Mondays and Tuesdays, so Mark and

I get some time for us. It's really important to have some week nights free to spend time being me, not a teacher or a mother, just me.

I prefer to stay late at work to do marking. This year I have created some success criteria stickers that I can stick into the work and so mark closely to the success criteria. I'm planning to use highlighters to show which aspects of the success criteria were met and then another colour highlighter for what I expected them to achieve and a target point to move the child forward. Because next year will be my second year with Year 5, I'm hoping to spend less time on planning and making resources. Hopefully I won't need to do more than an hour at the weekends.

Q. What's been the best thing about teaching for you so far?

Karen – This last year at Harefield Junior School has been very special for me, under the leadership of Gary Hampton. He has really made a difference! We have a strong team, and are going forward into amalgamation with the infants with excitement, happy that we can provide the children of Harefield with a great primary education.

Q. And what about the worst thing?

Karen – After Gary realized I was suffering from performance anxiety during lesson observations, he said I needed to get used to people in my room so it became second nature. He arranged for lots of different people to come into my room: from NQTS just walking through, to the maths advisor from the LEA carrying out formal observations, and then a visit from the senior inspector. By the time Paul came to observe me, I had spoken to loads of people. Paul said that my lesson was very good, and I was on my way to being a very effective teacher. Lesson observations are only horrible if you see them that way, and there are always people in your school able to share good practice and advice.

Q. What's the best thing about teaching in Key Stage 2?

Karen – No two days are ever the same, you can never predict what might happen next, or what might make you smile! My job is enjoyable, interesting and you really can make a difference. My favourite moment is when you watch a child gain in self-confidence, and realize they can do something.

Q. And the hardest thing?

Karen – Maintaining an organized and efficient classroom, that is also a stimulating environment. It is really difficult to keep yourself organized, but this year I have found the missing part – Sue Whitcombe my TA. She realized that I could easily put something down and not find it again. We put our heads together to work out how we could become more efficient, and stop me losing things.

Q. Could you tell me your thoughts on report writing? How do you format reports at your school?

Karen – I like reports to be personal and always try to write about the children and their progress rather than delving into a statement bank. I think reports get easier the more you write. It's good to share reports with colleagues because at first it is really difficult thinking of what to say. Zoe and I looked at the objectives for each of the subjects and the success criteria and wrote a selection of comments that related to what we had taught and what the children had achieved. This made our reports personal to Harefield and to the children they were written about. The blank report format is put onto the teacher drive for you to use. We don't use any report writing programs. Gary gets to take them all home to proofread for the weekend. I was very pleased this year as I only got one back with a mistake!

Q. And how does your school make and maintain contacts with parents?

Karen – Gary is very keen on getting the parents into school: we have open days and parents' evenings every term. I really enjoy having parents in the classroom, it's great to get them engaged and enjoying learning with their children. We all go out into the playground five minutes before the bell in the mornings and then again at the end of school. This gives parents a chance to catch you, tell you if there are any problems or just say hello.

Parents' evening used to be held in our classrooms but Gary changed this to us all being in the hall – it is far more efficient and even I can manage to keep on time! I give the parents a copy of the children's targets in reading, writing and maths, so that they know what their child is aiming for. Parents' evenings are a great opportunity to say how well a child is doing: I made one mum cry this year as she was so pleased to hear her son was making progress. Living close to my school has helped, and my eldest two daughters attend our feeder secondary. The parents see me as approachable, as someone from their community. One mum told me, 'You don't talk down to me, Mrs Garner, you talk to me with respect.'

It's very important to have a positive relationship with the parents and to listen to their concerns: being a parent is a difficult job and if you've got a teacher to help you that's a good thing.

Q. Have you been involved with any extracurricular activities during your teaching career? What benefits and drawbacks have you found with these?

Karen – Our head felt the children should have the opportunity to attend a variety of clubs. In the autumn term I run a drama club which is great fun and very popular with the children. They love doing voice exercises, exploring movement and developing characters. I also run a nature club in the summer. It's great fun, but it's important to put your teaching first. This year I was fortunate to get some library clubs, the most popular being comic club. As library subject leader I targeted reluctant boy readers and bought comics for them each week. They loved it and some of them even started making their own comics.

Q. Any thoughts on all those government initiatives and strategies? How have they affected you as a teacher?

Karen – I've found the introduction of SEAL (Social Emotional Aspects of Learning) absolutely brilliant. I've enjoyed the way that some of the units instil a positive approach to learning. My class wrote their class rules and these were then adopted by the whole school as a 'Code for Children'.

Q. Can you recommend any good resources for teachers?

Karen – Two books that have been extremely useful to me are *ALPS Approach*

(Alistair Smith) and *The Teachers' Toolkit* (Paul Ginnis). I have also been very impressed by some of the LEA websites. The *TES* website (www.tes.co.uk) is great, if you need any help the staff room is the place to go. I would also recommend their new resource bank. The Teacher Resource Exchange is a moderated database of resources that have been checked by specialists, (www.tre.ngfl.gov.uk). I like National Curriculum in Action (www.ncaction.org.uk) which has pupils' work with a commentary by the QCA. As RE coordinator www.juniors.reonline.org.uk is a fantastic place for anyone searching for online activities for a Smartboard. The National Whiteboard Network (www.nwnet.org.uk) is also an excellent resource.

Q. Would you recommend a teaching career to others?

Karen – Yes. Every day is different – you can never predict what might happen next, you have to be adaptable, think on your feet and enjoy the unexpected. But when you do make a difference you have the most amazing feeling of elation – teaching rocks!

Q. What could be done to improve teaching as a profession?

Karen – Naturally, you'd expect me to say a pay rise but I think I'd prefer respect for and appreciation of the hard work we do. This attitude that we only work 9 to 3 with long holidays needs to disappear. Most of the teachers at Harefield work until 5pm every night, either planning, marking or in meetings. Every holiday we all come into school for at least one day. This year I have probably spent 20 hours preparing my classroom during the summer holidays. To make a difference you need to realize that your hours of work are not just those in which you teach.

The introduction of PPA time has been good. I have used the time wisely, organizing intervention programmes for my TA to run, carrying out pupil interviews and arranging action plans for my class.

Q. Any tips for other teachers, anything you wish you'd known when you first started teaching?

Karen – Annotate your planning, photocopy whiteboards, and carry out pupil interviews in your PPA time – brilliant evidence to add to your assessment of the children.

Q. Finally, in your opinion, what kind of things do 'good teachers' do?

Karen – They provide a caring, supportive environment where children are respected and feel a sense of belonging. They believe that every child has the ability to learn and ensure that the children understand this. They involve children in making classroom rules that are clear and understandable to all.

Good teachers emphasize the children's strengths and exclude negativity from the classroom. They get to know the students' interests, talents, goals and the way each child learns best. They use the school behaviour policy consistently and maintain an organized, calm classroom that is conducive to concentration.

They try to make the lessons interesting and enjoyable by catering for learning styles and offering opportunities for everyone to engage with the lesson and take an active part. They define work in specific, short-term goals that help the children associate effort with success. They make expectations clear and provide feedback and credit for work well done. They acknowledge when a child gives 100 per cent effort.

Good teachers emphasize cooperation rather then competition; they find opportunities for students to help one another. They demystify the situation SEN children find themselves in, explaining that children learn in different ways, and that you will do your best to find the way they learn best. They encourage independence, and use a TA in a purposeful way. They use effective questioning – questions that encourage thinking and look for ways of finding solutions.

They encourage goal setting, and 1:1 target setting where the child is aware of what they need to do to make progress. They demystify level descriptors by putting them in child speak.

Good teachers use circle time to build self-esteem. They provide opportunities for discussions, a chance to engage in non-purposeful talk but interesting conversation. They are willing to adapt the timetable to ensure progress is made in basic skills.

Finally, good teachers show enthusiasm, commitment and dedication. They are efficient and caring. Plus, they enjoy the job!

NAME K. Garner	CLASS 5G	DATE 03.03.06	TIME 11:30 pm
			45-minute lesson

LESSON Numeracy group 3/3 – (school closed Monday) 1 lesson taught in classes

WALT Subtract using a written column method.

SUCCESS CRITERIA

MUST	SHOULD	COULD
make jump to and from hundreds and thousands	Estimate accurately	Check with number line

---

STARTER/INPUT <u>TIME 5 mins</u>

Number stick – counting on in groups of eights

Chant

Sequences of eight

Sequences in head, 321 what have I landed on

Give answers sing, rap and down low etc.

KEY QUESTIONS

Q what do I add to 867 to get to the nearest 100?

Q I'm on 900 what do I want to jump to? (1000) what do I need to add to 900?

Q How many thousands do I need to add?

Q What do I need to add now to get to 3450?

So how many people stay to the end of the match? 2583

MAIN   **SUPPORT**

1) Here is the problem: 3,450 people attend a football match. At half-time 867 people leave. How many people stay to the end of the match?

2) PT: What calculation do we need to do to work out the answer to this problem? Establish that the calculation is a subtraction problem.

3) Write number sentence. (Red group – write all 4 number sentences) . PT Estimate the answer 3450 – 900 (2500.)

4) Use whiteboards, have a go at   <u>TIME 30 mins</u>
solving this problem – look for
any errors and misconceptions and annotate on planning, intervene if possible, if not make note to intervene tomorrow.

5) Select chn to show and explain method – 3 max. (Look at method e.g. number line or someone with an error or misconception, someone might have used a column method)

6) On whiteboards use a number line to solve this problem. Check. Show

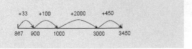

Remind the children that the jumps are to and from hundreds and thousands numbers as this helps

Explain that this can be set out using a column method. Work through the method and relate it to the jumps on the number line.

```
 3450
-  867
   33    to make 900
  100    to make 1000
 2000    to make 3000
  450    to make 3450
 2583    Answer is 2583.        Compare the answer with the estimate.
```

7) Go through again with this example if necessary:

Write on the board: 2340 – 758. Agree an estimate then work through the calculation. At each stage ask children for prompts

Set task Give the children subtractions, set out as practice and confident such as: 832 – 645; 2733 – 1609; 9876 – 543;

573 – 67. Must make an estimate first. Using AFL from point 4) allocate chn practice or confident questions

PLENARY   **KEY QUESTIONS**

Do another one together.

Look at your partner's book and look at the Success Criteria

Have they achieved M S C? If there are errors can they see where they have gone wrong? what target should they work on next?

(SATS Question if time available)   <u>TIME 10 mins</u>

Secondary 16

Secondary school science teacher

Turves Green Girls' School and Technology College, Birmingham

Carl Smith

Q. What made you decide to become a teacher?

Carl – I had gained a degree in chemistry at the age of 26. Six years later and the company that had sponsored me through college had no idea what to do with me. I had left the lab and was working as a foreman on the shop-floor and going nowhere. I had always thought that I could be a teacher since I first left school and spent four years working in a teacher training college as a lab tech.

Q. And how long have you been teaching now?

Carl – To date I have 16 years in the job.

Q. Tell me about how you qualified. What was teacher training like when you first came into the profession?

Carl – My degree was with the Royal Society of Chemistry (GRSC Pts I and II). At 32 I gained a place on the PGCE course at the University of Birmingham. The PGCE course had a good structure and was well presented by the science lecturers. Teaching practice was three weeks in the first term and 12 weeks after Christmas. On the down side was the EPS (education and professional studies) lectures. These were on the whole extremely boring, delivered by a bunch of out-of-touch academics who it seemed had not been inside a school for years. In many cases they just seemed to want to deliver their brand of political dogma, which, to me, bore no resemblance to the real world (the 21 and 22 year olds on the course lapped it up). This does not seem to be the case now and the PGCE students we have in our school seem much better prepared for the experience than we were.

Q. What would you say is the best way for trainees to learn how to teach?

Carl – The best training is to watch, assist and follow on from experienced teachers in real classrooms. Talk to them in the staff room and listen to what they have to say. This also applies to the first years in the job, and still applies for me today. Sadly we still sometimes get training videos where actors/teachers perform in front of 'Stepford Wives' type classes where the teacher raises an eyebrow and a pupil is immediately subjugated – good for a laugh at least!

Q. I understand that you now mentor the trainees at your school?

Carl – That's right. I'm a student mentor for my department and have had responsibility for several PGCE science students, of whom all bar one have become successful teachers in their own right. Teacher training students at my school are fortunate in being able to observe many fine practitioners in science and all other areas of the curriculum. One of 'my' students is now my boss, having taken on the role of 2nd in science when I stepped down.

Q. Could you tell me a bit about your first teaching job?

Carl – My initial post was at Lordswood Boys' School in Birmingham, where I stayed for five years. There I taught a mixed science, maths and games timetable. I was fortunate to work alongside a group of very strong teachers who taught me a lot. When I first started teaching I was really keen. I took on several unpaid responsibilities at my first school with the intention that the experience would stand me in good stead when I sought paid promotions. My only 'promotion' at my first school was as a temporary Year Head covering a term's medical leave. It was a Year 7 first term (September to Christmas) and included an Ofsted inspection!

Q. And where did you go next?

Carl – The experience I gained at Lordswood enabled me to apply successfully for the post of second in science at Turves Green Girls' School and Technology College, Birmingham. I'm still there 11 years later, teaching science at KS3 and KS4.

Q. You've stayed at the same school for a long time. How does that affect you and the way that the students (and staff) perceive you?

Carl – Well, given my age, the students think I have been there forever especially if I taught an elder sister before them. Actually on our staff 11 years still rates me as a relative newcomer given that we have quite a few teachers with over 20 years at the school, and a couple with 30 years in! It is that sort of school, no one wants to leave! However, younger colleagues do seem to regard me as an 'old hand'. Just recently one colleague told me that I reminded her of her dad! After the initial shock I realized that she is younger than my eldest child.

Q. What kind of developments have you been involved in since you've been at Turves Green? How has your job changed?

Carl – I introduced a bespoke KS3 science curriculum in my first year. Subsequent changes to the National Curriculum and then the introduction of the Science Strategy has seen that course change several times. Each time I have been involved in coordinating the changes within the department.

For two years I had extra responsibility in the department as the head of science went onto a part-time timetable leaving me in charge for half of the week. Last year I gave up my responsibility in the department and took up the dual roles of health and safety and trips coordinator. Under the new TLR arrangements this is now called 'environment and enrichment' coordinator!

The constant changes to the curriculum have meant a lot of time spent on courses to enable us to get to grips with the change. My new role with H&S means even more time out of the classroom trying to keep ahead of all the latest legislation. In addition I am responsible for the care and maintenance of the school minibuses and the coordination of driver training and certification. I am also one of the school's designated first aiders.

Q. What kind of CPD opportunities have you been offered during your career?

Carl – Over the years I've taken part in loads of CPD. Usually this is as a result of changes and initiatives coming from above. However, in 2005 I was fortunate to be given a chance to take part in a 'once in a lifetime' piece of CPD. The consortium of schools to which Turves Green belongs had established a link with a group of High Schools in Chicago, USA. I was chosen to visit these schools along with a group of colleagues. While I was there I was able to compare and contrast the two different education systems. They certainly do things differently over there. In particular was the high level of funding and resources that their schools have compared with ours. In 2006 the Americans came to visit us. Like we had been, they were blown away by our schools and could not get over how professional British teachers are. Some of the comments they made about our system really gave us a glow inside.

Q. And what are your plans and hopes for the future?

Carl – I have reached the stage in my career where I am pretty satisfied with what I have. I have enough responsibility and am not seeking more. My family is older now and so I am looking forward to using up some of those long school holidays travelling with my wife.

Q. What about the pastoral side of the job? Have you been a form tutor? What year groups have you worked with?

Carl – Up until the academic year 2005/6, I was always a lower school form tutor. However, I felt that I had built up such a good relationship with my Year 9 form that I requested to take them through to upper school. My wish was granted and so I am now the proud form tutor of a great bunch of young women. This could be quite daunting except that having been their tutor for the previous two years means I know them very well (and they know me).

Q. It sounds like you really enjoy this part of your work. What's the best thing about being a form tutor? How do you view your role?

Carl – There are a lot of good things about the job of form tutor: day-to-day interaction with the group, acting as an 'uncle' to one or two when trying to help with the many problems that modern pupils bring into school. I think of the role as being a mentor for the form and on occasions being their advocate. Obviously there are times when you need to be firm and 'heavy' but thankfully with my current form these have been rare. Attendance has improved at school in the last three or four years and my form in particular has an excellent attendance record. Because I know them so well now I can usually get to the bottom of any problems quite quickly.

Q. How about monitoring the progress of the students in your form group? How do you go about that at Turves Green?

Carl – The school instigated a 'target-setting' process in 2000 that entails the form tutor interviewing each of the form for fifteen minutes to discuss their progress and set some targets. The first interview takes place around October and the parents are invited into school (about 50 per cent come in). The second meeting takes place around April when targets can be reviewed and reset.

At first it seemed a little naff but having now done it for a few years we have become much smarter in using the process to encourage the students. As a form tutor the process seems worthwhile. You get the chance to sit down with each pupil in a quiet classroom on comfy chairs with soft music playing. You can discuss how they are finding school and find ways to praise and encourage them.

Frequently pupils will talk about or raise issues that they would not raise in the normal run of the school day. These interviews take a whole day (you usually get to see about 20 pupils in a day). Those students with SEN are usually seen by the SENCo and the 'Naughties' by a year head or SMT.

Q. Any exciting or unusual activities that you've done with a tutor group? Anything that sticks in your mind?

Carl – When I was a lower school form tutor we held a mock election at the end of Year 9 as part of our citizenship week. This was a great day when everyone in the form would get involved planning and carrying out an election campaign in an attempt to get our 'candidate' elected by the rest of the school. Everyone has a great time and you get to see the students in your form exhibit skills you didn't know they had.

Q. Tell me about the way that you plan.

Carl – When I first started teaching planning took up a huge amount of time. Every lesson went into pages of notes. Experience has shown that such detail is not necessary for individual lessons. A good scheme of work with a well-planned route through a topic is a better way to plan. Familiarity with resources and the content of the course also reduces the amount of detailed planning required. Long-term planning is more about setting markers to be reached as a department and making sure everyone is heading in the same direction.

Q. Can I see an example of the planning documents you use in your department?

Carl – Sure. Here's a Year 8 SoW (see the end of this chapter). On the surface it looks pretty thin but really it's just a document that ties together a whole host of resources and ideas.

When the new QCA curriculum came out we sat down and looked at the 12 topics for each year. There was a certain amount of duplication in the topics and also, we thought, some bits of the topic seemed out of sequence. So we paired the topics up and planned a route through each pair. Different members of staff took responsibility for a pair of topics and produced the schemes of work using our resources. We decided to have at least one Sc1 opportunity in each pair of topics. We also take each teaching group through the six pairs of topics in a different order so that we don't have two groups trying to use the same resources at the same time. Each pair of topics was planned to last for between eight and ten lessons, with the last lesson put aside for the test and feedback.

Q. What kind of resources do you use to help you deliver the schemes?

Carl – First and foremost we bought 'Exploring Science', which together with a teacher pack matched to QCA came with a whole host of differentiated resources. It also had loads of numeracy, literacy and citizenship opportunities listed. It also had most of the H&S stuff required for the practicals. This meant that our planning could be kept to a minimum which is why the schemes of work sometimes just refer to a page in the teacher's guide. This page will detail practicals, worksheets and have ideas and advice. It also lists equipment required for all practicals which makes the life of the lab techs easier. All we have to ask for is (for example) page 241/242 experiments 1 and 3 for twelve groups. The lab tech can then refer to a copy of the teacher guide for everything that needs to be prepared.

We also purchased a series of the Badger Starters. These are very useful although we found that they often made better plenaries than starters! Either way they are just referred to in the SoW as 'Starter 38a,' etc. As the SoW are usually written by subject specialists we can include favourite practicals that may not be in Exploring Science.

Q. How do you plan for assessment of what happens in science lessons?

Carl – A colleague has produced an Excel spreadsheet for Exploring Science. Each teaching group has a page with all that year's topics listed. Test marks can be recorded directly into the spreadsheet for each pupil. The spreadsheet will level the mark, aggregate it and produce an average level for each pupil and an average level for the class. We can input the target levels for each pupil and the spreadsheet will compare their current level with the target and by using colour indicate whether they are on, above or below target. A series of hidden sections can store levels from previous years and future targets based on KS2 data. Sc1 levels can also be recorded and the spreadsheet will collect those data and record best levels. Finally the sheet will group and average levels for Sc1, 2, 3 and 4 to enable end of Key Stage assessment.

These records are kept in a shared area so all science teachers can access and input. This is especially useful in Year 9 where we rotate groups. The KS3 coordinator can then look at progress at any time without having to ask individual teachers for their mark books. Print-offs can be used at parents' evening and also for passing on to SMT when necessary.

Q. Tell me about your views on the science strategy.

Carl – We decided early on that QCA made more sense to us than the Science Strategy (a decision that got us a lot of flak from the Science advisors) so we planned for QCA first and used the Strategy as a bolt-on where we thought it was needed. We have not changed our view on this after four years of using QCA. We still feel that the Science Strategy is just a mishmash of trendy ideas produced by people trying to justify their own existence.

Q. What are your thoughts about lesson delivery? What kind of activities do you use, and how do you adapt these for different kinds of students?

Carl – As a science teacher I enjoy practical work best and try to incorporate it at every opportunity. With higher-ability students I tend to use longer, more involved practical work. With the lower-ability groups I find short practicals work best. With some groups it may be possible to get three or four different short practicals into a lesson, with a break in between to consolidate the learning. I currently teach a bottom-set Year 7 group. Over the year they have got though a phenomenal amount of practical work and they really enjoy it. They are so good that I have tried practicals with them that I would think twice about using with some older groups!

Q. What impact has ICT had on the way that you go about teaching?

Carl – ICT has an increasing use in my lessons. Last year I had a data projector installed which enabled me to use various multimedia packages and the internet. The recent installation of speakers to the system means that I can use sound more. With many classes I use the PC to play music during lessons, particularly when the class is working on practicals or on self-directed learning. I have recently mastered the skill of adding music to my PowerPoint presentations. I am now trying to put some pictures and animations to a set of really cheesy 1950s science songs that I have found, so I can use them as lesson starters.

Q. What kind of relationships do you have with your classes?

Carl – I prefer to use a fairly informal approach with my classes, although this isn't always possible. I try to use humour and I have a supply of corny jokes which I can recycle year on year. You always have kids who say 'I can't do science' so it is a real challenge to find ways to let them succeed and to feel that science is relevant for them.

Q. Any thoughts on student behaviour? How has that changed over the years? What can be done to improve things?

Carl – Behaviour has definitely changed over the years I have been teaching. Firstly the government's inclusion policies mean that there are more pupils with behavioural problems in mainstream schools. Secondly there is also a general deterioration in behaviour in the school population.

When we were over in the States we were amazed by how well-behaved and how much respect the American students had for their teachers. However, we felt that much of this was due to the lack of challenge in the lessons. Over here we put our pupils under far more pressure to achieve targets and I think that this constant application of stress has a detrimental effect on behaviour. Also, modern kids spend a lot of time in front of the PC or Xbox which must affect their attention span and boredom threshold. Many seem to expect to be entertained rather than educated.

Q. What kind of strategies do you use to manage behaviour in your classroom? Any useful tips for teachers new to the profession?

Carl – I well remember the 'Don't smile until Christmas' maxim from when I first started. While I would not take it that far, I do think that you need to be firm with any new class. Make sure they know who is in charge. As time then goes by you can relax a bit (especially once you have learned their names). At Turves Green we have a rigidly enforced seating plan for all lessons. This sets the scene for lessons and gets classes off to a serious start. It prevents (usually) disruptive pairings of pupils. I always keep a seat or two empty at the front when I do my seating plan so that, if necessary, I can move a pupil nearer to the front.

Q. What about support for you in your classroom? How has that changed since you first started teaching?

Carl – When I began my career there was virtually no classroom support staff. Nowadays they are legion within schools. This year I have been lucky to have the support of a teaching assistant with one of my Year 7 classes. The extra pair of eyes and hands is very useful and she can give that bit of extra targeted support that some pupils need but can miss out on if there is just the teacher in the room. I don't tend to plan for my classroom support. I would rather let her have a roving brief in the lesson and pitch in to help any student that she feels needs it.

Q. What's a normal day at school like for you?

Carl – I'm an early bird and tend to arrive at school for 7.30am. There are usually two other teachers already there and both are fellow scientists! I see this early start as a 'golden hour' when I can get a lot of preparation done. I can make sure that all my resources are in place ready for the day. (And I get a decent spot in the car park!)

Staff briefing begins at 8.40am and registration at 8.50am. I have 20 minutes with my form and then straight into my lessons. We currently have eight 35-minute periods per day. In science we always teach doubles, so on a full day that would be four lots of 70-minute lessons. Any non-contact lessons are usually spent on my other responsibilities – organizing trips and overcoming H&S problems.

Q. Are you good at taking your breaks? I know how hard it can be to make time for relaxation during the day.

Carl – Whenever possible I do take my breaks in the staff room and sit for a few minutes with a coffee. It is a chance to share experiences with colleagues, have a moan and enjoy a joke. I am fortunate to share the staff room with a fine bunch of people. As I teach standing up all the time it is often the only chance I get to sit down. Also as the NASUWT rep for the school it can often be the only chance I might get to talk with other members.

Q. And how often do you have to take work home with you?

Carl – Frequently! There is always marking to do in the evenings. There is of course some PPA time in the week but nowhere near enough to do everything. I also use the evenings to surf the net searching for resources and interacting online with fellow teachers.

Q. Any 'magical moments' for you in your teaching career? What have been the best things for you about the job?

Carl – There have been quite a few of these but one that still sticks in my mind took place at my previous school (a boy's comp). There was a pupil who had been in my tutor group for Years 10 and 11 and who had had a very chequered school career. He came back to see me two years after he'd left to tell me how he'd got a job as a motor mechanic (using a reference I had given him) and was now at college on day release, had been promoted and was really doing well. In Year 10 he had been very close to total exclusion and even prison.

I always enjoy bumping into former students and seeing how they are getting on. A couple of years back I was even greeted in the staff room by a supply teacher who remembered me as being his science teacher when he was at school. This of course made me feel like Methuselah and was a source of great hilarity for my colleagues! He was a science teacher though, which was a bonus.

Q. And any particularly bad moments?

Carl – I can't really think of one really bad moment, although there have been one or two close calls. Walking into a room in my first weeks at my first school and finding two Year 10 boys fighting, being urged on by the rest of the class. Instinctively I grabbed both boys by the hair and pulled them apart (fortunately I am six feet tall and at the time played rugby) and held them until they stopped swinging. I remember sitting down in a quiet corner afterwards and I couldn't keep a limb still. I doubt a teacher would get away with that strategy these days! I also still get frustrated sometimes by the low aspirations some students have despite many of them having great ability.

Q. What's the best thing about being a science teacher?

Carl – When a pupil says that he or she would love a career in science, or when a pupil stays behind to ask about possible careers in science. Then I feel that I have enthused them.

Q. And the worst or hardest thing?

Carl – Trying to relate what we do to the real-life experiences of the pupils is always a challenge. Then there are those pupils (thankfully few and far between) who completely refuse to cooperate in their own learning and disrupt the education of others.

Q. What about the constant changes that seem to happen in education? How do you feel about those?

Carl – One thing you can be certain of in education is change. Most of it happens without consulting the teachers and you just have to get on with it. It is very frustrating to be given a half-complete syllabus, spend a couple of years actually getting it to work, only to find it all thrown away and you have to start again. It is particularly galling when the people making the changes don't even consult with each other. You end up in the situation we have at KS3, where the QCA curriculum is not compatible with the Science Strategy, and you have to spend a lot of time and effort trying to get them to work together. Like most science teachers these days we have to teach biology, chemistry and physics to GCSE, but the chemistry content seems to be reduced significantly in the latest GCSE syllabus.

Q. What changes would you make if you were given the opportunity?

Carl – If I was given the chance to change things I think I would introduce a two-tier curriculum. We need a curriculum that would give those who are able at science the change to forge ahead, with a view to filling the skills gap that has opened. Alongside this there could be a general science education for those who would not be taking it further. Perhaps something similar to the old model of O level and CSE?

Q. How does your school report on student progress to parents?

Carl – The school has refined its reporting procedures of late. All our profiles and effort reports are now done on the school computer system. We can access this from home using an online link as well which makes things even easier. A colleague who is a real whizz at ICT (another scientist as well)! has designed the profiles so that the number of keystrokes is kept to a minimum. Parents' evenings occur once a year for each year group, so that means a maximum of five evenings per year. These last three hours if you have a full appointment list. Of course it is often the parents you most wish to see who are not on the list.

Q. What about formal tests for the students? How does that work?

Carl – Over the last few years we have streamlined our assessments procedures. At KS3 we test at the end of around two-thirds of the topics to give us sufficient data to inform teaching and progress. At KS4 we hold a coursework day in Year 10 and another in Year 11. The pupils come into school for the whole day and carry out a full investigation, write it up and hand it in. This reduces the stress for the students and for the staff. We are not yet certain how the new KS4 assessment arrangements will work and whether they will be an improvement on current practice.

Q. Could you tell me about the kind of extracurricular things you've been involved with? What benefits have you found from working with the students outside the classroom setting?

Carl – I've been involved in quite a lot of extracurricular activities over the years. In my first school it was usually sports. Although employed mostly as a scientist I did have some periods of sport in my timetable and this led to my coaching of a school rugby XV and in the summer one of the cricket XIs. I also organized the annual 'industry day' within the school with the Year 10 pupils.

Getting involved in sport is far harder for a male in a girls' school, although I have supported the regular PE staff with the occasional hockey game or athletics meeting. When I first moved to Turves Green I was one of only two staff qualified to drive the newly acquired minibus. This meant that I was frequently asked to assist on trips as a driver. Even though we now have over 20 staff qualified to drive the buses, I still get to go on some of these trips with other subjects.

I am also always involved in the annual school residential trip that used to take place at the end of Year 7 but which now takes place at the start of Year 8. We take groups of girls to an activity centre to take part in challenges such as canoeing, abseiling, orienteering and many other things. The girls really enjoy it and it is usually great fun for the staff too!

The pupils really get a lot out of trips like this; they learn to work as a team and to be self-reliant. The staff gets to see the pupils in new situations and they get to see the staff away from school in a new setting. One thing the male staff try to do on these residentials is to break the stereotype; we do the lion's share of the cooking and clearing. In spite of it being the twenty-first century, many pupils do not see males doing this sort of stuff at home!

This year I am planning to take my bottom-set Year 7 group to the Royal Show as a reward for all the hard work they have put in.

Q. Have you been involved in any of those dreaded Ofsted inspections during your career? How did you find them?

Carl – I've seen four Ofsted inspections over my career. The lead-up to them was always more stressful than the actual inspection. The last one we had was the most stressful, it actually felt that the team were deliberately creating the stress hoping that we would somehow collapse when they were in. However, we got through it and passed with flying colours.

Q. Any thoughts on all those government initiatives and strategies? How have they affected you as a teacher?

Carl – When I first started teaching I took these constant initiatives really seriously, trying to put them into practice every time. However, experience has taught me not to rush in anymore. It is far better to take a step back and look more carefully at each new change. For a start most of them are things that have been tried before and are just resurrected with a new name. Nowadays I try out the bits I think will work and adapt them to my lessons. I exercise my 'professional experience' with the rest and ignore it.

Q. Can you recommend any good resources for other teachers?

Carl – The internet has opened up a huge array of resources for teachers. One of the best places I have found for sharing ideas and experience has been the *Times Educational Supplement* website. They have an online staff room where thousands of teachers communicate and share ideas. Whenever I get stuck for an idea I can usually get some advice and pointers on there. In return I am happy to share my thoughts and ideas with anyone asking for help.

Q. Would you recommend a teaching career?

Carl – Yes. Despite all of the bad publicity surrounding schools, teaching is still a career I would recommend. I do think that a few years in between leaving university and starting teaching is a good idea, though.

Q. What could be done to improve teaching as a profession?

Carl – Getting away from the 'one size fits all' model that still permeates secondary education. Grasping the nettle and acknowledging that some students are more able than others and would benefit from a school where they can be 'hot housed'.

Q. Any top tips for other teachers? Anything you wish you'd known when you first started teaching?

Carl – I can't think of any one tip I could give a new teacher. You have to go though the early stages to get the experience which enables you to survive in the classroom. After a few years you realize the job is a marathon and not a sprint so you have to pace yourself.

Q. You sound remarkably uncynical for a teacher with 16 years in the job. Any tips for NQTs on staying positive?

Carl – As one of the 'old codgers' I probably am a bit cynical these days. However, my advice to NQTs is probably what you would hear from any experienced teacher. Never be afraid to ask for help or advice from your colleagues, remember that they were in the same situation once. Don't try and run before you can walk. This is especially relevant now I think. As more staff leave, go part-time or opt for quality of life over promotion, the temptation is to load more responsibility onto younger (keener?) staff. To an NQT starting on the bottom of the scale I can see that an extra £1K or so can be very tempting.

Develop a healthy cynicism when someone tells you the latest idea for your lessons. Try things out with classes you can trust, but don't worry if it doesn't work for you, everyone is different and you will develop your own style. Always think of the good pupils you have taught that day. Remember that some of them are a lot cleverer than you are and will go a lot further, thanks to you. Remember that almost every child that you have taught today has made some progress, acquired some extra knowledge or skill that they didn't have yesterday.

There will always be pupils who drive you nuts, but let it go, don't allow that 5 per cent to dominate your thought or conversations (this is really difficult). Keep a sense of humour at all times and never take anything too seriously. After all, even in your worst lesson nobody died!

Q. Finally, in your opinion, what makes someone a good teacher?

Carl – You have to like kids!

Lesson	Exploring Science reference	Aim	Starter(s)	Main	Plenary
1	8La	To explore sounds and establish they are vibrations	Entrance into room with music playing. Discussion on what is making the sound and how it gets to your ears (pre-knowledge).	Sound circus. Selection of objects to shake, hit and pluck. What is making the sound. How can you make the sound louder/softer? Demo of 'twanging ruler'. Introduction of *vibration* and also *pitch*. Tuning forks. Showing vibration when ends dipped in water or placed against hanging polystyrene ball. Can the class play a scale using the forks? Relationship between *frequency* (vocab) of vibrations and pitch of note.	'Starter' 91
2	8Lb and 8Ld	To explore relationship between frequency and pitch. To discover the hearing range of a human. To learn how the human ear works		Class demo. How low and high can you hear. Use signal generator to establish range. Link the circuit into the *oscilloscope* to view the shape and size of waves. Introduce *wavelength* and show how it alters with pitch. Also introduce *amplitude* and show how that alters with volume. Use the ear model and diagrams to explain how sound enters our heads and we can interpret what we are hearing.	'Starter' 92a Could be a traffic-light activity.
3	8Le	Using sounds	Starter 96a and 96b to recap last lesson.	Noise. Unwanted/annoying sounds. Have the signal generator set at about 3kHz and ask them to listen to some music or read out loud!	'Starter' 97
4 and 5	8Ka	Shadows. Light travels in straight lines	Starter. Blinds down, lights off and class illuminated by 3 or 4 12V bulbs or candles. Starter for second lesson, no. 78.	Prove that light travels in straight lines. Give every child two pieces of paper (1 sheet of A4 should make 8 pieces). Poke a small hole in the centre of both with a pencil then get them to look at the nearest light through one of the holes holding the paper at arm's length. Then get them to hold the second piece halfway between their eye and the first piece so the light passes through both holes. A demo could be set up using several cards with holes held in clamp stands. All holes need to be lined up to see a light placed at one end. Use the projector to produce shadows. Sc1 The effect distance between light source, object and screen has on the shadow. Teacher's guide page 227 Ex 2 has the details. This could go	Plenary 'starter' no. 79.

6	Mirrors and reflections	Give everyone a plane mirror or piece of plastic mirror card. Stand behind class and get them to look at you in their mirrors. Tell them the aims of the lesson. You could hold coloured objects in your hand and ask them which hand is it in. They should get the idea that images are reversed horizontally but not vertically	Pinhole cameras Teacher guide page 229 Ex 3. Comparison of pinhole camera with eye. Model eye available.	Plenary 'starter' 80
7	Reflections	Have OHP on screen with small coloured spot in centre. Use a plane mirror to reflect the spot into different pupils' eyes. Why can everyone see the spot when the mirror isn't there but only one can see it when the mirror is used?	Teacher guide page 230 Ex 1 Ray boxes and plane mirrors. Measure angles or use angle sheets. Guide a ray round a brick or book. Demo of periscope (toy one available) Total internal reflection demo using 90 degree prisms and semicircular blocks.	
8	Refraction. Dispersion	Glass block and the broken pencil.	Refraction demo or class prac. Disappearing coin (done on a large scale using something big like a lead block and a bucket). You should be able to get quite a few kids around the bucket stood back far enough not the see the block. Fill the bucket carefully and they can see the block. Using a prism to get a spectrum (demo or whole class). ROYGBIV and Newton's disc to recombine colours.	Plenary 'starter' no. 83a
9	Colours	Starter 89 to recap last lesson.	Use filter gels on OHP and hold objects in front of screen. Why does a white object look red/green/blue? Etc. Plenary 'starter' No 88 Use ICT package to get pupils to predict colours	
10	Tests			

Part Six
TEACHER'S TOOLKIT

Sample documents

17

Job hunting

Job application form

The following generic job application form is from the *Times Educational Supplement* jobs website (www.jobs.tes.co.uk). It shows you the type of form that an LEA will send you when you apply for a teaching post, and the information that you will need to have to hand.

Post Applied For:	
School/College/Service	
Closing date for appliciations:	

1. PERSONAL DETAILS (PLEASE USE BLOCK CAPITALS)

Surname	Preferred Title
First Name(s)	Date of Birth
Address	N.I. Number
	DfEE Number
	Date of qualification
Postcode	Country of qualification
Tel (home)	E-mail
Tel (work)	Fax

2. EDUCATION AND ACADEMIC QUALIFICATIONS

School/College/University	From	To	Subject. Qualifications. Grades. Honours
Secondary (post 16)			
Higher Education			
Further postgraduate qualifications including PGCE)			

3. PRESENT APPOINTMENT (OR MOST RECENT)

Post Held:

School/College Address:

Number on Roll:	Age Range

Date Appointed:

LEA/Employer:

Responsibility Points: (if applicable)

Present or Final Salary/CPS:

Notice required:

Consent to contact place of employment.

4. PREVIOUS TEACHING APPOINTMENTS (PLEASE START WITH MOST RECENT)

Title of post and name of school/college/other employer	Status f/t or p/t	Type of School/College and age range	N.O.R.	Period of Service From	To

5. PROFESSIONAL DEVELOPMENT (PLEASE GIVE DETAILS OF COURSES RELEVANT TO THIS APPLICATION AND INDICATE ANY AWARDS EARNED)

Course title	Provider	Duration	Dates	Awards (if any)

6. OTHER RELEVANT WORK EXPERIENCE (PLEASE START WITH MOST RECENT)

Nature of Occupation	Employer	Period of Service From To	

7. INTERESTS (BOTH PROFESSIONAL AND LEISURE)

8. IF THIS APPLICATION IS FOR A SCHOOL OF A PARTICULAR RELIGIOUS AFFILIATION PLEASE INDICATE BELOW IF YOU ARE OF THAT AFFILIATION

9. LETTER OF APPLICATION

In support of your application, you are recommended to attach a statement giving your reasons for applying for this post. Include any information which you consider relevant to this application, addressing the key areas in the person specification.

10a) DECLARATION BY APPLICANT

As this post is classified as having substantial access to children, appointment will be subject to a police check of previous criminal convictions. You are required, before appointment, to disclose any conviction, caution or binding over including 'spent convictions' under the Rehabilitation of Offenders Act 1974 (Exemptions) Order 1975.
Disclosure will only be required following interview if it is considered that you are the most suitable candidate for the post.

10b)

I appreciate that I must declare any close relationship with a member of the school's Governing Body, or with a member or senior official of the local education authority which has responsibility for the school. I understand that failure to disclose such a relationship may result in my disqualification.

10c)

I declare that the information I have given on this form is correct and I understand that failure to complete the form fully and accurately could result in an incorrect assessment of salary, and/or exclusion from shortlisting, or may, in the event of employment, result in disciplinary action or dismissal.

Signature: Date:

11. REFERENCES

N.B. References will only be sought for shortlisted candidates.
May we approach your referees without further reference to you?

YES/NO

The first reference should be your present or most recent employer

(i)	(ii)
Name:	Name:
Position:	Position:
Address:	Address:
Telephone No:	Telephone No:
In what capacity do you know the above?	In what capacity do you know the above?

If you were known to either of your referees by another name, please give details:

12. EQUAL OPPORTUNITIES MONITORING

We aim to create the conditions in which all applicants and employees are treated solely on the basis of their merits, abilities and potential regardless of gender, colour, ethnic or national origin, age, socio-economic background, disability, religion, family circumstance, sexual orientation or other irrelevant distinction.

In order to carry out our equal opportunities policy, we must have some means of monitoring our recruitment and selection. Only by such measures will we be able to recognize potential sources of discrimination and take remedial action. The monitoring form will be separated from the application form and securely stored in the strictest confidence. It will be used for statistical monitoring only.

Please tick box as appropriate

Sex:	Female ☐ Male ☐	Marital Status: Married ☐ Single ☐	
Age:	Below 26 ☐ 26–35 ☐	46–55 ☐ 56–65 ☐	
How would you describe your ethnic origin?			
Black:	Caribbean ☐	African ☐	Other ☐
White:	European ☐	Other ☐	
Asian:	Indian ☐	Pakistani ☐	Bangladeshi ☐
Chinese: ☐		Other: ☐	Please specify:
Do you have any disability as described within the terms of the Disability Discrimination Act 1995	Yes ☐ No ☐		

Applying for jobs by letter

Two examples of letters of application are given below. The first is for a trainee applying for a first teaching post; the second is for an experienced teacher applying for promotion. For each of these examples, I have included a fictitious job description, to show how an application letter can be adapted to match a particular post.

Job description – NQT post

> ### Stanley Hill Primary School
> **Key Stage 2 Teacher**
>
> Stanley Hill is an inner-city school with a multicultural population. We are looking for a dedicated, enthusiastic teacher to teach Year 5. The successful applicant will be somebody who enjoys a challenge. Applications are particularly welcome from NQTs. We are hoping to appoint someone with a special interest in ICT.

Letter of application

Post: **Stanley Hill Primary School, Key Stage 2 Teacher**

Name: **Sally Jones**

I would describe myself as an enthusiastic, dedicated and caring teacher. I enjoy hard work and I am keen to build on my initial teacher training in an environment which offers a challenge. I feel that these qualities, and the experiences described below, mean that I am well suited to the post of Key Stage 2 teacher at Stanley Hill School.

My first teaching practice at Aldridge Primary School offered a supportive environment in which to begin my training. I worked with a Year 4 class, alongside the class teacher. I developed my lesson planning and classroom management skills, with a particular focus on differentiating for pupils with different learning needs. I learned a great deal about working with a mixed-ability class from my supervisory teacher. I also created a series of differentiated worksheets for developing literacy skills, in line with the National Literacy Strategy.

In my second placement at Keygate Infant School, I taught a Year 3 class, and I very much enjoyed working with this age group. My supervisory teacher was the ICT subject coordinator, and I had the chance to learn about planning for ICT across the curriculum. In addition to teaching the whole class, I also worked with a targeted group of children on developing literacy skills. I tested the new Liter-8 software program with this group, analysing the progress made by the children, and advising the school on whether to purchase a site licence for this program.

My third placement was at Findlay Primary and Junior School, where I had full responsibility for a Year 6 class. I consolidated my classroom and behaviour management skills, and worked closely with several children who had social, emotional and behaviour difficulties. I learned to use a range of teaching and learning strategies to help them access the curriculum. During this placement, I experimented with the use of digital cameras and video in the classroom, uploading some of the children's work to the school website.

My previous experience of working in an office has allowed me to make effective use of ICT in my teaching. I find that being able to use shorthand and to touch-type at 50 words a minute is very helpful in my teaching, particularly in keeping accurate records and in writing reports.

During my time at university, I took a particular interest in ICT, helping to write and maintain a new website for the education department. For one of my coursework units I developed a database to help analyse children's progress in numeracy.

I feel that the experiences outlined above mean that I am well suited to the post of Key Stage 2 teacher at Stanley Hill Primary School. I would welcome the opportunity to demonstrate my aptitude for the post at interview.

Job description – experienced teacher

Barr Wood Secondary School

Head of Faculty: Performing Arts

Barr Wood is an oversubscribed school with beacon status. We are looking for a manager with organizational skills, flair and leadership ability to develop the faculty further. Barr Wood has a long history of successful school productions, and we are looking for a candidate who could continue and build on this tradition.

Letter of application

Post: Head of Faculty: Performing Arts

Name: Ben Sampson

After two years in my present post as second in faculty at Newtown School, I believe I have the experience needed to make the move into a Head of Faculty role. I very much enjoy my current position: I take full responsibility for planning the delivery of drama at Key Stages 3 and 4, and I manage the work of two other drama teachers. I am also in charge of producing and directing the annual school production. I would describe myself as an enthusiastic, imaginative, hard-working and committed teacher. As second in faculty I have developed my leadership abilities and have also made some innovative changes to the curriculum we deliver. I am also an efficient and well-organized administrator.

My first teaching post at Camley School offered an exciting environment in which to consolidate and build on my training. I taught in the drama and music departments, in all years from 7 to 13. I developed the ability to cater for students with a wide range of learning needs, in mixed-ability classes. I also learnt a great deal about balanced lesson planning from my Head of Department, as we worked together to develop the departmental schemes of work.

I very much enjoyed taking my first GCSE drama group through to their examination. The students achieved excellent results (96 per cent A–C grades) and it gave me great pleasure to see all my students develop and learn through participating in the performing arts. While at Camley I was involved with three school productions. In my NQT year I worked as assistant director on *West Side Story*. In the two subsequent years I took full responsibility for directing *Little Shop of Horrors* and *Romeo and Juliet*.

In my current teaching post, my work as second in faculty has given me the chance to learn about managing staff, as well as developing a performing arts curriculum. I teach drama and music in Key Stage 3, and Expressive Arts at GCSE and A level. I also work as an induction tutor for NQTs, a role that I find particularly rewarding.

While at Newtown School, I have developed a partnership with the local theatre, Bromwich Arts Centre, creating a 'links' programme between the students at our school and professional actors and musicians. I have also maintained the school tradition of two annual drama productions: one a play, the other a musical. I have worked closely with teachers from art, music and dance departments, developing strong cross-curricular input in our school productions.

I do hope you feel, as I do, that I have the requisite experience and skills for the post of Head of Performing Arts at Barr Wood School. I would very much welcome the chance to demonstrate my suitability for the post at interview.

Teaching

Lesson plans

There really is no right or wrong way of going about planning: only you can know what is going to work for you. The sample lesson plans below give two possible formats for a teacher to use when planning his or her lessons: one brief, the other detailed. For each example I give a blank format then a sample of how a lesson plan might be written within this format.

A teacher with previous experience of working with the topics shown below would probably find sufficient detail to run the lesson in the brief plans. These are the type of plans that you might note down quickly in your teacher's planner. The more detailed versions give the less confident teacher, or the trainee, a great deal of additional information to use in preparing, presenting and assessing how well the lesson worked. These plans would be more appropriate for observed lessons or evaluated lessons, or for an Ofsted inspection.

Brief lesson plan (blank)

Topic/Class	
Objectives	
Activities	1.
	2.
	3.
	4.

Brief lesson plan (sample)

Topic/Class	*Twelfth Night* – Theme of love – Year 9 SATs
Objectives	Learning about themes Focus on specific theme (exam prep.) Develop/assess speaking and listening skills
Activities	1. Brainstorm types of love – discussion work in pairs. (Passion, friendship, male/female, family, self, forbidden.)
	2. Whole class share ideas on board.
	3. Pairs – choose one type of love, find examples and quotes from play. Make notes in exercise books.
	4. Oral presentations to class, others take notes.
	(Homework: write up notes into full paragraphs as though for essay.)

Detailed lesson plan

Subject	Lesson Topic	
Class	Date	
Objectives	NLS/NNS	
SEN	Differentiation	
Task	Timing	Equipment
1.		
2.		
3.		
4.		
Assessment	Homework/ Extension task	

Detailed lesson plan (sample)

Subject	Science	Lesson Topic	Sinking and Floating
Class	Year 1, mixed ability	Date	12 October 2006
Objectives	- Learning what sinks/floats and why - Predicting outcome of experiment - Discussing reasoning behind prediction - Testing hypothesis - Developing class discussion skills	NLS/NNS	Key terms – sink/float
SEN	Yellow Group – Jamie, Sam and Candice: weak literacy skills	Differentiation	Differentiated worksheet Tracing activity for Yellow Group
Task		Timing	Equipment
1.	Discuss words 'sink' and 'float' – what do they mean? Write on board.	5 mins	Board, marker.
2.	Show range of materials – predict whether they will float or sink and discuss why	10 mins	Materials: wood, plastic, metal, polystyrene, stone, paper, sponge.
3.	Volunteers to come to tank and try each material. Discuss prediction and results. Were we right? If wrong, why?	15 mins	Materials, tank filled with water.
4.	Complete differentiated worksheet about experiment. Work individually/in pairs.	20 mins	Differentiated worksheets.
Assessment	Mark worksheet – check understanding of task/activities.	Homework/ Extension task	Find 3 more materials to try (from classroom or at home).

Schemes of work

The medium-term plan below provides a very useful outline for a primary school scheme of work. I would like to thank Bentinck Primary School, Nottingham, for agreeing to share this document. (Please note that the format is the copyright of the school.) In the secondary school, the content of medium-term plans will depend a great deal on the subject being taught.

© Bentinck Primary & Nursery School

Unit title: Class: Term: Teacher:

Learning Objectives	Main Activity — Differentiation – EMTAG – Assessment			Resources	Vocabulary
	Introduction	Main Activity	Plenary		

Lesson 1 Lesson 2 Lesson 3 Lesson 4 Lesson 5 Lesson 6

Marking work

There is no one right or definitive way of marking work: much will depend on the individual needs and ideas of the child, class, subject and teacher. The examples below show you how different pieces of writing could be marked. You can find more information about marking, and an explanation of the different marking styles in the section on marking in Chapter 7 (pp. 133–6).

'Close' marking

> Jamie whent to the park with his freind Ben
> they play on the slide and they play in the
> sand. Ben fell of the slide and hurt his
> nee Jamie whent to get help. It was geting
> dark and Jamie was frightend.

> Jamie whent to the park with his freind Ben
> They play on the slide and they play in the
> sand. Ben fell off the slide and hurt his
> knee Jamie whent to get help. It was geting
> dark and Jamie was frightend.

Well done, you have tried very hard to improve your punctuation. Now take care to stick to the same tense throughout and check your spelling in the dictionary.

Marking for specific errors

Note: in this example the teacher has set the marking focus as layout and punctuation.

> What do plants need to grow
>
> in our expriment we looked at what
> plants need to grow properley we
> found that they need water and light
> we did our expriment by puting some
> seeds on a peace of bloting paper
> then we gave one lot of seeds no
> water or light, the next lot just
> water and the last lot water and
> light.

What do plants need to grow?

<u>In</u> our expriment we looked at what plants need to grow properley<u>.</u> <u>We</u> found that they need water and light<u>.</u>

We did our expriment by<u>:</u>
1<u>.</u> <u>P</u>uting some seeds on a peace of bloting paper<u>.</u>
2<u>.</u> <u>G</u>iving one lot of seeds no water or light<u>.</u>
3<u>.</u> <u>G</u>iving the next lot just water<u>.</u>
4<u>.</u> <u>G</u>iving the last lot water and light.

You include all the right information, but remember to take care with the way you lay out your work, as we discussed. Experiments should be written as a series of points (see my corrections above).

Teacher's mark book

The sample mark book page below shows how a teacher might use his or her mark book to record a range of information about the students in a class. In the sample shown, the teacher records a number of different pieces of data about the children.

- *Column 1*: Surname.
- *Column 2*: First name.
- *Column 3*: Students who were present '/' or absent 'O' on 09.09.06.
- *Column 4*: A list of textbooks issued, which gives the number noted in each book. In this way, the teacher has a record of which child was given which book, for when they are collected back in. If a book is vandalized, or missing, the teacher can pinpoint which child is responsible.
- *Column 5*: Register of present/absent on 10.09.06.
- *Column 6*: Effort and attainment grades for the homework set on that date. See the 'Teachers' notes' for details of what these effort and attainment grades mean. (Note: because the teacher has placed the homework column beside the present/absent column, she knows which students were absent on that day, and consequently who would not have done the homework.)

- *Column 7*: Register of present/absent on 12.09.06.
- *Column 8*: Register of present/absent on 16.09.06.
- *Column 9*: Effort and attainment grades for the homework set on that date

ST PATRICK'S 2002 – MARK BOOK FOR CLASS E10 (SAMPLE PAGE)

		Register	Texts Issued	Register	HOMEWORK 1	Register	Register	HOMEWORK 2
SURNAME	FIRST NAME	09.09.06	No. in book	10.09.06	Effort/ Attainment	12.09.06 x	16.09.06	Effort/ Attainment
Baggio	Andrea	/	N1	/	B/5	/	/	B/4
Bayer	Frans	/	N2	O	O	/	/	C/3
Benson	Sally	/	N3	/	C/3	/	/	B/3
Davies	Jennifer	/	N4	/	A/2	/	/	A/2
Du Morier	Nicole	/	N5	/	D/3	O	/	C/3
Gomez	Maria	/	N6	O	O	/	/	A/3
Jones	Owen	/	N7	/	B/4	/	/	B/3
Mckay	Angus	/	N8	/	A/1	/	O	O
Singh	Amjan	/	N9	/	A/2	/	/	A/1
Smith	Bob	/	N10	/	A/3	/	O	O

Teachers' Notes

Effort grades:	Attainment grades:
A – Excellent	1 – High
B – Good	2 – Above average
C – Average	3 – Average for class
D – Below average	4 – Below average
E – Poor	5 – Low

18 Checklists

The '10 tip' checklists in this chapter are designed to give you 'at a glance' advice for when you're in need of a quick boost. They include practical, realistic and honest ideas for dealing with the trickiest aspects of the job. Turn to them for some tips when you need them, for inspiration when things are going wrong, or for support when your children simply won't do as they're told.

10 tips for surviving your first year in teaching

1 If at all possible, find yourself a job at a decent school, where NQTs are well supported and helped to develop. There are some schools out there (thankfully rare) that view NQTs as a 'cheap option'. Ask about support for NQTs at your interview, and make sure your school lives up to its obligations (after all, they're getting extra money to support you).

2 Don't make an enemy of your induction tutor or mentor. Regardless of whether you like this person or not, he or she is the one who will be responsible for helping you pass or fail that vital first year in teaching.

3 Know about your rights and responsibilities are as an NQT, particularly as concerns your induction. Read the induction guidelines, or look closely at Chapter 5 of this book.

4 Don't take on too much. No matter how tempting it is to direct the school play, run a football team and sit on three or four different working parties, you are far better off dedicating yourself to becoming the best teacher you can be, and to passing your induction year.

5 Ask for help when you need it. Teachers are, on the whole, superb at supporting each other. We've all been there, through the ups and downs of our own first year in teaching. Turn to your colleagues for advice and support – don't keep your problems to yourself.

6 Take a break when you need it, and don't allow yourself to be consumed by guilt when you do. A few sessions in the computer room, or a couple of lessons watching a video, can be educational for the students and restful for you. Taking a break also means making a real effort to get to the staff room during break and lunchtime.

7 If you're too sick to work properly, don't come into school and spread your germs around. Many people find that they pick up every bug going in their first year of teaching. This is probably due to a combination of tiredness and stress, plus the fact that schools are great places for germs to breed. Don't feel guilty about taking time off when you're ill.

8 Be careful where you sit in the staff room. Teachers are notoriously territorial, and you don't want to sit in the chair that has been Mr Smith's for the last ten years. The same applies to mugs – bring in one or two of your own and never, ever leave someone else's mug unwashed.

9 Strike a balance between your enthusiasm and a realistic workload. Have at least one night a week when you don't take any marking home. Try to take one full day off from work at the weekend.

10 And finally, the 'old chestnut'. Start out as strict as you can – you can always relax with your children later on, but you can never get them back once you've lost them (at least until next year, that is). You might be advised not to smile until after the Christmas holidays. I disagree – you can smile and still be strict.

10 tips for better behaviour

1 Make it your number one aim to never, ever talk to a class until every child is sitting in silence, eyes focused on you and ready to listen. It's nerve-racking at first, but once you've set and achieved this expectation, your life will be 100 per cent easier.

2 Set the boundaries for your children right from the start. Let them know what you expect from them, and what will happen if they don't comply. Your school will have a set of 'official' boundaries (i.e. the school rules), but there will also be 'unofficial' boundaries – expectations that you as a teacher have of how your students will behave. Try to find time to have a chat with an experienced teacher about some suitable boundaries before you meet your students for the first time.

3 Keep your voice calm and quiet as far as is humanly possible, and avoid shouting at all costs. Shouting demonstrates a loss of control, it has a tendency to escalate problems and can sometimes lead to serious confrontations. Shouting can also be very damaging for your voice.

4 Perfect the 'deadly stare' and other forms of non-verbal communication. These can be wonderfully effective, and are far less stressful and tiring than using your voice all the time. When you become very skilled at non-verbal communication, you may find that a raised eyebrow is enough to silence a whole class.

5 Find out what sanctions the children want to avoid and use these when necessary. However, don't forget that rewards are usually far more effective than punishments. A positive atmosphere, in which you focus on those children who are behaving, is much more beneficial than a negative focus on constant punishment.

6 Look for what's going right, rather than what's going wrong. Praise a child who's working well, rather than punishing one who's being silly. Along the same lines, focus on what you're doing right in the classroom, rather than beating yourself up about what isn't working yet.

7 Talk to your children as you would speak to any adult. Try not to use phrases like 'don't be so stupid', or 'shut up'. On the other hand, do accept that you are human and that these things may slip out of your mouth on occasions.

8 When a lesson or activity isn't working, and the students are mucking around, put yourself in your children's shoes and think about how they might be feeling. Sometimes school can be boring, no matter how good the teacher is.

9 Ask your colleagues (particularly the SEN staff) for help when dealing with very difficult individuals. They may have some excellent tips and advice that could save you a lot of heartache.

10 Don't bottle up your feelings. Find a sympathetic shoulder to cry on or a friend to rant at, preferably in the privacy of the staff room. There's nothing shameful about getting upset or irritated when a child has been abusive towards you, but try not to let your students see you becoming emotional.

10 tips for dealing with marking

1 No matter how tempting it is to have your class sitting in silence for an hour doing a test, don't set too many of them – they take ages to mark!

2 Get your students to help out with marking each other's work whenever possible. They love 'playing teacher', and it can be very educational for them to see the standard that others in the class are achieving.

3 Target your marking – mark for a specific skill, such as good spelling or imaginative ideas, rather than trying to close-mark all the time.

4   Don't make promises you can't keep. It will damage your reputation if you say you will mark a set of books or a piece of work, then have to explain to your class that you just couldn't do it in time.

5   Marking expands to fill the time you allow for it. Don't give up every evening of the week to marking – you're entitled to a life outside of school.

6   Do try to avoid spilling coffee on that beautiful set of projects that your Year 5 children spent weeks completing.

7   Set some pieces of homework which don't involve any writing, and consequently need no marking. For instance, researching a topic, memorizing a passage, learning times tables and so on.

8   Mark exercise books regularly, rather than letting the work build up. Don't forget that parents and Ofsted inspectors will be looking through the books to make judgements about your effectiveness as a teacher.

9   Keep a record of the marks you give – exercise books are easily lost, and this excuse is very convenient for a student with poor grades.

10   Prioritize your marking load – GCSE coursework wins over Year 7 exercise books every time.

10 tips for getting on with your colleagues

1   Gossip is rife in some schools. Try not to gossip about other teachers, but if you do feel the urge, make sure that the person you're talking to will keep their mouth shut afterwards. Ensure, too, that you're not gossiping about somebody to his or her best friend.

2   If you borrow somebody else's equipment, lesson plans or room, make sure you return them in their original condition. Say 'thank you' afterwards, and offer your own services in return. That way, you will build up a network of support and help.

3   Be generous: offer your own resources to others (but keep a copy or a record and make sure that you get them back eventually).

4   Don't photocopy large quantities of worksheets either before school or during break time. The large queue of people forming behind you will not be happy. If someone else is waiting to use the photocopier, offer them the chance to jump in, as long as they only have a few copies to make. This will gain you many Brownie points.

5   Never ask pointless questions in meetings. It's a guaranteed way to make the meeting go on longer than necessary, and will not make you popular.

6   Don't plan noisy lessons when:
   • the person next door to you is setting a test

- you are going to be observed
- the head is doing his/her rounds
- you're in the middle of an Ofsted inspection

7 Always, always check the cover list. Not turning up to cover a class or lesson is a fast and efficient way to make enemies and get a bad reputation.

8 Always, always hand in your reports on time. Not doing so causes problems right along the chain of command, especially in a secondary school where a long line of people may have to read and approve them.

9 Don't leave unwashed coffee mugs in the staff room, then claim that you are conducting an important experiment on growing mould.

10. And finally … make a special effort to get on with the non-teaching staff at your school. Remember, the headteacher's secretary is one of the most powerful (and knowledgeable) people in the school. The caretaker, office staff, librarians, catering staff can all make your life a hell of a lot easier, or an awful lot harder.

10 tips for getting on with your students

1 Show that you're a human being with a decent sense of humour. Laugh at yourself if you do something stupid – better that they laugh with you than at you.

2 Make at least some of your lessons fun, exciting, imaginative or unusual. This may take a little more time in preparation, but it will help engage your class or classes and will gain you a reputation for being a good, 'fun' teacher.

3 Be in a good mood for as much of the time as is possible. There's surely nothing worse than having to face a moaning, miserable teacher every day of the week. Always try to focus on the positive, on what the children are doing right, rather than what they are doing wrong.

4 Don't shout unless you really can't help it, or you feel that it's essential. Nobody enjoys being shouted at, and it shows the children that you are a teacher who cannot control his or her emotional responses. Even if a fair few students are misbehaving, remember that the majority are probably not doing anything wrong, and do not deserve to be on the receiving end of your anger.

5 Don't say anything to your students that you would object to them saying to you. Never call a child 'stupid' or 'an idiot'. Many of your 'difficult' students are probably spoken to rudely at home; you should provide them with a different, and better, role model.

6 Despite its stress-alleviating results, try to avoid using sarcasm if at all possible. Many children will take you seriously, rather than understanding what you imagine to be your sparkling sense of humour.

7 Take time to listen to your children as individuals, and show an interest in them as people. Find out what they really enjoy and aim to incorporate it occasionally into your lesson planning. Taking time to get involved in extracurricular activities can be very helpful in getting to know your children properly outside the classroom environment.

8 Show your students that you want them to succeed, and that's why you make them work and behave as well as possible. Have the highest possible expectations of them, and express surprise if they don't achieve what they could.

9 Don't punish a whole class for the sins of one individual, either by giving out a whole-class punishment, such as a detention, or by shouting at a whole class of children because one student angers you.

10 Remember what it was like to be young, and bring some of that childlike quality to your teaching, your classroom and your lessons. When your children do 'muck around' try to put yourself in their shoes – school can be boring sometimes, no matter how wonderful the teacher.

10 tips for dealing with stress

1 Take your breaks, rather than working through the day without a rest. You'll be a much more effective teacher as a result, and it'll give you the chance to blow off steam with other adults.

2 Join in with some extracurricular activities. Although it's a drain on your time, it gives you a chance to have some fun, and to see a different side to your kids. This applies to school trips too – they can be very enjoyable, and the children will really respect you for showing them 'another side' of you as their teacher. The time spent will usually have a very positive impact in your classroom.

3 Don't take insults or abuse personally. No matter how hard it is, remember that a child who behaves in this way usually has serious problems. 99 per cent of the time the student's anger is not directed at you as a person, but is a result of issues from outside school.

4 Aim to take part in some form of physical or social activity after school hours to help you unwind. This could be playing in a teachers' football or netball team, or simply heading down the pub with your friends on a Friday evening.

5 Share your worries with other teachers – they are probably experiencing the same fears and stresses as you, or have done so in the past. There's

a lot of truth behind the old cliché: a problem shared is a problem halved.

6 Try to avoid talking about work all the time – it's vital that you learn to 'switch off' in the evenings. Remember that your husband/wife/partner/parents/friends may not be all that interested in how little Johnny misbehaved in your lesson that day. Switching off is probably even more vital if you live with another teacher.

7 If your school environment is conducive, and your commitments allow, stay behind after school to complete your marking, planning and paperwork. That way, when you leave school for the day you can leave 'work' behind.

8 When a child or class is stressing you out, learn to react from your head and not from your heart. This means respond intellectually, rather emotionally, and never let a bunch of naughty kids wind you up. They're not worth it – focus on the well-behaved ones instead.

9 Keep a sense of perspective, and learn to laugh at yourself when things do go wrong. A great quote to remember in times of tribulation: 'Even in your worst lesson, nobody died.'

10 If you're really at the end of your tether, go and see a doctor. Stress can be a genuine issue that requires medical treatment.

10 tips for successful lessons

1 Set out your aims or objectives at the start of the lesson. Like a group setting off on an expedition, your children need a 'map' of where they are headed, they need to know what the purpose of their journey is and what to expect while they are travelling.

2 Make at least some of your lessons really exciting and engaging. Bring in an unusual object to use as a starting point, or take a lateral approach to a boring topic. Remember, the more engaged your students, the better they'll behave and work.

3 Give your children the sense that you are energized by and interested in the tasks you are asking them to complete. The best teachers convey a sense of their love for the particular subject they are teaching.

4 Use short, focused tasks and reward your children for completing each one. Although this takes more energy from you as a teacher, you'll get a much better quality of work and behaviour from your class as a result.

5 Use a good mix of tasks, such as writing, reading, discussion, practical activities and group work. This will help your students retain their interest and focus, as well as developing a range of different skills.

6 Ensure that you have a good 'opening' to your lessons. When you invite your class into the room, give a sense of pace and energy about what is going to happen. Get them settled quickly, and ready to start with the appropriate equipment on their tables.

7 Similarly, make sure that the end of every lesson is well structured. Take time to look back on what has been achieved, and praise your children if they have worked well. Standing behind chairs is a wonderfully controlled way to finish a lesson or to end the school day. From this position you can hand out praise and reminders about homework, keep behind any troublemakers, and please the caretaker and cleaners by checking for litter.

8 Don't be afraid to make up the occasional lesson on the spot, for instance throwing out that carefully planned lesson in favour of exploring a topical issue raised by the children. Flexibility is the key to good teaching.

9 Use lessons and tasks that will stretch the most able, as well as giving the least able a chance to succeed. Set 'extension activities' to offer your gifted students a chance to shine.

10 Find out what really interests your children, whether it is a particular subject area, such as IT or art, or the latest craze. Try to incorporate this into at least some of the work that you ask your classes to do, and you'll gain a reputation as a fun and interesting teacher.

10 tips for dealing with paperwork

1 Deal with as much paperwork as you can the minute you receive it. If a form needs filling in, do it on the spot, rather than adding it to the towering pile on your desk.

2 Don't file a resource unless you're sure you'll use it again. The same applies to meaningless bits of paper that you're unlikely to reuse, such as meeting agendas.

3 When you file a piece of paper, make sure you know where it is so that you can access it again. Work out a reasonably organized filing system early on in the year, for instance dividing resources into different curriculum or topic areas, or by year groups.

4 There will be centrally kept copies of a lot of paperwork you receive. If someone else is likely to have a copy of a piece of paper, you can bin the one that you've been given to save space and effort.

5 Have a yearly 'chuck-out' session. Otherwise you'll end up with that exam syllabus from 1987 that you really, honestly don't need anymore.

6 With paperwork that you need to access daily, keep things in one place as far as possible. The teacher's planner is a wonderful way of organizing your school life. If these are not provided at your school, ask if you can order one for yourself and get your school or department to pay for it.

7 Don't leave copies of confidential material, such as SEN reports, lying around where children might be able to find them. As a professional, you have a responsibility for the confidentiality of your students.

8 Beware of the pile entitled 'to do'. When exactly are you going to 'do' it?

9 Prioritize your admin. If a piece of paperwork comes from the headteacher, deal with it swiftly.

10 Empty your pigeonhole on a daily, or at least weekly, basis. Otherwise it's sod's law that a crucial bit of paper will get crushed at the back, only to be discovered on the last day of term, when it simply has to be dealt with immediately.

10 tips for writing reports

1 Computerized reports make life much easier. If your school doesn't use a computer system, in most cases you will still be able to prepare and print out your reports using a word-processing program.

2 If you are typing your reports, and you have a lot of them to write, create a 'bank' of comments for poor, average and good students. You can then cut and paste these comments, adding a more individualized sentence to each one.

3 If you are printing out your reports, check them very carefully for errors first. That way you will save yourself from printing out 500 reports, each one with a spelling mistake.

4 Get your reports in on time. The names of the teachers who are always late with reports will be well known in your school. Don't add your name to the list.

5 Take care over the content and presentation of your reports: they are one of the main types of formal communication with the home. Make sure that you give parents or guardians a good impression of their child's teacher.

6 Be very wary of children with 'androgynous' names. It's incredibly embarrassing to send out a report in which you call a 'he' a 'she'! If there are any children whose names you're uncertain about, confirm their gender in the weeks leading up to report writing.

7 Avoid negative comments in your reports. Although it's important to give a realistic assessment of a child, phrase your comments so that they give positive ideas for improvement. For instance, instead of saying

'Jimmy never listens in class and doesn't follow my instructions', you could say 'Jimmy has trouble listening in class, and he needs to concentrate fully when he is being given instructions'.

8 Set some targets in your reports, and use these as a part of your daily teaching. For instance, you might set a target for behaviour, which you refer to when a child first arrives at your class each day. Alongside the target you could also set a reward that the child will earn for achieving it.

9 The parents' evening is a very good time to refer to reports, especially if they have been sent out recently. Talk through the targets you have set with the parents or guardians (and the child if he or she is there) and ask for support in ensuring these targets are met.

10 If possible, spend some time discussing the reports with the children after they've been handed out. It's important for reports to be an effective tool in improving learning, rather than simply gathering dust in a drawer somewhere.

10 tips for surviving parents' evening

[Note: the term 'parents' is used here to cover guardians of any kind. Be aware that some children will attend parents' evening with a foster carer, older brother or sister, etc.]

1 If at all possible, find time to take a break before the parents' evening starts. After a full day at school, you will not be at your best unless you spend some time refreshing yourself. Have something to eat to sustain you through the evening.

2 Wear your best suit or outfit. You are a professional and should put forward a professional appearance on such 'public' occasions.

3 Remember that the parents are likely to be as scared as you are, if not more so. Aim to make them feel relaxed and comfortable during your discussion. Despite all the damage that has been done to teachers' images over the years, we are still 'authority figures' of a kind.

4 If the child attends with the parents, focus the discussion on making the child aware of his or her strengths and weaknesses. A good question to ask when starting the discussion is 'How do you think you've been getting on this year?' Involve the child in setting areas for further improvement, and ask the parents to help the child stick to these targets.

5 Keep the discussion brief and focused, rather than feeling the need to waffle on endlessly. This is especially important if you have large numbers of parents to see. Keeping people waiting for ages suggests a

lack of professionalism. Plus, you really don't want to end up with a huge queue of parents still waiting to see you at the end of the evening, when everyone else is heading home.

6 Set some targets for areas where you want the child to improve, as well as discussing the present levels of attainment. You might link this to a discussion of the child's latest report.

7 You might like to have some work to show the parents, but don't focus your discussion simply on going through the marks that the student has achieved. It's far better to talk from your own impressions and knowledge of how the child is getting on.

8 If you get the chance to meet with the parents of a child who is badly behaved (often these are the parents who don't show up), then ask if you can contact them directly if the student continues to misbehave. This is a wonderful way of motivating a child to improve his or her behaviour.

9 A good way to end your discussion is to ask 'Do you have any questions?' This gives the parents a chance to raise any concerns or queries, and if they don't have any questions to ask, brings the discussion to a neat conclusion.

10 If you do encounter any parents who become abusive (and this is, thankfully, relatively rare), then direct them to your line manager rather than trying to deal with them yourself. You could also suggest a meeting at another time to sort out their concerns. Above all, refuse to descend to their level, remaining relentlessly calm, polite and professional.

10 tips for getting and dealing with promotion

1 If are you hoping to find a promoted post, show a willingness to do things that are outside of your actual job description. For instance, you might sit on a working party or take on some responsibility for co-ordinating a curriculum subject. Make sure, though, that you don't show too much willing – you do want paying for the extra work eventually.

2 Look at what Chris Pickering (headteacher) says in Part Three, Anatomy of a School (p. 179) about the type of teachers he would look to employ, and to promote.

3 Before you make that application for a promoted post, think carefully about the direction that you want your career in teaching to take. It is very tempting to take a promotion, especially if it means a salary increase, but do consider how far up the ladder you envisage yourself going first.

4 Consider your priorities and what you really enjoy about the job. Be aware that a move into the higher echelons of management will mean that you spend less time in the classroom, with the kids, and more time dealing with bits of paper.

5 Be aware that your relationship with your colleagues will change once you are promoted. You will be in a position where you must tell people what they should do. It can sometimes be difficult for others to adapt to seeing you in a new light.

6 Remember that the higher up you go, the more time you spend 'on the job'. A headteacher is always a headteacher, whether inside or outside of school, and will probably play a significant role within the local community.

7 Consider your professional development, and look at the type of training and further education you might need. In some schools, you may be given support to do a further qualification, such as an MA.

8 If you are interested in becoming a senior manager or headteacher, contact the National College for School Leadership (see the Directory for details).

9 Sometimes, a teacher looking for promotion will need to move schools in order to progress. Once you have a few years' experience, look carefully at the opportunities available in your present school, and consider whether you need to move on.

10 Not all promotions or career opportunities take place within the school environment. Consider your career from a wider perspective — you may wish to move into LEA inspection services, freelance writing or consultancy work, or other fields within education.

10 tips for surviving Ofsted

1 Try not to spend the time before Ofsted arrives getting worked up about what is going to happen. Don't believe all the scare stories that you will hear. You know already if you're an effective teacher, so focus on gaining something positive from the experience.

2 Don't take the whole process too seriously. An inspection can only ever provide a 'snapshot' of a school, and of you as a teacher. Have confidence in your own abilities within the classroom, and try not to allow a negative judgement of your work to get you down. You know the truth.

3 Think carefully about health and safety in your classroom. Look around with 'fresh' eyes and check carefully for any potential hazards. Consider what your children do with their bags and

equipment when they come into the classroom, and any safety implications this may have.

4 Get your lesson planning done in advance, so you don't have lots of last-minute stress. If your school has designed a format that will prove 'acceptable' to Ofsted, use this for your plans. Although it can feel irritating and contrived to plan in lots of detail when you don't normally do this, accept that this is all part of 'playing the game' of inspection.

5 Try to strike a balance in the lessons that you plan. Don't play it too safe, and end up boring your children to tears. On the other hand, this is probably not the time to try out that experimental and whacky new approach to learning.

6 Consider the needs of all the children in your class. Show that you are aware of those students who have SEN, and what their particular learning needs are. Think carefully about inclusion, equal opportunities and differentiation.

7 Don't expect the inspectors to turn up for a whole lesson (or even to turn up at all). With the new inspection format this will not necessarily happen. Accept that it is 'sod's law' that they will turn up in the really tricky part of your lesson, or when the children have just decided to riot.

8 Have a copy of your lesson plan to hand, and pass it to the inspector if he or she comes into the room. That way, you can demonstrate the overall structure of the lesson.

9 Make sure the students' exercise books are marked.

10 If you are observed, ask for some feedback afterwards. Get the inspector to discuss your lesson with you after the observation, and talk to your line manager if you have any concerns or questions.

10 tips for long-term survival in the profession

1 Find that crucial work/life balance early, and be ruthless with yourself about sticking to it. Don't let teaching become your whole world – you are entitled to a life of your own outside of school.

2 Make the most of your holidays. If it works for you, spend the first day or two of the holiday catching up on planning and paperwork, then leave school behind and go and relax.

3 Take advantage of every opportunity you are offered for a bit of time out of the classroom to relax and reflect. Book a training course for the time in the term when you know you are most likely to need a break.

4 Develop a good, solid support network and spend time maintaining your contacts. Other teachers are a particularly useful source of support, help and advice.

5 Focus on what is going well, rather than allowing the difficult students or tough times to drag you down. This is particularly important if you teach in a 'challenging' school.

6 Retain a belief in yourself as an effective teacher, even if a class riots or a lesson goes badly wrong. Don't allow the opinions of others, who don't really know you and your teaching, to cloud your judgement.

7 Take a 'lesson off' when it all gets too much. A session watching a video or taking the children into the ICT room can be just what is needed to give you a rest.

8 Remember, 'The caring stops at 5 o'clock'. Don't allow your children's problems to come home with you. No matter how difficult their lives are, you cannot change the world.

9 Keep a 'bank' of all those activities and lessons that have worked well for you in the past. Reuse and refine these over the years, so that your life becomes progressively easier.

10 Have fun whenever possible (both in and out of the classroom). Aim to retain the 'big kid' that lurks inside all teachers. Refuse to allow cynicism to creep in – remember that you *are* making a difference.

Part Seven
ICT

Part Seven

ICT and the teacher

This chapter deals with ways that you might use ICT to make your teaching more effective: the background work such as planning, preparation and assessment, and using computers and other technological equipment in the classroom. You'll find information here about the advantages of using computers, both for the teacher and for the student. You'll also get some 'top tips' for working with ICT, and learn about some of the potential hazards of ICT-based learning.

Using ICT

There are many different ways that teachers can use ICT at work. Here are just some ideas:

ICT for teachers

- Lesson and scheme planning.
- Undertaking research for lessons.
- Accessing a huge range of educational resources and different types of information on the internet.
- Creating differentiated worksheets.
- Keeping records of student grades.
- Keeping records of textbooks and other resources.
- Writing reports and other communications with the home.
- Communicating with students, teachers and schools via email.
- Using digital cameras and video to make lessons more engaging and to create impressive displays.
- Working with an interactive whiteboard in your classroom.
- Using a school or your own website to enhance your teaching.

ICT with students

- Creating paper-based materials, such as books, newspapers and magazines.

- Editing large pieces of text, for instance coursework assignments.
- Presenting work in a smart and adaptable format.
- Calculating data using spreadsheets.
- Storing and accessing information on a database.
- Researching and downloading information via the internet.
- Communicating globally via the internet and email.
- Adding photos and images to work.
- Creating web pages and sites.

The advantages of ICT

Using ICT is now such a natural part of the way that we teach, it is hard to believe that only twenty or so years ago there was little or no use of computers in the average classroom. ICT really does bring many advantages to the world of education: I've listed just a few of these below:

For the teacher

- The ability to create, edit, save and change worksheets, lesson plans and other computerized resources.
- The ease with which a single worksheet can be differentiated for children with different learning needs.
- The motivational qualities of resources that are well presented.
- The generally better behaviour and focus that children have when working on computers.
- The ability to keep, change and work with data and records, for instance of assessments.
- The opportunity to calculate scores and percentages with ease, using spreadsheets.
- The time-saving nature of writing reports on the computer, as well as the more professional-looking presentation.
- The huge store of knowledge and information available via the internet.

For the students

- The ability to build a piece of written work, for instance creating an outline of each paragraph then filling in the text.
- The ease with which changes can be made, without the need for laborious rewrites.
- The ability to make work look good and be professionally finished with pictures and other presentational devices.
- The motivational aspects of creating polished and professional-looking pieces of work.

- The help that ICT offers for children who have SEN, for instance weak spellers, those with poor handwriting, etc.
- The vast store of knowledge and information available on CD-ROMs and the internet.
- The ability to communicate quickly and efficiently around the world, via email.
- The importance of being able to use ICT for future career prospects.

Top tips for ICT

Learn to type

It's worth putting in the effort, because being able to touch-type will save you a huge amount of time. It will also get you massive kudos with your students. There are lots of free programs on the internet: try www.typeonline.co.uk.

Use the 'advanced' functions

If it feels like there should be an easy or quick way of doing a task, there probably is. Use the 'Help' function to find out.

Ask your students for advice and help

They probably know more than you, and will welcome the chance to share their expertise.

Get to know the ICT teacher or technician

It's a great idea to have the ICT teacher or technician 'on side' for those times when you most need help.

Store your work with care

It's easy to forget the name you've given a document, or for it to get lost on a big network. If possible, store your resources on your own PC or portable, or create your own folder.

Managing ICT use

Using any type of equipment in the classroom inevitably leads to management issues; perhaps nowhere is this more so than with electrical and electronic equipment, which can so easily be misused or go wrong in the middle of a lesson. If you have only a limited number of computers at your school, you'll find some ideas in the section that follows about how you can go about maximizing these resources. Other general tips about managing ICT use in the classroom are given below:

- Set out the 'ground rules' for handling equipment right from the start, before you allow the students actually to use it. This will help them focus their attention fully on what you are saying.

- Make the boundaries very clear and the sanctions for misuse of the machines equally apparent. Have an alternative task or activity available in case you do need a child to sit away from the computers.
- If space allows, have the children sitting at tables to explain the lesson, before setting them loose on the machines. It is much harder to maintain a group's attention once they have their hands on the equipment. If there is an electronic whiteboard available, you could demonstrate the work to the whole class on this.
- Explain carefully to your children how delicate computers and other electronic equipment can be. Although frustration is often understandable, let them know that computers respond badly to being bashed about and will end up freezing, crashing or going out of action.
- Spend at least one or two lessons with a class teaching them about the correct use of word processors, spreadsheets, etc. (See the next chapter for some useful tips.) Many of us use only the absolute minimum of the full range of functions available.
- Think of activities designed to introduce some advanced functions to the class, such as section breaks, columns, creating tables, formulating sums and so on.

Maximizing your resources

There is still a definite disparity between the ICT resources that teachers and their students are offered from school to school. In some large secondary schools, especially those with specialist ICT status, there are numerous computers, laptops, digital cameras, etc. that teachers can use whenever they need. In other small primary schools, a number of children have to share a limited number of computers and other equipment. Here are some tips for maximizing the resources available at your school:

- If you do not have enough computers for one each, encourage your students to find different ways of sharing the machines.
- One idea for this is to work in pairs, taking it in turns with one student acting as 'reader', the other as 'writer'.
- Make ICT time about learning the technologies, rather than about creating pretty work for displays. Try not to use computers for simply typing up work.
- Encourage your students to take very good care of the equipment that is available.
- Book time in a computer room early on in the term – ICT suddenly becomes very popular when teachers are tired.

ICT hazards

Alongside an awareness of how useful and advantageous ICT can be, the wise teacher also has an understanding of the downsides and potential hazards. Many of these hazards are actually to do with the way that you plan for ICT use in your classroom or subject, and the way that you encourage your students to work with ICT. Some of the potential dangers are listed below:

- Viewing word processing as simply a way of presenting work, rather than as a tool for building and editing writing.
- The dangers of time wasting and distraction for your students. These dangers come from a variety of sources, including:
  - The internet (e.g. chat rooms)
  - The excessive editing of written work
  - The overuse of ClipArt
- An easy sense of achievement, when the presentation looks good, but the content is actually weak.
- The possibility (indeed likelihood) of plagiarism from some students.
- A lack of decent, reliable and up to date resources.
- Computers which break down, freeze, or crash, causing students to lose their work.
- The abuse of computers by the students, for instance the theft of mouse balls.
- Internet connection problems which can lead to real frustration and in turn to poor behaviour.
- 'Print-out mania', whereby the students send endless copies of the same page to the printer.
- Safety issues, for instance relating to use of the internet (e.g. the dangers of giving out personal information).
- A lack of a really deep knowledge about exactly what computer programs have to offer.

The internet in teaching

At the moment, we're right at the start of internet use in teaching. The full extent of what the net and all the associated technologies really offer us still awaits discovery. There's no doubt, though, that whatever age group or subject you teach, there is plenty of potential for teaching and learning via the internet. Some of the possible uses of the internet for the teacher are listed below:

- Publishing children's writing, for example via a school website or an educational site using student contributors.
- Researching and finding information on pretty much anything under the sun, both for the teacher and for the student.
- Downloading programs, documents, etc. Also copying chunks of text from the net onto your own computer.
- Educational websites that offer interactive activities with which students can learn.
- Distance teaching and learning, for instance the use of video conferencing.
- Communication locally, nationally and globally via email.
- Setting up a school or class website of your own.

Of course, alongside the many potential benefits that the internet offers, there are also a number of downsides that the wary teacher needs to look out for. Some of these are listed below:

- The ease with which work can be plagiarized. Some sites even offer essays for sale.
- The proliferation of advertising on the internet, both in terms of how irritating it is, and also because of the teacher's responsibility not to expose students to this type of material.
- The huge range of 'adult' sites available, and the need to be fully aware of the content to which our children may be exposed.
- The huge quantity of information available, which may lead to research time being ill-spent or wasted.

There are a good number of ways in which many of these problems can be overcome, or at least the difficulties minimized. The tips below focus on ways that the individual teacher can avoid squandering lesson time when using the internet:

- Find a good search engine to avoid wasted time when research is being done. I recommend the very popular Google (www.google.co.uk) for the relevance of its search results and its minimal advertising content.
- Teach your children how to go about using a search engine, e.g. the use of quotation marks to indicate 'search for this entire phrase'.
- Undertake some background research yourself, before the lesson, so that you can give the class a list of websites to visit. This will help you encourage focused research and prevent your children wasting time visiting unsuitable sites.
- Give your students a list of questions to answer during the lesson, to encourage them to focus on the task in hand, and to avoid distraction.

Safety on the internet

Of course, when we use the internet in the classroom, we have a responsibility to be fully aware of the dangers that exist for our children. Before letting them loose to wander the web, we need to take the time to advise our students about what is and is not acceptable and sensible behaviour. The majority of schools now have an effective filtering system for the internet (in fact, sometimes too effective, barring you from some useful or at least fun sites). The advice below for teachers to give their children in school is equally applicable to internet use at home:

- Advise your children that it is essential to keep personal information to themselves, and not to give out their name, address or telephone number over the internet.
- Warn the class that people on the internet can take on false personae, and that the 'child' they meet in a chat room may not be what he or she appears.
- Make it crystal clear to your children that they should never arrange to meet up with someone via the internet.
- Talk about how easy it is for viruses to find their way onto a PC or network. Tell your students to guard against downloading files, unless they are certain about the source. The same applies to opening attachments that arrive with emails.
- Discuss the sanctions that the school imposes for those visiting 'adult' sites. (It is inevitable, particularly with teenagers, that at least some will try getting away with this.)

Interactive whiteboards

Interactive whiteboards (IWBs) are a relatively recent innovation in education, but one that is increasingly making its mark. In some schools, particularly at primary level, every classroom will have an IWB of its own. An IWB is a touch-sensitive projection screen. It allows you to control a computer or laptop by using either a special 'pen', mouse or simply your finger. IWBs can help teachers and students use interactive teaching and learning activities.

A basic IWB kit consists of three main components: a computer, a projector and a whiteboard. The computer is connected to the projector and whiteboard, and the projector can then display an image of the computer screen on the board. There are three main types of IWB:

- Passive whiteboard – these have a touch-sensitive dual-membrane resistive board. They can sense pressure from an object such as a finger or marker.

- Active whiteboard – these are operated with an electronic or cordless device. They can 'draw' the content onto the board via a projector (the pen does not actually mark the board).
- Infrared/ultrasound kits – these fix to any normal whiteboard or hard surface using clips or suckers. They use special pens and can be used with or without a projector.

You can also buy whiteboard emulators which work with existing non-electronic whiteboards. These allow you to convert a standard board into an interactive whiteboard by applying a small device. You can see some different IWBs at:

- Easiteach (www.easiteach.co.uk)
- Smartboard (www.smarttech.com)
- Promethean (www.prometheanworld.com/uk)

For more general information about using IWBs, see:

- www.nwnet.org.uk/
- www.schools.becta.org.uk
- www.teachernet.gov.uk/wholeschool/ictis/infrastructure/iwb/
- www.e-learningcentre.co.uk
- www.schoolzone.co.uk/resources/IWB/index.asp

The advantages and disadvantages of IWBs

There are some very positive benefits of using IWBs, although it is also worth being aware of the potential drawbacks (see below). The advantages include:

- Opportunities for active involvement from your students.
- Lessons can be made more interactive and 'hands on'.
- Boards can be used for more effective modelling, assessment and planning.
- They can help with understanding new or unfamiliar concepts.
- If well used, they can make your students feel more motivated and involved.
- Boards can speed up the flow and pace of the lesson.
- Content developed during a lesson can be edited and saved for future use.
- This can make lesson planning less stressful, and cut down preparation time.
- They can enhance literacy and numeracy lessons at both primary and secondary level.

- Boards can increase accessibility and interaction for disabled or SEN students.
- Students are given the chance to experience, use and expand upon essential ICT skills.

As with any new technology, there will always be some downfalls, particularly when teachers are first incorporating a new approach into their lessons. Here are a few potential downsides to keep in mind:

- The majority of the class watching while a few individuals use the board.
- A lack of confidence from teachers who have relatively little experience in using the new technology.
- The teacher getting 'stuck' at the front of the room, beside the whiteboard, rather than moving around the space.
- The teacher spending (at first) lots of time designing and rewriting lesson plans to incorporate use of the board.

IWB software

Most IWBs come with their own software, which includes the basics of what you might need. These usually include a design page or blank sheet, various templates such as graph paper, pens or pointers to control the board, and some interactive activities to get you started. There are lots of sites offering software, both free and for purchase. You might like to look at:

- Boardworks (www.theboardworks.co.uk/)
- Usable Software Company (www.usablesoftwarecompany.com/)
- Notatelt (www.notateit.com/)
- SMART Education (www.smart-education.org/uk/)

20 Software

This chapter gives you some general tips about working with software, and specific information about using two common types of computer software: the word processor and the spreadsheet. The tips and instructions given will be helpful to the inexperienced computer user, and also to those hoping to build on a reasonable level of knowledge. (Please note: I deal with the Microsoft programs here, as these are the most commonly used in schools.)

Some general tips

The tips below should prove useful both for teachers working on their own documents, and also when using ICT in the classroom. Some of these tips cover general good practice, others are based on the most common errors made by students.

- Always save your document a few minutes after you have started working on it and keep saving it as you go along. There really is nothing quite as frustrating as losing a piece of work because the computer crashes or freezes before you have saved it.
- Aim to type your work first and worry about detailed formatting later. This is especially important if you are using a number of different fonts on one page. If you format as you go along you might find that 'glitches' appear on the page where the computer defaults to the standard formatting (for instance dropping out of a chosen font and into default Times Roman).
- Use the layout functions of left/right, justify and centre, rather than using the space bar or tab button.
- When word processing, only put a return at the end of a paragraph, rather than at the end of each line. Allow the computer's wrap-around function to do its work. Many students make this error because they don't know what wrap around does.
- Use 'Ctrl + return' to create a new page instead of adding returns.

- Use the 'Print preview' function to see what a document looks like before sending it to the printer.
- Check at the end of your document for blank pages before sending your work to print.
- Name your documents sensibly, preferably using a separate folder for work in different topic areas.
- Use the shortcut functions, such as 'Ctrl + S' for save, and 'Ctrl + B' for bold. These functions can save a great deal of time and effort, especially once they become second nature. It should become a natural part of working on a document to hit 'Ctrl + S' every couple of minutes.
- Learn to use more advanced functions, such as section breaks, columns, adapting page layout, creating tables, formulating calculations and so on. A good way to start working with these functions is by using the 'Help' menus which take you step by step through the processes involved.

Word processing

The word processor really is a wonderful tool for the teacher and the student (and of course for the writer!), because of the endless hours of rewriting that it saves us. The word processor also enables us to create professional looking documents relatively easily. You can find information below about putting together a worksheet that will look good and also prove easily accessible for your students.

Creating a worksheet

The instructions that follow give you guidance in creating a professional-looking worksheet to use with your students, using MS Word.

How do I get started?

- Use your mouse to point your cursor at the 'start' button on the bottom left of your screen.
- Click once with the mouse to open up the menu.
- Point your cursor to 'Programs', across to 'Word', then click.
- Alternatively, click on the 'Word' icon on this menu or on your desktop.

What happens next?

- You will see a blank page, like a clean sheet of paper.
- You can view your page in various different layouts, using the 'View' function on the pull-down menus.

- You can also use different-sized views of your page, using the ' per cent' box on your toolbar. 100 per cent shows the full-sized page, 50 per cent the page at half size and so on.

How do I create the 'WordArt' title?

- There are a range of pre-formatted 'WordArt' titles available to use, which will make your work look more interesting.
- To add a 'WordArt' title, go to the drop down menu 'Insert', then drag down to 'Picture', then across to click on 'WordArt'.
- You will see a range of different title styles. Click on your selection, then on 'OK'. A box will appear in which you can type the required text. This box also gives you options for font size and other formatting.
- Click on 'OK' once you are happy with your text. Your title will be inserted onto your blank page, with a 'WordArt' toolbar at the bottom, which you can use to manipulate the title.
- To make any further changes to the title, double click over it and the 'WordArt' editing box will appear.

How do I format text to add bold, underlining, centering, etc?

- To add formatting to a line of text, position your cursor just to the left of the line, then click once. You will find that the whole line is highlighted.
- Alternatively, position your cursor near the line, click down your mouse button and hold, then drag the mouse so that the text is highlighted.
- To add bold, either use the shortcut 'Ctrl + B' or the **B** icon on your toolbar.
- To add italics, use the shortcut 'Ctrl + I', or the *I* icon on your toolbar.
- To align your text (for instance centering), again use the icons on the toolbar. These show a series of lines which offer align left, centre, align right or justify.
- To add bullet points, click on the bullet icon on your toolbar. You can change the type of bullet point used with the drop-down menus. To do this, go to 'Format', then 'Bullets and Numbering'.

How do I add and manipulate a text box?

- To enclose text in a box, highlight the text that you wish to appear in the box.
- Now use the pull-down menus to click on 'Insert', then 'Text box'. A box will appear around the text.

- You can resize the text box to fit your text. Hold your cursor over one of the lines of the box until you see a symbol with four arrows appear.
- Click once and you will see the box highlighted, and eight small empty boxes appear on the lines. You can now manipulate the size of the box.
- Do this by holding your cursor over one of these boxes until a line with two arrows appears. Now click once, hold down the mouse button and drag the box out or in.
- You can also move the text box around the page. To do this, position your cursor so the four arrows appear. Then click and hold down your mouse button and drag the box to its new position.
- In addition, you can change the formatting of the box. To do this, double click with the four arrows showing, and you will be given a number of options for changing the format.
- A good idea is to change the box fill and line weight to highlight a box giving activities on a worksheet. This helps focus the weaker student on this part of the sheet.

How do I add and edit a table?

- To add a table to your worksheet, use the drop-down menus. Go to 'Table', 'Insert', then drag across to 'Table'.
- A box will appear giving you different options for your table. You can choose the number of columns and rows. You can also use a number of different auto formats.
- To change your table once it has been inserted, again use the 'Table' drop-down menu. You can delete or insert rows or columns. There is also a function to sort the text, and various other features.

How do I add AutoShapes to my work?

- To add AutoShapes, view the Drawing toolbar by going to 'View', 'Toolbars', then dragging across to 'Drawing'.
- The toolbar will appear at the bottom of your screen.
- You can use this toolbar to do a number of different things within your document, including changing text colour, adding lines and arrows, 'ordering' your text and pictures (for instance so that a box appears behind or in front of a piece of text), and so on.

How do I add a border to my page?

- To add a border to the page, use the drop-down menus. Go to 'Format', then click on 'Borders and Shading'. Now click on 'Page Border'.

- Here you will find a number of different options for adding borders to your page. You can choose an 'Art' border, which features pictures or other frames, or you can use a more straightforward line.
- You can also alter the size of border that will appear.

Spreadsheets

The instructions that follow give you all the information you need to create two basic spreadsheets using the Microsoft Excel program. The spreadsheets that are created will do some basic calculations of student assessments. You can see an example of the finished spreadsheets below (pp. 337–8).

How do I get started?

- Use your mouse to point your cursor at the 'start' button on the bottom left of your screen.
- Click once with the mouse to open up the menu.
- Find the 'Excel' icon (through the programs menu, or using your desktop), then click on it to begin.

What happens next?

- A blank workbook (series of spreadsheets) will automatically open, ready for you to use.
- On the top line you will see the workbook's current document name (the default will be book1.xls).
- To change the name of your document, use the pull down menus at the top of your screen. Go to 'File', then 'Save as', and type in the new name of your document.
- The workbook is made up of worksheets (or spreadsheets).

What are worksheets and how do I use them?

- The worksheets are a series of blank spreadsheets, stacked one behind the other like the pages of a book.
- The worksheets are called Sheet 1, Sheet 2, Sheet 3 and so on. The default setting is to open 8 worksheets within each workbook.
- You will see the series of worksheets listed at the bottom left of the page on tabs.
- You can move between the worksheets by clicking on these tabs.

- Alternatively, use the shortcut 'Ctrl + Pg Up' (hit both these keys together) to move from sheet 1, to 2, to 3, etc. Use the shortcut 'Ctrl + Pg Dn' to go in reverse order.
- The worksheets allow you to have a range of information within one workbook, and then to formulate sums involving all the worksheets (for instance, finding out average grades over several different classes).
- To rename the worksheets within your workbook:
  - Double click on the worksheet tab
  - The original name will be highlighted in black
  - Type over the original name with the new name you want

How do I move around the worksheet?

- On the worksheet you'll see letters going across the top, starting with 'A' and moving alphabetically.
- You'll also see numbers going downwards on the left, in order.
- Each box or 'cell' consequently has an identifying letter/number. The first cell is called A1.
- You can type text or numbers in the cells (or both).
- To move to a cell, click on the box so that it is highlighted. You can then type the text or numbers which you want to appear at that point.

How do I type on the worksheet?

- Click on the cell to highlight the point where you want to type. Now simply type in the text or numbers that you want.
- Note: it doesn't matter if the text you type in is too big for the cell, because you can resize them.
- In the example spreadsheets, the information typed in is:
  - Title of worksheet
  - Student's surname
  - Student's first name
  - Grades and percentages for assignments 1–5
  - Total column (for marks and sum formula)
  - Exclusion of one assignment from the marking (for formula, see below).

How do I resize the columns to fit my text?

- To resize columns individually, move your cursor to the top of the sheet into the gap between the letters, and hold it there until you see a line with two arrows facing left/right.

- Now hold down your mouse button and pull the column width out until the text fits.
- Alternatively, you can automatically size the columns so that the text fits them exactly. To do this, go to the letter row at the top of the worksheet (A, B, C ...). Click with your mouse in this row and hold down the button.
- Now mark the columns you want to resize by pulling the mouse across until they are highlighted.
- Then simply double click on one of the lines between the columns. The cells will automatically resize to fit your text.

How do I use the sum formula?

- To use the 'sum' (or addition) formula, type the marks out of 20 in each of the assignment columns.
- In the 'total' column, type '=sum ('. Once you have typed this the computer knows that you are going to add something up to create a formula.
- Now move the cursor to the first point from where you want to add up. In the example this was cell 'C6'.
- Hold the shift button down and mark all the columns you want to add together by moving the cursor along.
- You will see a box with a flashing dotted line around it. Ensure that this box is expanded to cover the area you want to add up. Then hit the 'Enter' or 'Return' button.
- Note: you can add a series of numbers vertically as well as horizontally.

Is there another way to add up?

- You can also use the sum icon. This is a Greek 'Epsilon' symbol on the toolbar at the top of your screen (which looks like a funny 'E').
- Click your cursor so that the 'Total' column is highlighted, then double click the 'Epsilon' icon.
- This function will automatically sum up the most logical sequence of numbers from the cell where your cursor is.
- In the example given, the computer works out that you want to add up the five assignment columns to create your total.
- Another method is to use the '+' key. Hit the '+' while in the 'Total' cell.
- Now move the cursor to the cells you want to add together in turn, each time putting a + sign in front of the cell reference. The computer will automatically add up these cells.
- Other keys that work in the same way are divide '/', multiply '*' and minus '−'.

How do I remove one cell from the calculation?

- In the examples, you will see that there is a final column with the marks for Assignment 4 excluded. This might come in useful if, for instance, you suspected a student of cheating in that assignment, or if you felt that the assignment had been too difficult for the class.
- To take out a cell use the '−' key in the same way that you used the '+' key above.
- Alternatively, type a formula into the relevant cell. In this case '+H6' (the name of our total column) '− F6' (the name of the Assignment 4 column).

How do I put in and add up percentages?

- In the second example worksheet, you will see that percentages are used, rather than marks.
- To put in a percentage, type the number in the relevant cell, putting a percentage sign after it. The computer will automatically know that this number is a percentage, and must be treated as such.
- In the total column at the end of the example worksheet, the percentages are added together and then averaged out.
- To do this, type '=sum(' in the 'Total' box. Now use one of the functions described above to add up the columns.
- Click on the 'Total' cell, then in the formula line that appears at the top of your page, showing the current formula. Add '/5' after the brackets to tell the computer to divide the sum by 5 (to create an average of the 5 assignments).

How do I format the text on my spreadsheet?

- To format the text, click your cursor in the relevant box, then click on the bold (**B**), italic (*I*) or underline (U) icons (normally on the toolbar at the top right of your screen).
- Alternatively, you can use the drag-down menus as you would in a word-processing document.
- To format a group of cells, mark the area you want to format by clicking on the cell, holding down and dragging mouse across. Then click the relevant formatting icon.
- The large and small 'A' icons can be used to increase and decrease text size.
- To add a box around the spreadsheet, mark the cells to go within the box, then use the icons with borders at the top of the screen.

How do I sort out the layout of my document?

- Use the print preview function (either the icon of a document with a magnifying glass, or the function on the pull-down 'File' menu).
- Excel should automatically format your document so that it looks 'correct' on the screen.
- If you are not happy with how it looks, click on the 'Set up' button at the top of the 'Print preview' screen.
- Here you will find options to change the page layout to landscape format, or to fit the text to one page.

ST PATRICK'S 2006 – ASSIGNMENT MARKS

SURNAME	FIRST NAME	ASSIGNMENT 1 mark out of 20	ASSIGNMENT 2 mark out of 20	ASSIGNMENT 3 mark out of 20	ASSIGNMENT 4 mark out of 20	ASSIGNMENT 5 mark out of 20	TOTAL mark out of 100	excl assign 4 mark out of 80
Baggio	Andrea	1	5	10	5	6	27	22
Bayer	Frans	14	16	11	12	14	67	55
Benson	Sally	9	11	10	10	8	48	38
Davies	Jennifer	18	16	15	17	20	86	69
Du Morier	Nicole	11	9	10	9	12	51	42
Gomez	Maria	14	12	11	12	15	64	52
Jones	Owen	8	9	7	4	9	37	33
Mckay	Angus	17	19	16	17	19	88	71
Singh	Amjan	18	19	18	14	17	86	72
Smith	Bob	13	11	12	11	15	62	51

ST PATRICK'S 2006 – ASSIGNMENT MARKS

SURNAME	FIRST NAME	ASSIGNMENT 1 as percentage	ASSIGNMENT 2 as percentage	ASSIGNMENT 3 as percentage	ASSIGNMENT 4 as percentage	ASSIGNMENT 5 as percentage	TOTAL as percentage	excl assign 4 as percentage
Baggio	Andrea	5 %	25 %	50 %	25 %	30 %	27 %	28 %
Bayer	Frans	70 %	80 %	55 %	60 %	70 %	67 %	69 %
Benson	Sally	45 %	55 %	50 %	50 %	40 %	48 %	48 %
Davies	Jennifer	90 %	80 %	75 %	85 %	100 %	86 %	86 %
Du Morier	Nicole	55 %	45 %	50 %	45 %	60 %	51 %	53 %
Gomez	Maria	70 %	60 %	55 %	60 %	75 %	64 %	65 %
Jones	Owen	40 %	45 %	35 %	20 %	45 %	37%	41 %
Mckay	Angus	85 %	95 %	80 %	85 %	95 %	88 %	89 %
Singh	Amjan	90 %	95 %	90 %	70 %	85 %	86 %	90 %
Smith	Bob	65 %	55 %	60 %	55 %	75 %	62 %	64 %

Part Eight
DIRECTORY

art

assessment

business studies

careers

citizenship

curriculum

design and technology

drama

English

examination boards

examinations

further education

general

geography

government

history

ICT

independent schools

inspection

international education

jobs

languages

library

management

maths

media

online education

parents

pensions

PE

PSHE

primary

professional development

publications

RE

schools information

science

secondary

special educational needs

suppliers (educational products)

supply teaching agencies

support organizations

teacher training

teaching forums and communities

teaching resources

unions

Art

Arts Council England
14 Great Peter Street
London SW1P 3NQ
Website: www.artscouncil.org.uk
Email: enquiries@artscouncil.org.uk
Tel: 0845 300 6200
Fax: 020 7973 6590
Textphone: 020 7973 6564

National Society for Education in Art
and Design (NSEAD)
The Gatehouse
Corsham Court
Corsham
Wiltshire SN13 OBZ
Website: www.nsead.org
Email: johnsteers@nsead.org
Tel: 01249 714825
Fax: 01249 716138

Assessment

Assessment and Qualifications
Alliance (AQA)
Contact local offices via details on
Contacts page
Website: www.aqa.org.uk
Email: mailbox@aqa.org.uk

Association of Assessment Inspectors
and Advisors (AAIA)
East Kent Area Education Office
Clover House
John Wilson Industrial Estate
Thanet Way
Whistable
Kent CT5 3QZ
Website: www.aaia.org.uk
Email: vice-president@aaia.org.uk

See also: Examinations

Business Studies

Biz/ed
Website: www.bized.ac.uk
Email: bized-info@bized.ac.uk

The Economics and Business
Education Association (EBEA)
The Forum
277 London Road
Burgess Hill
West Sussex RH15 9QU
Website: www.ebea.org.uk
Email: office@ebea.org.uk
Tel: 01444 240150
Fax: 01444 240101

Just Business
Department of Teacher Education
McMillan Building
Bradford College
St Horton Road
Bradford BD7 1AY
Website: www.jusbiz.org
Email: s.fairbrass@bilk.ac.uk
Tel: 01274 436456

National Education Business
Partnership Network (NEBPN)
188 Main Street
New Greenham Park
Thatcham
Berkshire RG19 6HW
Website: www.nebpn.org
Email: office@nebpn.org
Tel: 01635 279914
Fax: 01635 279919

Careers

Association for Careers Education and
Guidance
9 Lawrence Leys
Bloxham
Banbury
Oxon OX15 4NU
Website: www.aceg.org.uk
Email: info@aceg.org.uk
Tel: 01295 720809
Fax: 01295 720809

Careers Research Advisory Centre
(CRAC)
2nd Floor
Sheraton House
Castle Park
Cambridge CB3 0AX
Website: www.crac.org.uk
Email: web.enquiries@crac.org.uk
Tel: 01223 460277
Fax: 01223 311708

Connexions
Contact your local offices for further
details.
Website: www.connexions-direct.com/
Email: via local offices

Institute of Careers Guidance (ICG)
Third Floor
Copthall House
1 New Road
Stourbridge DY8 1PH
Website: www.icg-uk.org
Email: hq@icg-uk.org
Tel: 01384 376464

Citizenship

The Citizenship Foundation
Citizenship Foundation
63 Gee Street
London EC1V 3RS
Website: www.citfou.org.uk
Email:
info@citizenshipfoundation.org.uk
Tel: 020 7566 4130

Council for Education in World
Citizenship (CEWC)
Hampton Community College
Hanworth Road
Hampton
Middlesex TW12 3HB
Website: www.cewc.org
Email: info@cewc.org.uk

Institute for Citizenship
20 Old Bailey
London EC4M 7AN
Website: www.citizen.org.uk
Email: info@citizen.org.uk
Tel: 020 7844 5444
Fax: 020 7844 5541

Curriculum

The Basic Skills Agency (BSA)
Commonwealth House
1–19 New Oxford Street
London WC1A 1NU
Website: www.basic-skills.co.uk
Email: enquires@basic-skills.co.uk
Tel: 020 7405 4017
Fax: 020 7440 6626

National Curriculum online
Website: www.nc.uk.net
Email: via QCA feedback form –
www.qca.org.uk/contact.html

National Curriculum in Action
Website: www.ncaction.org.uk

Design and Technology

Design Technology Department
Website: www.design-technology.org
Email: a.davies@design-
technology.org

The Design and Technology
Association (DATA)
16 Wellesbourne House
Walton Road
Wellesbourne
Warwickshire CV35 9JB
Website: www.data.org.uk
Email: DATA@data.org.uk
Tel: 01789 470007
Fax: 01789 841955

Design and Tech.com
Website: www.designandtech.com
Email:
postmaster@designandtech.com

Design & Technology Online
Website: www.dtonline.org
Email: dtonline@dialsolutions.co.uk

The National Association of Advisers
and Inspectors in Design and
Technology (NAAIDT)
c/o John Culpin, Admin Officer
Hallgate, 26 Back Lane
Glapwell

Chesterfield
Derbyshire
S44 5PX
Website: www.naaidt.org.uk
Email: john.culpin@naaidt.org.uk

Drama

Drama Online
Website: www.dramamagazine.co.uk
Email: via details on contacts page

National Association for Youth Drama
(Ireland) (NAYD)
34 Upper Gardiner Street
Dublin 1
Ireland
Website: www.youthdrama.ie
Email info@nayd.ie
Tel: 353 1 878 1301
Fax: 353 1 878 1302

National Council for Drama Training
(NCDT)
1–7 Woburn Walk
London WC1H 0JJ
Website: www.ncdt.co.uk
Email: info@ncdt.co.uk
Tel: 020 7387 3650
Fax: 020 7387 3860

National Drama
Website: www.nationaldrama.co.uk
Email: via details on contacts page

The Royal National Theatre
Royal National Theatre
South Bank
London SE1 9PX
Website: www.nationaltheatre.org.uk
Email: info@nationaltheatre.org.uk
Tel: 020 7452 3400

The Society of Teachers of Speech and
Drama (STSD)
73 Berry Hill Road
Mansfield
Nottinghamshire NG18 4RU
Website: www.stsd.org.uk
Email: stsd@stsd.org.uk

English

British Council Teaching English
10 Spring Gardens
London SW1A 2BN
Website: www.teachingenglish.org.uk
Email:
teachingenglish@britishcouncil.org

The English Speaking Union (ESU)
Dartmouth House
37 Charles Street
London W1J 5ED
Website: www.esu.org.uk
Email: esu@esu.org
Tel: 020 7529 1550
Fax: 020 7495 6108

National Association for the Teaching
of English (NATE)
50 Broadfield Road
Sheffield S8 OXJ
Website: www.nate.org.uk
Email: info@nate.org.uk
Tel: 0114 255 5419
Fax: 0114 255 5296

The National Literacy Association
(NLA)
1st Floor of Leonard House
321 Bradford Street
Digbeth
Birmingham B5 6ET
Website: www.nla.org.uk

Email: mail@nla.org.uk
Tel/Fax: 0121 6225143

The National Literacy Trust
Swire House
59 Buckingham Gate
London SW1E 6AJ
Website: www.literacytrust.org.uk
Email: contact@literacytrust.org.uk
Tel: 020 7828 2435
Fax: 020 7931 9986

The United Kingdom Literacy
Association
Upton House
Baldock Street
Royston
Herts SG8 5AY
Website: www.ukla.org
Email: admin@ukla.org
Tel: 01763 241188
Fax: 01763 243785

Examination boards

City and Guilds
Customer Relations
1 Giltspur Street
London EC1A 9DD
Website: www.city-and-guilds.co.uk
Email: via online form
Tel: 020 7294 2800
Fax: 020 7294 2405

Edexcel
One90 High Holborn
London
WC1V 7BH
Website: www.edexcel.org.uk
Email: via online enquiries form
Tel: 0870 240 9800

Joint Examining Board (JEB)
30a Dyer Street
Cirencester
Gloucestershire GL7 2PF
Website: www.jeb.co.uk
Email: jeb@jeb.co.uk
Tel: 01285 641747
Fax: 01285 650449

Oxford Cambridge and RSA
Examinations (OCR)
Website: www.ocr.org.uk
Email:
OCRNewMediaTeam@ocr.org.uk

Welsh Joint Education Committee
245 Western Avenue
Cardiff CF5 2YX
Website: www.wjec.co.uk
Tel: 029 2026 5000

Examinations

The Examination Officers Association
4th Floor
29 Bolton Street
London W1J 8BT
Website: www.examofficers.org
Email: info@examofficers.org
Tel: 020 7509 5817

The Qualifications and Curriculum
Authority (QCA)
83 Piccadilly
London W1J 8QA
Website: www.qca.org.uk
Email: info@qca.org.uk
Tel: 020 7509 5555
Fax: 020 7509 6666

QCA Northern Ireland
Website: www.qca.org.uk/ni
Email: info@qcani.org.uk

Northern Ireland Council for the
Curriculum, Examinations and
Assessment (CCEA)
29 Clarendon Road
Clarendon Dock
Belfast BT1 3BG
Website:
E-mail: info@ccea.org.uk
Telephone: 028 9026 1200
Textphone: 028 9024 2063
Fax: 028 9026 1234

Scottish Qualifications Authority
The Optima Building
58 Robertson Street
Glasgow G2 8DQ
Also at:
Ironmills Road
Dalkeith
Midlothian EH22 1LE
Website: www.sqa.org.uk
Email: customer@sqa.org.uk
Tel: 0845 279 1000
Fax: 0141 242 2244

Further education

Association of Colleges (AOC)
5th Floor, Centre Point
103 New Oxford Street
London WC1A 1RG
Website: www.aoc.co.uk
Email: enquiries@aoc.co.uk
Tel: 020 7827 4600
Fax: 020 7827 4650

The Learning and Skills Council (LSC)
National Office:
Cheylesmore House
Quinton Road
Coventry CV1 2WT

London Office:
8–10 Grosvenor Gardens
London SW1W 0DH
Website: www.lsc.gov.uk
Email: info@lsc.gov.uk
Tel: 0845 019 4170
Fax: 024 7649 3600

Learning and Skills Network (LSN)
Regent Arcade House
19–25 Argyll Street
London W1F 7LS
Website: www.lsneducation.org.uk
Email: enquiries@LSNeducation.org.uk
Tel: 020 7297 9000
Fax: 020 7297 9001

Quality Improvement Agency (QIA)
Friars House
Manor House Drive
Coventry CV1 2TE
Website: www.qia.org.uk
Email: via online form
Tel: 0870 1620 632
Fax: 0870 1620 633

General

The British Council
10 Spring Gardens
London SW1A 2BN
Website: www.britishcouncil.org
Email:
general.enquiries@britishcouncil.org
Tel: 020 7930 8466
Fax: 020 7839 6347

British Educational Research
Association (BERA)
No 3 The Stable
Hall Farm Yard
Main Street

Kirklington (near Southwell)
Nottinghamshire NG22 8NN
Website: www.bera.ac.uk
Email: admin@bera.ac.uk
Tel: 01636 819090
Fax: 01636 819090

Childline
45 Folgate Street
London E1 6GL
Website: www.childline.org.uk
Tel: 020 7650 3200
(Media and PR) 020 7650 3240
Fax: 020 7650 3201
Childline Helpline: 0800 1111

The Commission for Racial Equality
In England:
St Dunstan's House
201–211 Borough High Street
London SE1 1GZ
Website: www.cre.gov.uk
Email: info@cre.gov.uk
Tel: 020 7939 0000
Fax: 020 7939 0004
In Scotland:
The Tun
12 Jackson's Entry
off Holyrood Road
Edinburgh EH8 8PJ
Email: scotland@cre.gov.uk
Tel: 0131 524 2000
Fax: 0131 524 2001
Textphone: 0131 524 2018
In Wales:
3rd Floor
Capital Tower
Greyfriars Road
Cardiff CF10 3AG
Email: InformationWales@cre.gov.uk
Tel: 02920 729 200
Fax 02920 729 220

Development Education Association
(DEA)
1st Floor
River House
143–145 Farringdon Road
London EC1R 3AB
Website: www.dea.org.uk
Email: dea@dea.org.uk
Tel: 020 7812 1282
Fax: 020 7812 1272

The Duke of Edinburgh's Award
Gulliver House
Madeira Walk
Windsor
Berkshire SL4 1EU
Website: www.theaward.org
Email: info@theaward.org
Tel: 01753 727400
Fax: 01753 810666

National Confederation of Parent
Teacher Associations (NCPTA)
18 St Johns Hill
Sevenoaks
Kent TN13 3NP
Website: www.ncpta.org.uk
Email: info@ncpta.org.uk
Tel: 01732 748850
Fax: 01732 748851

National Foundation for Educational
Research (NFER)
The Mere
Upton Park
Slough
Berkshire SL1 2DQ
Website: www.nfer.ac.uk
Email: enquiries@nfer.ac.uk
Tel: 01753 574123
Fax: 01753 691632

National Society for the Prevention of
Cruelty to Children (NSPCC)
Weston House
42 Curtain Road
London EC2A 3NH
Website: www.nspcc.org.uk
Email: via the website
Tel: 020 7825 2500
Fax: 020 7825 2525
Child Protection Helpline: 0800 800
5000

Geography

Association for Geographic
Information (AGI)
Block C, 4th Floor
Morelands
5–23 Old Street
London EC1V 9HL
Website: www.agi.org.uk
Email: info@agi.org.uk
Tel: 020 7253 5211
Fax: 020 7251 4505

The Council for Environmental
Education (CEE)
94 London Street
Reading RG1 4SJ
Website: www.cee.org.uk
Email: info@cee.org.uk
Tel: 0118 950 2550
Fax: 0118 959 1955

The Geographical Association
160 Solly Street
Sheffield SB1 4BF
Website: www.geography.org.uk
Email: ga@geography.org.uk
Tel: 0114 296 0088
Fax: 0114 296 7176

Ordnance Survey
Customer Contact Centre
Romsey Road
Southampton SO16 4GU
Website: www.ordnancesurvey.co.uk
Email:
customerservices@ordnancesurvey.co.
uk
Tel: 08456 050505
Fax: 023 8079 2615

Royal Geographical Society
1 Kensington Gore
London SW7 2AR
Website: www.rgs.org
Email: via online form

Government

Department for Education and Skills
(DfES)
Sanctuary Buildings
Great Smith Street
London SW1P 3BT
Website: www.dfes.gov.uk
Email: info@dfes.gsi.gov.uk
DfES Ministers:
dfes.ministers@dfes.gsi.gov.uk
Tel: 0870 001 2345
Fax: 01928 79 4248
Tel (public enquiries): 0870 000 2288
Textphone: 01928 794274

Department for Education Lifelong
Learning and Skills (DELLS) (Wales)
Welsh Assembly Government
Cathays Park
Cardiff CF10 3NQ
Website: http://new.wales.gov.uk
Tel: 0845 010 3300

Department of Education Northern
Ireland
Rathgael House
Balloo Road
Bangor BT19 7PR
Website: www.deni.gov.uk
Email: mail@deni.gov.uk
Tel: 028 9127 9279
Fax: 028 9127 9100

Directgov
Website: www.direct.gov.uk
Email: via online form

General Teaching Council for England
(GTCE)
Victoria Square House
Victoria Square
Birmingham B2 4AJ
Website: www.gtce.org.uk
Email: info@gtce.org.uk
Tel: 0870 001 0308
Fax: 0121 345 0100
Also at:
Whittington House
19–30 Alfred Place
London WC1E 7EA
Fax: 020 7023 3909

General Teaching Council for Scotland
(GTCS)
Clerwood House
96 Clermiston Road
Edinburgh EH12 6UT
Website: www.gtcs.org.uk
Email: gtcs@gtcs.org.uk
Tel: 0131 314 6000
Fax: 0131 314 6001

Higher Education Funding Council for
England (HEFCE)
Northavon House
Coldharbour Lane
Bristol BS16 1QD
Website: www.hefce.ac.uk
Email: hefce@hefce.ac.uk
Tel: 0117 931 7317
Fax: 0117 931 7203

National Recognition Information
Centre for the United Kingdom
(NARIC)
Oriels House
Oriels Road
Cheltenham
Gloucestershire GL50 1XP
Website: www.naric.org.uk
Email: info@naric.org.uk
Tel: 0870 990 4088
Fax: 0870 990 1560

Scottish Executive (Education
Department)
Victoria Quay
Edinburgh EH6 6QQ
Website:
www.scotland.gov.uk/education/teach
ing/scotexec.html
Email: ceu@scotland.gov.uk
Tel: 0131 556 8400
Fax: 0131 244 8240

Secretary of State for Education and
Skills
Rt Hon Alan Johnson MP
House of Commons
London SW1A 0AA
Email: johnsona@parliament.uk

Sure Start
(via DfES and DWP)
Level 2 Caxton house
Tothill Street
London SW1H 9NA
Website: www.dfes.gov.uk
Email: info@dfes.gsi.gov.uk
Tel: (public enquiry unit)
0870 000 2288

Teachernet
Website: www.teachernet.gov.uk
Email: info@dfes.gsi.gov.uk
Tel: 0870 000 2288
Fax: 01928 794 248

Welsh Joint Education Committee
(WJEC)
245 Western Avenue
Cardiff CF5 2YX
Website: www.wjec.co.uk
Email: info@wjec.co.uk
Tel: 029 2026 5000

History

British Association for Local History
PO Box 6549
Somersal Herbert
Ashbourne DE6 5WH
Website: www.balh.co.uk
Email: info@balh.co.uk
Tel: 01283 585947

The British Museum
Great Russell Street
London WC1B 3DG
Website:
www.thebritishmuseum.ac.uk
Email: visitorinformation@
thebritishmuseum.ac.uk
Tel: 020 7323 8000

English Heritage
Customer Services Department
PO Box 569
Swindon SN2 2YP
Website: www.english-heritage.org.uk
Email: customers@english-heritage.org.uk
Tel: 0870 3331181
Fax: 01793 414926

The Historical Association
59a Kennington Park Road
London SE11 4JH
Website: www.history.org.uk
Email: enquiry@history.org.uk
Tel: 020 7735 3901
Fax: 020 7582 4989

History.Uk.Com
Tallow House
Lower Galdeford
Ludlow
Shropshire SY8 1RU
Website: www.history.uk.com
Email: via online form

National Archives
Kew
Richmond
Surrey TW9 4DU
Website: www.nationalarchives.gov.uk
Email: via online contact form
Tel: 020 8876 3444

The National Trust
PO Box 39
Warrington WA5 7WD
Website: www.nationaltrust.org.uk
Email: enquiries@thenationaltrust.org.uk
Tel: 0870 458 4000
Fax: 020 8466 6824

ICT

Association for Information
Technology in Teacher Education (ITTE)
Website: www.itte.org.uk

British Computer Society (BCS)
1st Floor, Block D
North Star House
North Star Avenue
Swindon SN2 1FA
Website: www.bcs.org
Email: bcshq@hq.bcs.org.uk
Tel: 0845 300 4417

British Educational Communications
and Technology Agency (BECTA)
Milburn Hill Road
Science Park
Coventry CV4 7JJ
Website: www.becta.org.uk
Email: becta@becta.org.uk
Tel: 024 7641 6994
Fax: 024 7641 1418

The IT Network
Website: www.itnetwork.org.uk
Email: itn@itnetwork.org.uk

MirandaNet
15 Stratton Street
London WLJ 8LQ
Also at:
10 Manor Way
South Croydon
Surrey CR2 7BQ
Website: www.mirandanet.ac.uk
Email: enquiries@mirandanet.ac.uk
Tel: 020 8686 8769
Fax: 020 8686 8768

The National Association of Advisers
for Computers in Education (NAACE)
PO Box 6511
Nottingham NG11 8TN
Website: www.naace.org
Email: office@naace.org
Tel: 0870 2400480
Fax: 0870 2414115

National Association for coordinators
and Teachers of IT (ACITT)
Website: www.acitt.org.uk

Independent schools

Boarding Schools' Association
The Boarding Schools' Association
Grosvenor Gardens House
35–37 Grosvenor Gardens
London SW1W 0BS
Website: www.boarding.org.uk
Email: bsa@boarding.org.uk
Tel: 020 7798 1580
Fax: 020 7798 1581

The Girls' Schools Association (GSA)
130 Regent Road
Leicester LE1 7PG
Website: www.gsa.uk.com
Email: office@gsa.uk.com
Tel: 0116 254 1619
Fax: 0116 255 3792

Independent Schools' Association
Boys' British School
East Street
Saffron Walden
Essex CB10 1LS
Website: www.isaschools.org.uk
Email: isa@isaschools.org.uk
Tel: 01799 523619
Fax: 01799 524892

Independent Schools Council (ISC)
St Vincent House
30 Orange Street
London WC2H 7HH
Website: www.isc.co.uk
Email: office@isc.co.uk
Tel: 020 7766 7070
Fax: 020 7766 7071

Scottish Council of Independent
Schools (SCIS)
21 Melville Street
Edinburgh EH3 7PE
Website: www.scis.org.uk
Email: information@scis.org.uk
Tel: 0131 220 2106
Fax: 0131 225 8594

Inspection

HMIe (Scotland)
Website: www.hmie.gov.uk
Email: through website
Tel: 01506 600200

Independent Schools Inspectorate
CAP House
9–12 Long Lane
London EC1A 9HA
Website: www.isinspect.org.uk
Email: info@isinspect.org.uk
Tel: 020 7600 0100
Fax: 020 7776 8849

The Office for Standards in Education
(Ofsted)
Alexandra House
33 Kingsway
London WC2B 6SE
Website: www.ofsted.gov.uk
Email: enquiries@ofsted.gov.uk
Tel: 020 7421 6800

Also at:
Royal Exchange Buildings
St Ann's Square
Manchester M2 7LA

International education

Council for International Education
(UK COSA)
9–17 St Albans Place
London N1 0NX
Website: www.ukcosa.org.uk
Email: info@ukcosa.org.uk
Tel: 020 7288 4330
Fax: 020 7288 4360

European Council of International
Schools (ECIS)
21B Lavant Street
Petersfield
Hampshire GU32 3EL
Website: www.ecis.org
Email: ecis@ecis.org
Tel: 01730 268244
Fax: 01730 267914

Voluntary Service Overseas (VSO)
317 Putney Bridge Road
London SW15 2PN
Website: www.vso.org.uk
Email: infoservices@vso.org.uk
Tel: 020 8780 7200
Fax: 020 8780 7300

Jobs

Acquire A Teacher
The Stables
Leighton Road
Northall
Buckinghamshire LU6 2EZ

Website: www.acquireateacher.com
Email: enquiries@acquireateacher.com
Tel: 01525 220 050

Capita Education Resourcing
Website: www.capitaers.co.uk
Email: enquiry.ers@capita.co.uk
Tel: 0800 731 6871 – Primary
0800 731 6872 – Secondary
0800 731 6873 – Nursery Nurses,
SEN & Support Staff
0800 316 1332 – Further Education

Education Jobs
21 St Martins Street
Wallingford
Oxfordshire OX10 0DE
Website: www.education-jobs.co.uk
Email: info@education-jobs.co.uk
Tel: 01491 834966

Education Lecturing Services
(ELS – jobs in further education)
Website: els.co.uk

ETeach
Website: www.eteach.com

The Guardian
Education section published weekly
on Tuesdays
Website:
http://jobs.guardian.co.uk/browse/edu
cation

Hays Education
Website: www.hays.com/education
Email: customerservice@hays.com

The Independent
Education section published weekly
on Thursdays

Jobs in Education
Website: www.jobsineducation.co.uk/

The Times Educational Supplement
(TES)
Published weekly on Fridays
Website: www.jobs.tes.co.uk

Teacher Recruitment Solutions
Pennineway Offices (1)
87–89 Saffron Hill
London EC1N 8QU
Website: www.teachers.eu.com/
Email: via website
Tel: 0845 8331934

Languages

Association for Language Learning
(ALL)
150 Railway Terrace
Rugby CV21 3HN
Website: www.all-languages.org.uk
Email: info@ALL-languages.org.uk
Tel: 01788 546443
Fax: 01788 544149

Centre for Information on Language
Teaching and Research (CiLT)
20 Bedfordbury
London WC2N 4LB
Website: www.cilt.org.uk
Email: library@cilt.org.uk
Tel: 020 7379 5110
Fax: 020 7379 5082

International Association of Teachers
of English as a Foreign Language
(IATEFL)
Darwin College
University of Kent
Canterbury
Kent CT2 7NY
Website: www.iatefl.org
Email: generalenquiries@iatefl.org
Tel: 01227 824430
Fax: 01227 824431

Languages Linguistics Area Studies
(LLAS)
School of Modern Languages
University of Southampton
Highfield
Southampton SO17 1BJ
Website: www.llas.ac.uk
Email: llas@soton.ac.uk
Tel: 023 8059 4814
Fax: 023 8059 4815

Library

Belfast Education and Library Board
(BELB)
Education Department
40 Academy Street
Belfast BT1 2NQ
Website: www.belb.org.uk
Email: info@belb.co.uk
Tel: 028 9056 4000
Fax: 028 9033 1714

The British Library
Location 1:
The British Library
St Pancras
96 Euston Road
London NW1 2DB

Location 2:
British Library Newspapers
Colindale Avenue
London NW9 5HE
Location 3:
The British Library
Boston Spa
Wetherby
West Yorkshire LS23 7BQ
Website: www.bl.uk
Email: Visitor-Services@bl.uk
Tel: 0870 444 1500 (Switchboard)

National Library of Scotland
George IV Bridge
Edinburgh EH1 1EW
Website: www.nls.uk
Email: enquiries@nls.uk
Tel: 0131 623 3700
Fax: 0131 623 3701

National Library of Wales
Aberystwyth
Ceredigion
Wales SY23 3BU
Website: www.llgc.org.uk
Email: via website
Tel: 01970 632 800
Fax: 01970 615 709

School Library Association (SLA)
Unit 2
Lotmead Business Village
Lotmead Farm
Wanborough
Swindon SN4 0UY
Website: www.sla.org.uk
Email: info@sla.org.uk
Tel: 0870 777 0979
Fax: 0870 777 0987

Management

National College for School
Leadership
Triumph Road
Nottingham NG8 1DH
Website: www.ncsl.org.uk
Email: ncsl-office@ncsl.org.uk
Tel: 0870 001 1155
Fax: 0115 872 2001

Maths

Advisory Committee on Mathematics
Education (ACME)
The Royal Society
6–9 Carlton House Terrace
London SW1Y 5AG
Website: www.royalsoc.ac.uk/acme
Email: via online form
Tel: 020 7451 2571
Fax: 020 7451 2693

Association of Teachers of
Mathematics (ATM)
7 Shaftesbury Street
Derby DE23 8YB
Website: www.atm.org.uk
Email: admin@atm.org.uk
Tel: 01332 346599
Fax: 01332 204357

The Institute of Mathematics and its
Applications
Catherine Richards House
16 Nelson Street
Southend-on-Sea
Essex SS1 1EF
Website: www.ima.org.uk
Email: post@ima.org.uk
Tel: 01702 354020
Fax: 01702 354111

Media

British Broadcasting Corporation
(BBC)
Website: www.bbc.co.uk
Email: via online form

The British Film Institute (BFI)
National Film Theatre
Belvedere Road
South Bank
London SE1 8XT
Website: www.bfi.org.uk
Email: via online form
Tel: 020 7928 3535

Education Guardian
Website:
www.guardian.education.co.uk

MediaEd
Website: www.mediaed.org.uk

Media Education
9 South College Street
Edinburgh EH8 9AA
Website: www.mediaeducation.co.uk
Email:
enquiries@mediaeducation.co.uk
Tel: 0131 662 8844
Fax: 0131 662 8833

Online education

Actis Ltd
Website: www.actis.co.uk
Also curriculum websites for various
subjects
Email: welcome@actis.co.uk
Tel: 0800 587 8032

BBC
Website: www.bbc.co.uk/education
Email:
homepage.education@bbc.co.uk

Channel 4
Website: www.4learning.co.uk
Email: via online links

Homework High
Website: www.homeworkhigh.com

Learn.co.uk (from *The Guardian*)
Website: www.learn.co.uk
Email: contact@learn.co.uk

Learning and Teaching Scotland
Website: www.ltscotland.com
Email: enquiries@ltscotland.com

Parents

Advisory Centre for Education (ACE)
1c Aberdeen Studios
22 Highbury Grove
London N5 2DQ
Website: www.ace-ed.org.uk
Email: enquiries@ace-ed.org.uk
Tel (exclusion): 020 7704 9822
Tel (general): 0808 800 5793

Bullying Online
PO Box 552
Harrogate
North Yorkshire HG1 9BF
Website: www.bullying.co.uk
Email: help@bullying.co.uk

ParentsCentre
Public Enquiry Unit
Sanctuary Buildings
Great Smith Street
London SW1P 3BT
Website: www.parentscentre.gov.uk
Email: via feedback form on website
Tel: 0870 000 2288

Parentline Plus
Website: www.parentlineplus.org.uk
Email:
parentsupport@parentlineplus.org.uk
Also via online form
Tel: 020 7284 5500
Helpline: 0808 800 2222

Pensions

Scottish Public Pensions Agency
7 Tweedside Park
Tweedbank
Galashiels TD1 3TE
Website: www.sppa.gov.uk
Email:
christine.marr@scotland.gsi.gov.uk
(Policy Manager)
Tel: 01896 893225
Fax: 01896 893230

Teachers' Pensions England and Wales
Capita Teachers' Pensions
Mowden Hall
Darlington DL3 9EE
Website: www.teacherspensions.co.uk
Email: via website
Tel: 0845 6066166
Fax: 01325 745789
Minicom: 0845 6099899

Teachers' Pensions Northern Ireland
Department of Education
Teachers' Pensions Branch
Waterside House
75 Duke Street
Londonderry BT47 6FP
Tel: 028 7131 9000

PE

Association of Physical Education
(AfPE)
Building 25
London Road
Reading RG1 5AQ
Website: www.afpe.org.uk
Email: enquiries@afpe.org.uk
Tel: 0118 378 6240
Fax: 0118 378 6242

Central Council of Physical Recreation
(CCPR)
Francis House
Francis Street
London SW1P 1DE
Website: www.ccpr.org.uk
Email: info@ccpr.org.uk
Tel: 020 7854 8500
Fax: 020 7854 8501

PSHE

DrugScope
32–36 Loman Street
London SE1 0EE
Website: www.drugscope.org.uk
Email: info@drugscope.org.uk
Tel: 020 7928 1211
Fax: 020 7928 1771

FRANK
Website: www.talktofrank.com
Email: frank@talktofrank.com
Tel: 0800 77 66 00 (Helpline)

Kidscape
2 Grosvenor Gardens
London SW1W 0DH
Website: www.kidscape.org.uk
Email: webinfo@kidscape.org.uk
Tel: 020 7730 3300
Fax: 020 7730 7081

Mind, Body and Soul
Website: www.mindbodysoul.gov.uk
Email: wfh@dh.gsi.gov.uk

Schools Councils UK
3rd Floor
108–110 Camden High Street
London NW1 0LU
Website: www.schoolcouncils.org
Email: info@schoolcouncils.org
Tel: 0845 456 9428
Fax: 0845 456 9429

Teachernet PSHE
via DfES:
Sanctuary Buildings
Great Smith Street
London SW1P 3BT
Website:
www.teachernet.gov.uk/pshe
Email: PSHE.TEAM@dfes.gsi.gov.uk

Primary

The British Association for Early
Childhood Education
136 Cavell Street
London E1 2JA

Website: www.early-education.org.uk
Email: office@early-education.org.uk
Tel: 020 7539 5400
Fax: 020 7539 5409

The Centre for Language in Primary
Education (CLPE)
Webber Street
London SE1 8QW
Website: www.clpe.co.uk
Email: info@clpe.co.uk
Tel: 020 7401 3382/3
020 7633 0840
Fax: 020 7928 4624

National Association for Primary
Education (NAPE)
Information Officer
John Coe
155 High Street
Chalgrove
Oxford OX44 7ST
Website: www.nape.org.uk
Email: nape@onetel.com
Tel: 01865 890281

The Pre-school Learning Alliance
The Fitzpatrick Building
188 York Way
London N7 9AD
Website: www.pre-school.org.uk
Email: info@pre-school.org.uk
Tel: 020 7697 2500
Fax: 020 7770 0319

Professional development

Chartered London Teacher Status
(Part of the College of Teachers)
Website: www.clt.ac.uk
Email: support@clt.ac.uk

The College of Teachers
Institute of Education
University of London
57 Gordon Square
London WC1H 0NU
Website:
www.collegeofteachers.ac.uk
Email: info@cot.ac.uk
Tel: 020 7911 5536
Fax: 020 7612 6482

Publications

The Education Guardian
Website:
http://education.guardian.co.uk

*The Independent Education
Supplement*
Website:
http://education.independent.co.uk

The Times Educational Supplement
Admiral House
66–68 East Smithfield
London E1W 1BX
Website: www.tes.co.uk
Email: via online form
Tel: 020 7782 3000
Fax: 020 7782 3200

The Times Educational Supplement
(Scotland)
Website: www.tes.co.uk/scotland

*The Times Higher Education
Supplement*
Website: www.thes.co.uk

RE

The Inter Faith Network
8a Lower Grosvenor Place
London SW1W 0EN
Website: www.interfaith.org.uk
Email: ifnet@interfaith.org.uk
Tel: 020 7931 7766
Fax: 020 7931 7722

The Professional Council for Religious
Education (PCfRE)
1020 Bristol Road
Selly Oak
Birmingham B29 6LB
Website: www.pcfre.org.uk
Email: retoday@retoday.org.uk
Tel: 0121 472 4242
Fax: 0121 472 7575

RE Online
Website: www.reonline.org.uk
Email: comment@reonline.org.uk

RE Quest
Website: www.request.org.uk
Email: office@request.org.uk

RE Today (part of PCfRE)
Website: www.retoday.org.uk

Schools information

DfES School and College Performance
Tables
Website:
www.dfes.gov.uk/performancetables

Specialist Schools and Academies
Trust
16th Floor, Millbank Tower
21–24 Millbank
London SW1P 4QP
Website:
www.specialistschools.org.uk/
Email: info@ssatrust.org.uk
Tel: 020 7802 2300
Fax: 020 7802 2345
Video Conferencing: 020 7828 8024

Science

Association for Science Education
(ASE)
College Lane
Hatfield
Herts AL10 9AA
Website: www.ase.org.uk
Email: info@ase.org.uk
Tel: 01707 283000
Fax: 01707 266532

Institute of Biology (IOB)
Institute of Biology
9 Red Lion Court
London EC4A 3EF
Website: www.iob.org
Email: info@iob.org
Tel: 020 7936 5900
Fax: 020 7936 5901

Institute of Physics (IOP)
76 Portland Place
London W1B 1NT
Website: www.iop.org
Email: physics@iop.org
Tel: 020 7470 4800
Fax: 020 7470 4848

Secondary

English Secondary Students
Association
3rd Floor
Downstream Building
1 London Bridge
London SE1 9BG
Website: www.studentvoice.co.uk
Email: enquiries@studentvoice.co.uk
Tel: 020 7022 1911 or
020 7022 1910

Special educational needs

The British Association of Teachers of
the Deaf (BATOD)
Mr Paul A. Simpson (Secretary)
175 Dashwood Avenue
High Wycombe
Buckinghamshire HP12 3DB
Website: www.batod.org.uk
Email: secretary@batod.org.uk
Tel: 01494 464190

The British Dyslexia Association (BDA)
98 London Road
Reading RG1 5AU
Website: www.bdadyslexia.org.uk
Email: via the website
Tel: 0118 966 2677
Fax: 0118 935 1927
Helpline: 0118 966 8271

British Institute of Learning Disabilities
Campion House
Green Street
Kidderminster
Worcestershire DY10 1JL
Website: www.bild.org.uk
Email: enquiries@bild.org.uk
Tel: 01562 723 010
Fax: 01562 723 029

Dyslexia Action
(formerly The Dyslexia Institute)
2 Grosvenor Gardens
London SW1W 0DH
Website: www.dyslexiaaction.org.uk
Email: info@dyslexia-inst.org.uk
Tel: 020 7730 8890
Fax: 020 7730 0273

The National Association for Gifted
Children (NAGC)
Suite 14
Challenge House
Sherwood Drive
Bletchley
Bucks MK3 6DP
Website: www.nagcbritain.org.uk
Email:
amazingchildren@nagcbritain.org.uk
Tel: 0870 7703217
Fax: 0870 7703219

The National Association for Special
Educational Needs (NASEN)
NASEN House
4–5 Amber Business Village
Amber Close
Amington
Tamworth B77 4RP
Website: www.nasen.org.uk
Email: welcome@nasen.org.uk
Tel: 01827 311500
Fax: 01827 313005

The National Autistic Society (NAS)
393 City Road
London EC1V 1NG
Website: www.nas.org.uk
Email: nas@nas.org.uk
Tel: 020 7833 2299
Fax: 020 7833 9666

The National Deaf Children's Society
15 Dufferin Street
London EC1Y 8UR
Website: www.ndcs.org.uk
Email: ndcs@ndcs.org.uk
Tel: 020 7490 8656
Fax: 020 7251 5020
Minicom: 020 7490 8656

Suppliers (Educational Products)

The Consortium
Hammond Way
Trowbridge
Wiltshire BA14 8RR
Website: www.theconsortium.co.uk
Email: enquiries@theconsortium.co.uk
Tel: 0845 3307750
Fax: 0845 3307785

Hope Education
Hyde Buildings
Ashton Road
Hyde
Cheshire SK14 4SH
Website: www.hope-education.co.uk
Email: enquiries@hope-
education.co.uk
Tel: 0870 2412308
Fax: 0800 929139

Supply Teaching Agencies

Note: Some supply agencies only
deal with a small geographical area
of the UK. Where this is the case,
the areas covered are noted below.
Some agencies also offer permanent
vacancies. Teachers wishing to do
supply work in Scotland would
normally register for work via
their LEA.

Capita Education Resourcing
Website: www.capitaers.co.uk
Email: enquiry.ers@capita.co.uk
Tel: 0800 731 6871 (primary)
0800 731 6872 (secondary)

Castle Recruitment
Website: www.castlerecruitment.com
Email: info@castlerecruitment.com
Tel: 020 8514 3888
Areas – London (secondary teachers)

Concorde Teaching Bank
Website:
www.concordeteachingbank.co.uk
Email: concordeteachingbank@
cornwall.ac.uk
Tel: 01872 262033
Areas – Cornwall

Cover Teachers
5 Westfield Park
Bristol BS6 6LT
Website: www.coverteachers.co.uk
Email: enquiries@coverteachers.co.uk
Tel: 0117 973 5695
Areas – South-west England

Dream Education
Dean Clough
Halifax HX3 5AX
Website: www.dream-education.co.uk
Email: education@dream-group.com
Tel: 0142 238 4100
Fax: 0207 747 3064

Education Recruitment Network
Website: www.ernteachers.com
Email: via online form
Newport, covering Wales and South
West: 0800 0154 358

Wakefield, covering Yorkshire:
0800 0154 352
Areas – Southern England, Wales

Education VIPs
Website: www.educationvips.com
Email: teach@educationvips.com
Tel: Lewisham/Greenwich/Kent
020 8402 9164
Bromley/Croydon/Surrey 020 8289
3753
Areas – London and Southern
England

Hays Education
Website: www.hays.com
Email: customerservice@hays.com
Tel: 0800 716026

Head Line Teacher Supply Service
Roman House
49 Spencer Street
St Albans
Hertfordshire AL3 5EH
Website: www.headline-uk.com
Email: teachers@headline-uk.com
Tel : 0870 240 3759
Fax : 01727 840019
Areas – Bedfordshire, Berkshire,
Buckinghamshire, Essex, Greater
London, Hertfordshire.

International Supply Teachers
Website:
www.teachersonthemove.com
Email: ist@teachersonthemove.com
Fax: 020 7681 2110
Note: This agency charges a
registration fee

Key Stage Teacher Supply
First Floor
9 Preston New Road
Blackburn
Lancashire BB2 1AR
Website: www.keystagesupply.co.uk
Email: info@keystagesupply.co.uk
Tel: 01254 507210
Fax: 01254 507211
Areas – Blackburn, Burnley, Chorley,
Preston

Link Education
61a High Street
Orpington
Kent BR6 0JF
Website: www.linkteacher.com
Email: linkeducation@btconnect.com
Tel: 01689 878565
Fax: 01689 839668
Areas – Bexley, Bromley, Essex County,
Greenwich, Kent County, Lewisham
and the Medway towns.

Locum Group Education
1 Wells Yard
High Street
Ware
Hertfordshire SG12 9AS
Website: www.teachers-uk.co.uk
Email: info.south@teachers-uk.co.uk
Tel: 01920 484415
Fax: 01920 486692

Longterm Teachers
The Space
57–61 Mortimer Street
London W1W 8HS
Website: www.longtermteachers.com
Email: info@longtermteachers.com
Tel: 0845 130 6149
Fax: 0871 250 6193

Mark Education
Tannery Court
Tanners Lane
Warrington WA2 7NA
Website: www.markltd.com
Email: info@markeducation.co.uk
Tel: 01925 241115

Masterlock Education
32 Queensway
London W2 3RX
Website: www.masterlock.co.uk
Email: info@masterlock.co.uk
Tel: 020 7229 6699
Fax: 020 7229 6464
Areas – Bristol, Hertfordshire, London

Opus Educational
75 Saltergate
Chesterfield S40 1JS
Website: www.opuseducational.co.uk
Email: via online form
Tel: 01246 224288
Fax: 01246 221283
Areas – East Midlands

Protocol Teachers
Website: www.protocol-teachers.com
Email: via online form
Tel: 0845 450 8450

Quality Education
Turnford Place
Great Cambridge Road
Turnford
Broxbourne
Hertfordshire EN10 6NH
Website:
www.qualitylocums.com/education
Email: education@qualitylocums.com
Tel: 0800 043 7320
Fax: 01992 305 631

Reed Education
Website: www.reed.co.uk/education
Contact your local office direct

Select Education
Regent Court
Laporte Way
Luton
Bedfordshire LU4 8SB
Website: www.selecteducation.co.uk
Email:
education@selecteducation.com
Tel: 01582 406800
Fax. 01582 406815

Standby Teacher Services
Sanderson House
119 Main Street
Burley-in-Wharfedale
Ilkley
West Yorkshire LS29 7JN
Website: www.standbyteachers.com
Email: info@standbyteachers.com
Tel: 01943 864677
Fax: 01943 864353
Areas – North-east England

STEP Teachers
The Grange
100 High Street
Southgate
London N14 6BN
Website: www.stepteachers.co.uk
Email: info@stepteachers.co.uk
Tel: 0800 026 9222
Fax: 0870 1422 994

Supply Desk
Fives Court
Hillsborough Barracks
Penistone Road
Sheffield S6 2GZ
Website: www.thesupplydesk.co.uk

Email: info@thesupplydesk.co.uk
Tel: 0114 2834900
Fax: 0114 2834908
Switchboard: 0800 0272737

Supply Teachers
32 Smarts Road
Gravesend
Kent DA12 5AQ
Website: www.supplyteachers.com
Email: info@supplyteachers.com
Tel: 01474 328635
Fax: 01474 328635

Teaching Personnel
Website:
www.teachingpersonnel.com
Email: via online form
Tel: 0800 980 8935

The Teaching Supply Agency
Website: www.teaching-agency.co.uk
Email: supply@teaching-agency.co.uk
Tel: 01344 482708
Areas – Berkshire, Hampshire, Surrey

TimePlan
Website: www.timeplan.com
Email: via online form
Tel: 0800 358 8040

Support Organizations

Teacher Support Network
Hamilton House
Mabledon Place
London WC1H 9BE
Website: www.teacherline.org.uk
Email: enquiries@teachersupport.info
Tel: 020 7554 5200
Fax: 020 7554 5239

Teacher Training

Graduate Teacher Training Registry
(GTTR)
Rosehill
New Barn Lane
Cheltenham
Gloucestershire GL52 3LZ
Website: www.gttr.ac.uk
Tel: 0870 1122205
Minicom: 01242 544942

National Union of Students (NUS)
2nd floor, Centro 3
Mandela Street
London NW1 0DU
Website: www.nus.org.uk
Email: nusuk@nus.org.uk
Tel: 0871 221 8221
Fax: 0871 221 8222
Textphone: 020 7561 6577

The Training and Development
Agency for Schools (TDA)
Portland House
Bressenden Place
London SW1E 5TT
Website: www.tda.gov.uk
Tel (general enquiries):
0870 4960 123
Tel (teaching information line):
0845 6000 991 (for English speakers)
0845 6000 992 (for Welsh speakers)

Universities and Colleges Admissions
Service (UCAS)
Rosehill
New Barn Lane
Cheltenham
Gloucestershire GL52 3LZ
Website: www.ucas.ac.uk

Email: enquiries@ucas.ac.uk
Tel: 0870 1122211
Minicom: 01242 544942

Universities Council for the Education
of Teachers (UCET)
Whittington House
19–30 Alfred Place
London WC1E 7EA
Website: www.ucet.ac.uk
Email: ucet@ioe.ac.uk
Tel: 020 7580 8000
Fax: 020 7323 0577

Teaching Forums and Communities

Education.com
Website: www.education.com
Email: via online form

Talking Teaching
Website: www.talkingteaching.co.uk
Email: via online form

TES Staffroom
Website: www.tes.co.uk/staffroom

Teaching Resources

By Teachers
Website: www.byteachers.org.uk

Clickteaching
Unit 102
5 Charter House
Lord Montgomery Way
Portsmouth PO1 2SN
Website: www.clickteaching.com
Email: support@clickteaching.com

English Teaching
Website: www.english-teaching.co.uk
Email: feedback@
englishteaching.co.uk

Primary Resources
Website: www.primaryresources.co.uk
Email: via online form

Quality Teaching Resources
Website:
www.qualityteachingresources.co.uk
Email: via online form

Schoolzone
Website: www.schoolzone.co.uk
Email: mail@schoolzone.co.uk

Tagteacher
Website: www.tagteacher.net
Email: feedback@tagteacher.net

Teaching Ideas for Primary Teachers
Website: www.teachingideas.co.uk
Email: mark@teachingideas.co.uk

Teachit (English teaching online)
Website: www.teachit.co.uk
Email: mail@teachit.co.uk

Topmarks
Website: www.topmarks.co.uk
Email: education@topmarks.co.uk

Unions

Association of School and College
Leaders (ASCL)
130 Regent Road
Leicester LE1 7PG
Website: www.ascl.org.uk

Email: info@ascl.org.uk
Tel: 0116 299 1122
Fax: 0116 299 1123

Association of Teachers and Lecturers
(ATL)
London Headquarters:
7 Northumberland Street
London WC2N 5RD
Website: www.askatl.org.uk
Email: info@atl.org.uk
Tel: 020 7930 6441
Fax: 020 7930 1359
Wales Office:
1st Floor, Empire House
Mount Stuart Square
Cardiff CF10 5FN
Email: cymru@atl.org.uk
Tel: 029 2046 5000
Fax: 029 2046 2000
Northern Ireland Office:
The Gas Office
10 Cromac Quay Ormeau Road
Belfast BT7 2JD
Northern Ireland
Email: ni@atl.org.uk
Tel: 02890 327 990
Fax: 02890 327 992

Headteachers' Association of Scotland
(HAS)
University of Strathclyde
Jordanhill Campus
Southbrae Drive
Glasgow G13 1PP
Website: www.has-scotland.co.uk
Email: head.teachers@strath.ac.uk

National Association of Headteachers
(NAHT)
1 Heath Square
Boltro Road

Haywards Heath
West Sussex RH16 1BL
Website: www.naht.org.uk
Email: info@naht.org.uk
Tel: 01444 472472

National Association of Schoolmasters
Union of Women Teachers (NASUWT)
Headquarters:
Hillscourt Education Centre
Rose Hill
Rednal
Birmingham B45 8RS
Website: www.nasuwt.org.uk
Email: nasuwt@mail.nasuwt.org.uk
Tel: 0121 453 6150
Fax: 0121 457 6208/9
Wales Office:
Greenwood Close
Cardiff Gate Business Park
Cardiff CF23 8RD
Website: www.nasuwt.org.uk/Cymru
Email: rc-wales-cymru@
mail.nasuwt.org.uk
Tel: 029 2054 6080
Fax: 029 2054 6089
Scotland Office:
6 Waterloo Place
Edinburgh EH1 3BG
Website:
www.nasuwt.org.uk/Scotland
Email: rc-scotland@
mail.nasuwt.org.uk
Tel: 0131 523 1110
Fax: 0131 523 1119
Northern Ireland Office:
Ben Madigan House
Edgewater Office Park
Edgewater Road
Belfast BT3 9JQ
Website:
www.nasuwt.org.uk/NorthernIreland

Email: rc-nireland@mail.nasuwt.org.uk
Tel: 028 9078 4480
Fax: 028 9078 4489

National Union of Teachers (NUT)
Hamilton House
Mabledon Place
London WC1H 9BD
Website: www.teachers.org.uk
Email: contact your local office
Tel: 020 7388 6191
(Membership) 0845 300 1666
Fax: 020 7387 8458

Professional Association of Teachers
(PAT)
2 St James' Court
Friar Gate
Derby DE1 1BT
Website: www.pat.org.uk
Email: hq@pat.org.uk
Tel: 01332 372337
Fax: 01332 290310

PAT Scotland
1–3 St Colme Street
Edinburgh EH3 6AA
Email: scotland@pat.org.uk
Tel: 0131 220 8241
Fax: 0131 220 8350

Scottish Secondary Teachers'
Association (SSTA)
14 West End Place
Edinburgh EH11 2ED
Website: www.ssta.org.uk
Email: info@ssta.org.uk
Tel: 0131 313 7300
Fax: 0131 346 8057

Society of Headmasters and
Headmistresses of Independent
Schools (SHMIS)
12 The Point
Rockingham Road
Market Harborough
Leicestershire LE16 7QU
Website: www.shmis.org.uk
Email: gensec@shmis.org.uk
Tel: 01858 433760
Fax: 01858 461413

University and College Union
(formerly the AUT and NATFHE)
Website: www.ucu.org.uk
Email: hq@ucu.org.uk
AUT website: www.aut.org.uk
NATFHE website: www.natfhe.org.uk

Index